PINK

First published in the French language by Editions du Seuil, Paris, under the title *Rose. Histoire d'une couleur* by Michel Pastoureau
Copyright © 2025 Editions du Seuil, Paris
English translation copyright © 2025 by Princeton University Press

Requests for permission to reproduce material from this work should be sent to permissions@press.princeton.edu
Published by Princeton University Press, 41 William Street, Princeton, New Jersey 08540
In the United Kingdom: Princeton University Press, 99 Banbury Road, Oxford OX2 6JX
press.princeton.edu
Jacket image: Lawrence Alma-Tadema, *The Roses of Heliogabalus* (detail), 1888. Photo: incamerastock / Alamy Stock Photo.

ISBN 9780691266268
ISBN (ebook) 9780691269375

Library of Congress Control Number: 2024936698

British Library Cataloging-in-Publication Data is available
This book has been composed in Tiempos
Printed in Slovenia
1 3 5 7 9 10 8 6 4 2

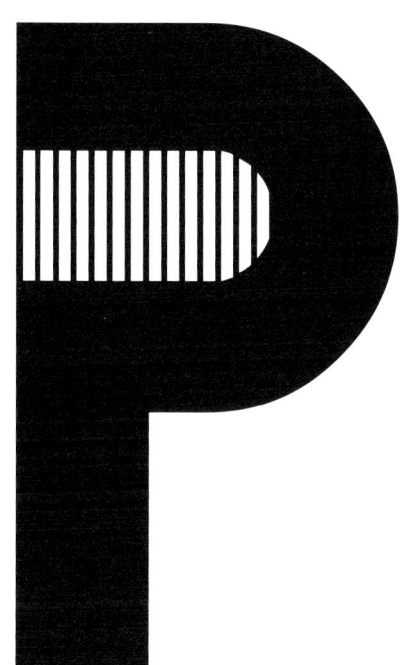

P I

THE HISTORY OF A COLOR

MICHEL PASTOUREAU

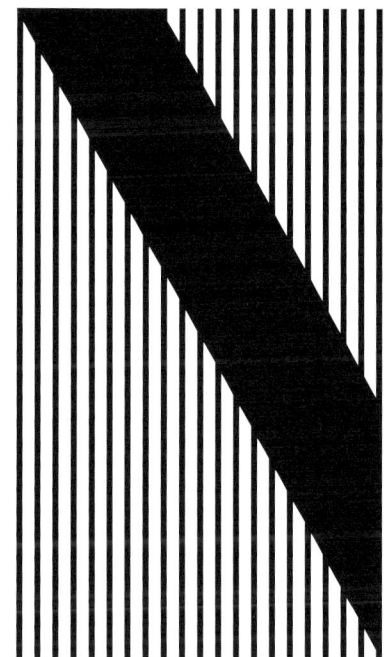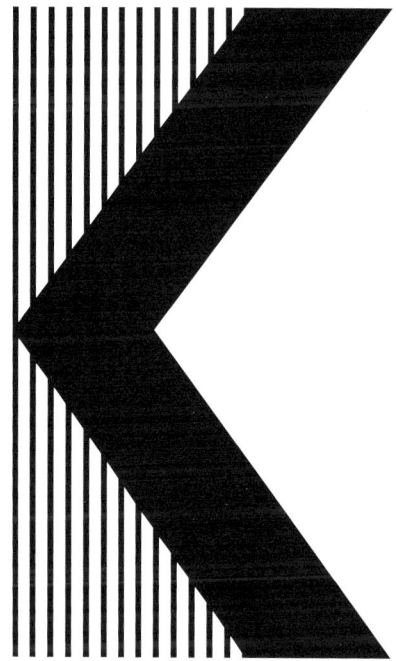

N K

Translated by
Jody Gladding

Princeton University Press
Princeton and Oxford

Introduction

Is pink a color in its own right? There are grounds for doubting this or at least asking the question. Contemporary science refuses to grant it that status; for science, it is neither a color in terms of material nor light, but simply a shade of red, absent from the solar spectrum. In 1666, when Isaac Newton succeeded in breaking down white light into colored rays, he did not find pink, although in addition to red, yellow, green, and blue, he found purple and orange. Following his lead, physics and all the related sciences have continually refused to see pink as a true color, or even as a half color, but only as a shade.

For the historian, the issue is more complex. While it is clear that human beings only began to produce pink quite late, both in painting and dyeing, it is just as apparent that early on they observed this color in nature, and sought to both name and classify it. How to describe this shade that was visible on various plants and minerals, on the fur and feathers of many animals, and even in the sky when the sun rose or set? For a long time the lexicon was powerless to do so, as neither Greek nor Latin had a standard word for *pink*. Then it was a slow, halting process, with vernacular languages only adopting a basic term for it in the eighteenth century when a flower finally gave its name to the color: the rose in French, German, and Italian, and the pink in English. And moreover, where to locate this color in the *ordo colorum* of scientists or on any chromatic scale? For centuries, nowhere, since it had no name, and to classify is, above all, a matter of vocabulary. In fact, pink is absent from all color lists left to us by antiquity and the Middle Ages as well as from poems, chronicles, treatises, or encyclopedias that speak of colors.

Beginning in the 1450s, things would change. Chromatic repertoires became matters of hues, not just words; pink finally found its place there, a discreet place admittedly, but well attested. It is surprising for us, incidentally, to see that before being included in the range of reds, pink was classed among the yellows—a pale yellow tending more or less toward orange, as neither dyeing nor painting yet knew how to make vivid, saturated pink tones. It was not until the eighteenth century that people learned how to do so, and that pink was definitively considered to be a mix of red and white, after which it would be grouped with the "mixed" colors, along with purple, gray, brown, and orange.

The history of pink, as we will see, is an uncertain and tumultuous one, difficult to trace because for so long this color seemed elusive, fragile, ephemeral, and as resistant to analysis as to synthesis. No doubt that is why there are so few studies on it, at least with regard to its history. Most of the works available address only the last few decades. They are often disappointing, focusing most of their remarks on gender issues alone: feminine pink and masculine blue. That is a shame because this issue of sexual distinction involves only a short period of time and represents only one aspect of the rich symbolism of pink. Beginning in the eighteenth century, pink finally occupied a place in everyday life and started to possess its own symbolism, independent from that of red, yellow, or white. It deserves our sustained attention, and all the more so because the shades of pink then diversified and even multiplied in contact with other shades, while its name grew rich with various figurative meanings and was adopted in many expressions and idioms, sometimes positive ("to see the world through rose-colored glasses") and sometimes negative (*l'eau de rose*, meaning mawkish or sentimental). If pink is not a color for the sciences, it is undeniably one in the material culture, in its uses in clothing, and the social codes accompanying them. There, it is autonomous and significant.

In all of these ways, pink can serve as an example to illustrate and underline the divide that exists in the domain of colors between scientific theories and social practices. In various domains, physics and chemistry too often dictate their truths to society. With regard to colors, this is clearly not the case. Far from regretting that, the historian can only rejoice: whatever the hard sciences

say, pink, like white and black moreover, is very much a color in its own right.

*

The present book is the seventh in a series begun almost twenty-five years ago. *Pink* was preceded by *Blue: The History of a Color* (2001), *Black: The History of a Color* (2009), *Green: The History of a Color* (2014), *Red: The History of a Color* (2017), *Yellow: The History of a Color* (2019), and *White: The History of a Color* (2023), all published by Seuil and Princeton University Press. As with the preceding books, the plan for this one is chronological; it is very much a history of the color pink, not an encyclopedia of pink, and even less a study of pink in the contemporary world alone, as are those rare works devoted to it. I have tried to study this color over the long term and in all of its aspects, from lexicon to symbols, and by way of everyday life, social practices, scientific knowledge, technical applications, religious values, artistic creations, the world of emblems, and representations. Too often works that claim to discuss the history of colors are limited to artistic stakes alone, which is very reductive. The history of painting is one thing; the history of colors is another, and much more vast, and there is absolutely no reason to limit it to the contemporary era.

That said, as with the six preceding works, this one only appears to be a monograph. A color never occurs alone; it only derives its meaning, it only fully "functions" from the social, lexical, artistic, or symbolic perspective insofar as it is combined or contrasted with one or many other colors. Hence it is impossible to consider it in isolation. To speak of pink necessarily leads to speaking of red, white, blue, and even green and yellow.

These seven works now form an edifice I have been working to build for more than half a century: the history of colors in European societies, from Roman antiquity to the end of the eighteenth century. Although, as readers will find in the pages that follow and the other volumes, I range considerably beyond and before those two periods, it is within that—already quite ample—slice of time that the essence of my research lies. Similarly, I have deliberately limited my research to European societies because for me the issues of color are first of all social ones. As a historian, I am not competent to speak about the whole planet, and not interested in compiling, second- or thirdhand, works by other researchers on non-European cultures. In order to avoid making foolish claims, plagiarizing, or recopying the books of others, I have limited myself to what I know, and what was the subject of my seminars at the École Practique des Hautes Études and École des Hautes Études en Sciences Sociales for four decades, starting in 1983. A warm thanks to all of my students, doctoral students, assistants, and auditors for the fruitful exchanges we had then, and that I hope will continue in different places and institutions. Color concerns everyone and touches on all the issues of life in society, whether material or cultural. Pink is no exception.

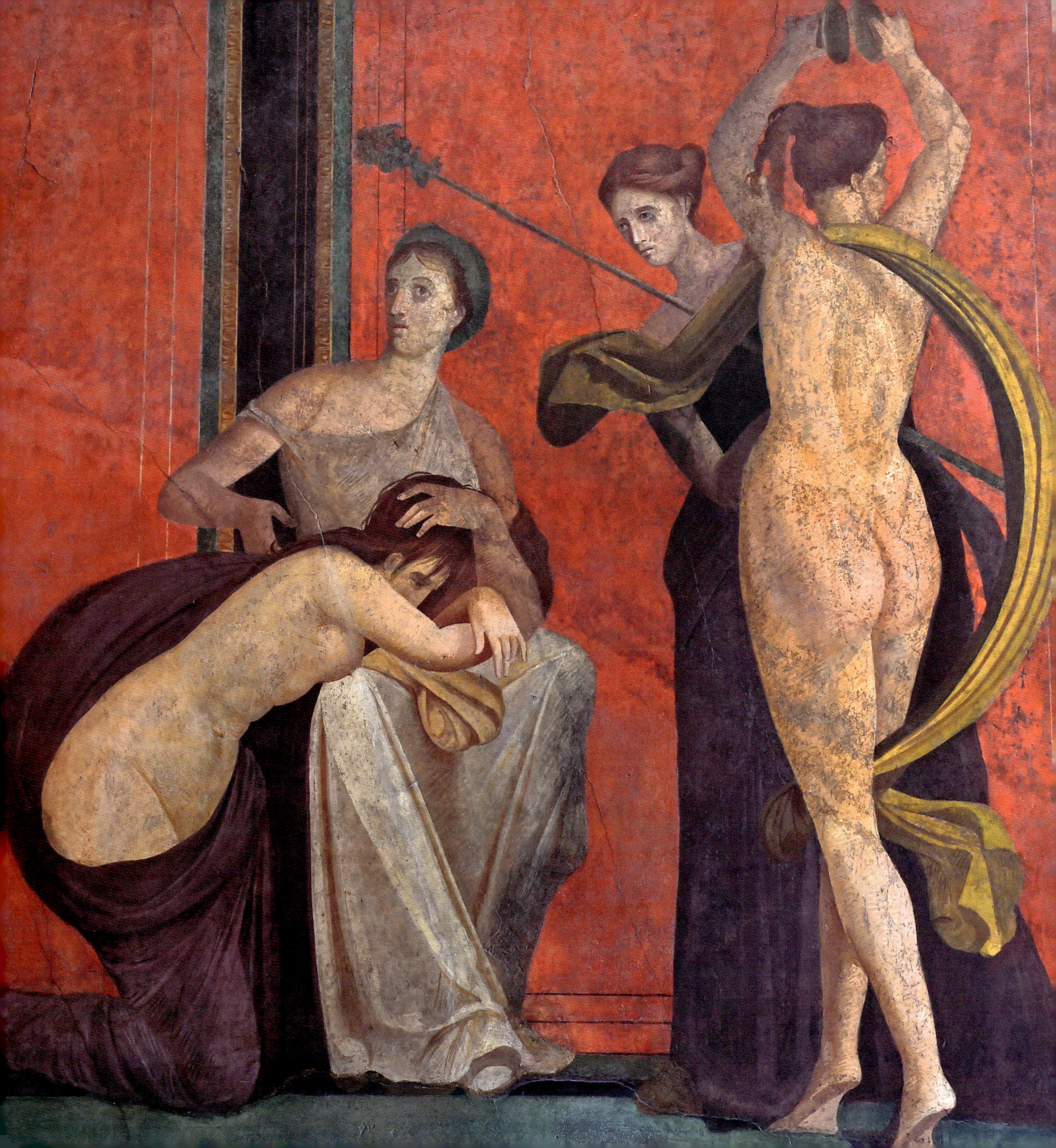

A DISCREET COLOR

(FROM EARLIEST TIMES TO THE 14TH CENTURY)

The Pinks of Pompeii

The walls of Pompeii display many red tones as well as a certain number of pinks. Sometimes it is a matter of cinnabar-based red pigments that were transformed under the lava and ashes. Sometimes and more frequently it is a matter of actual pink pigments, produced by painters to convey the flesh tones of nudity. These tones are always lighter for female nudes than for male ones.

Cult initiation scene, first century BCE. Villa of the Mysteries, Pompeii.

Appearing on the walls of caves as early as the Paleolithic age, red is the first color that painters learned to break down into an array of different shades. Nevertheless, for the ranges of pinks, they did so only relatively recently, at least in Europe: the fourth century BCE. The few traces of this color that we can discover dating back to earlier times, on walls or movable objects, are not due to the work of painters but instead to the work of time, which has sometimes transformed into various pinks tones that were originally red, brown, or orange.[1] This late appearance of pink in European painting is somewhat surprising because nature offers various examples of this color, not only present in many plants, minerals, and shells, the fur and feathers of some animals, but also resulting, in a more fleeting way, from light effects tied to the course of the sun, the cycles of the moon, and even natural phenomena like thunderstorms and volcanic eruptions. Artists and artisans of antiquity rarely sought to reproduce these shades, and it was even later still that European societies began to categorize and name them.

OPPOSITE

The Pink of the Paleolithic?

The palette of prehistoric painters is relatively limited: red, black, yellow, a little brown and orange, and sometimes white, but never green or blue. The shades of these different colors are quite numerous, but they are often the result of time rather than the painters' intentions. That is true, notably, for the few pinkish reds that appear in many caves, like the Cave of Altamira in northern Spain.

The great bison of Altamira, 15,500–13,500 BCE. Cave of Altamira, Hall of the Bisons, Santillana del Mar (Spain).

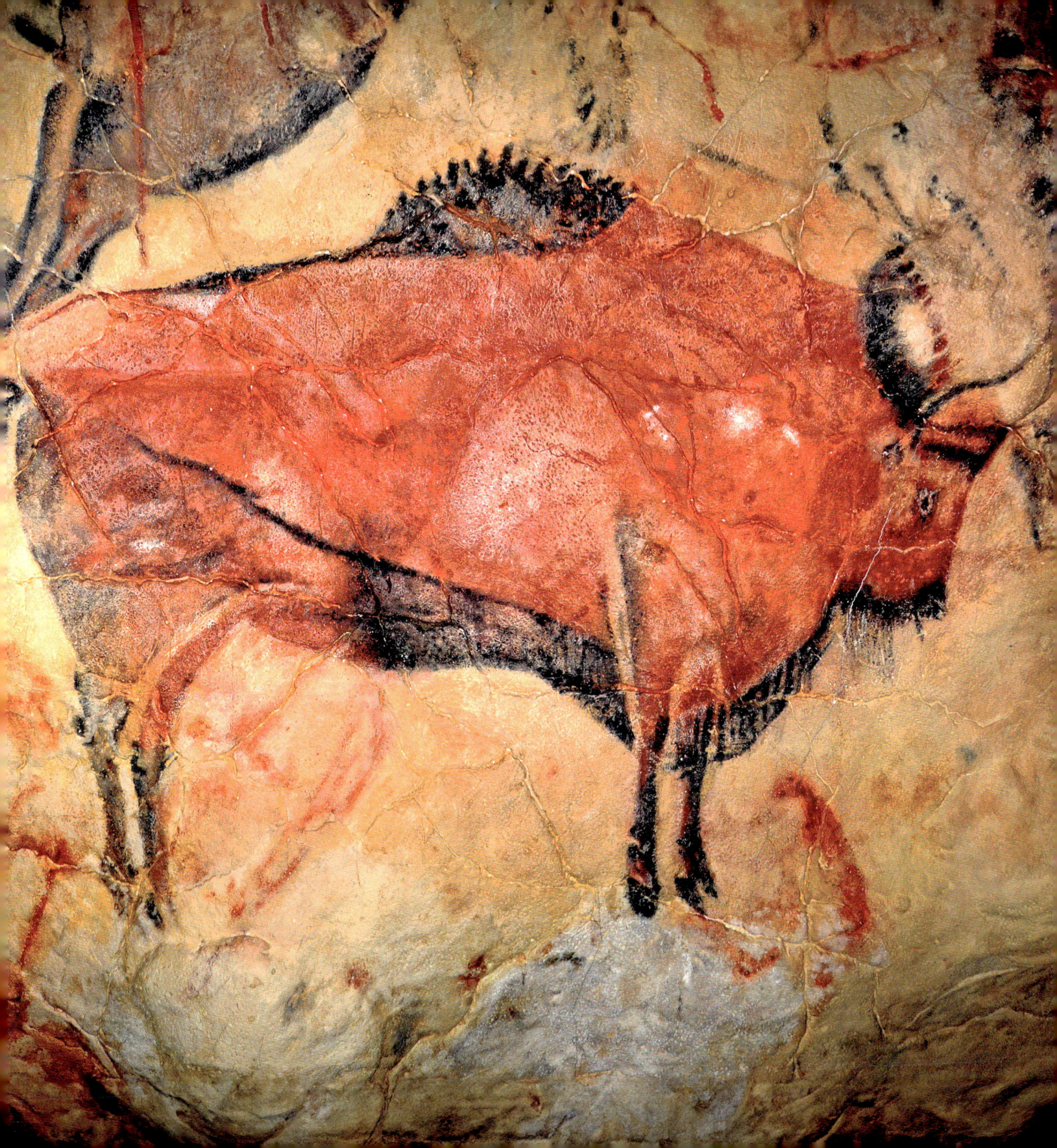

The First Pink Pigments

In ancient Greece, there are recent discoveries of Macedonian paintings that date to the late fourth and early third centuries, and provide the first incontestable evidence of the use of pink by painters. Here, pinks are finally truly pink, and not the more or less light reds or oranges tending toward crimson that we see in figures on vases where, during firing, they took on shades similar to those of brick or tile. Let us cite, for instance, a famous Attic kylix from the years 500 to 480 attributed to the painter Onesimos: on the base of the cup appears a nude woman—a rare theme on Greek vases—her reclining body an attractive pink tone, unusual even for representing female flesh, which was often shown as paler than male flesh. But this is a ceramic piece, not a mural.

The discoveries made in Macedonia over the course of recent decades involve actual polychrome interiors. They have created difficulties for the idea of a Greek palette limited to four colors (red, white, black, and yellow)—a notion inherited from Pliny and his modern commentators that must be definitively abandoned. This painted decor comes from a palace in ruins, funeral temples, and especially, princely tombs from the late classical and early Hellenistic periods, dating from the years 330 to 280. Conducted in several stages between 1977 and 2014,

excavations unearthed abundant archaeological material (jewels, weapons, and precious objects), and brought to light a whole group of painted scenes and motifs that constitute an exceptional contribution to our knowledge of fourth- and third-century painting. Bedrooms, beds, stelae, thrones, royal furnishings, walls, and facades: all are decorated in vivid and varied colors, the stone as well as the marble, ivory, metal, or simple surface coatings. The most lavish decor is found in four large tombs located in the village of Vergina, not far from Aigai, the first capital of Macedonian kings: the tomb of Alexander the Great's

Kylix with Pink Figures

A kylix is a wide, shallow drinking cup, generally used for enjoying wine at banquets. This one shows an entirely nude courtesan–a rare theme in Greek ceramics–playing the game of kottabos. Kottabos consisted of trying to throw the wine lees from the cup into a receptacle situated at a certain distance while invoking the name of a certain person. If the player was successful, the match with that person would be favorable. Here the figures are matched by pink, a fairly common color in Attic ceramics, resulting from the nature of the clay used and degree to which it was fired.

Attic ceramic kylix, ca. 500 BCE. J. Paul Getty Museum, Villa Getty Collection, Los Angeles.

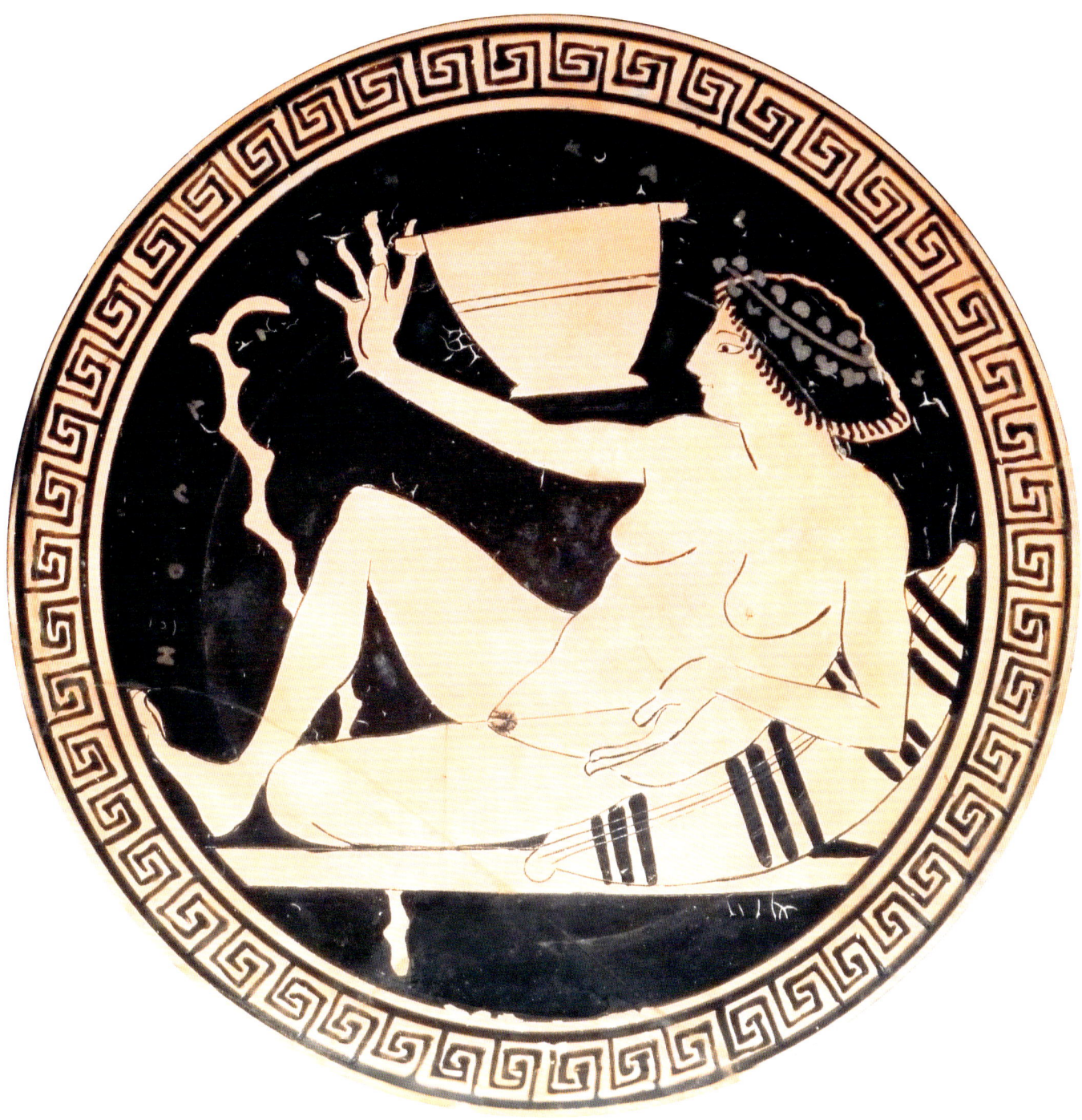

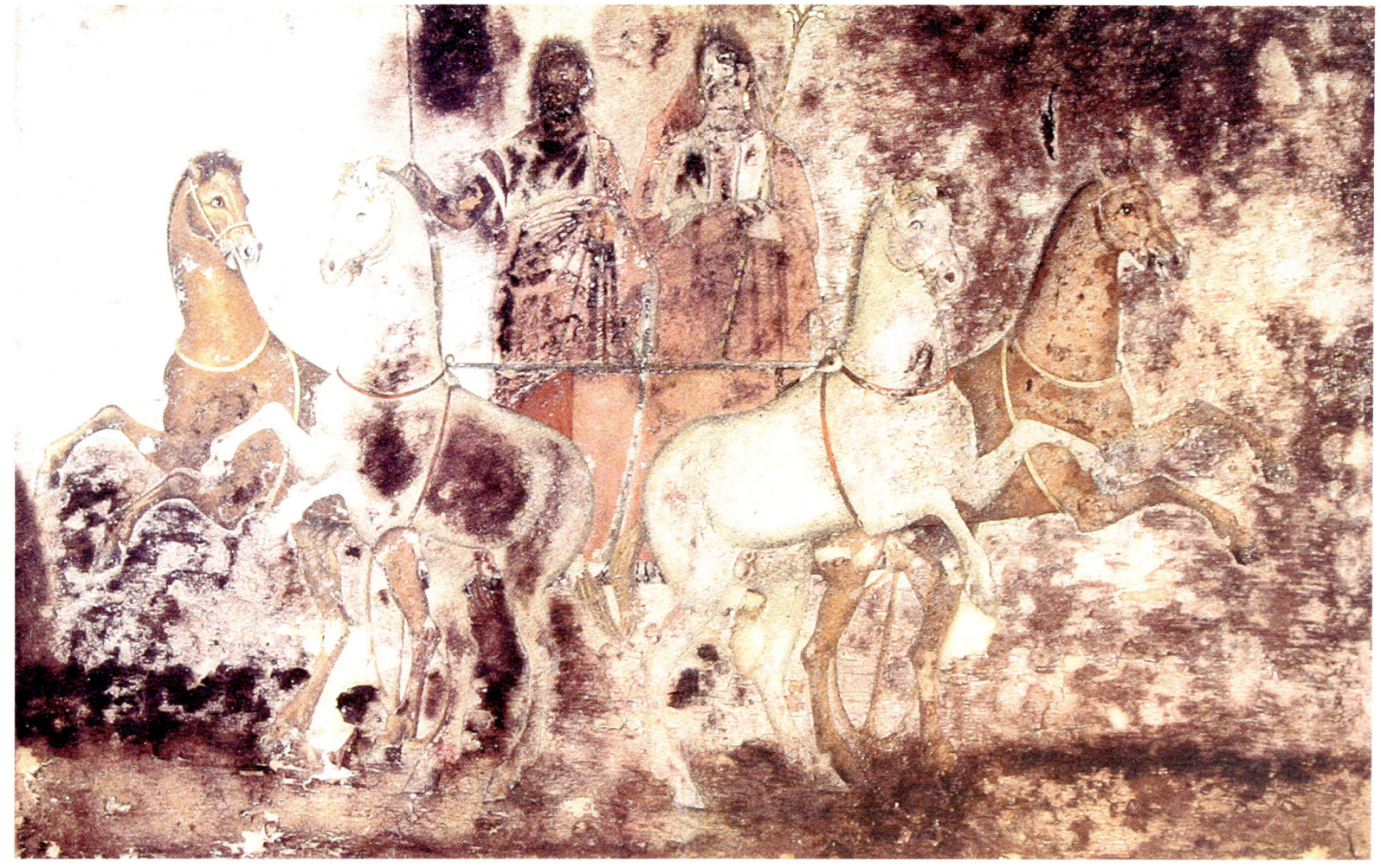

father, Philip II, who died in 336; the tomb of Philip II's mother, Eurydice, who died a generation earlier; and the tombs of two other younger princes or princesses, both unidentified. There are many other tombs in addition to those four, in Vergina and elsewhere, as well as more or less significant fragments of painted walls and objects.[2]

Studying these tombs has added immensely to our knowledge of the pictorial practices of ancient Greece.[3] Not only is the palette much broader, offering eleven rather than only a few colors—red, black, yellow, white, blue, green, gray, purple, orange, brown, and pink—but those eleven colors are each broken down into multiple shades thanks to the mixing of pigments and superimposition of colored layers forming a kind of glaze. We can even note that painters were already using a technique we find much later in Roman painting: "optical mixing." To make pink, for example, they could certainly mix or superimpose white, but they could also juxtapose those two colors in small touches, thus letting the eye of the viewer mix them and see pink. That procedure, perfectly familiar to the ancients, would not become theory until 1839 when Michel-Eugène Chevreul included it in his famous work *De la loi du contraste simultané des couleurs*,

a copious and difficult book that nevertheless exerted great influence on the impressionist painters thanks to a synopsis of it provided by Charles Blanc in 1867 in his *Grammaire des arts du dessin*.[4]

The analyses done on these various Macedonian decors have shed light on the use of numerous pigments, more varied than those we know were used in earlier Greek painting. Let us cite here only the ones employed in producing pink tones by mixing, superimposition, or juxtaposition. The whites have a base of chalk or chalky materials, kaolin (white clay), and sometimes calcined bones—three natural substances that were already used by Paleolithic painters. But we also find abundant use of a product destined for lasting success: ceruse, an artificial pigment with a lead base. To make it, the simplest method consisted of exploiting the oxidizing action of an acid on thin strips of lead, tightly sealed in a receptacle containing organic matter ready to ferment and release carbon dioxide. Once collected, the ceruse was washed, crushed, dried, and stored in the form of powder. Despite ceruse's toxic nature, until right up to the modern period, all artists appreciated its covering power, stability in light, low cost, adaptability, and the quality of tones it provided once mixed with other pigments. This was especially true of pink tones, created with the simple addition of a bit of red ocher or hematite powder (a mineral compound rich in iron oxide), or even lacquers made from plants (madder) or animals (murex).[5] On the other hand, Greek and Roman painters never combined ceruse with cinnabar (naturally occurring mercury sulfide), a costly pigment that they otherwise used and abused (in Pompeii, for example). Like all lead-based products, ceruse could not be mixed with or adjacent to pigments containing sulfur.

In relation to the painting of the classical period, the great innovations of the Macedonian painters lay in both the variety of their pigments and their way of using them to obtain different effects. The colors were applied in light touches and not on uniform, flat surfaces, thus allowing

OPPOSITE AND NEXT PAGE SPREAD

Macedonian Funeral Paintings

Over the last half century, the paintings revealed on the walls of royal tombs in Vergina, Macedonia, have greatly increased our knowledge of the materials and processes used by Greek painters at the beginning of the Hellenistic period. Their rich and varied palette includes eleven different colors. The pinks were obtained by either mixing lead white, bone white, and a little red ocher, or juxtaposing small touches of cinnabar and white clay, leaving the mixing of the two colors to the eye of the viewer.

Hades abducting Persephone, funerary paintings in the tomb of Eurydice, mother of Philip II, king of Macedonia, ca. 340 BCE. Necropolis of Aigai, Vergina (Greece).

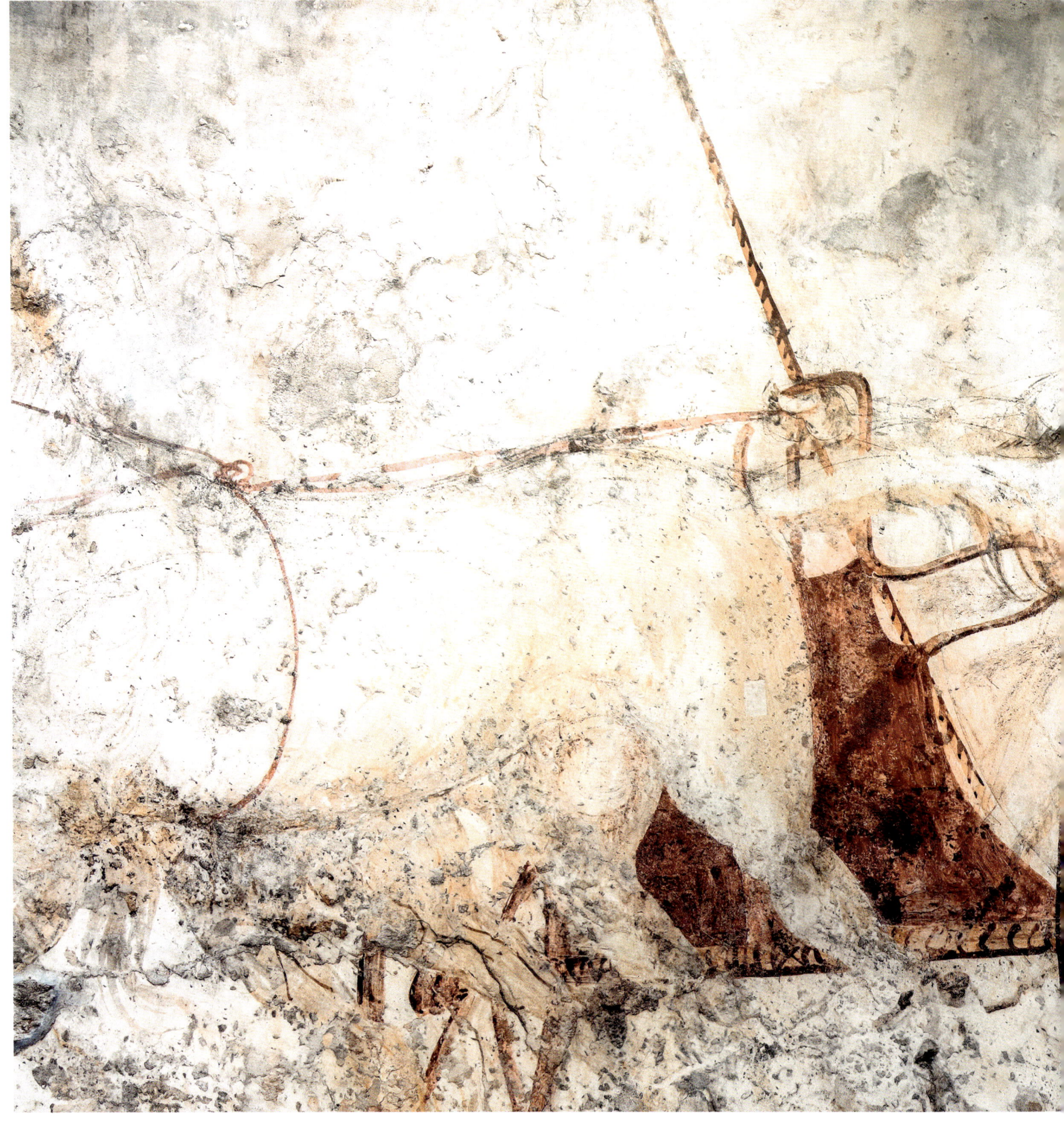

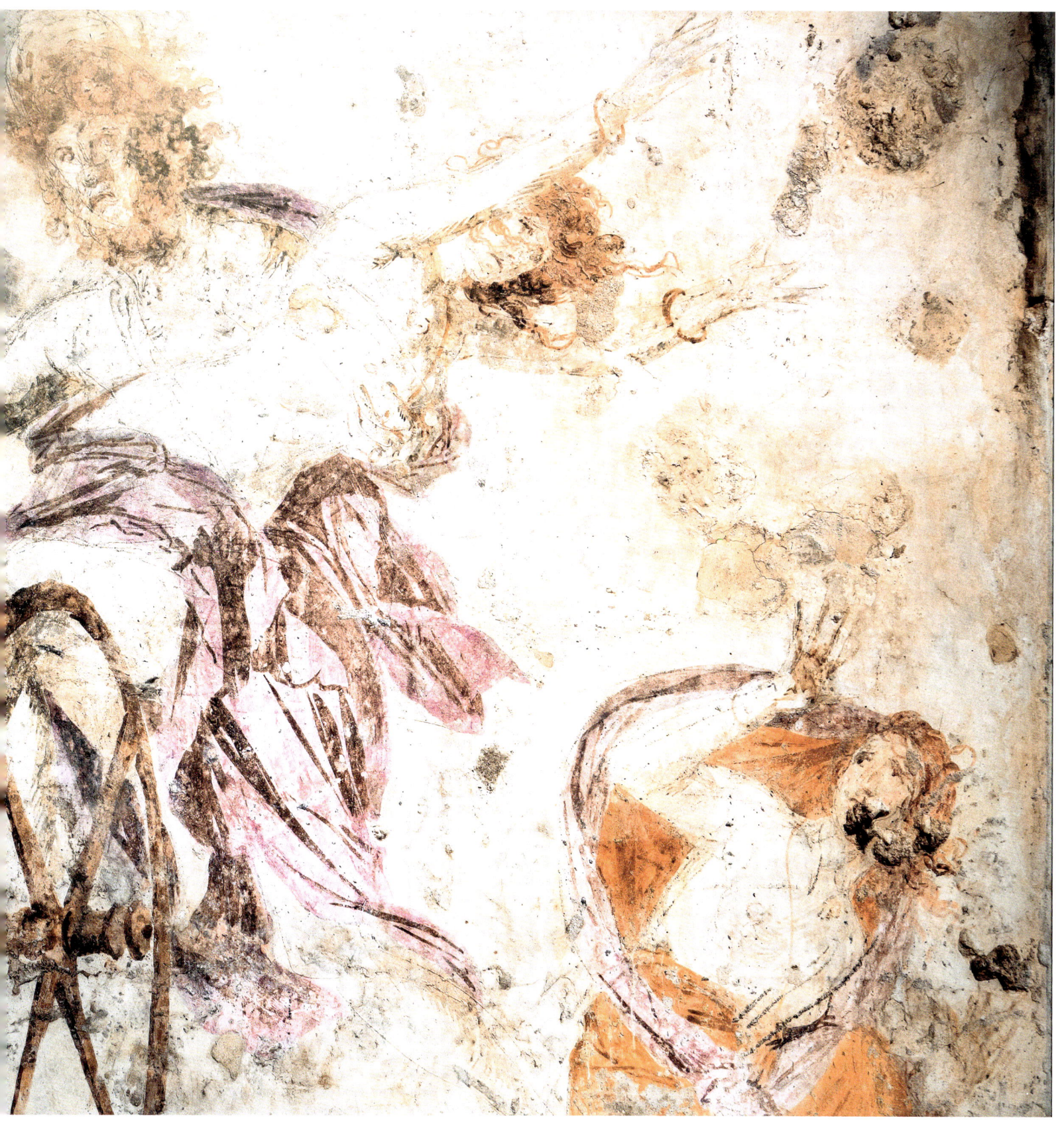

for nuanced shades, graduated tones, and sometimes subtle plays of transparency, which we will find more abundantly in Roman painting. Thanks to these variations in the application of pigments, the artists also learned how to manipulate relationships between shadow and light, to create illusions of volume, and even how to model, as in sculpture, the pose of a figure on a background, especially a human figure. Most of the painters working in Macedonia paid special attention to how they rendered flesh, mixing and superimposing pigments to vary skin tones, reserving the lightest for women and the darkest for men, and possibly distinguishing social status or ethnic origin through particular shades of skin.[6] Moreover, in a more general way, the delicacy of the skin tones brought to life the faces and bodies, not by making them more realistic, but on the contrary by idealizing them. In this domain, pink tones played a major role, and were broken down into subtle shades, more or less saturated, and lightly tinted with other colors: orange pink, beige pink, brownish pink, greenish pink, or bluish pink. This was an innovation, at least on this scale. In Western painting, pink would henceforth maintain a privileged relationship with skin, flesh, and nudity.

Stag Hunt

This famous mosaic was found in Pella, the birthplace of Alexander the Great, in a wealthy patrician's house that was known as the "House of the Abduction of Helen," the subject of another enormous mosaic. The artist, Gnosis, signed his work, but we know nothing about him. The two figures represented here are probably Alexander along with his general and favorite companion, Hephaistion. Marble tesserae provide the pink tones—a much more costly artistic material than molten glass.

Gnosis, Stag hunt, mosaic, late fourth century BCE. Archaeological Museum, Pella (Greece).

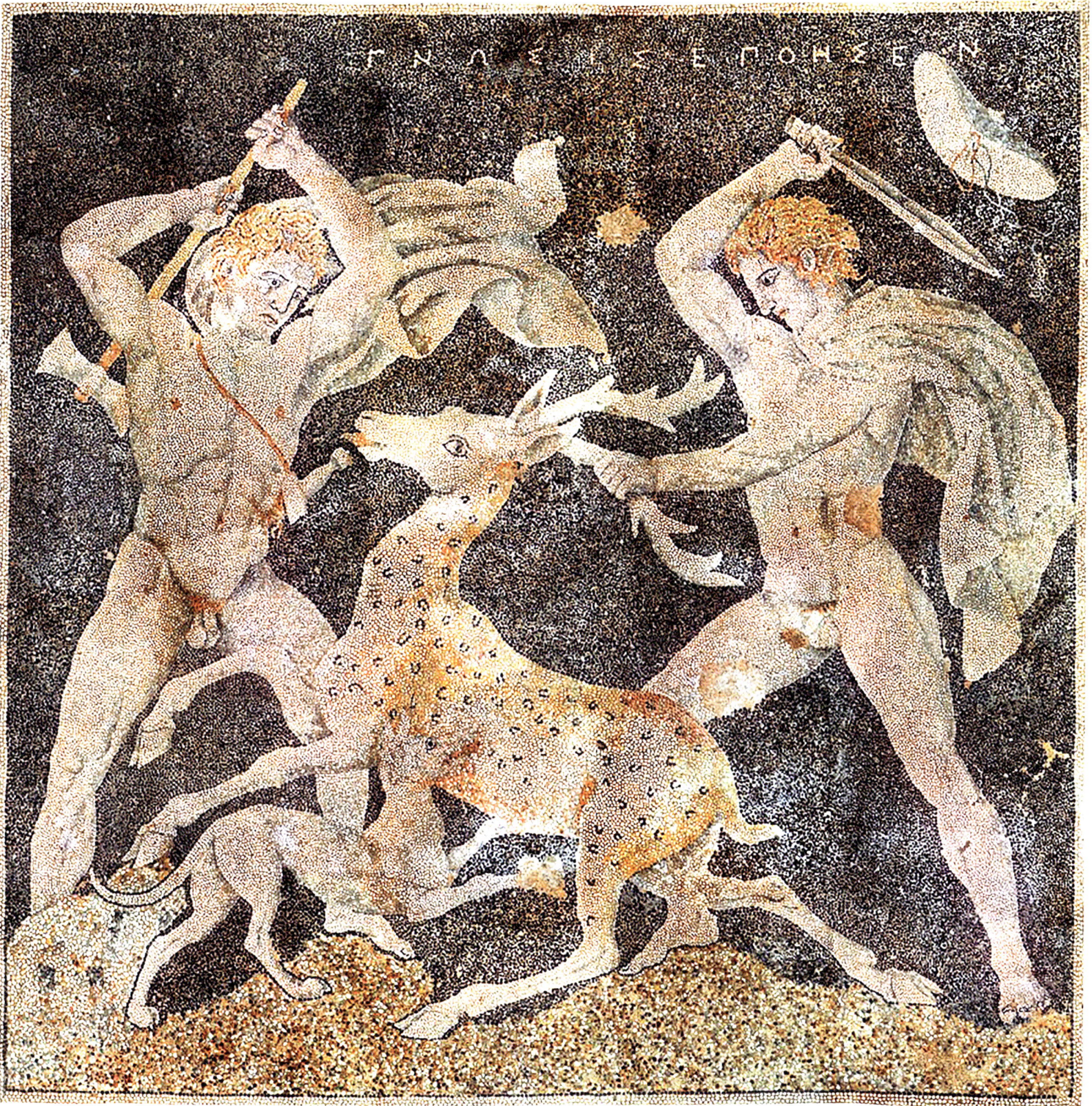

Ancient Flesh Tones

This close relationship between the color pink and nudity emerges fully in Roman painting. More frequently than in Greek painting, Roman painting presents the human body nude or seminude, notably in representations of the divinities and erotic art, abundant in the painted interiors of sumptuous patrician villas beginning in the first century BCE. The most famous examples come from the cities that fell victim to the eruption of Vesuvius around the Bay of Naples on August 24, 79, one of the most important dates in the entire history of painting. On that day, the volcano began erupting, and within a few hours, it had covered or destroyed four flourishing cities erected on its borders: Herculaneum, Pompeii, Oplontis, and Stabiae. Everything was engulfed or fixed in its current state at the moment of the eruption. Of course many inhabitants had time to flee—deaths totaled between 10 and 15 percent of the population—but public buildings, houses, workshops, shops, chariots, tools, instruments, merchandise, provisions, animals, vineyards, and gardens were covered and buried under stone, mud, lava, and ash, until the sixteenth century initially, and then crucially, the eighteenth century, when the first archaeological excavations began to extricate what could be unearthed.

Continuing to the present day—and far from being completed—these excavations have increasingly offered archaeologists and historians abundant materials for studying the material culture, urban life, and professional activities in the Roman Empire in the first century CE. And their contribution does not end there; they have also offered art historians an exceptional group of painted interiors, some of them remarkably well preserved, that have served for the past 250 years as our major source for studying Roman painting. Thanks to Vesuvius, Roman painting is the best known and best preserved of all ancient artwork.

Venus at Her Toilet

Roman mosaics often offer a palette of more diverse tones than do wall paintings. In particular, blues, greens, grays, and pinks are more abundant, more delicate, and lighter. This mosaic from a Roman villa is a beautiful example. It represents Venus at her toilet and is part of a series, following two other scenes: Artemis bathing, and Thetis, goddess of the sea, surrounded by sea creatures and sea monsters.

Pavement mosaic (detail), third century. As-Suwayda Museum (Municipality Building), As-Suwayda (Syria).

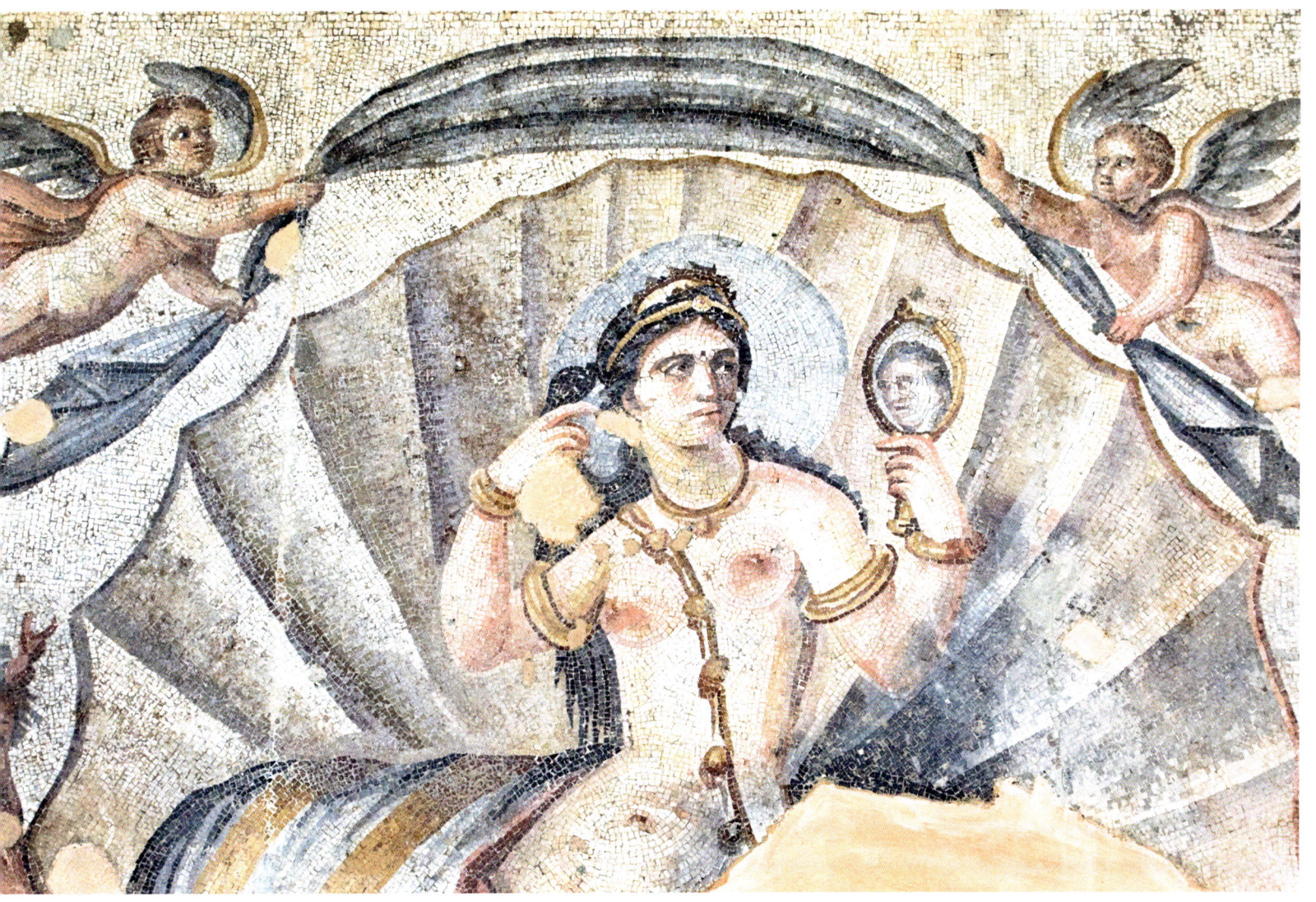

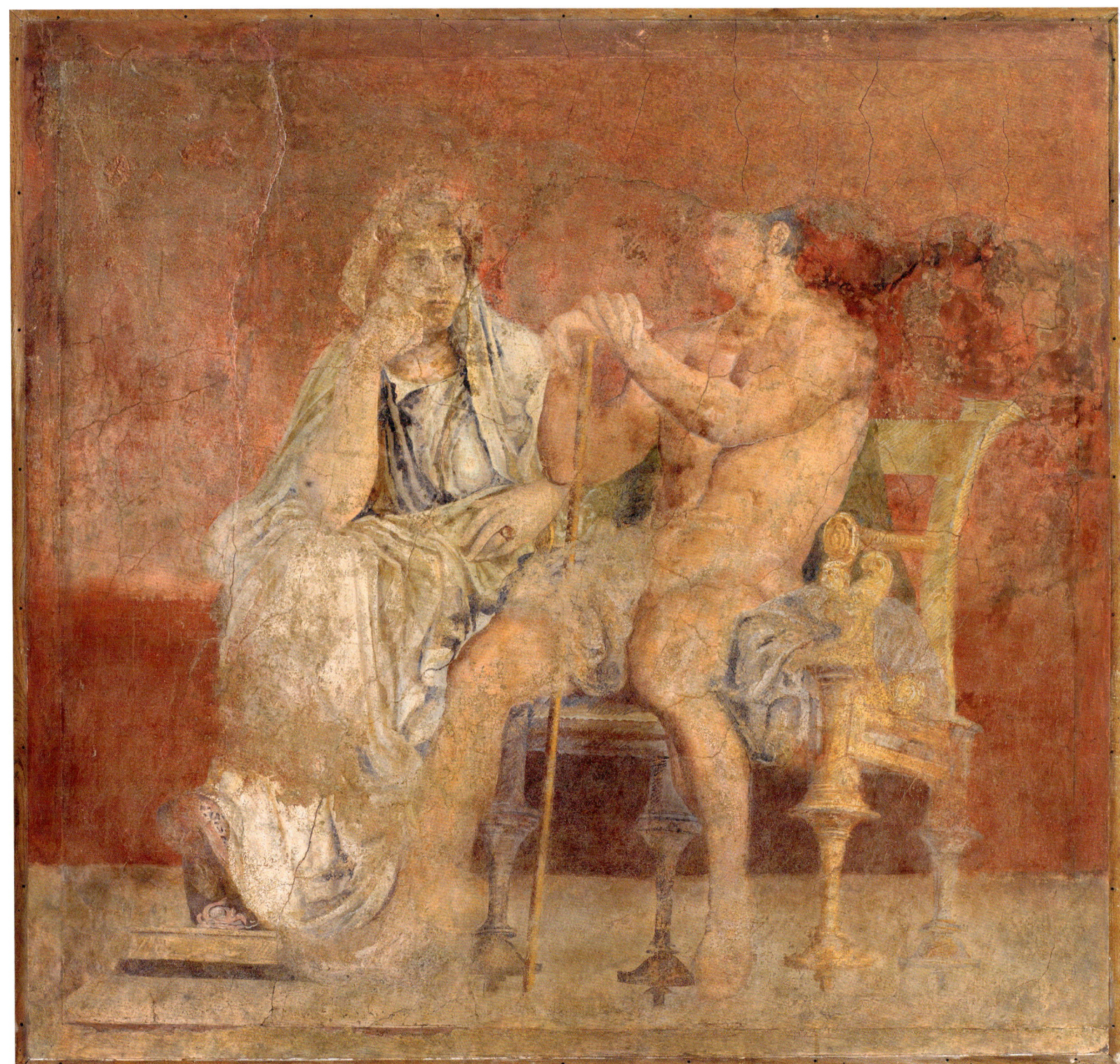

Sometimes extraordinarily sumptuous and refined, these murals are found in various villas that were owned by the wealthiest patricians in Herculaneum, Pompeii, and Stabiae. They mostly date from the first century BCE and first century CE. There is no comparison between what they offer us and what we can learn about ancient Roman mural painting otherwise from studying a few temples and villas located in Rome or its surroundings, or even in numerous cities in southern Italy, Sicily, and the provinces.

In Pompeii and other Vesuvian cities, red is ubiquitous, but pink is hardly less so, in a variety of tones. In some cases, it is a matter of yellows, reds, or purples that the heat of the eruption may have transformed into pinks (on friezes or columns, for instance), but generally these were the original tones: the flesh tones of faces, hands, arms, legs, and other parts of the body not covered by clothing. The wealth of examples is all the richer because the human figure is abundantly represented and erotic scenes are common, notably in bedrooms and brothels. Beginning in the eighteenth century, these scenes prompted surprise, alarm, and interrogation; they continue to do so today at the National Archaeological Museum of Naples, where one room (not always open) is devoted specifically to them. Not all the nudes in Pompeii are associated with Eros, however; a good number of the gods are naked for no particular reason, as are certain glorified or deified heroes. As for female nudity, it does not always evoke love or carnal relationships but more simply, beauty, fertility, prosperity, or even happiness or good luck. In Rome, Pompeii, and elsewhere, there is a great temptation to overanalyze or misinterpret such nudes anachronistically if the modern observer is too eager for spicy or transgressive content. How many historians of antiquity have thus gone astray, seeing "sex" where there is none!

Whatever the case, such a wealth of nudes provides us remarkable material for studying the range of pinks presented by these painters. There are many diverse tones. Some are pale and tend toward white or a very soft yellow; others are more saturated and tend more toward red, salmon, or orange; and still others are downright beige or even bister. Were they so before the eruption? It is hard to say. Furthermore, many of the flesh tones are not one uniform color but instead enhanced with glazes or highlights that are slightly amber, greenish, bluish, or even purplish. Just by itself, the Roman palette of pinks is almost a rainbow.

To obtain that palette, artists had many pigments available to them, which they were skilled at combining. There are the ones we have already encountered in Macedonia: chalk and ground limestone, kaolin, plaster, and ceruse for the whites; red ocher, hematite, and lacquers made from madder, kermes, or murex for the reds. Heating together ceruse and a bit of clay rich in iron oxide (*sinopia*) was a common method in Greece and Rome for making a pigment that offered lovely pink tones, although they had the disadvantage of being dull. Now in Herculaneum, Pompeii, and Stabiae, the preference was for high gloss, for what was bright, shiny, iridescent, and nacreous. Thus to make pinks, sulfur-based red pigments were used, like realgar, a natural arsenic sulfide already present in Egyptian painting, and especially cinnabar, the natural mercuric sulfide that we have already mentioned.

Banquet Room Decor

The eruption of Vesuvius in 79 CE not only engulfed the cities located at the foot of the volcano but also buried the villas owned by wealthy patricians and scattered throughout the surrounding countryside. That was the case with the villa belonging to Publius Fannius Synistor, a figure about whom we know nothing, although his residence, with its abundant, lavish, painted decor, leads us to believe he was wealthy. Now housed in various museums, these paintings are, for the most part, remarkably well preserved. Pink tones appear in numerous shades, lighter for the flesh of women, and more orange for that of men.

Wall painting from the dining room of the villa of Publius Fannius Synistor at Boscoreale (Campania). Metropolitan Museum of Art, New York.

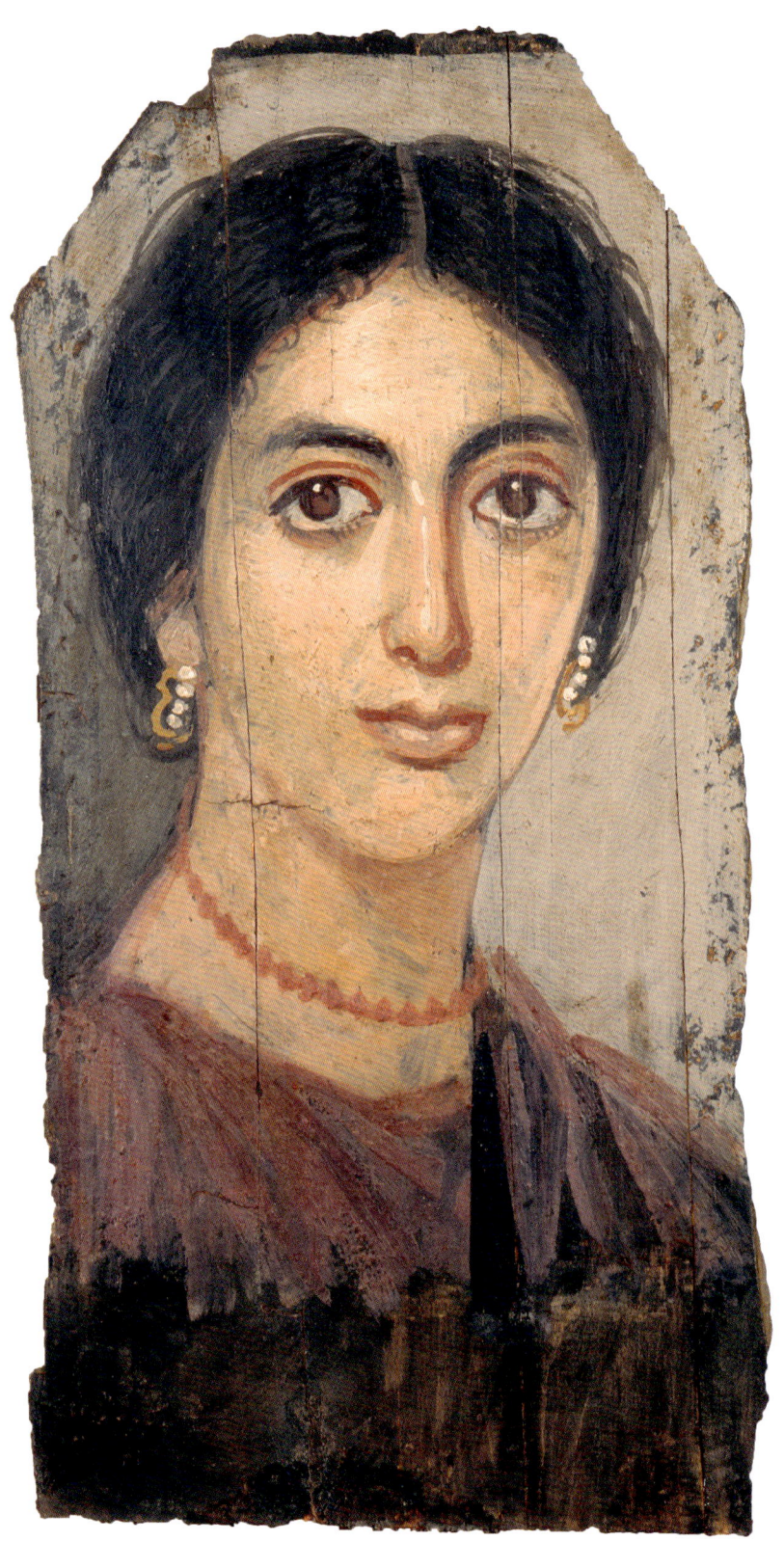

Encaustic Funerary Portrait Paintings

Inserted over the face of the mummified body, Egyptian funerary portraits from the Roman period could be stereotypical, or else as here, more or less realistic. For women, special attention was paid to makeup and jewelry, and for men, to the beard and hair. As in wall paintings, the female complexion is lighter and less orange than the male one.

Two Fayum funerary portraits (Egypt). The one of a mother, second century CE. Milwaukee Art Museum. The one of a bearded man, mid-third century CE. Roemer-Pelizaeus Museum, Hildesheim.

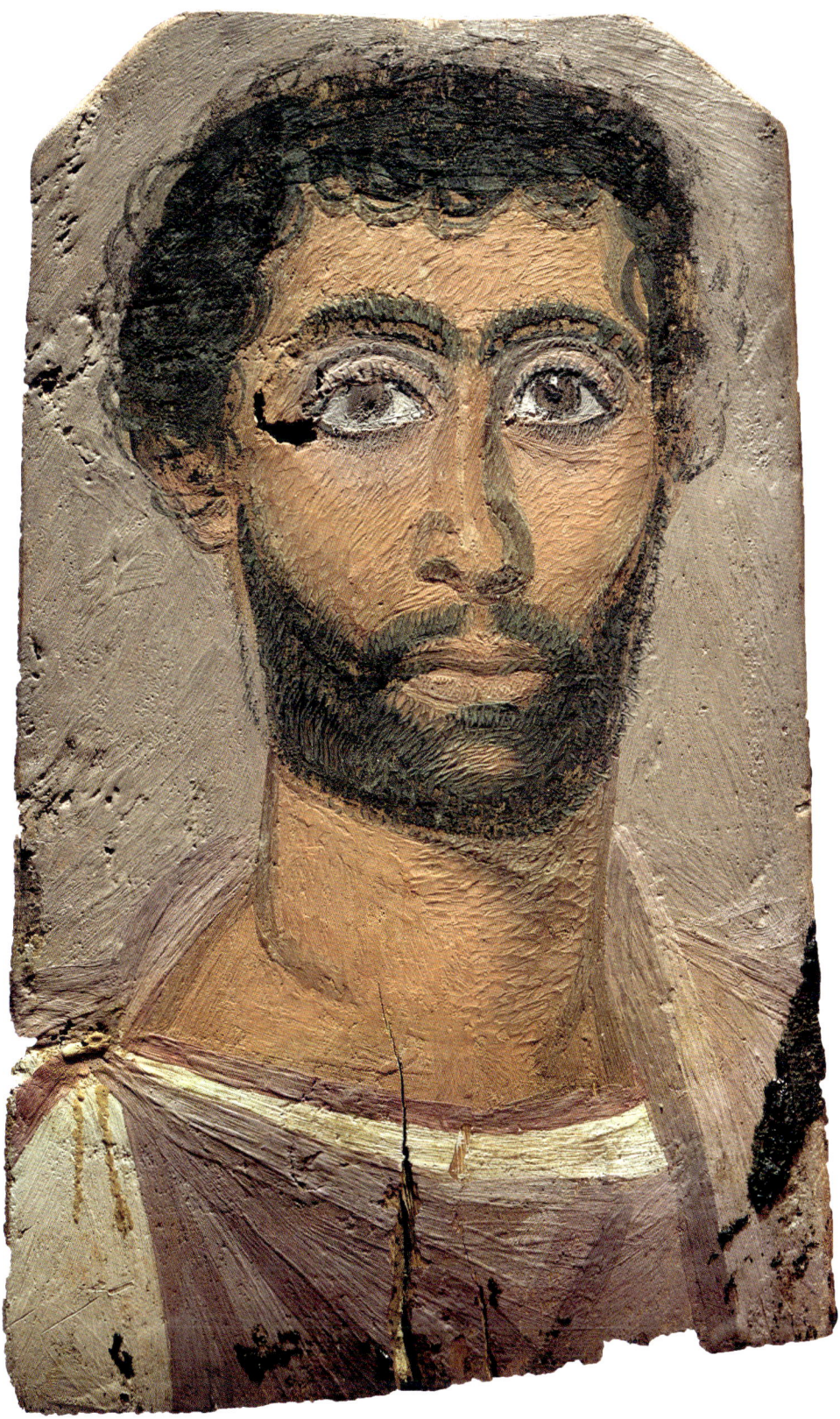

Despite its high price and dangerous nature (it is extremely toxic), cinnabar is everywhere in Pompeii, where it was used in an ostentatious way for painting backgrounds. Hence the dominant red appearing on the wall of many villas whose owners would have been considered "nouveaux riches" in the eyes of their contemporaries. In his *Natural History*, where Pliny is happy to inform his readers about prices, we learn that cinnabar cost "fifteen times more than red ocher from Africa," and that its price was even equal to that of "blue from Alexandria" (the famous Egyptian blue), the most expensive pigment of his time.[7] This luxury cinnabar was extracted from the mines of Almaden, located in the heart of Spain. Shipped to Rome in its raw mineral form, it was processed in many workshops operating at the foot of the Quirinal, an active industrial neighborhood, noisy and foul smelling, with a bad reputation. There was another, more ordinary kind of cinnabar that came from mines located below the volcanic mountains of the Apennines, but the painters of Pompeii seemed to disdain it. The artists' rich sponsors wanted whatever was most beautiful, expensive, and ostentatious. The fortune and rank of these sponsors had to be displayed on the walls of the lavish villas that they had rebuilt after the earthquakes of the years 61 and 62. The abundant use of cinnabar was a means of conveying their vast wealth.

It is to this cinnabar that we owe the lovely vivid, saturated shade that since the early nineteenth century has been called, a bit improperly, "Pompeian red," and goes perfectly with gold or gilt. We also owe to cinnabar— and this is where our interest here lies—a great number of flesh tones in which small amounts of it were combined with chalky materials or kaolin. Sometimes a few grains of hematite were added to tone down its excessive brilliance. On faces, the tones thus obtained were often veined or shadowed with green earth or Egyptian blue. In the Vesuvian cities as throughout the Roman Empire, painting practices were already sophisticated, and the boundary separating them from chemistry, or rather alchemy, seemed fluid. Moreover, authors like Vitruvius and Pliny make that clear in the passages they devote to painting—Vitruvius in his treatise on architecture written about 30 or 25 BCE, and Pliny in the famous thirty-fifth book of his *Natural History*, compiled a century later.

Another important group of ancient flesh tones is provided to historians of painting by the famous "Fayum" funerary portraits (named for the rich agricultural oasis located in the western desert of Egypt). These portraits generally date from the second to fourth centuries CE. Painted on wood (sycamore, linden, oak, or cedar), less frequently on linen canvas, representing the bust of the deceased, head facing forward, they were meant to be inserted in wrappings over the face of the mummy. In Egypt under Roman rule, mummification was practiced much more often than cremation. These are the oldest painted portraits left to us by antiquity, and the most numerous as well; more than two thousand exist. Painted while their subjects were alive, the portraits were touched up at the time of their deaths, and served as both a means of identification and commemoration, and thus as a kind of survival for them. The most debated issue is clearly the one of resemblance: Are these realistic or idealized portraits? A little of both, probably, at least in most cases. Because although the body of work divides equally between men and women, and although it is relatively homogeneous from a social perspective (the wealthy classes, with clothing and hair styled in Roman fashion), there are no children or old people, and only a few adolescent boys and girls.

It is as if most of the dead had been represented at an ideal age, with traits that were certainly theirs, but more or less idealized as well.

Two techniques were used to paint these portraits: encaustic and tempera. The first technique, used in the majority of the paintings, offers less flat faces and a greater variety of skin tones. Pink tones abound, but these pinks are less "rosy" than in Pompeii or Rome; they are whiter, yellower, duller, and never uniform, but shadowed and accentuated or sharpened with other colors to model depths or emphasize an expression. The complexion is often darker for men than for women, who are made up and adorned with jewelry. Women's cheeks are of a more saturated skin tone than the rest of the face, and their lips are frequently bright pink or even fully red. The female complexion also seems smoother than the male one thanks to more finely ground pigments and smaller touches. All the faces contrast with the black or dark colors of the hair, eyebrows, and beards as well as with those of the background, generally neutral or summarily painted in beige, brown, grayish or greenish tones. Such a variety of flesh tones, otherwise unknown in ancient art, helps to make these portraits lifelike. Some of them seem to portray our contemporaries, to the point of having sometimes cast doubt—wrongly—on their antiquity or authenticity.

Dyes, Finery, and Clothing

L et us return to Rome, where the place of pink in everyday life was much more discreet than in Pompeiian painting. Only brick and tile sometimes introduced a bit of this color in street scenes, where reds, yellows, and oranges were much more present. The same is true for objects. None have survived that are truly pink, not even ceramic ones where the various shades of fired clay nevertheless formed a wide palette of rosy and orange tones. On murals, pinks were primarily flesh tones or else reds that became lighter over time. Mosaics, on the other hand, offered a slightly greater wealth of pinks, and these were the original colors. As for clothing—the first medium for color in all social life—pink was unknown there. There was no place for it in female attire during the successive waves of new fashions arriving from the East beginning in the first century CE. This introduction of frivolous colors (*colores floridi*), completely new to Rome, scandalized the old Romans (beginning with Pliny): blues, greens, blacks, purples, stripes, and brightly colored patterns, but no pink.

Moreover, naming such a shade would have been difficult. Latin possesses no word that means *pink*. The adjective *roseus* is a false friend that describes a bright red or vermilion tone, but not a pink in the sense that we understand it today. As for *rosaceus*, it refers only to the flower, to its beauty or scent, but never to its color. As it happens, that may be the reason why pink is absent from all color lists left to us by Latin antiquity; regardless the domain, pink is absent from any catalog or list of pigments, dyes, or colors. The same is true in the Middle Ages until the fourteenth century.

What documents we possess on the dyeing trade confirm this lack of interest in the color pink. Roman artisans nonetheless inherited solid technical knowledge in such

A Prelate Dressed in Pink

Ottonian illumination features more pink tones than do those from the Carolingian or Romanesque periods. In this regard, it may have been influenced by Byzantine illumination. In this frontispiece miniature, the archbishop Egbert of Trier (ca. 950–93) receives an illuminated lectionary that he himself commissioned from the monks of the Reichenau Abbey. He is entirely dressed in and surrounded by pink, a color present in images but not actually worn, especially by a high-ranking prelate.

Codex Egberti, Reichenau, ca. 980. Stadtbibliothek, Trier (Germany), HS 24, folio 2.

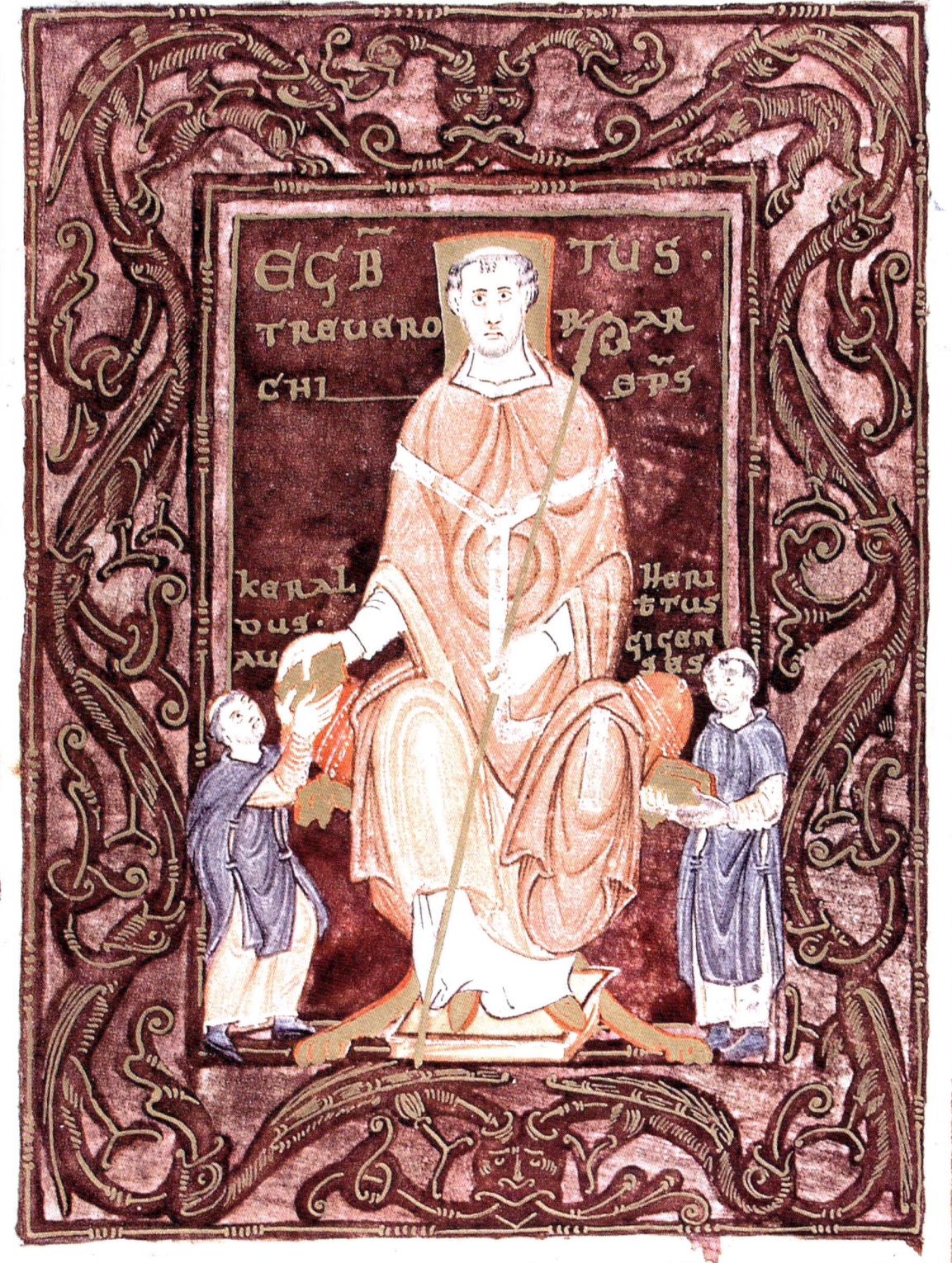

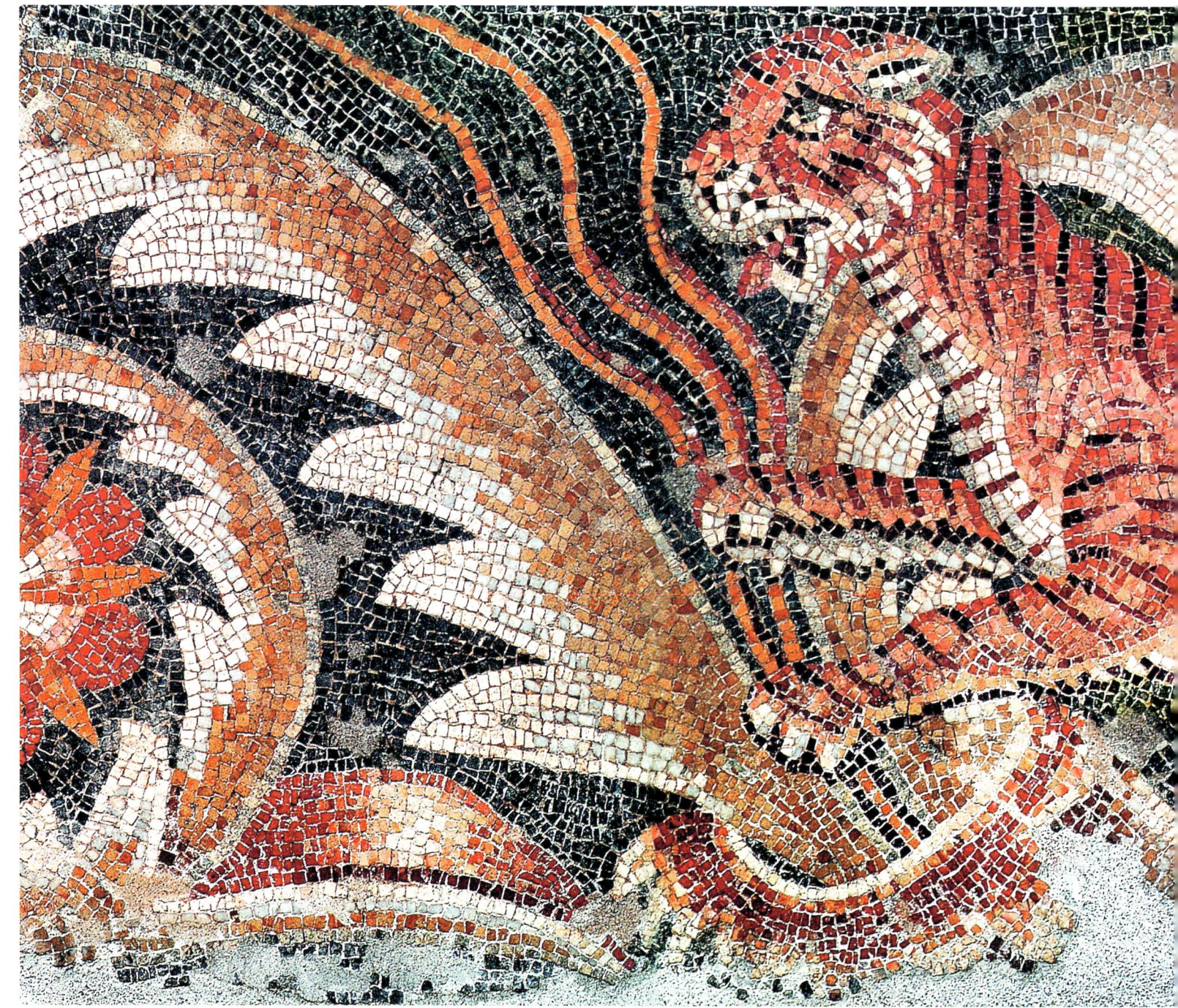

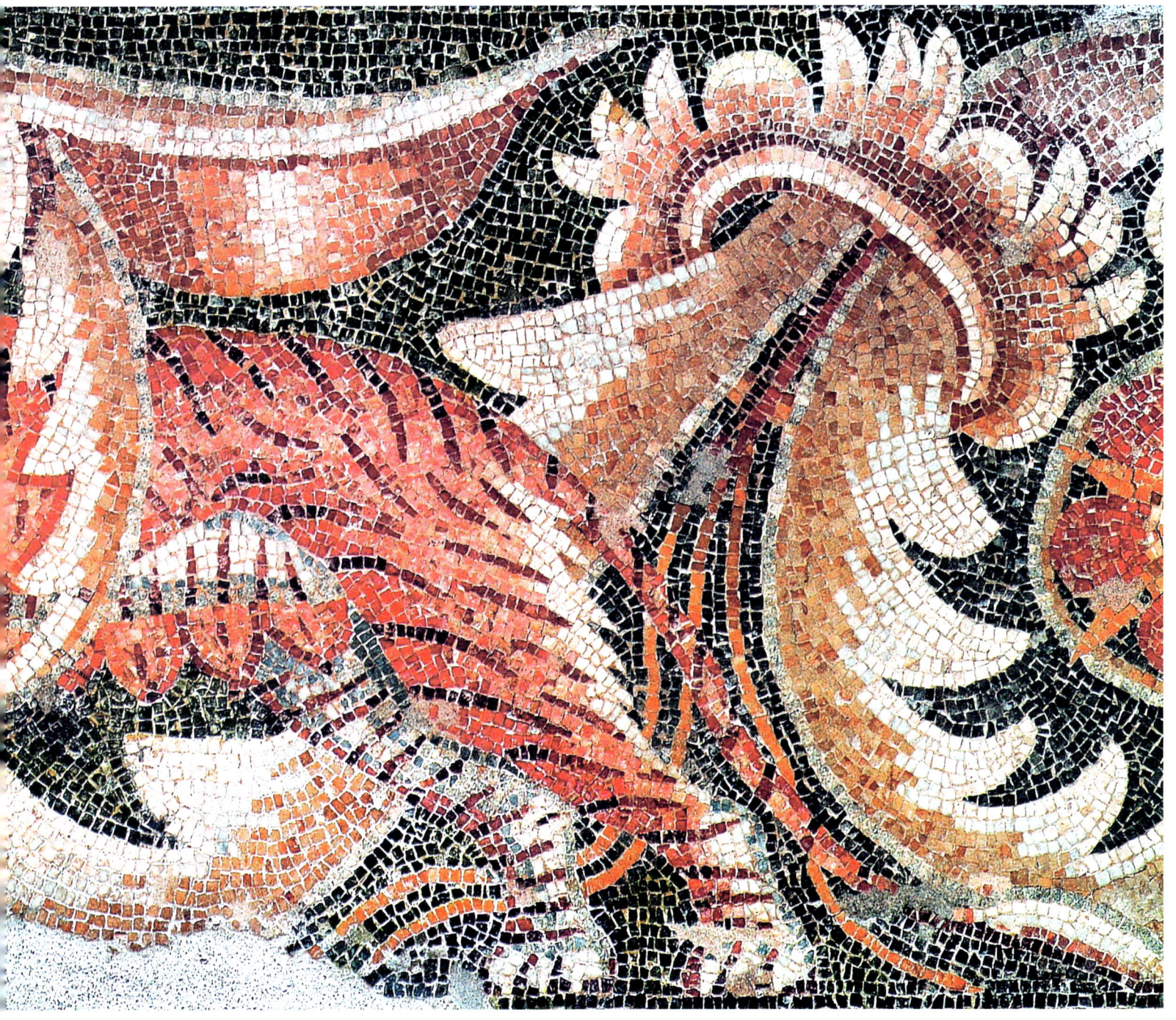

PREVIOUS PAGE SPREAD

A Polychrome Tiger

The colors of the fur or feathers of animals are frequently more varied in mosaics than in murals. On the other hand, they are less realistic, like the coat of this tiger, which is not really striped but instead polychrome. The Romans admired these wild animals, which they imported from great distances to display at the circus. For the Romans, tigers symbolized beauty, speed, and pride. The tigress in particular seemed to them especially proud of her coat.

Mosaic from a Roman villa, fourth century CE. Noto (Sicily).

matters from the Egyptians, Greeks, and Etruscans. They advanced it, and by the end of the Roman Republic, had become specialized according to color and dyestuffs. Thus in Marcus Tullius Cicero's time, the *collegium tinctorum*, an ancient artisans' guild, distinguished no less than six categories of artisans for reds and related colors. The *sandicinii* produced the many madder-based reds; the *coccinarii* produced the much more costly reds that were kermes based; the *purpurarii* made all the brilliant and changeable reds derived from murex; the *spardicarii* made a few brownish reds from various woods; the *flammarii* produced the bright and dark oranges derived from carthamin; and last, the *crocotarii* made the wonderful, luxurious yellow oranges that were saffron based. In total, that is, reds, yellows, russets, oranges, browns, and even purples, but no pink!

To find such a color in the appearance of Romans, we need to look to makeup and jewelry. Roman matrons in the time of the empire tended to use makeup excessively, combining three contrasting colors: white (chalk or ceruse) on the forehead, cheeks, and arms; red (*rubrica* or cinnabar) on the cheekbones and lips; and black (ash, various charcoals, or antimony powder) on eyelashes and around the eyes.[8] Many authors condemned excessively made-up female faces, and denounced the arsenal of jars and bottles that every woman possessed for making herself beautiful. Like Ovid, an expert on female beauty, they preferred a

few traces of "light red" (*fucus subrubeus*), which young women used to highlight their lips and cheekbones.[9] Regarding makeup, Ovid wrote, "The art is to conceal the art."[10] Must we read this line as praise for pink?

Regarding jewelry, for the rings and pendants that Romans—both women and men—wore in the time of the empire, red dominated, not only because it was considered alluring, but because it was supposed to bring good luck. Sometimes these reds were light in color (as with different kinds of rubies and garnets), and sometimes stones tending distinctly toward pink were used as substitutes (certain agates or tourmalines, for example). Added to these were pieces of cinnabar, coral (then likened to stone), or quartz set in rings of precious metal or else worn by themselves under clothing as talismans. In Rome, red stones had protective properties; they were supposed to ward off the forces of evil. Did the occasional pinks appearing in jewelry or amulets have these same properties? It is difficult to answer that question.

Pink's unobtrusiveness in everyday life and material culture extended throughout and even beyond the early Middle Ages. The fashions and dyeing techniques brought to Rome by the Germans certainly favored the new and

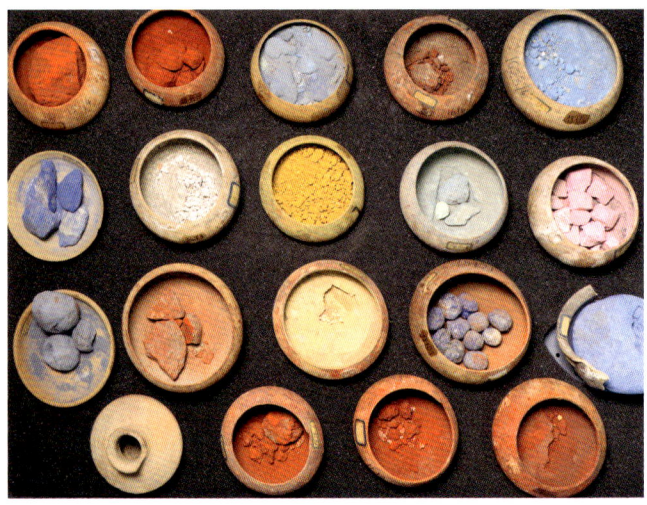

OPPOSITE PAGE

Pigments Used in Roman Painting

Roman painting used more pigments than Egyptian and Greek painting did. Among the coloring materials found at the sites of Pompeii and Oplontis, cities engulfed when Vesuvius erupted in 79 CE, we can identify red ocher, hematite, minium, and cinnabar for the reds; lime, gypsum, ceruse, and chalk for the whites; calcined plant matter and clays rich in manganese oxide or lead for the blacks; ocher and orpiment for the yellows; green earths, malachite, and oxidized coppers for the greens; and lapis lazuli, Egyptian blue, and azurite for the blues.

Pigments from the Villa Poppea. Oplontis (Italy).

OPPOSITE

The Virtues of Carnelian

For the Romans, carnelian was a stone that brought happiness, warded off evil, and gave strength and courage to those who made use of it. Thus it was worn as jewelry by both men and women. Relatively easy to work, it was turned into cameos and intaglios. Inserted into rings, these latter were used as wax seals. The most beautiful stones came from the Near East and Indies. Their colors varied from red orange to red violet, and included various shades of vermilion, pink, and purple.

Personification of Libya, with an elephant skin headdress, carnelian stone, first century. Metropolitan Museum of Art, New York.

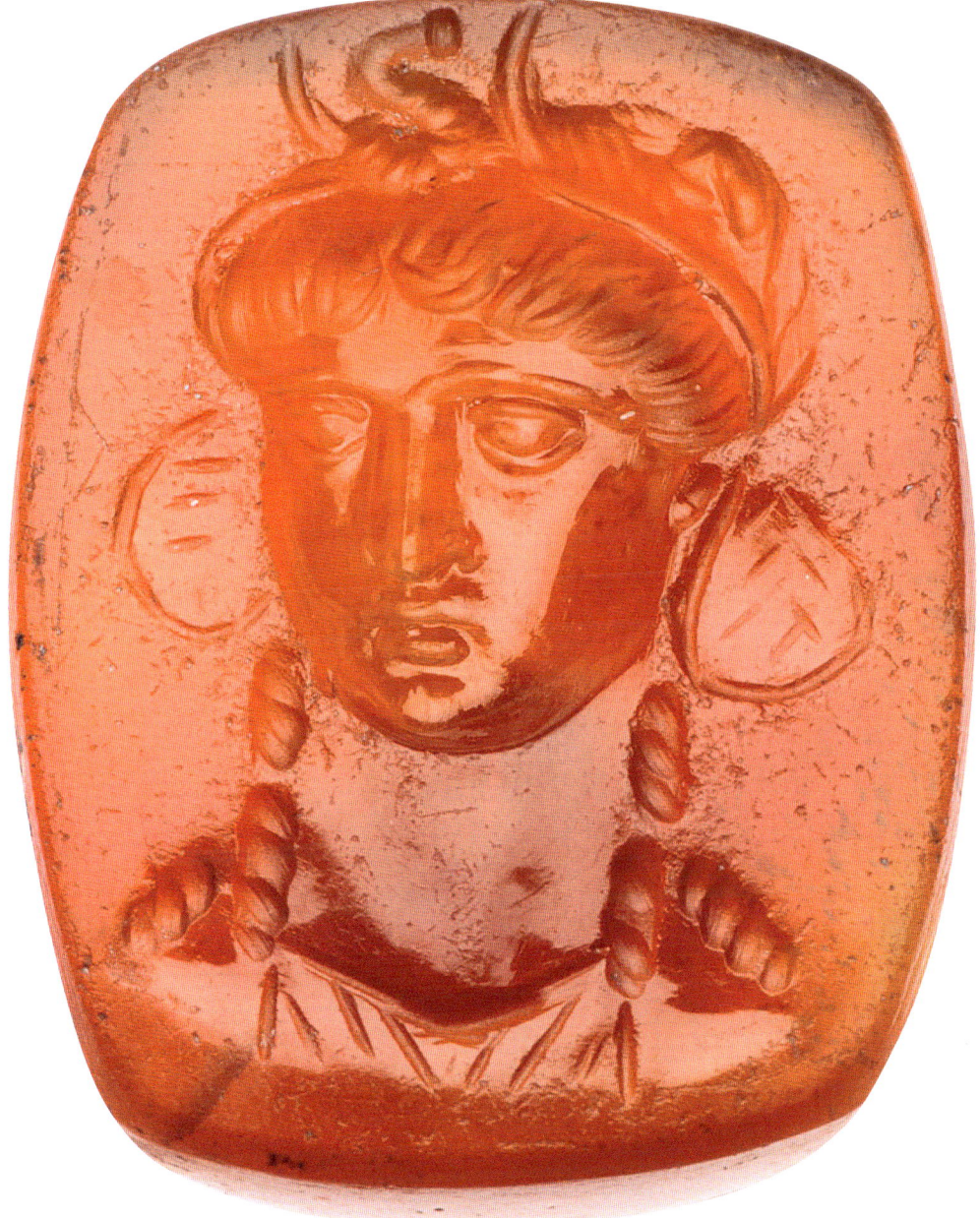

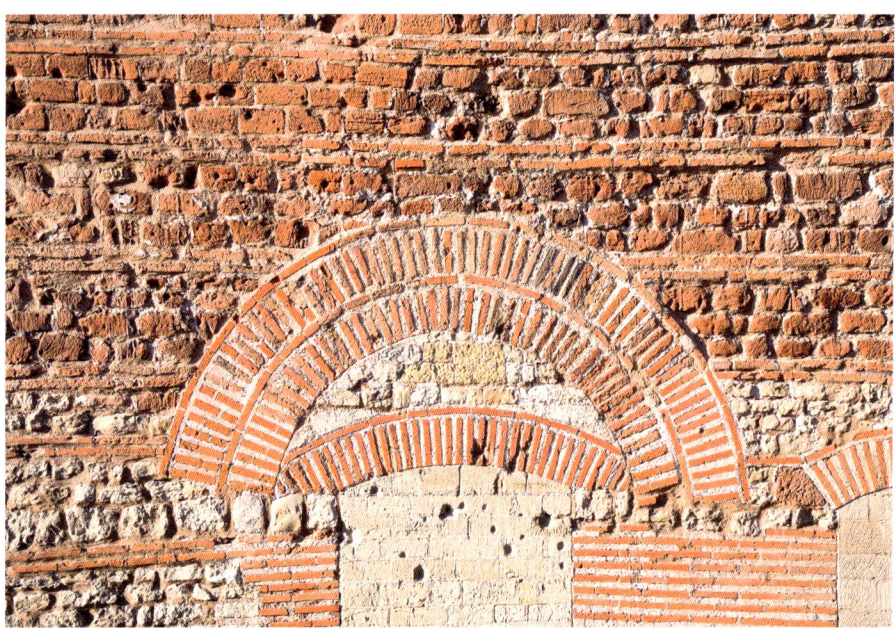

Roman Bricks

Fired solid bricks were the construction material most commonly used in the Roman period, both for buildings and everything related to civil engineering. Many areas of the Roman Empire were indeed rich in clay soils. Unlike the Greeks, the Romans did not cover over bricks but instead usually left them bare, which explains the red, pink, or orange look—rather than white—of most Roman cities.

Remains of a wall and door in Trier (Germany), third century.

lasting taste for green tones (and, to a lesser extent, blue tones) in the realms of textile and clothing, but pinks were not favored in the least. It is true that from the fall of the Roman Empire to the mid-twelfth century, few documents survive to give the historian an accurate idea of the palette of colors worn by each class or social category. We know that all clothing was dyed, including the most modest attire, but texts and images offer little information.[11]

After that time, documents are more forthcoming, but have not yet been systematically studied. That is no easy task because in this area, the only source allowing quantitative studies is the body of miniatures. They are certainly abundant for the twelfth and thirteenth centuries, but they are hardly photographic images of the actual clothing worn then, either in terms of fashions or colors. It would be naive to think that a given figure dressed in pink in a miniature really wore pink in some actual circumstance or even that such a color had a place in the wardrobes of a particular time period. With regard to colors, the illuminators of the central Middle Ages did what they liked and rarely painted what they actually saw. And what is true of miniatures is just as true of stained glass, enamel work, murals, and, later, tapestry. In the medieval image, any element can be any color. Thus a famous window

appearing in the nave of Chartres Cathedral features an enormous crow with splendid pink plumage; this is the crow released by Noah to go see if the floodwaters had begun to recede. Rather than returning to the ark with good news, this strange and seductive crow preferred to linger to eat cadavers, starting, as always, with the eyes in order to access more easily its choice delicacy, the brain. This necrophagous crow is not black as we would expect but rather very much pink.[12]

The preceding remarks pertain not only to medieval iconography but also to all the figurative sources used by historians of clothing. The colors reproduced by images only rarely correspond to those that were actually worn, whether the context is Roman antiquity, the height of the Middles Ages, the Enlightenment, or the twenty-first century. Even the most recent color photography does not give an accurate idea of the colors worn every day by ordinary people. Let us think of the historians who, in two or three centuries, will have our fashion magazines among their figurative sources. Let us hope they will not be so naive as to believe that in 2024, we were really dressed as those magazines portray us. For proof, let us sit down in a bus or subway car with a publication like that and observe how passengers are dressed. Nobody is

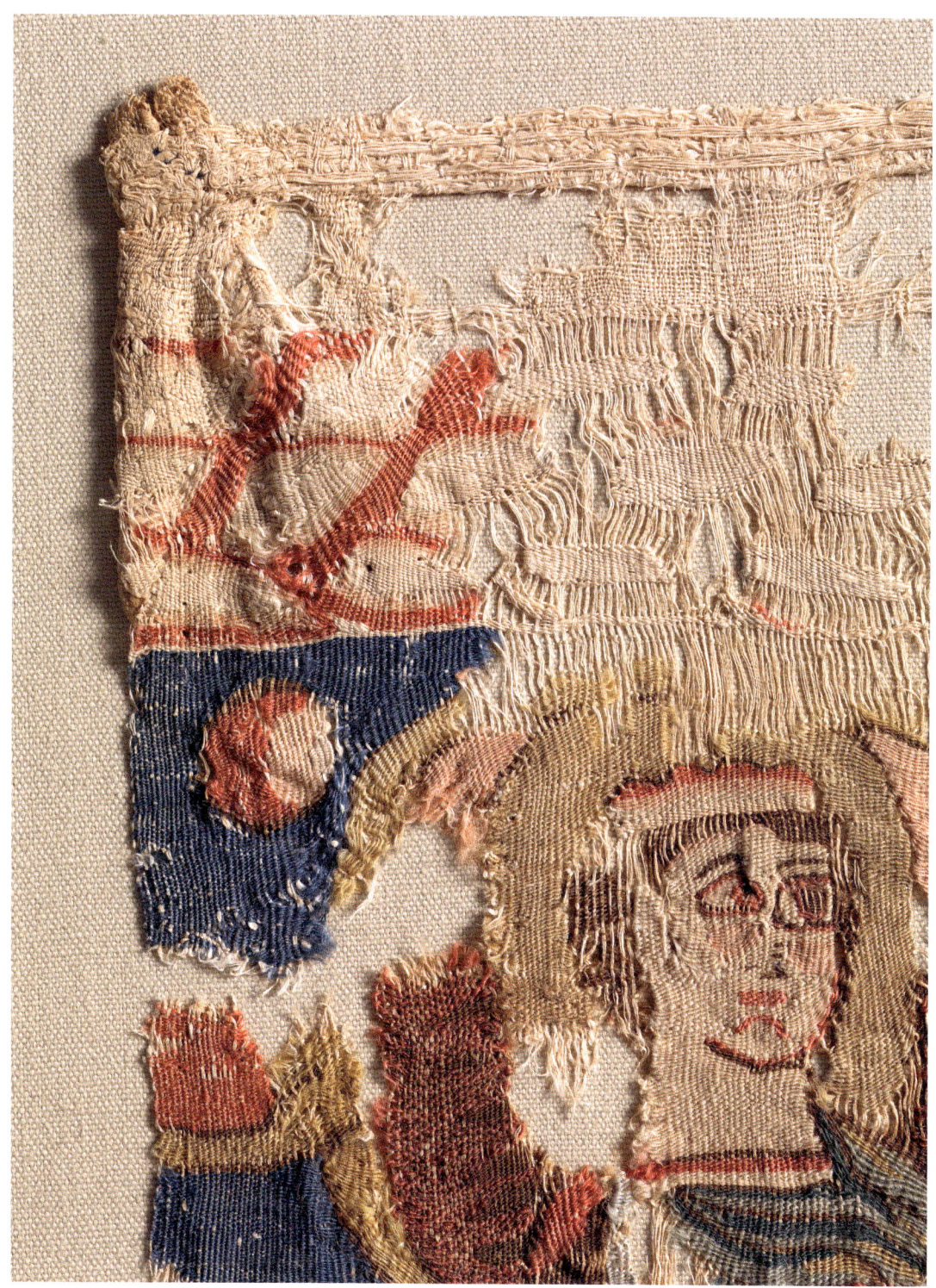

Coptic Cloth?

In the rare ancient textiles remaining to us, the colors are never in their original state but rather have been transformed by time. Although the reds are often more resistant than other shades, they have faded and taken on pink or orange tones that did not originally exist. Thus, for the historian, ancient and medieval fabrics are always difficult documents to study.

Fragment of funeral cloth, woven by Coptic Christians, Egypt, fifth century. Metropolitan Museum of Art, New York.

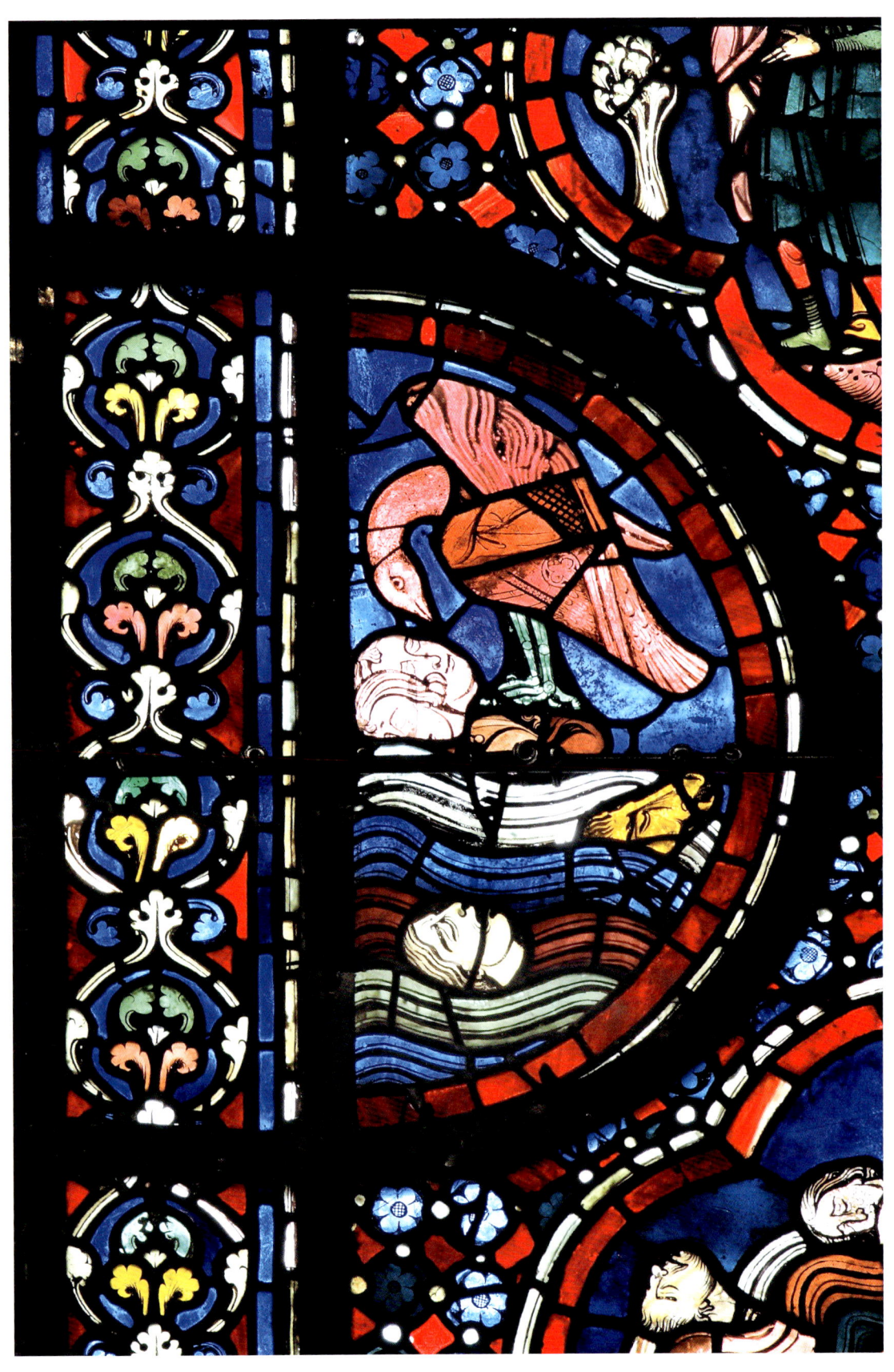

A Crow of an Unusual Color

In medieval stained glass as in miniatures, any animal can be any color, even the crow, the black bird par excellence. On this window of the Chartres Cathedral that relates the story of the Flood, the crow (who preferred to linger and eat cadavers, rather than return to Noah's ark and announce that the flood waters were receding) is not black but instead a splendid pink. Indeed, medieval glassworkers never used black glass.

Story of Noah, bay 47, medallion 17, ca. 1210–15. Our Lady of Chartres Cathedral, north window of the nave, Chartres (France).

dressed as in the magazine photographs, not with regard to styles or colors. That does not mean that the magazine photographs are not interesting to study, very much to the contrary. But it is a matter of the imagination or ideology of color, not of the colors that are actually worn.

The same is true for miniatures, enamel work, and stained glass of the feudal period. The few pink tones we see there must not be considered realistic. These are artistic signs, conventions, and devices that take on meaning only in relation to other tones of the same color or another color, as a pink dress is only pink because it is worn by a woman appearing against a blue background. In a miniature from the next folio, that same dress worn by that same woman will become green or yellow because the background of the miniature will no longer be blue but instead red. That is how colors are constructed in medieval images. Realism plays no part in it.

Around the year 1000, a form of artistic product existed in which pink tones were more numerous than elsewhere and therefore intriguing: Ottonian illumination. The painted miniatures in books from the Germanic Holy Roman Empire, between the late tenth and mid-eleventh centuries, present a greater number of figures dressed in this color than in the preceding Carolingian illuminations and especially in the Romanesque ones that followed. Often lavish, these books were produced in the scriptoria connected to the wealthy archdioceses of Trèves, Mainz, and Cologne as well as particularly the scriptoria of the great Benedictine abbeys (Fulda, Reichenau, Echternach, Saint Gull, Lorsch, and Ratisbonne) in Germany, Switzerland, and northern Italy. In addition to portraying the evangelists and church fathers, the paintings provided "portraits" of emperors and empresses, endowed with all the insignia of their power, sometimes accompanied or surrounded by the most powerful figures of the court, both laity and clergy. Why are some of them partially or entirely dressed in pink? Around the year 1000, this very discreet color played no symbolic or emblematic role whatsoever, neither in the Holy Roman Empire nor the other Western realms. Must we see Byzantine fashions here, whether in clothing or insignia? Or, more simply, just artistic influences? In Byzantium, pink seems not to have played any role in paintings, mosaics, or displays of power. Citing "Byzantine influences" in Carolingian or Ottonian art is a convenient ploy historians use too readily to avoid admitting their ignorance. Let us not follow their example. Must we search further, in the direction of a Sassanid, Persian, or Indian East where the textile palette was richer and more diversified than in the West in these same periods? In fact, some treasuries in churches and abbeys housed lavish silks from near or distant Asia. Were the pink tones they offered particularly appealing, if not to the emperors, at least to the illuminators? It is impossible to answer that question, but it is clear that to paint pink clothing, the illuminators did not use the same pigments as they did to convey the flesh tones of faces, hands, and feet. A bit of minium with a few grains of green earth was mixed with a large quantity of ceruse for the pink tones of the skin; cinnabar or a murex lacquer was mixed with yellow ocher or saffron yellow along with diluted chalk to produce the more saturated pinks of clothing.[13] As early as the Ottonian period in painting, there is pink and then there is pink.

First Classifications, First Systems

Discreet as it is in images, pink is even harder to find in early medieval texts. Nevertheless many such texts do speak of colors, including patristic, liturgical, exegetic, hagiographic, poetic, narrative, encyclopedic, and even technical texts. But never is it a question of pink, not even in simple lists of tints or shades. The same is true for the first classification systems that tried to bring a bit of order to the few color groups proposed by the lexicon, or emphasized by different codes and practices. For instance, that is what the liturgy tried to do before and after the year 1000, and later, what the nascent heraldry attempted in the second half of the twelfth century. Neither of them used pink, nor would they do so before the modern or even contemporary era. Moreover, the use of pink would always constitute an exception, contrary to what some ill-informed authors have written.[14]

Before turning to what pink we can find in these two domains, let us see if a color "system" that predates them—as perhaps the oldest one ever observed and described by humans—grants pink a place or not: the rainbow.

Ancient and medieval rainbows have hardly anything in common with the one we know today.[15] We nonetheless have access to numerous descriptions and representations of them, and never, in the texts or images, is the rainbow presented as a sequence of seven colors ordered as ours is: purple, indigo, blue, green, yellow, orange, and red. For that to happen, we must wait for Newton's discovery of the spectrum in 1666, or even for the early or mid-eighteenth century. Why do we observe such differences between earlier rainbows and our modern one? Between antiquity and today, the meteorologic phenomenon has not changed; neither has our visual apparatus as humans. That is evident. But vision is not the same as perception—far from it—and representation, even more than perception, is a completely cultural phenomenon.

The Path of the Chosen toward the Crucified One

Copied and painted in Reichenau like the *Codex Egberti*, this lavish manuscript also makes abundant use of pink for the clothing of divine figures, high-ranking dignitaries, and the chosen ones. It is hard to say if that chromatic feature, belonging to a few manuscripts from that same prestigious scriptorium, corresponds to an aesthetic choice or artistic style, or constitutes a true iconographic code.

Commentaries on the Old Testament, Reichenau, ca. 1000. Staatsbibliothek, Bamberg (Germany), Msc. Bibl. 22, folio 4.

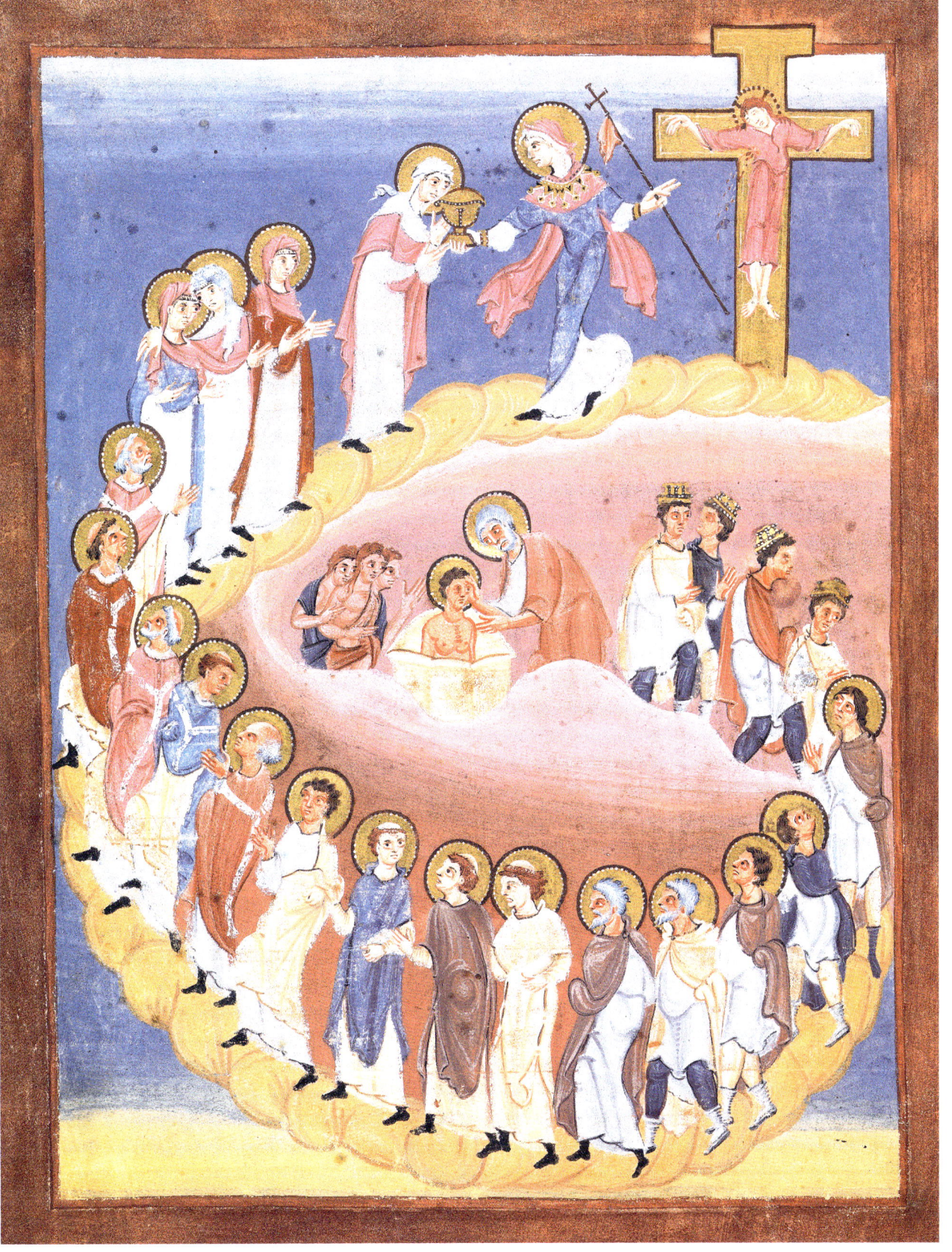

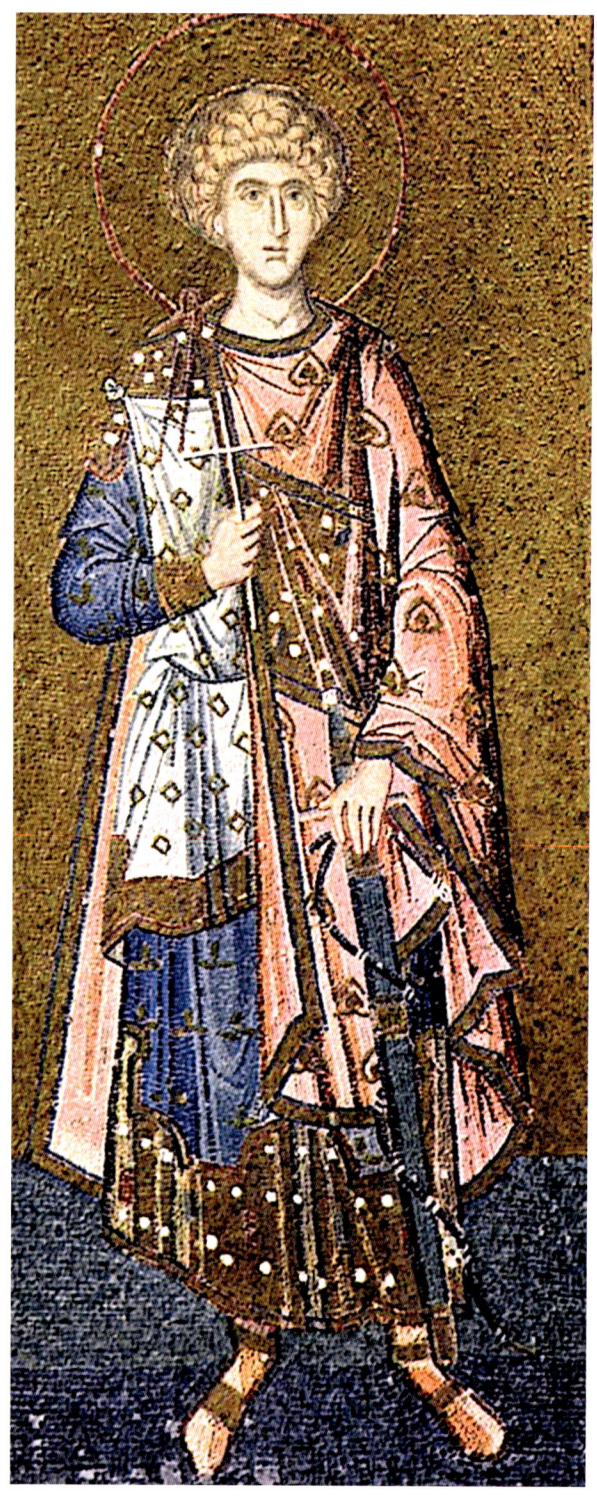

Let us remain with the Middle Ages, a time when many authors had much to say about the rainbow, especially in the Carolingian period and thirteenth century, the great century of optics. The rainbow captured the attention of scientists, who had rediscovered Aristotle's *Meteorology* and Arab optics.[16] They all tried to determine the number of colors visible in the rainbow and the sequence those colors formed within it. None of them, however, proposed a sequence or part of one that bore any relationship to the spectrum. They all saw the rainbow as an attenuation of solar light crossing through an aqueous medium denser than air, and thus as a gradation going from light to dark. But more controversial than the visible colors proposed were the phenomena of reflection, refraction, and absorption of light rays, and how to measure them and their angles. Most of the arguments and demonstrations, moreover, were drawn from ancient culture or Arab science, as were the explanations advanced by doctors regarding color vision. As for the images that represent the rainbow, the distribution of colors in them is very variable; as a general rule, there are only four colors, sometimes three or five, rarely more, and always assembled in an uncertain manner. Gold is often present, as is red. As for the rest, there are many diverse shades, including white, black, gray, and brown. Only pink never appears there, despite the sometimes rosy appearance of the dawn or dusk sky. Pink is a color unknown to physics and optics, as much in the Middle Ages as in modern or contemporary times. Whatever the time period, science has ignored pink!

A Martyr Dressed in Pink

Byzantine art draws on pink more often than Western art does. In mosaics and illuminations, many types of important figures are dressed in pink, men as well as women: emperors, dignitaries, divine beings, saints, martyrs, and the chosen ones. It is a color that seems to have been reserved for clothing, perhaps in imitation of the many silks imported from the Sasanian Empire, India, and even China.

Martyr, mosaic in the Byzantine church of St. Saviour-in-Chora, 1315–20. Istanbul.

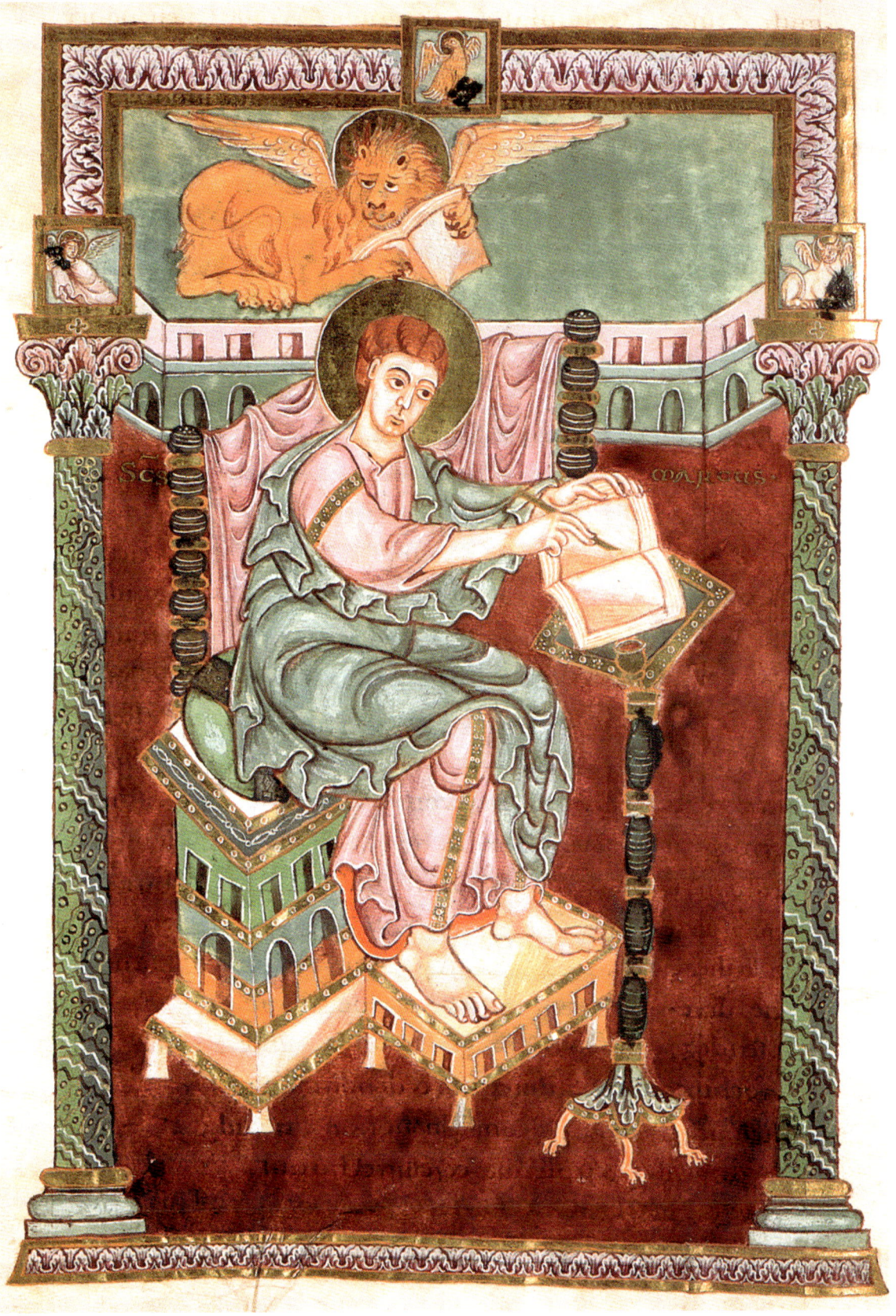

The Apostle Mark Writing

In the great Germanic scriptoria of the late tenth century, the color pink was much in evidence. This evangeliarium copied and painted at the Fulda Abbey is a fine example. The beginning of each Gospel is transcribed in gold letters on a crimson background and appears opposite a large painting showing its author in the process of writing. Mark and Luke are dressed in pink and green. A later tradition holds that Widukind, a powerful Saxon leader defeated and converted by Charlemagne, commissioned this lavish codex, but he lived much too early to have done so.

Codex Wittekindeus, ca. 970–80. Staatsbibliothek, Berlin, Codex Theol. Lat. Fol. 1, folio 45 verso.

So has the liturgy, at least until the nineteenth century. It is worth pausing here because many allegations with no historical basis have circulated in this regard, associating pink with certain feast days of the liturgical calendar. Now, as we are going to see, that association involves only the most contemporary era.

Strange as it may seem, there are no in-depth studies on the origin, establishment, and subsequent diffusion of the liturgical color system.[17] It is true that it is a difficult issue, and on many points, there are gaps in our knowledge, not only for the early Middle Ages, but even for the entire medieval period. In the earliest Christian times, priests celebrated the Mass wearing their ordinary clothes; hence there was a certain unity across Christendom as well as a predominance of white or undyed vestments. Then gradually white was reserved for Easter and the high holidays of the Christian year. Saint Jerome, Gregory of Tours, and many other church fathers agreed on making white the color possessing the greatest dignity. Nonetheless, liturgical customs varied according to diocese and were placed under the control of the bishops, who rarely legislated in matters of color, and were content, as were the provincial councils, to condemn colorful clothing and underscore the primacy of white.

Beginning in the ninth century, luxury made its appearance, with gold and brilliant, saturated colors finding their way into liturgical vestments and cloths. This fairly widespread movement was accompanied by the compilation of many speculative treatises on the symbolism of these items—treatises that sometimes mentioned colors. Their number varies, as does their distribution throughout the liturgical calendar, but pink is never among them.[18] There is some question, of course, about whether these texts—anonymous, often difficult to date and place, and sometimes difficult to understand—have any significance whatsoever with regard to actual practices. If the ritual consisting of associating a color to a holiday or time in the liturgical calendar is already well attested by this period, great differences remained between one diocese and another.

Then came Cardinal Lothar of Segni, the future Pope Innocent III. Around 1195, when he was still only a cardinal deacon and Pope Celestine III, an enemy of his family, had removed him for the moment from the church government, he wrote many treatises, among them one on the Mass titled *De sacro sancti altaris mysterio*.[19] This is a youthful work, sometimes considered unworthy of the great Innocent III. In accordance with scholastic practices, the author did much quoting and compiling, thus proving consistent with his time. For us, his work has the merit of summarizing what was written before him. Moreover, with regard to the colors of liturgical cloths and vestments, his testimony is all the more invaluable for describing the practices of the Roman diocese just prior to his own pontificate. Until that time the Roman practices might serve as a reference, but they hardly carried weight throughout Christendom, as bishops and believers often remained faithful to local traditions. Thanks to the immense prestige of Innocent III, things changed over the course of the thirteenth century. Gradually the idea took hold that what was done in Rome should carry close to the weight of law.

We do not have room here to describe in detail the distribution and symbolism of the colors throughout the liturgical year as Cardinal Lothar elaborated them. Briefly, white, the symbol of purity, was used for the feasts of the angels, virgins, and confessors, Christmas and Epiphany, and Holy Thursday and Easter Sunday, the Ascension, and All Saints' Day. Red, which evokes the blood spilled by and for Christ, was used for the feasts of the apostles and martyrs as well as those of the Cross and for Pentecost. Black, associated with mourning and penitence, served for funeral masses as well as throughout Advent and Lent.

The Trinity

Christ is rarely dressed in pink in medieval miniatures. It is not his liturgical color (white) or one of his usual iconographic colors (red, blue, and gold). But in the fifteenth and sixteenth centuries, the fashion for pink was so prevalent that even the son of God could be dressed in it.

The Princess Joan Psalter, ca. 1560. British Library, London, MS Royal 2 B VIII, folio 101 verso.

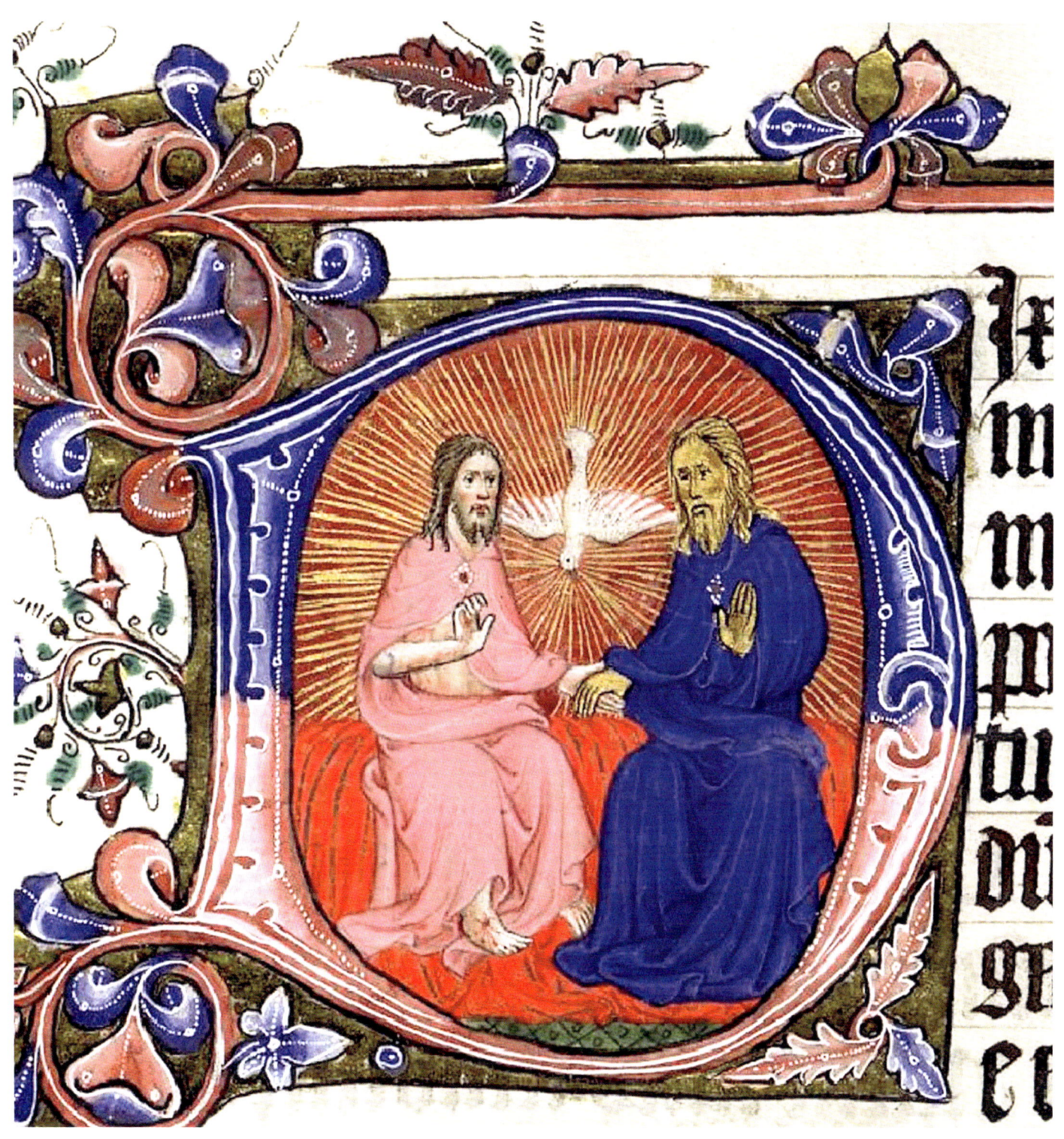

And finally, green was called for on the days when white, red, and black were not suitable, because—and this is an original touch—"green is a middle color between white, red, and black."[20] As for pink, it is never mentioned.

Although more descriptive than normative, Lothar's text on the colors went in the direction of unifying the liturgy. His words were amplified and codified in the famous *Rationale divinorum officiorum* compiled by Guillaume Durand, bishop of Mende around 1285–86. This work in eight books, constituting the most extensive medieval encyclopedia on all the objects, signs, and symbols linked to the celebration of divine worship, repeats Lothar's chapter on the liturgical colors, completes the cycle of feast days, and establishes as a system what for Lothar was initially only a depiction of Roman practices. When we consider that many hundreds of manuscripts of the *Rationale* survive to this day, that it was the third book to be printed, preceded only by the Bible and the psalter, and that there were forty-three incunabula editions of it, we can appreciate what an influence such a normative and practical work on colors could have had in the West.[21]

If Durand, like Lothar, never mentions pink, he does have much to say about purple, explaining notably that it could replace black during Advent and Lent. Furthermore, he specifies that during the observation of important fasting holidays, it was possible to use not only black or ordinary purple but also a "pale, slightly pallid purple." This ambiguous expression later led to various misinterpretations, especially since, beginning in the thirteenth century, a few other liturgical holy days were assigned this same "pale purple," mainly the third Sunday in Advent and fourth Sunday in Lent. Both of them were (and still are) usually designated by the first words of the introit for that day's Mass: *Gaudete* Sunday and *Laetare* Sunday, two imperative verbs evoking joy—"rejoice" in second-person plural for the first, and in second-person singular for the second.

In the Latin texts preceding and following the Council of Trent, it is always a matter of "pale purple," never pink. But in the nineteenth century, many authors thought it was a good idea to translate the various words and expressions used (*violaceus pallidus*, *hyacinthinus*, and *subviolaceus*) with the adjective "pink," as pale—that is to say, light and unsaturated—purple was, in their eyes, very close to pink. Following them, the rare holidays that were celebrated in that pale purple gradually shifted to pink, and that is still the case today. Now this was a matter not only of a false meaning but even of a nonsensical one. In the old color classification system as it existed in Roman antiquity, the Middle Ages, and the beginning of the modern period, purple was never situated between red and blue, but rather between blue and black. Thus it had no relationship with red, crimson, or pink. When it was "pale," it was closer to a bluish gray or mauve. It was only after Newton's discovery of the spectrum, and then the adoption in the eighteenth century of a new color order, that purple found its new place between red and blue—a place it still occupies today, allowing us to see perhaps a kind of pink in pale purple. Before the spectrum was adopted to classify the colors, though, that was absolutely impossible. There was no red in purple, and when it became lighter or faded, it could never have taken on a more or less pinkish shade.[22]

Hence the present-day Roman Catholic liturgy rests on a mistranslation and misunderstanding of the history of colors when the priest and church are adorned in pink on Gaudete and Laetare Sundays. It is also possible that the recent association of pink with ideas of joy and happiness—life "looking rosy"—helped promote this chromatic and liturgical anachronism starting in the late nineteenth century. Those two Sundays do indeed mark a pause in the periods of waiting and penitence that Advent and Lent represent. The entrance hymn for the Mass those days expressly invites rejoicing. What color better lends itself to joy today than pink? Perhaps none of them. Yet that was not the case in the Middle Ages or even during the ancien régime.

After the liturgy, heraldry is the other great color system created by medieval culture. Appearing in the twelfth century, coats of arms were composed of two elements: colors and figures. But colors probably constitute the more important element because while many coats of arms exist that lack figures, none lack colors.[23] For the first two centuries of its history, heraldry used only six colors: white, black, red, blue, green, and yellow—that is, the six basic colors of European culture. From this perspective, early heraldry added nothing new to color practices predating or contemporary to it. On the other hand, and this is more innovative, the colors of heraldry were uniform, conceptual, and almost abstract; their shades did not count. The *azur* in the coat of arms for the king of France, for instance, could be either light or dark blue. It could tend toward green or purple. It could be dull or glossy, saturated or faded. None of that mattered or meant anything; all that counted was the idea of blue, not its material representation. The same was true for the other five colors.[24]

These colors bore specific names in the French language of heraldry, the most widely used in the Middle Ages: *or* (yellow), *argent* (white), *gueules* (red), *azur* (blue), *sable* (black), and *sinople* (green).[25] If the words *or*, *argent*, and *azur* pose no particular problems semantically or etymologically, the others demand some explanation. The term *sable* is related to a family of Germanic and Slavic words that designate the sable martin, whose fur, an intense black, was the most expensive in the medieval West. *Sinople* is more ambiguous. It comes from the name of the city of Sinop (originally called Sinopa) in today's Turkey on the shores of the Black Sea. In antiquity, the red ocher collected in that region served as a pigment and gave rise to the Latin noun *sinopis* (the color red), and later the French word *sinople*. Why this term lost the meaning of "red" to take on that of "green" over the course of the fourteenth century, when it was adopted by heraldry, remains a mystery. Similarly mysterious is the etymology of the word *gueules*, which also designates the color red in heraldry. There are hypotheses that make it a derivation from Gallic, Hebrew, Armenian, or Persian terms, all equally fanciful, as is the one that sees the word evoking the pink throats of certain animals.[26] Many heraldists and philologists in the nineteenth century indeed imagined that the first knights were in the habit of attaching the heads of their most beautiful prey to the upper edge of their garments after a hunt. With an animal's throat (*gula*) wide open, the flesh of its gullet was very apparent and formed a kind of collar. Hence the temptation to see the *gueules* of heraldry not as red but rather as pink or even a flesh tone. This hypothesis is far-fetched, but it enjoyed a certain success among the general public, especially since it was taken up by various dictionaries, and then many editions of the *Petit Larousse* between the years 1920 and 1950.[27] Less tenuous, all things considered, is the connection between the Old French *gueules* and the Latin *tegulatus* (red like tile or brick), but the loss of the first syllable is difficult to explain.

Toward the end of the thirteenth century, a seventh color made its timid appearance in heraldry: purple (called *pourpre*), although its use would always and everywhere remain limited. Likewise, in the modern period, to represent the parts of the human body used as heraldic figures (the head of a crowned king, an arm holding a sword, or two hands joined), a more or less pinkish color was sometimes employed, meant to evoke the skin and designated as *carnation*.[28] But that is rare and comes quite late. That is why it is false to say that heraldry completely ignores pink, just as it is false to consider it a heraldic color in its own right. The same is true for the liturgy: pink is present there, but in so tentative and recent a manner that it would be wrong to call it an authentic liturgical color.

No Pink in Heraldry

Originally heraldry only employed six colors, which in the French language of heraldry had these specific names: *argent* (white), *or* (yellow), *gueules* (red), *azur* (blue), *sable* (black), and *sinople* (green). Toward the end of the Middle Ages, a seventh color, rarely used, was added to them to form a septenary: *pourpre* (purple). These are absolute colors; their shades do not matter. If red, for example, tends toward orange, brown, or pink, that is of no importance and has no meaning.

Page from the coats of arms of *Chronica majora* by Matthew Paris, ca. 1250. British Library, London, MS Cotton, Nero D I folio 171 verso.

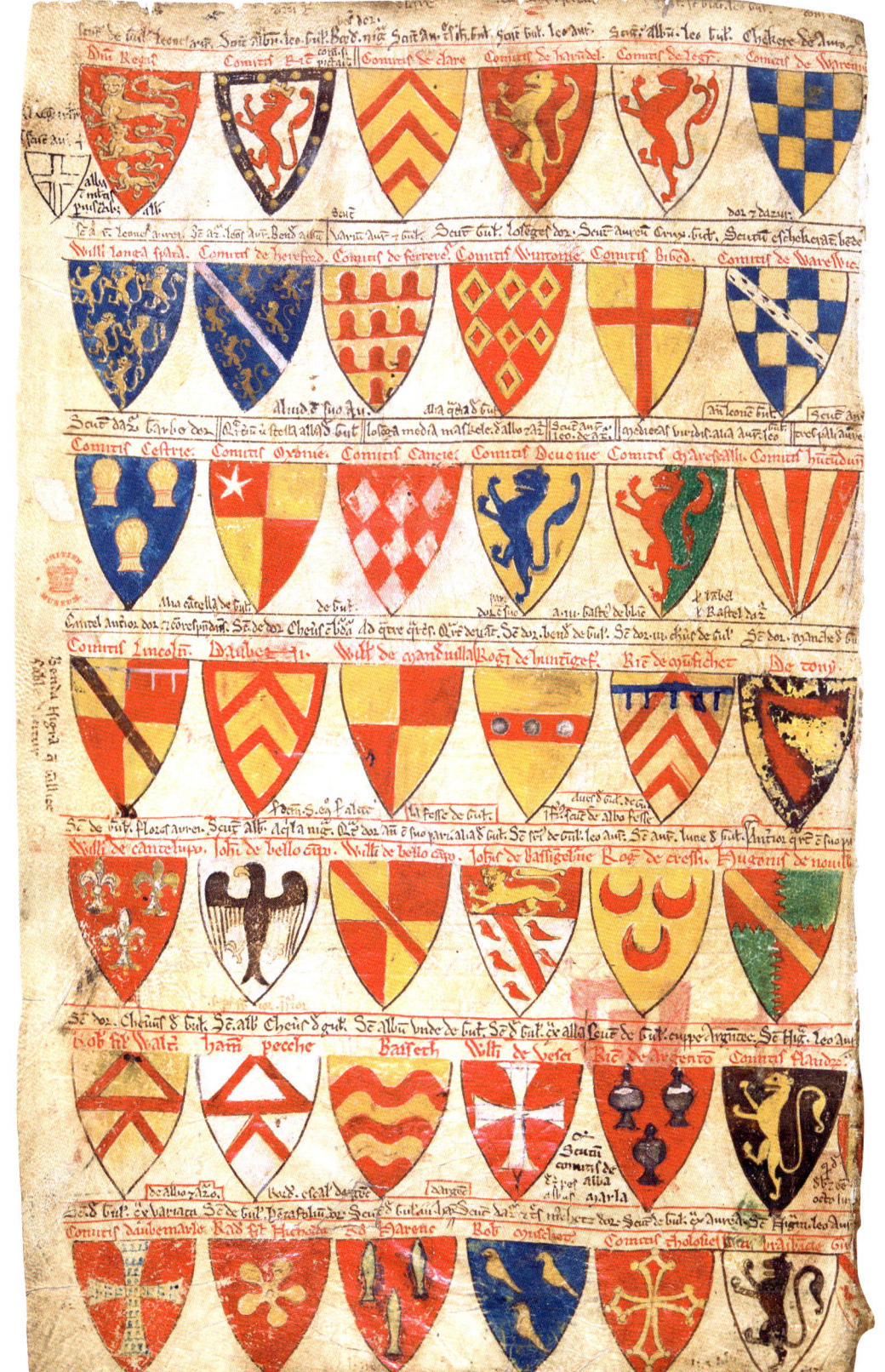

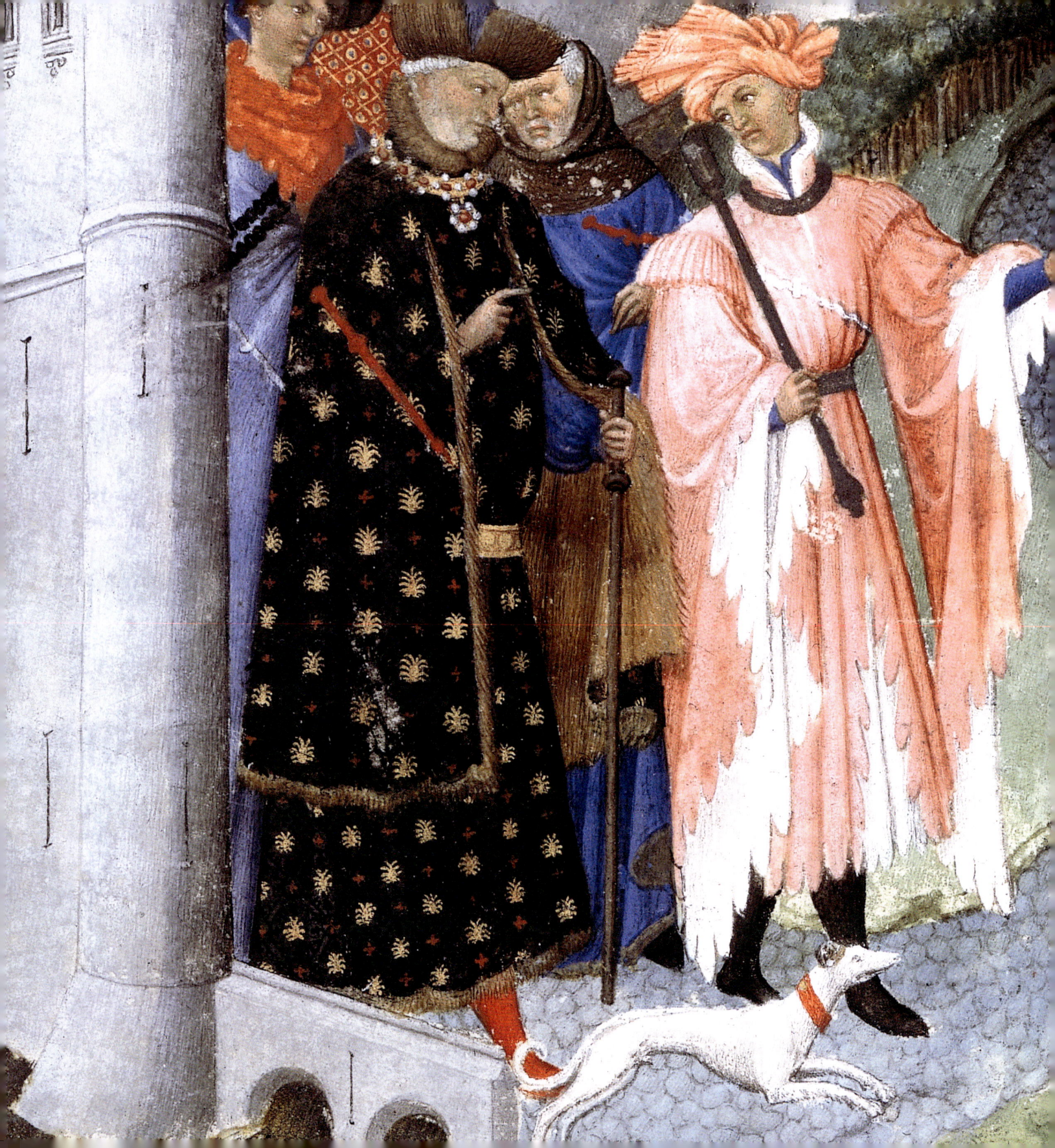

AN ADMIRED COLOR

(14TH TO 16TH CENTURIES)

An Enigmatic Figure Dressed All in Pink

This famous miniature attributed to the Limbourg brothers, painters by appointment to Jean de Berry after having been in the service of his brother Duke Philip the Bold of Burgundy, was inserted around 1412 into a manuscript begun in 1375: *Les Petites Heures*. The duke, elderly and wearing his famous bearskin hat, seems to have left his castle to depart on a journey, followed by an escort. But he is on foot and carrying a staff, the usual attribute of a pilgrim. Is he going on a pilgrimage? He appears too richly attired to be doing that, as does the man who precedes him and seems to be clearing the way for him; this is probably the most lavish figure in all medieval illumination. He cannot be a sergeant or usher; he must be an envoy from God, as he wears a pink like the angels in the sky (not shown here). Is the duke embarking on his last journey, toward the celestial Jerusalem?

Miniature added to *Les Petites Heures* of Jean de Berry, ca. 1412. Bibliothèque Nationale de France, Paris, ms. Latin 18014, folio 288 verso.

A Changeable Color

In the late Middle Ages, pink was admired in both painting and dyeing, where it was relatively easy to produce thanks to brazilwood, although difficult to fix. Unstable, especially in dyeing, pink was therefore associated with everything changeable such as love, beauty, luck, and fortune. In images, the goddess Fortuna frequently wears a striped dress, a symbol of instability that is sometimes replaced with a pink dress.

Giovanni Boccaccio, *Des cas des nobles femmes*, ca. 1410. Bibliothèque de Genève, Geneva, ms. fr. 190/2, folio 30 verso.

Rare in European clothing in the early Middle Ages and feudal period, at least if we stick to the few written sources (inventories and bookkeeping documents, dress laws and decrees, and recipes meant for dyers), which are more reliable than miniatures, pink becomes less discreet beginning in the fourteenth century, first in Italy, and then later in France and England. One might think that the black death in the middle of the century, which killed almost half the European population in five years, played a decisive role here. After the pandemic and all the hardships accompanying it, a newfound joie de vivre might have favored new clothing fashions and a trend toward lighter or livelier colors than worn in the past. That was not the case at all. The infatuation with pink preceded the plague. Moreover, it is not clear that this color was considered particularly cheerful or comforting at the time. New, pleasant, and young? Yes. But soothing or joyful? That is not at all certain. Let us avoid anachronism; to "see the world through rose-colored glasses" must wait for the eighteenth century, a decidedly more recent date. For the moment, let us stay with the fourteenth century.

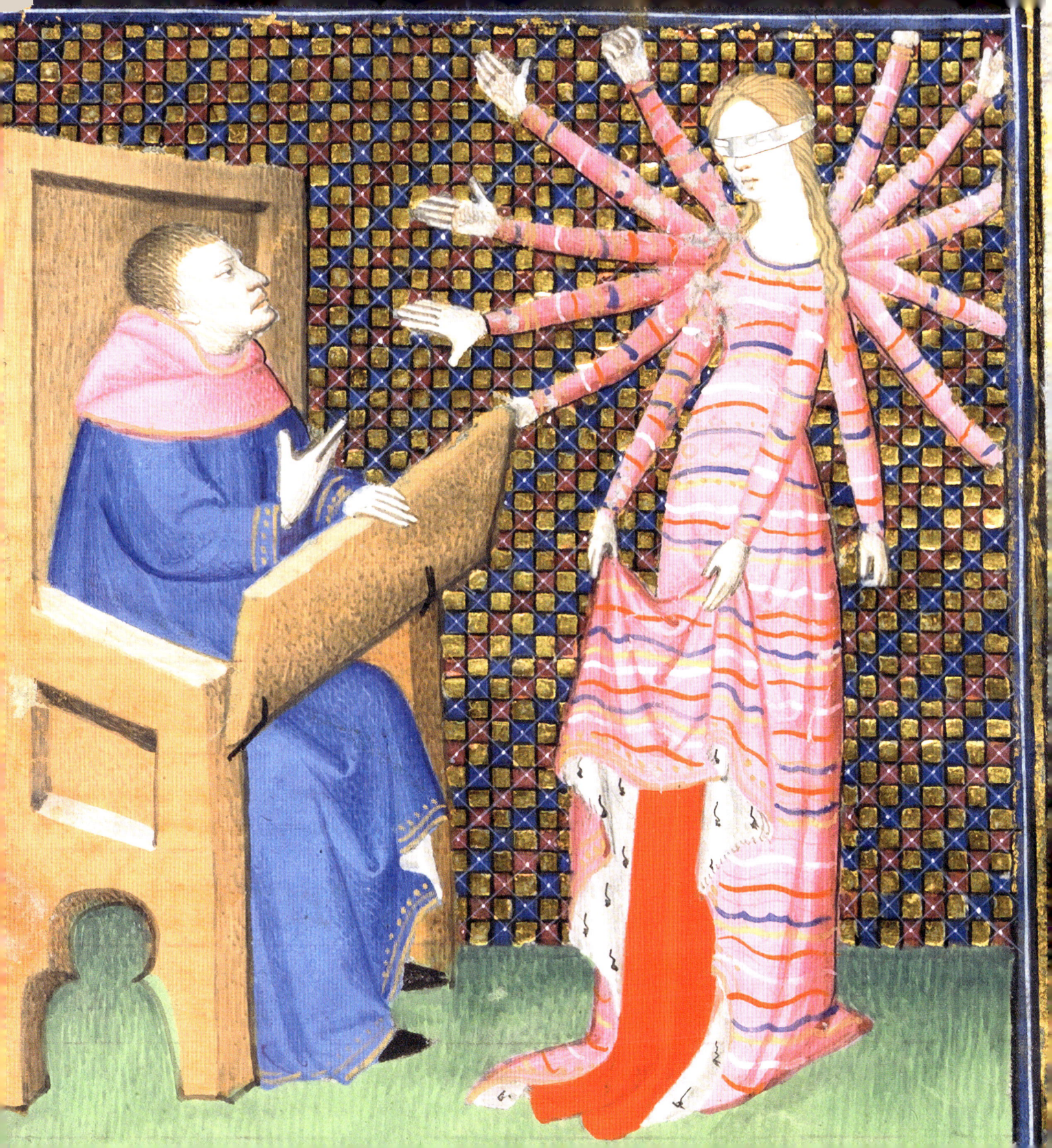

New Fashions

We are lucky to have access to an exceptional document that gives us a good picture of the wardrobes of the great ladies of Florence in the years 1343 to 1345, just before the ravages of the plague: the *Prammatica del vestire*.[1] It is a general inventory of the wardrobes of all women belonging to the wealthy classes (nobility, the patrician class, and the *popolo grasso*)—an inventory carried out by various lawyers in order to implement recent sumptuary laws and tax all of those who must be taxed.[2] The authorities' aim was to reduce luxury expenditures because they considered these to be unproductive investments. With regard to clothing, they also wanted to combat the new fashions, which they deemed indecent or outlandish (brightly colored, tight-fitting dresses with low necklines). And finally, they wanted to maintain the barriers that separated the various social classes; members of each class should remain in their place, and dress according to their condition, rank, fortune, name, and reputation. Medieval sumptuary laws were moralizing, reactionary, segregationist, and misogynist.[3]

From autumn 1343 until spring 1345, every Florentine woman of good society had to present her trousseau before her district's lawyer, who counted, named, and described the various items found there, trying in faltering, tortured Latin to provide as much detail as possible: kinds of fabric, styles, cuts, dimensions, colors, decorations, linings, and accessories. This information was transcribed into various notebooks, now gathered into a single volume, in handwriting that was not neat, full of abbreviations, and difficult to read.[4] In total, 3,257 entries inventoried 6,874 dresses and coats, 276 headpieces, and a large number of accessories of all kinds, all of which belonged to 2,420 women, some of whom appeared multiple times. The whole thing constitutes a document

A Fashionable Young Woman

Painted in about 1410–11 for Louis de Guyenne, son of King Charles VI of France and lover of books, this sumptuous manuscript uses pink extensively, as much for the painting of clothing as for the painting of architecture. The fashion for pink had appeared a few decades earlier in Italian painting and illumination. In about 1400, it reached its height throughout western Europe in illumination, the precious arts, and life at court.

Terence, *Comediae*, Paris, ca. 1410–11. Bibliothèque Nationale de France, Bibliothèque de l'Arsenal, Paris, ms. 664, folio 75 verso.

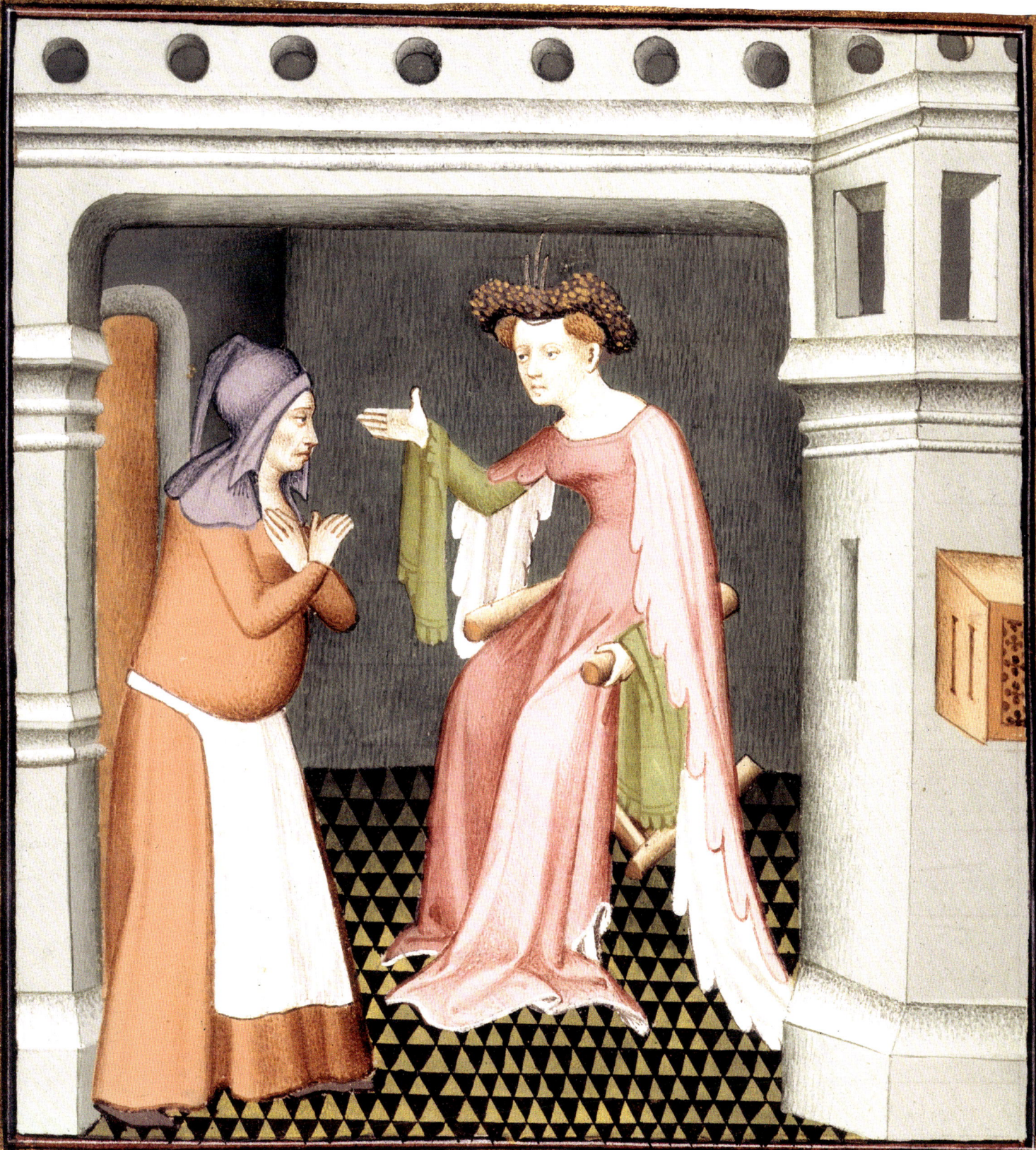

unique in every way, not only for the history of clothing and society, but also for the history of description and vocabulary of colors.[5]

Studying this incomparable document gives us an accurate idea of the colors then in fashion in Florence. The colors were varied, but red tones clearly dominated, sometimes alone, and sometimes combined with another color (in checks, stripes, or vertical halves), with yellows or greens, sometimes with whites, rarely with blues or blacks. The great fashion for blacks, then emerging in Milan, would not reach Tuscany until the end of the century. With the help of a varied lexicon that mixed Latin and vernacular words, dialectical and technical terms, convoluted wording and neologisms, the lawyers strove to name with precision the different nuances of all of those reds. There is a wide palette: light and dark reds; drab and bright reds; plain and mixed reds; reds tending toward orange, purple, and crimson; and most important for our subject here, reds tending toward pink. Florentine dyers seem to have become skilled in the range of light reds—unfashionable in earlier centuries—and were able to offer their clientele a diverse repertoire in pink tones. From there it is a short step to thinking how supply responds to demand; on the eve of the black death, the beautiful ladies of Florence seemed to appreciate pink.

To obtain and produce pinks in a range of shades, the dyers of Tuscany had many dyestuffs at their disposal, beginning with those we have already mentioned with regard to reds. The two principal ones were madder and kermes. Madder (*Rubia*) is a tall perennial plant that grows wild in many areas, especially in damp or marshy ground, and its roots have powerful dyeing properties. It is likely that madder provided the first-known dye, perhaps as early as the Neolithic period, producing red tones that dyers subsequently learned to vary by using different mordants (chalk, urine, vinegar, tartar, and alum).[6] In the fourteenth century, Florentine artisans knew how to obtain various pink tones from madder, which was stable for cloth, but dull or even drab.

That is why, for luxury fabrics, the dyers preferred a much more expensive dyestuff: kermes (*coccum*). This was

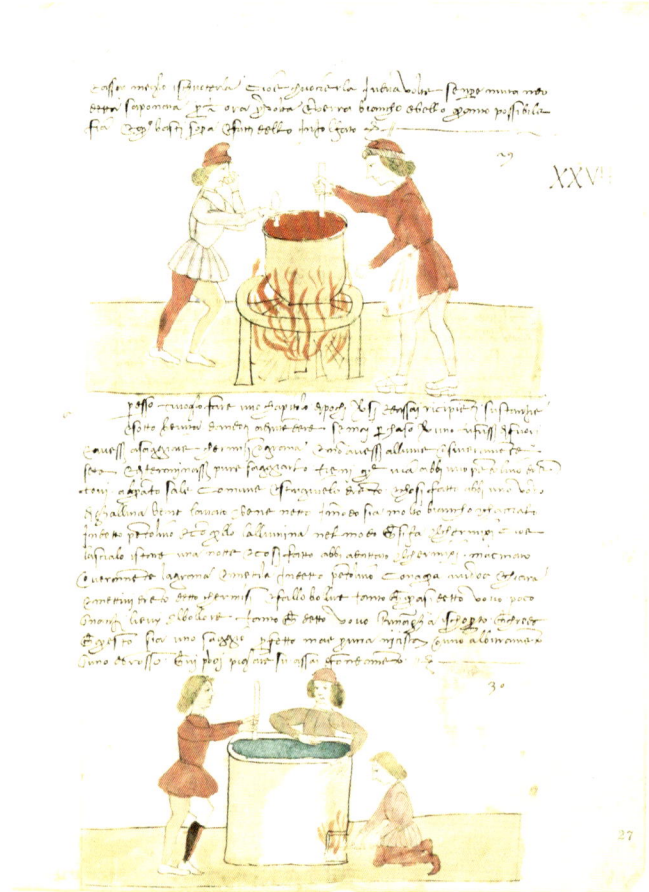

animal matter, extracted from the dried bodies of certain insects collected from the leaves of many varieties of oaks growing in eastern Europe and the Near East.[7] Only the female insect was used and had to be caught at the moment she was preparing to lay her eggs. Exposure to vinegar vapors and then drying in the sun transformed the insects into a sort of brownish seed (*granum*) that, when crushed, secreted a bit of intense red juice that was used as a dye. The result was a solid, intense color, but it took considerable quantities of insects to obtain a small amount of dyestuff. Hence the high price of kermes, the use of which was reserved for expensive cloth. The palette ranged from the most flamboyant red orange to deep and luminous pinks.

OPPOSITE PAGE

Dyers at Work

Although they are barely present in images, beginning in the late thirteenth century, dyers left us a considerable number of bookkeeping, legal, and professional documents. Consulting them provides the color historian with a wide range of information, often richer than what paintings and illuminations supply because it is information that relates directly to social practices, rules of the trade, fashion phenomena, and the histories of techniques and dyestuffs.

Precetti dell'Arte della Seta, Florence, ca. 1450. Biblioteca Medicea Laurenziana, Florence, Codex 2580, folio 27.

OPPOSITE

Brazilwood Gives Its Name to a Country

Brazilwood (*brasileum*) is a red dyestuff that comes from different tropical woods that, in their natural state, resemble glowing embers. In the Middle Ages, it was imported from India, Ceylon, and even Sumatra. Dyers were able to derive from it attractive reds, oranges, and pinks. Hence the fashion for this last color in princely circles starting in the mid-fourteenth century. Two centuries later, the wood gave its name to a country in the New World. The Portuguese had indeed discovered in the northern part of South America tropical trees whose wood possessed the same dyeing properties as the trees of Asia.

Portuguese map of Brazil, representing a family of Indigenous people, one of whom is collecting wood from brazilwood trees, 1565.

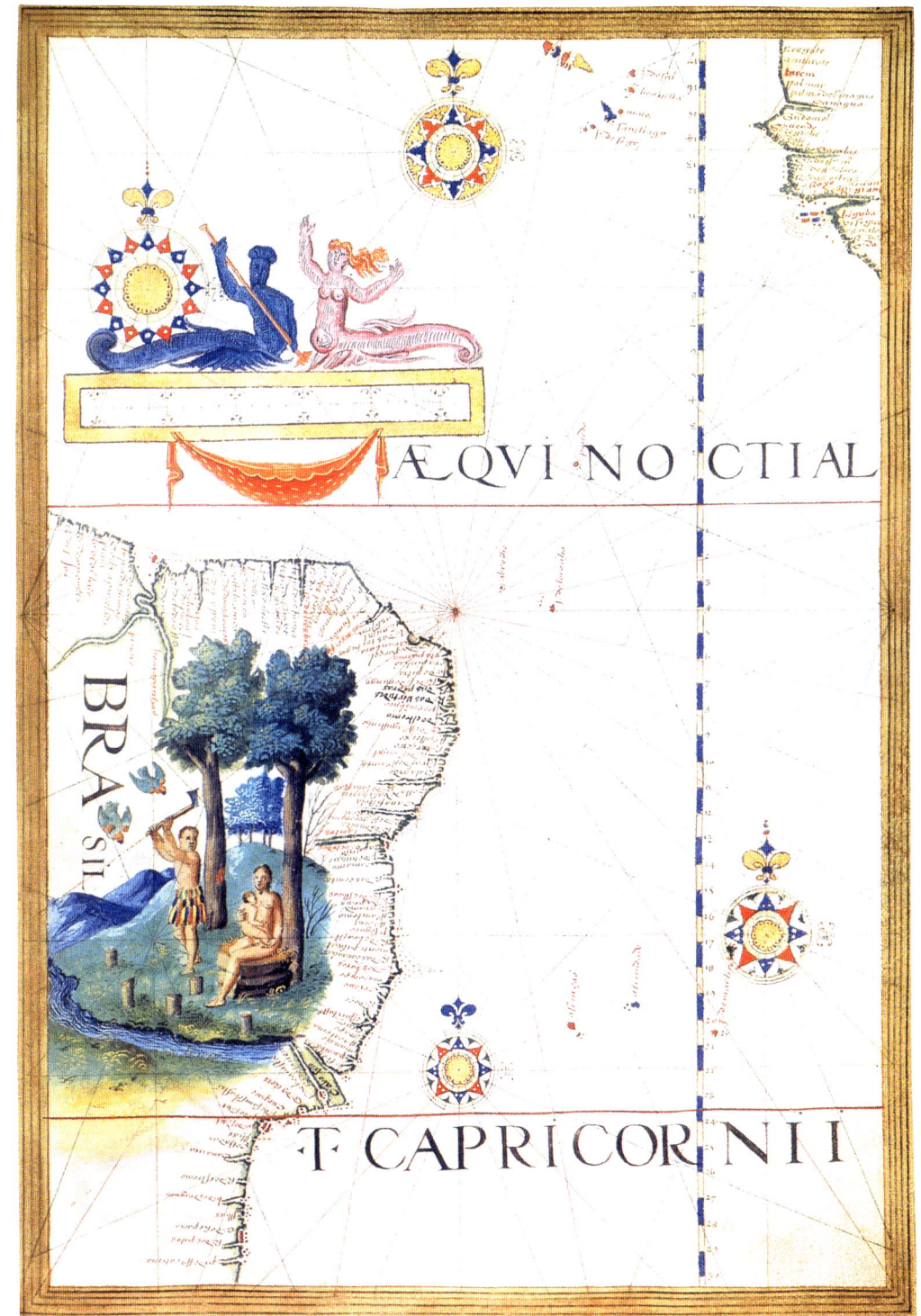

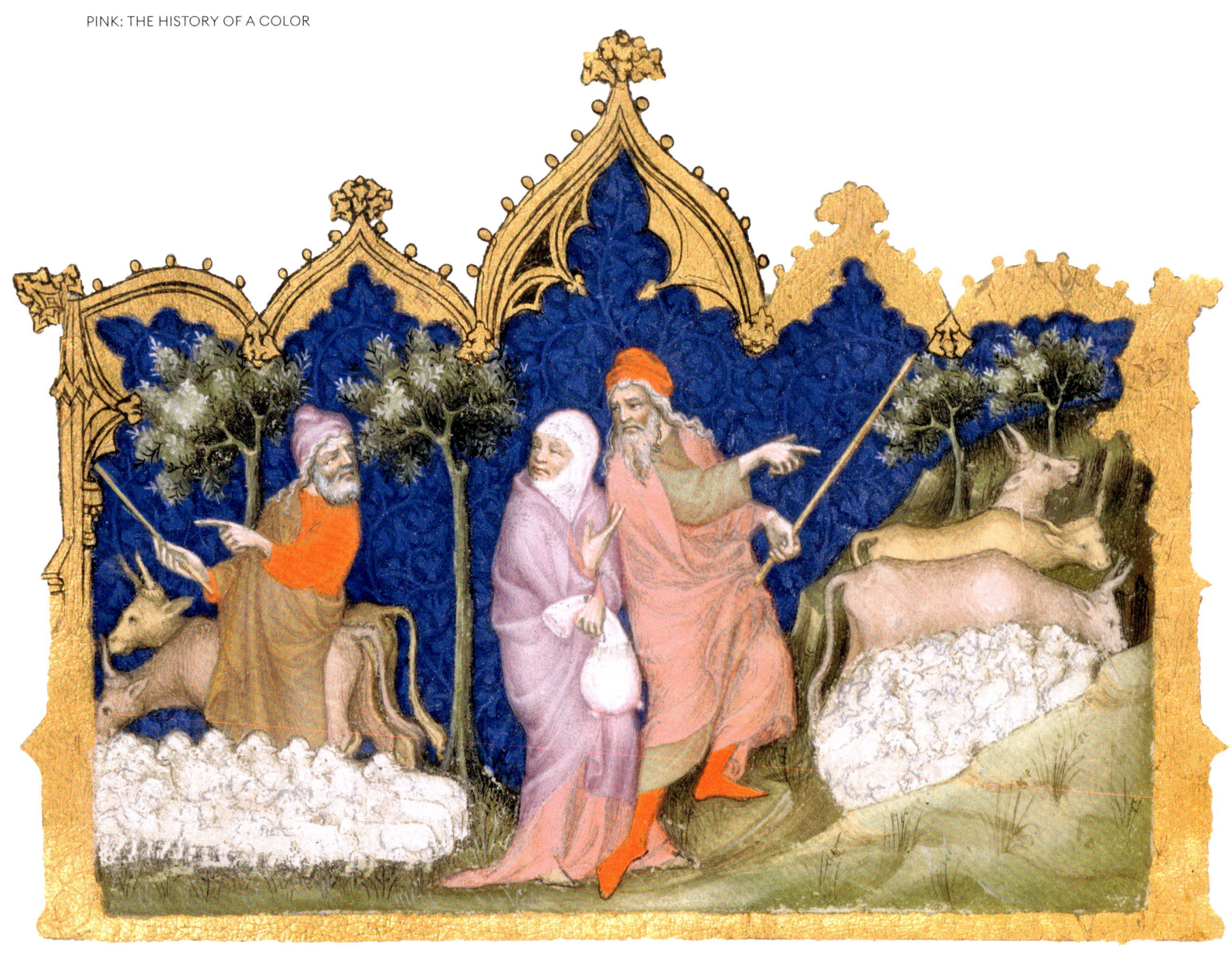

Pink in the Old Testament

As early as the mid-fourteenth century, illuminated manuscripts commissioned by monarchs and princes attested to the fashion for pink clothing just then beginning to take hold. Even biblical figures–like Abraham and Sarah seen here–could be dressed in pink. That fashion would last for about three generations before becoming less prevalent.

Separation of Abraham and Lot, Bible of Jean de Sy, Paris, 1355–56. Bibliothèque Nationale de France, Paris, ms. français 15397, folio 14.

To these two materials, dyers sometimes added orcinol, a material provided by certain lichens growing on rocks (hence its Latin name *roccella*).[8] More rarely they used carthamus (safflower), a plant whose flowers have dyeing properties in the range of reds and oranges. And most important, they used brazilwood (*brasileum*), which all by itself directly provided truly pink tones. This was a dyestuff derived from exotic trees, stiff and thorny, in the sappan family (*Biancae sappan*). In its natural state, the wood of these trees is the red of glowing embers; hence its name in the vernacular language: *brésil*. Imported from southern India, Ceylon, and even distant Sumatra, this wood arrived in Europe through Alexandria and then Venice in the form of logs, sticks, and wood shavings. It was then reduced to a powder—with much effort because it is a very hard material—that was then steeped in water for a long time to obtain the dye. A powerful mordant had to be used to make it penetrate wool fibers.

The Romans already recognized the dyeing properties of brazilwood, but they considered it too unreliable and unstable to be used on a large scale in dyeing. Moreover, this was a semiprecious wood for them, imported from far away and difficult to work with. They used it for decoration more than for dyes or pigments. In the feudal period, little had changed; brazilwood was familiar, but used only in a limited way as dye—much less so than in the East. Not only was it expensive, but European artisans, unlike artisans in the Indies or Middle East, were not skilled at using it. They did not use effective mordants, and the dye did not really take.[9] Thus in Europe, for many centuries brazilwood had a bad reputation, supposedly providing a "false color"—that is, a shade that faded easily.

Contact with Islamic societies, the Crusades, and travels to Persia or India introduced the Europeans to magnificent shades of pink, though, and prompted their desire to imitate them, especially with regard to textiles. For a long time, their efforts failed, mostly due to their lack of an effective mordant. But as demand became insistent, dyers increasingly tried different experiments, paying closer attention to advice obtained from Greek, Arab, and Persian counterparts, so that they finally achieved their first successes in Tuscany in the early fourteenth century. But this was not so much thanks to madder or kermes as to orcein and especially brazilwood. The dyers of Lucca and Florence now knew how to mordant brazilwood correctly using tartar or alum, as well as how to derive from it lovely light, luminous tones in the range of pinks and even oranges, thereby starting a new trend for clothes of these colors among the wealthy classes in northern Italy. In Florence and the cities of Tuscany, this happened early, in the years 1320 to 1340; in Milan and Venice, it took place a bit later, about midcentury; and in France and England, it occurred later still, beginning in the 1380s. Yet from then on, the craze for pink increased on both sides of the Alps. In princely circles, there were many men—more than women—who wanted to wear this new color that had come from far away, and was considered delicate, subtle, and a bit mysterious.

In Italy, pink was in fashion throughout the fifteenth century, and despite a few eclipses, remained so until just before the modern period. At the French court, it was the duke Jean de Berry (1340–1416), uncle of King Charles VI as well as a great patron and lover of what we would call today "contemporary art," who launched the pink craze in the years 1380 to 1390—a fashion that involved not only fabric and clothing but also the pictorial arts. Quickly, the painters and illuminators were imitating the dyers, transforming brazilwood into lacquer and introducing into their palettes different shades of this color, rarely used before, at least in France.[10] In England, pink as a clothing fashion was at its height at the turn of the century, then subsided, but reappeared occasionally during the sixteenth century. Nonetheless, it was more discreet because for a long time it had to compete with yellow, a color then considered beneficial and joyous (unlike in France and Italy, where it was discredited). As for Portugal and Spain, brazilwood experienced such a wave of success in the early sixteenth century for dyeing in pink and orange that it eventually gave its name to a huge territory in the New World: Brazil. The Portuguese had indeed discovered, in the northern part of South America, tropical trees whose precious wood possessed the same properties as those of the Indies, Ceylon, and Sumatra, but with more intense dyeing properties, and benefiting from less costly conditions for exploitation and transport. For the first and only time in history, a dyestuff gave its name to a country.

This new taste for pink beginning in the fourteenth century is instructive in many ways, but especially because it confirms how in the area of clothing colors, demand always precedes supply. In the late Middle Ages, it was demand that required artisans and merchants to make the necessary advances to satisfy their customers. These advances, in turn, led to a subsequent increase in demand, and so on. If the patrician class of Florence had not first demanded pink, followed by the courts of Milan, France, and England, dyers would never have perfected new methods for obtaining such a color from madder or kermes originally, and then, a bit later and on a much greater scale, from brazilwood. A similar process had already been witnessed in the late twelfth century with the promotion of blue shades. Demand from kings and princes, who now wanted to dress like the Virgin Mary, obliged dyers to make rapid progress in that color range, which had eluded them for centuries. No new dyestuff appeared, but they made advances because the demands of their wealthy clientele forced them to use their skills

Celestial Jerusalem

Created for Louis I of Anjou, brother of King Charles V of France, this immense tapestry of the Apocalypse (probably 6 meters by 140 meters in its original state) faithfully follows the biblical text. Here a section of the tenth panel depicts the appearance of the celestial Jerusalem after the opening of the last seal. Saint John, dressed in pink, watches the city descend from the sky. The roofs are pink like the garment of God, who, from the heavens above, blesses the scene.

Apocalypse Tapestry, ca. 1373–82. Château d'Angers, Musée de la Tapisserie, Angers.

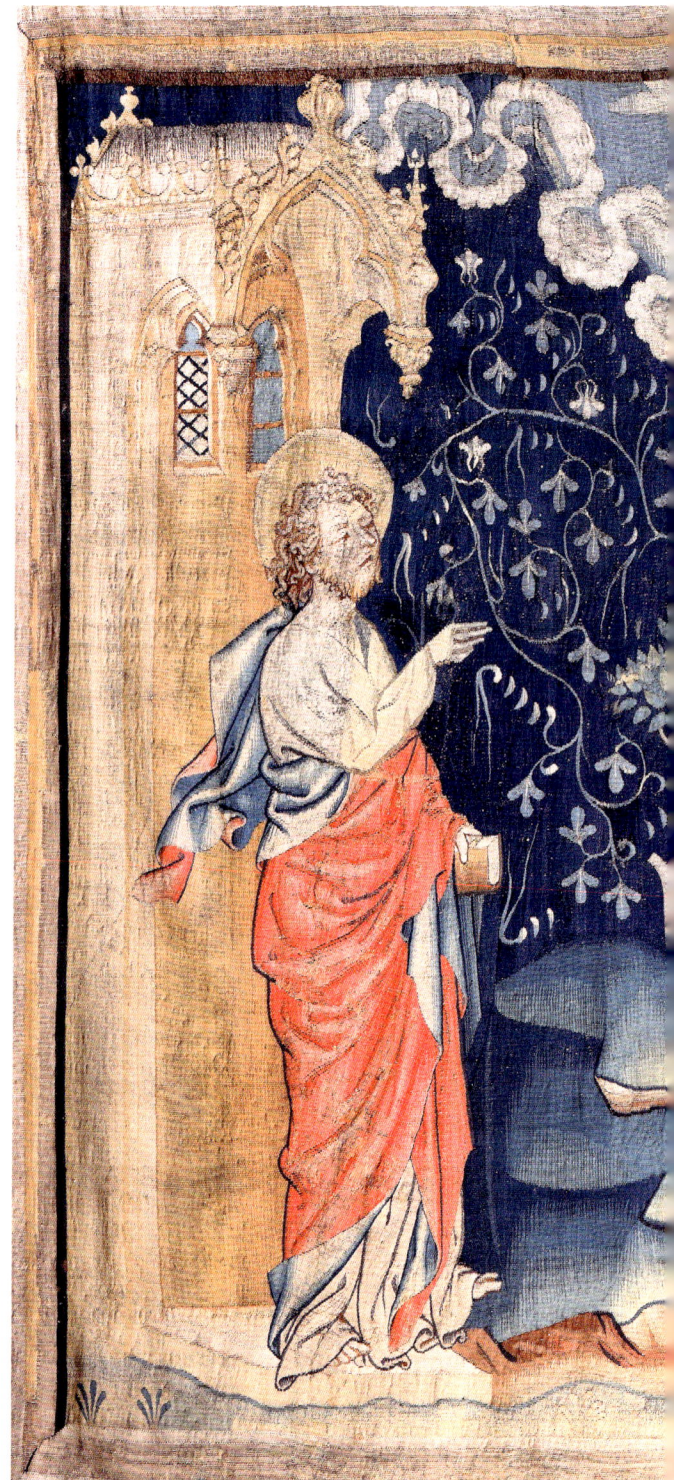

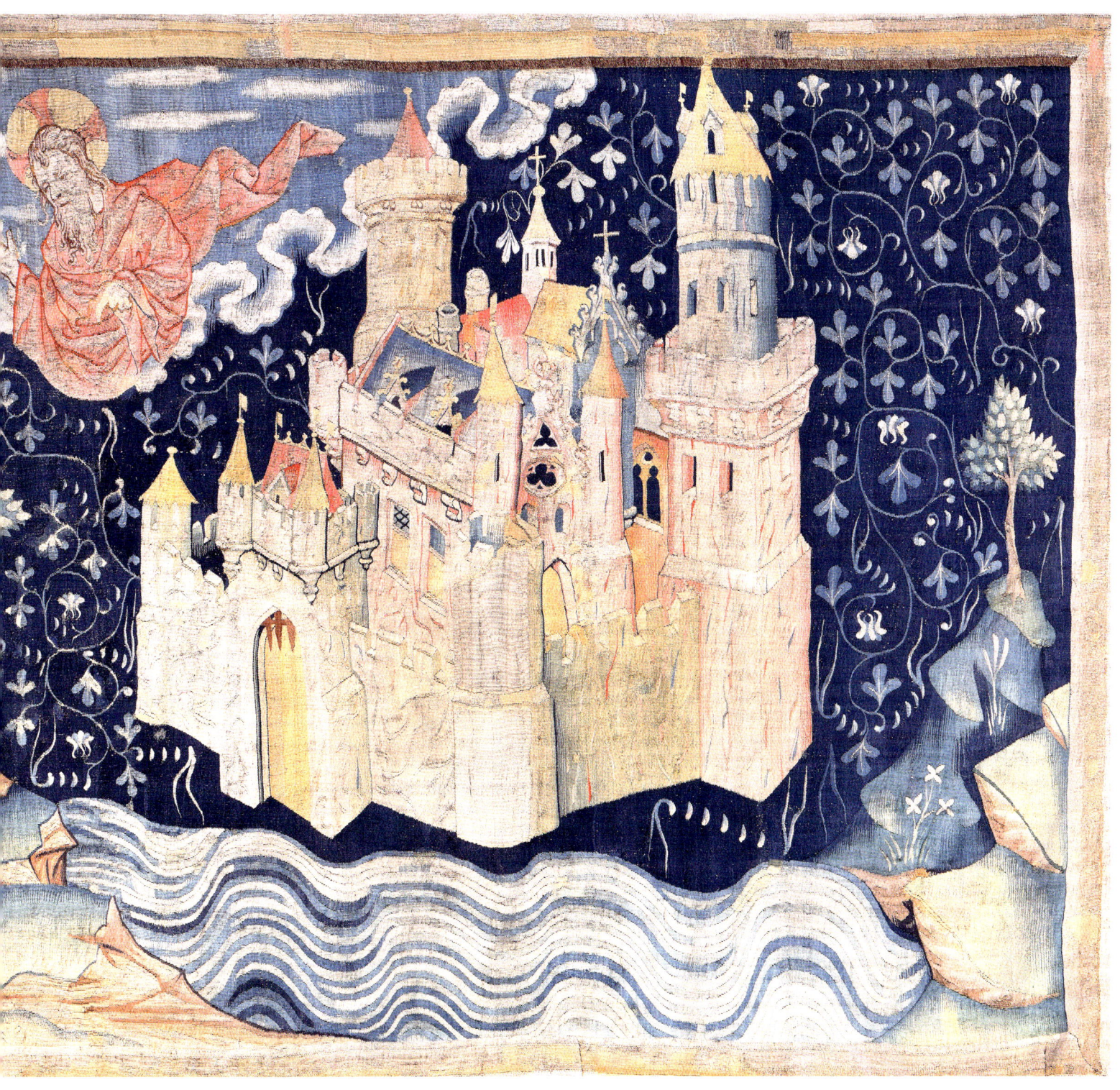

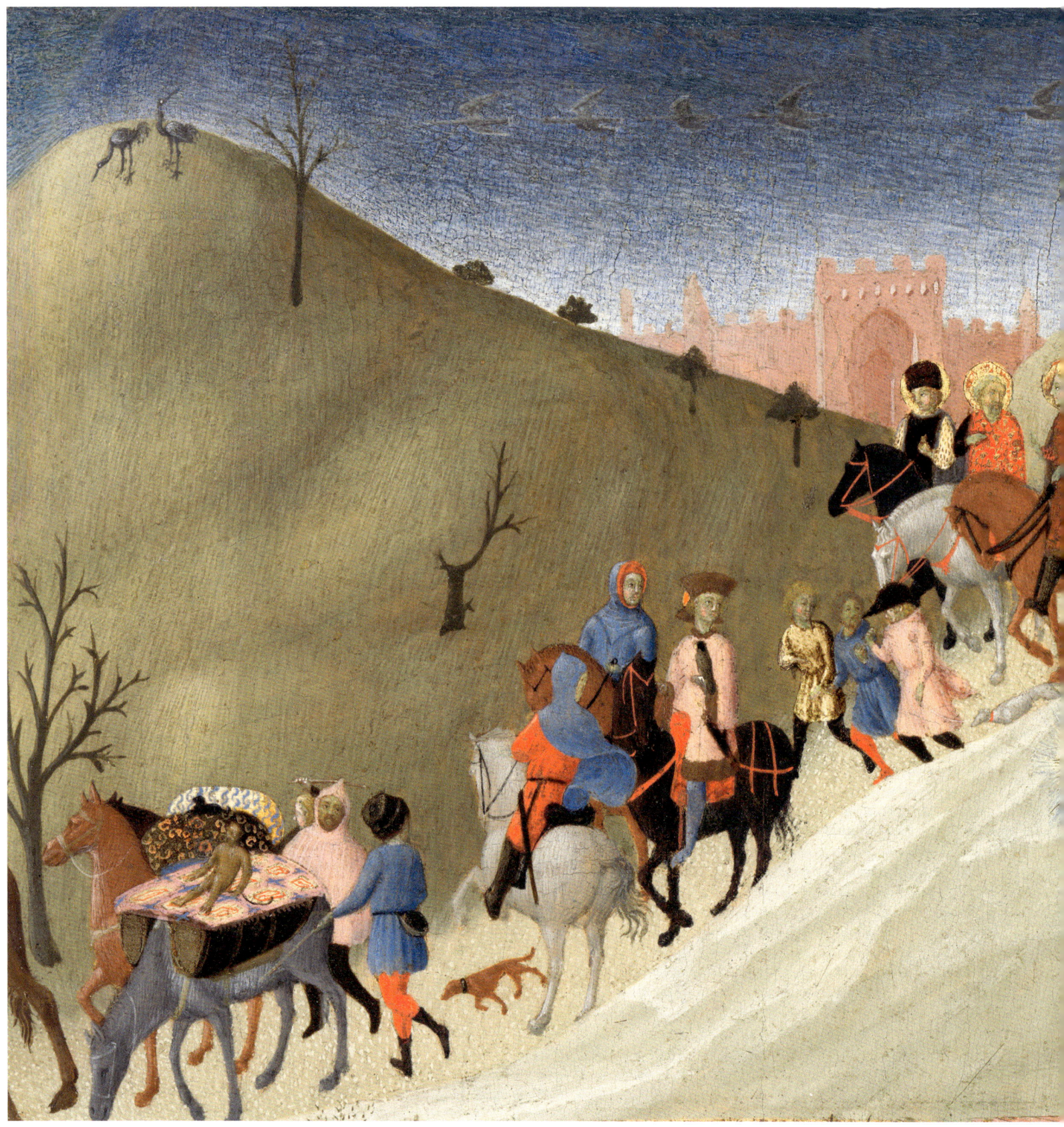

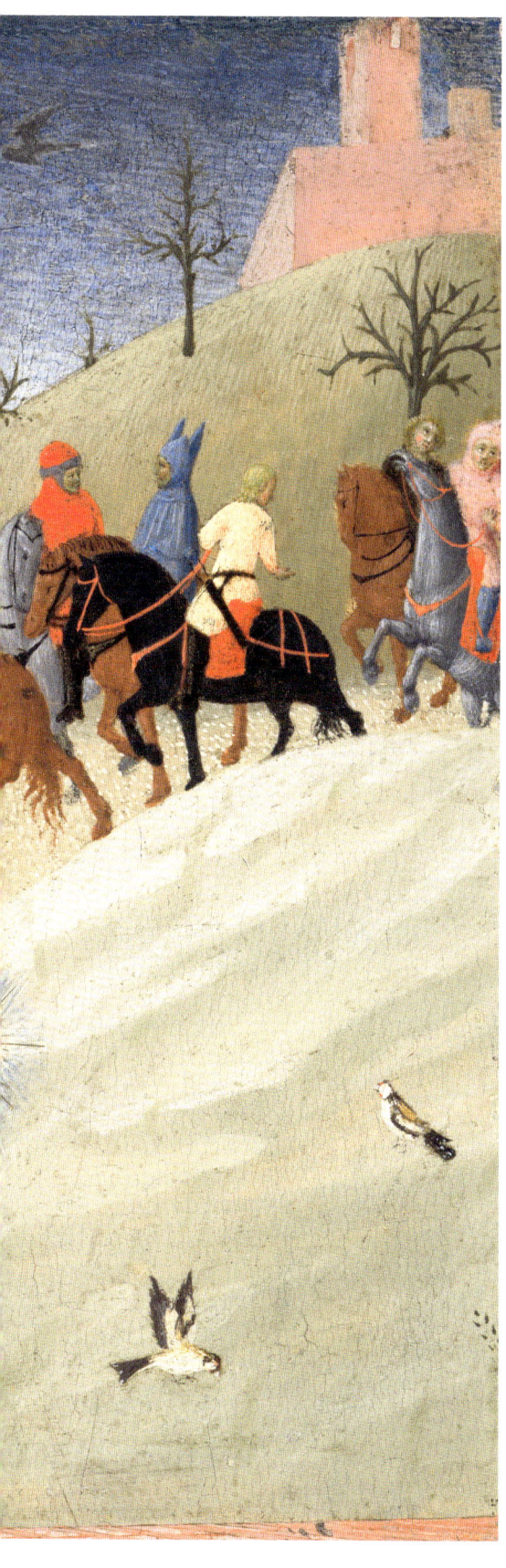

and products more effectively. A similar mechanism can be noted in the fifteenth century with the birth of the fashion for black tones at the Burgundy court, and then in the seventeenth century with the rage for dark greens in France under Louis XIII, and finally in the Enlightenment, when the elite almost everywhere in Europe demanded pastel shades and halftones to distinguish themselves from the middle classes, which had started to dress in bright colors. Moreover, it is rare in history for any sort of technical progress to precede rather than follow a social, moral, or ideological change.

OPPOSITE

The Journey of the Magi

Like the figures of the Old Testament, those of the New Testament could also sometimes be dressed in pink in illuminations and paintings. Thus they took part in a fashion trend that affected all aristocratic society in western Europe between the mid-fourteenth century and the 1430s. For painters, this was an opportunity to experiment with new pigments, notably those with a brazilwood lacquer base that provided them with a new range of pink and orange tones.

Stefano di Sassetta, *The Journey of the Magi*, Siena, ca. 1433–35. Metropolitan Museum of Art, New York.

NEXT PAGE SPREAD

From the Carole to the Farandole

The carole was the most popular group dance in the late Middle Ages. It began in a circle and then ended in a farandole, accompanied by leaping and singing. High nobility disdained it, but everyone else in society participated with pleasure. It was the custom to wear beautiful clothes for dancing, in the latest style if possible. That is what this miniature shows: the men are dressed in pink, a new color at that time and considered elegant.

Roman de la Rose, Paris, ca. 1345–50. Bibliothèque Nationale de France, Paris, ms. français 1567, folio 7.

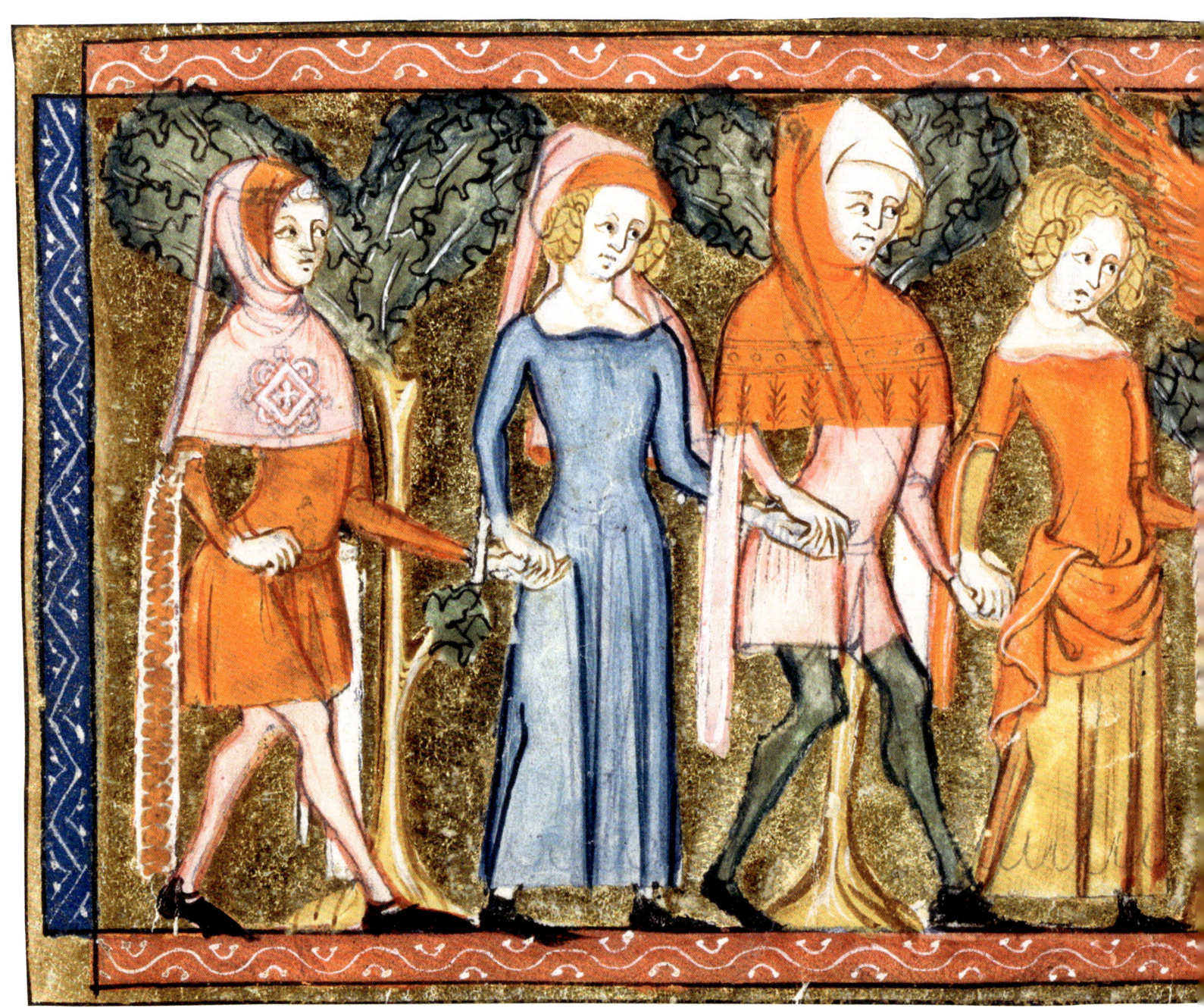

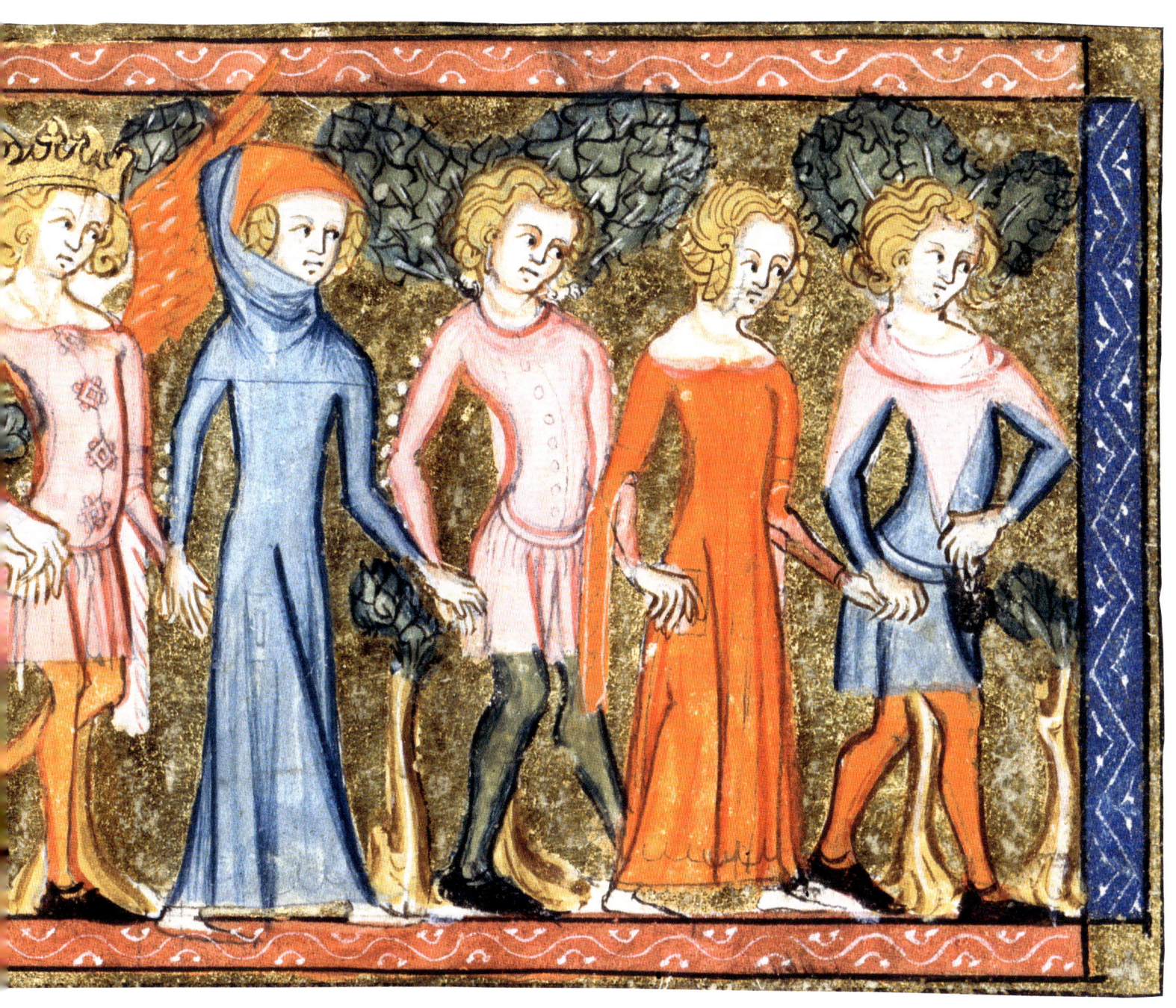

First Recipes

L et us stay with pink at the end of the Middle Ages. Studying the recipe collections for making colors, intended for dyers, illuminators, and painters, helps the historian to discern more clearly the evolution of this fashion wave, and gauge the distance between practice and discourse. A great number of these collections from the fourteenth and fifteenth centuries survive, but in terms of artisanal techniques, they are difficult documents to put to use.[11] Not only were they all recopied, with each new copy offering a new version of the text, but they are consistently imprecise in terms of quantities and proportions as well as cooking, decoction, and maceration times. Here is an example translated from Tuscan according to a manuscript from 1480:

> Take a good portion of brazilwood and immerse it in a certain quantity of water to which a bit of chalk has been added; add as much tartar as needed, and if you can, the urine of an ass, but moderately. If you do not have ass urine, that of a drunk man will do. Then heat it all long enough and place your cloth in the bath; you will obtain a beautiful rosy hue.[12]

The Scent of the Rose

Among the five senses, sight and hearing were most valued by medieval culture because they functioned from a distance, whereas touch, taste, and smell were somewhat disdained for working only in close proximity. Nevertheless, an exception was made for the scent of flowers, more pleasing than all other odors. The rose's fragrance was considered the most noble of all. Certain authors even went so far as to establish a link between the color and the odor; for them, the scent of a red rose was superior to that of a white rose.

Guillaume de Lorris and Jehan de Meung, *Le Roman de la Rose*, 1340–60. Bibliothèque Nationale de France, Paris, ms. Français 1567, folio 26 verso.

Such a recipe, however, does not date from the fourteenth century but instead only from the second half of the fifteenth century. In fact, difficult to date as they are, the recipes meant for dyers seem to be silent on the color pink until the years 1460 to 1480, although by that time, this color had been worn as clothing for almost 150 years, especially in Tuscany and northern Italy. There is a considerable chronological gap here between practices and the technical discourse.

That gap is slightly less wide with regard to painting and illuminating. Recipes for making pink are attested in Milan and Paris as early as the 1400s, and isolated examples of them may occur even earlier. They are all anonymous, brief, and involve a mix of red and white

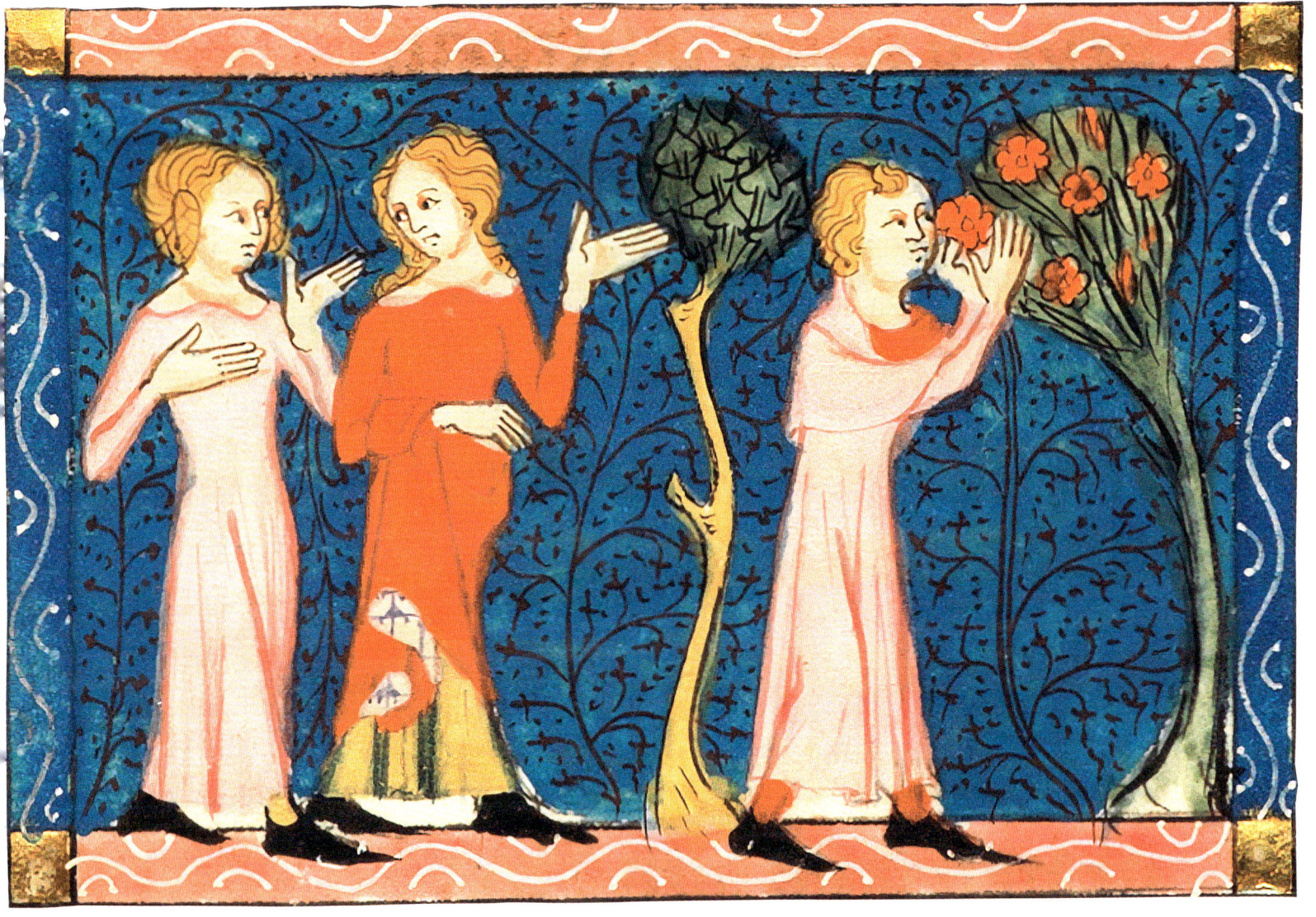

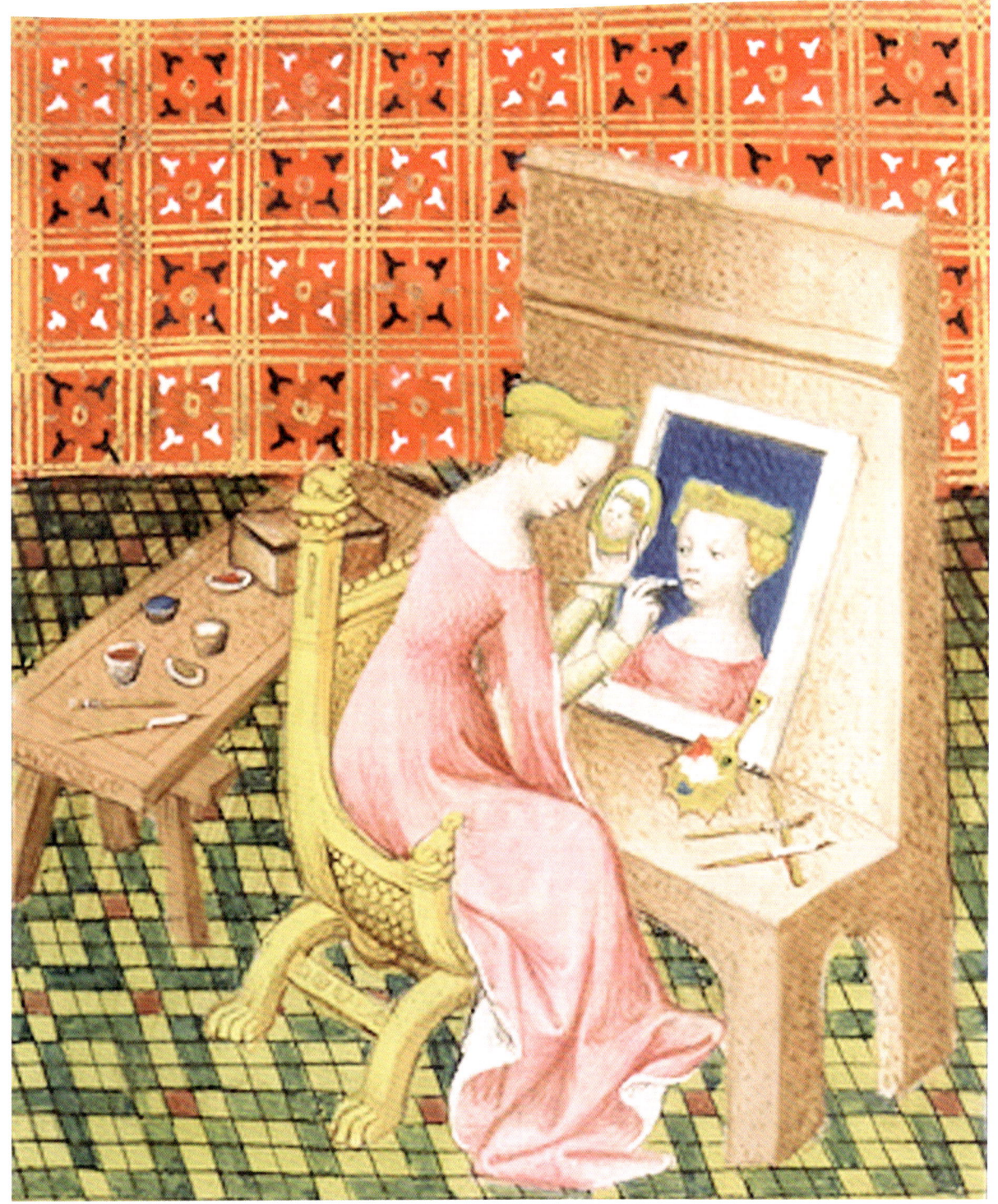

OPPOSITE PAGE

A Woman Illuminator

Contrary to a widely held view, the late Middle Ages are relatively rich in documents related to the work of women, notably in textile and luxury crafts. Bookkeeping documents thus inform us about the existence of fairly many *enlumineresses*, who, like embroideresses, worked either at home or in workshops. Much more rare, on the other hand, were women painters of murals or panels.

Boccacio, *Des cleres et nobles femmes* (translation by Laurent de Premierfait). Marcia (alias Iaia) creating her self-portrait, early fifteenth century. Bibliothèque Nationale de France, Paris, ms. français 12420, folio 101 verso.

pigments in variable quantities. The first author to go on at length is the Tuscan Cennino Cennini (ca. 1360–ca. 1440) in his famous *Libro dell'arte*, compiled in the first decades of the fifteenth century.[13] The work offers good evidence of workshop practices in Florence and Padua in that time period. Cennini was a painter and thus knew what he was talking about. Moreover, he is very articulate, his language—a Tuscan dialect—clear and elegant, and he gives his reader much advice even as he explains the different steps the artist must follow.[14]

Cennini begins by discussing drawing and the choice of medium, and then goes on at length about the grinding of pigments, their qualities and faults, their stability, and ways of using them. He then pauses on mural painting, its various techniques, the mixing of colors, the rendering of flesh, proportions of bodies, and representation of clothing and landscapes. Then, turning to painting *a tempera*

OPPOSITE

The First Painting Handbook

The *Libro dell'arte* by Tuscan painter Cennino Cennini (ca. 1360–ca. 1440) is the earliest actual treatise on painting that the Middle Ages has left to us. It was begun in the last decades of the fourteenth century or first years of the fifteenth century, perhaps in Padua. Based on workshop practices, the manual gives the reader much advice and explains the different stages of work, both for painting murals and panels (illumination gets the smallest share of attention).

Cennino Cennini, *Libro dell'arte*, signed (?) manuscript, ca. 1400. Biblioteca Medicea Laurenziana, Florence

on panels, Cennini offers quite a lot of information on glues and coatings, varnishes, and gold and gilding. He insists on binders, makes various allusions to the use of oil, and explains how the delicate work must be done to render the facial complexion, body hair, hair, and different textile materials. The last part of the treatise is shorter and concerns painting in books. It is with regard to the flesh tones that Cennini discusses the mix of pigments used to obtain shades of pink. He does this twice, the first time in a general way for fresco painting, for any kind of flesh, by using a mix of red ocher and lime—a mix he calls by a Tuscan term well attested elsewhere: *cinabrese*. The base of this mineral compound is not cinnabar at all (the natural mercuric sulfide that was discussed with regard to Roman painting) but instead simple red ocher clays rich in iron oxide:

The light red comes from a color called cinabrese, and I do not believe that it is used anywhere but in Florence. It is perfect for painting flesh. On walls it is painted fresco. This color is made with sinopia (red ocher clay) of good quality and very luminous if possible. It is ground, then mixed with the white of Saint John. It seems to me that is what this white is called only In Florence. It comes from slaked lime, very white and very pure. When these two materials are properly mixed, according to the proportion of two parts of cinabrese to one part of white of Saint John, you must make the mixture into small cakes, the size of half a walnut, and let them dry. When you need it, take only the quantity that you think necessary. This color will serve you magnificently for coloring faces as well as hands and the body when it is nude. Sometimes you can also use it to paint beautiful clothing.[15]

Further on Cennini explains how to paint flesh tones on faces in panel paintings a tempera. He even explains how to distinguish the rosy complexion of a young man from the darker one of an old man by choosing different egg yolks to make the binder to be used:

When you have finished painting the clothing, trees, and mountains, you will come to the most difficult part: coloring the faces. It is useful to begin in this way: mix a little green earth and more white with a good binder, add water, then spread this mixture on the face twice. . . . If these are young faces that have fresh complexions, the yolks of eggs laid in the city must be used as a binder, because they are whiter than those of eggs laid by hens in the country. Those yolks, because of their color, are especially good as a binder for the complexions of old men and swarthy men. Although on walls you can make flesh tones with cinabrese, here, on the panel, you must make it with true cinnabar; above all, it must not be pure but instead mixed with much white. Also put a bit of white in the *verdaccio* that you use to shade the faces.[16] In the same way as you worked on the wall, prepare three degrees of flesh tones here, from the lightest to the darkest, and apply each tone on the different faces as appropriate. . . .

When you have applied your different flesh colors and the faces are painted, make a much lighter flesh tone and apply it over the most rounded parts of the faces, always whitening them gradually, delicately, until you can apply white in small touches on the most protruding contours. Finally, take a bit of dark sinopia, even with a touch of black, and accentuate the contours of the nose and eyes, as I taught you to do it for the wall.[17]

Most of the recipes from the fifteenth century that explain how to make pink or flesh tones in painting follow the same process as Cennini does: grinding red pigments and white pigments, possibly adding a little yellow ocher, and mixing it all together using egg or casein as a binder. Depending on whether there is more red or white, the pink obtained will be more or less light or dark. Similarly, depending on the pigments used and how finely ground they are, the resulting pink will be smooth and glossy, or alternatively a bit harsh and dull. The red pigments most often cited for use are minium, hematite, and various red ocher clays all coming under the generic name of sinopia; more rarely, madder or brazilwood lacquers; and never cinnabar or vermilion. For white pigments, chalk, lime, plaster, various crushed shells, and particularly ceruse (white lead) are used. Such recipes would hardly vary before the end of the eighteenth century.

Nativity of the Virgin

Cennino Cennini left us not only his *Libro dell'arte* but also many panel paintings. Here as with other painters, there is a wide gap between what the artist writes and what he implements on the wall, panel, or canvas. Most important with regard to color, analyses of the pigments used reveal certain products not mentioned in the texts. All painters developed their own "recipes" and were not anxious to share them.

Cennino Cennini, *Nativity of the Virgin*, ca. 1390–1400. Pinacoteca Nazionale, Siena.

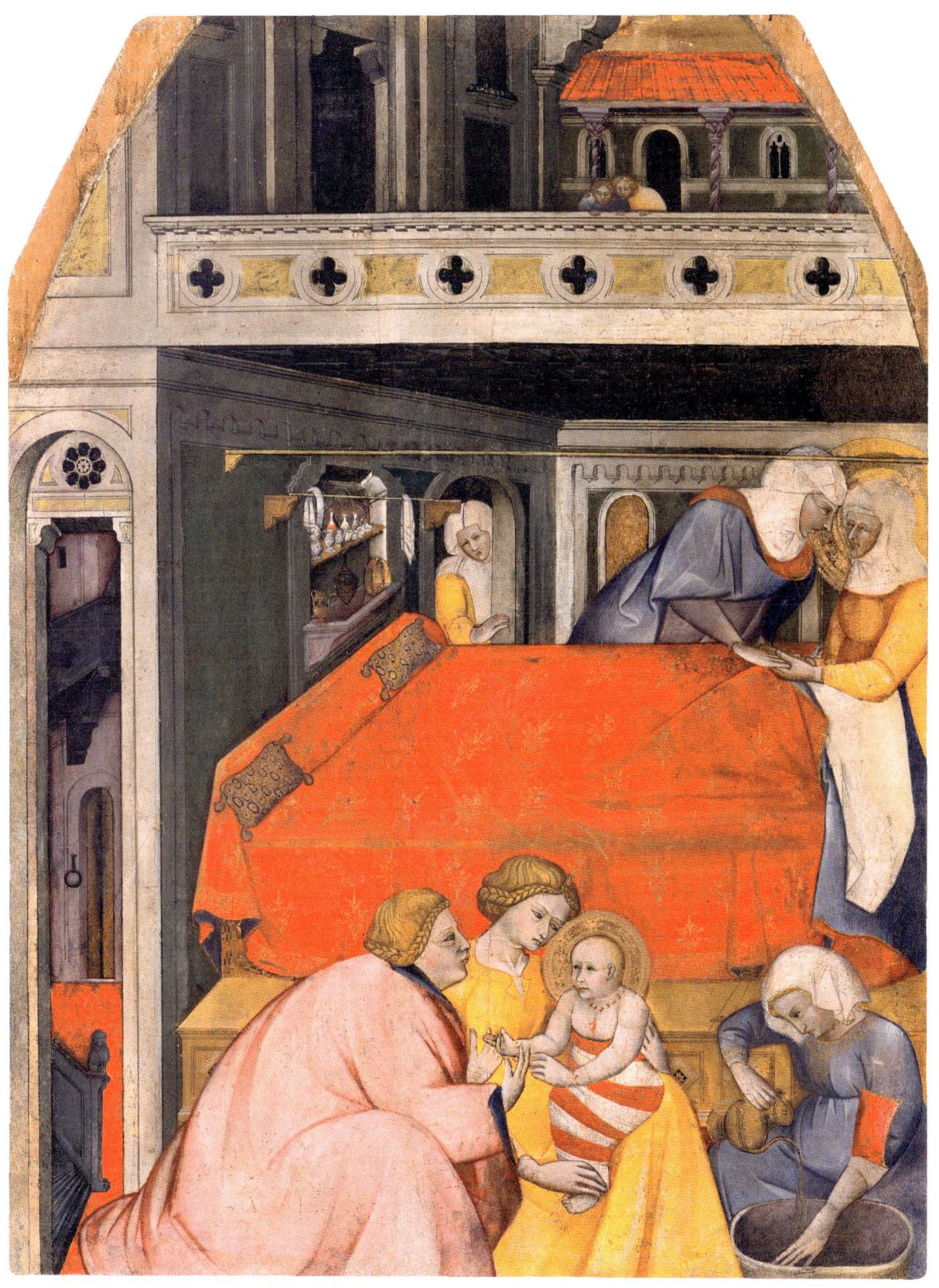

The Most Beautiful of the Colors

Having long remained reticent on colors, didactic texts became more loquacious in the late Middle Ages, not only encyclopedias and works on natural philosophy, but medical books, pharmacopoeias, alchemical treatises, and liturgical handbooks, not to mention the collections of recipes meant for painters and dyers that we have just discussed. Whether it was a matter of rainbows, flowers, stones, pigments, urine, or even the Mass, the discourse on colors became verbose and varied. This is especially so given that in addition to this literature, there were normative texts on the body and clothing: *specula principum*, treatises on curial etiquette, books on manners and social customs, sumptuary laws and clothing decrees, sermons and diatribes by moralists, and observations and commentaries by chroniclers.

And then there were literary texts, sometimes abounding in color notations, and in certain cases, delighting in holding forth on the hierarchy and symbolism of colors. The courtly lyrics and chivalric romances of the twelfth and thirteenth centuries were hardly expansive on this matter; only the nascent heraldic tradition introduced a bit of color into the horizon of a landscape in which light played a more important role than color did. That all changed at the end of the Middle Ages. Poets and romancers loved to discuss colors along with their beauty and meanings. In doing so, they added an aesthetic and affective dimension to the technical discourse of the scholarly and normative texts. For this period, historians have at their disposal documentation that allows them to identify preferences or aversions, and study combinations, hierarchies, and correspondences. In the feudal period, judgments on the beauty or ugliness of particular colors had primarily been a matter of moral or social considerations. The beautiful was almost always the suitable, temperate, and customary. Of course the purely aesthetic

The Chiaroscuro Effect in Pink

Giovanni Savoldo (ca. 1480–1548), a Venetian painter originally from Lombardy, like all Venetian artists, is a great master of color. He loved contrasts, backlighting, and especially nocturnal effects. In that way he seems to have influenced Michelangelo da Caravaggio and many of his followers. Moreover, it is possible that Georges de La Tour knew his *Saint Matthew* and was inspired by it. Here the pink of the robe, intensely lit, contrasts with the saint's face, remaining in shadow, and particularly with the face of the angel, hardly visible.

Giovanni Gerolamo Savoldo, *Saint Matthew and the Angel*, 1534. Metropolitan Museum of Art, New York.

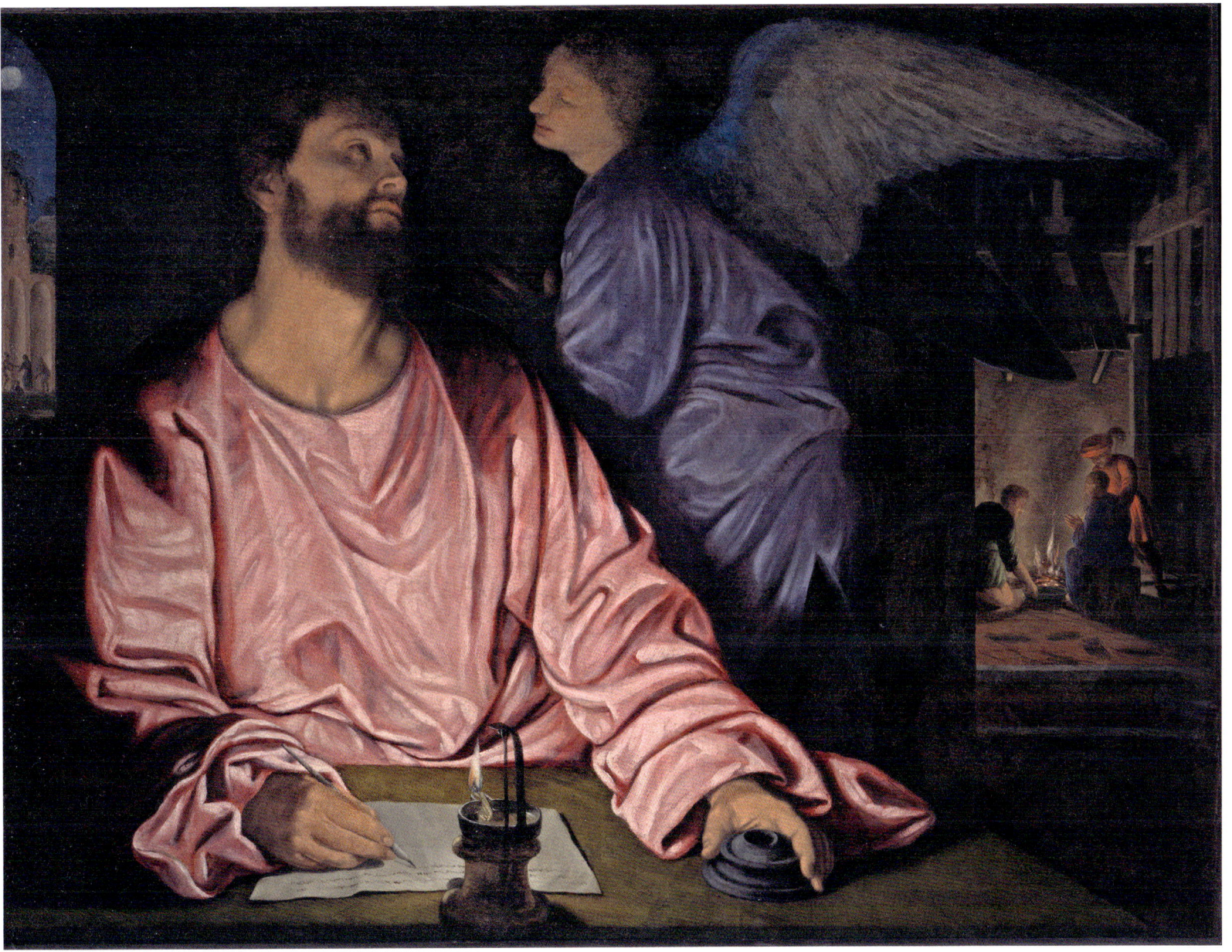

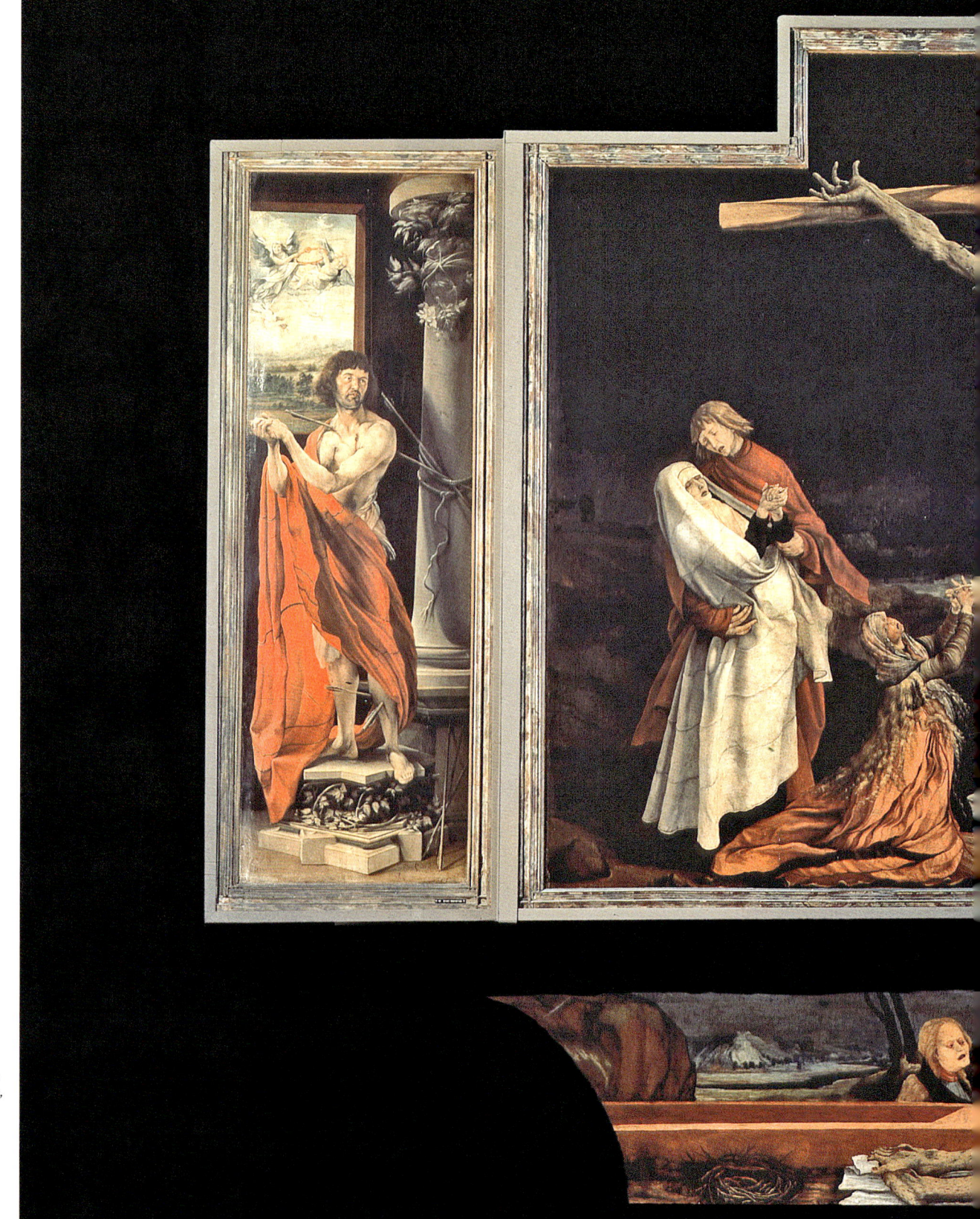

Nikolaus of
Haguenau and
Matthias Grünewald,
Issenheim Altarpiece,
1512–16. Unterlinden
Museum, Colmar
(Alsace, France).

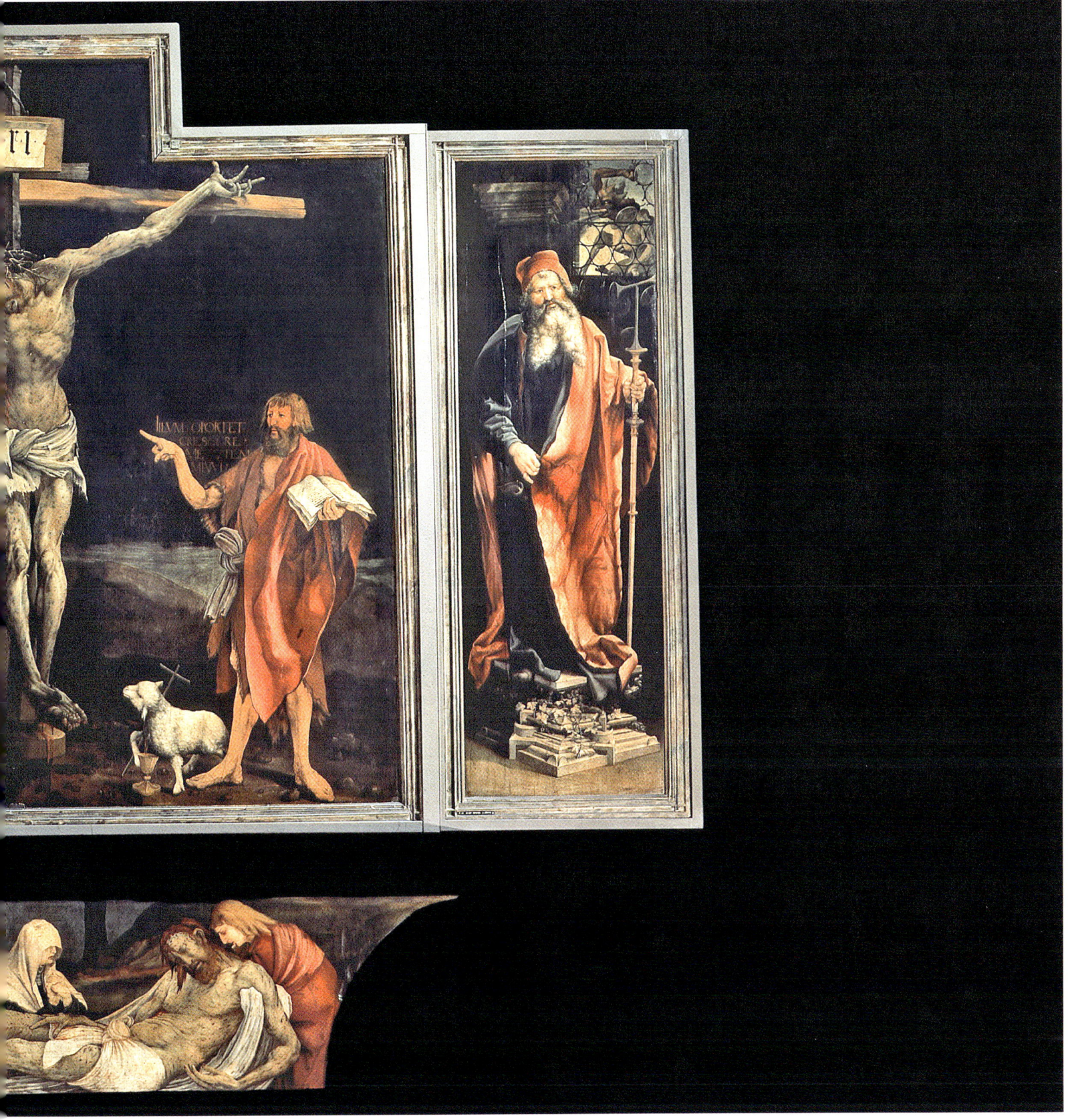

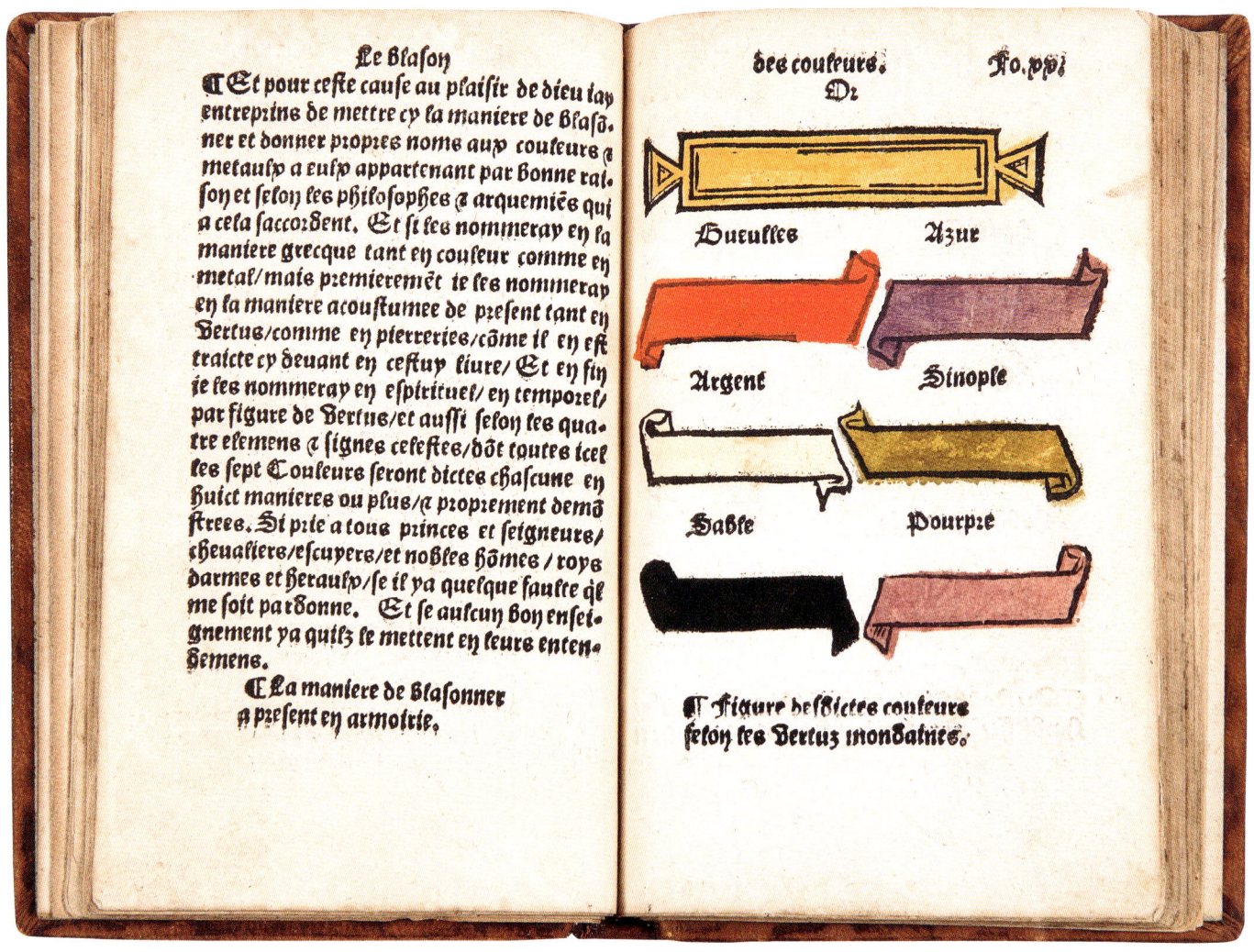

Le Blaſon

Et pour ceſte cauſe au plaiſir de dieu iay entreprins de mettre cy la maniere de Blaſonner et donner propres noms aux couleurs ꝗ metaulx a eulx appartenant par bonne raiſon et ſelon les phiIoſophes ꝗ arquemiẽs qui a cela ſaccordent. Et ſi les nommeray en la maniere grecque tant en couleur comme en metal/mais premieremẽt ie les nommeray en la maniere acouſtumee de preſent tant en Vertus/comme en pierreries/cõme il en eſt traicte cy deuant en ceſtuy liure/Et en ſin ie les nommeray en eſpirituel/en temporel/par figure de Vertus/et auſſi ſelon les quatre elemens ꝗ ſignes celeſtes/dõt toutes icelles ſept Couleurs ſeront dictes chaſcune en huict manieres ou plus/ꝗ proprement demõſtrees. Si prie a tous princes et ſeigneurs/cheualiers/eſcuyers/et nobles hõmes / roys darmes et heraulx/ſe il ya quelque faulte q͠ me ſoit pardonne. Et ſe aulcun bon enſeignement ya quilz le mettent en leurs entendemens.

La maniere de Blaſonner a preſent en armoirie.

Gueulles   **Azur**

Argent   **Sinople**

Sable   **Pourpre**

Figure deſdictes couleurs ſelon les Vertuz mondaines.

Le Blason des couleurs, en armes, livrées et devises

The first part of this work, which enjoyed great success when it was printed in the early sixteenth century, is a treatise on heraldry compiled about 1435 by Jean Courtois, known as the Sicily Herald. The second part, more developed, discusses the symbolism of the colors and their role in dress codes. Written in about 1480–90, it is attributed to an anonymous author originally from Brussels or Lille.

Double-page spread devoted to the colors in a copy of the book printed for Parisian bookseller Jean Janot, rue Neuve-Notre-Dame, established 1521 or 1522.

pleasure of contemplation existed, but it essentially involved the colors of nature, the only truly beautiful, pure, licit, and harmonious ones, because they were the work of the Creator. At the dawn of modernity, that was no longer the case. Colors manufactured by humans could also be attractive.

In this domain, there are a few treatises on heraldry that best express the transition from the symbolic to the aesthetic. One of them is *Le Blason des couleurs*, a compilation attributed to a herald who was famous in his time, Jean Courtois, known as the Sicily Herald, the title of his position in the service of King René of Anjou and then King Alphonso V of Aragon. Born around 1380 near Mons in Hainaut, he died in 1437 or 1438. Toward the end of his life, he composed a treatise in French that is devoted almost entirely to colors, and comes down to us through about twenty manuscripts and many printed copies.[18]

Actually, the Sicily Herald is the author of only the first part of that work. Half a century later, an anonymous author, perhaps from Lille or Brussels, added a second, more developed part, discussing in detail livery and the symbolism of colors in clothing. The work then took on a more complete title, *Le Blason des couleurs en armes, livrées et devises*. It enjoyed considerable success. Printed in Paris in 1495, it was reprinted in 1501, and then six more times until 1614. Meanwhile, it was translated or adapted into various languages, first Venetian, and then Tuscan, German, Dutch, and Castilian.[19] It had great influence in various domains, notably literary and pictorial ones. Some poets and artists followed it to the letter and presented figures dressed according to the color codes proposed by this small work. The second author does, in fact, recommend colors for each social condition, age, and life circumstance, promoting certain combinations and advising against others. His choices are based on the "virtues, properties, and meanings" of these different colors. Thus he asserts that incarnadine—our saturated pink—is

Venice, the Capital of Printing and Color

Venice is not only a city of art but also a city of printing. Throughout the sixteenth century, Venetian presses published painting treatises, dyeing manuals, and works on the nature and symbolism of colors as well as books on coats of arms and the rules of heraldry. In the city of the doges, color was ubiquitous, including in books.

Lodovico Dolce, *Dialogo nel quale si ragiona della qualità, diversità e proprietà dei colori*, Venice, 1565, title page.

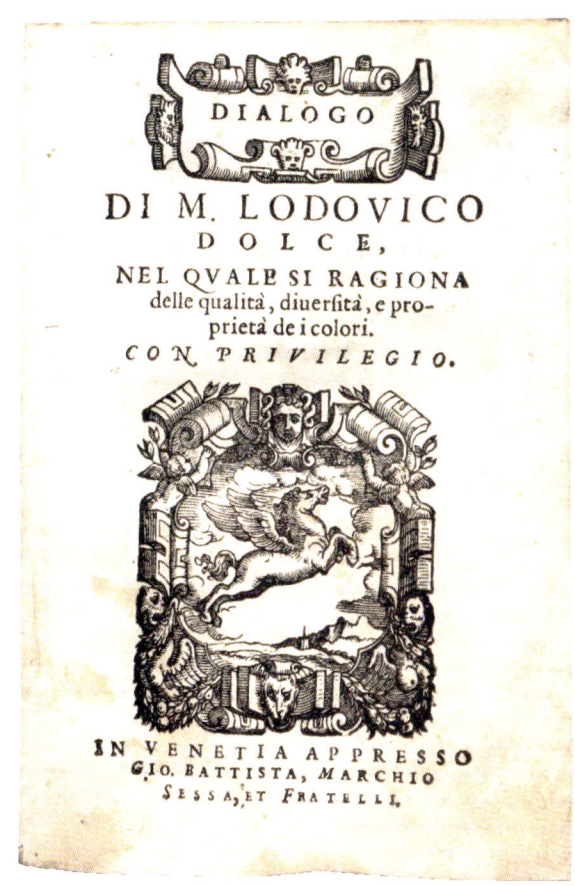

worn "by amorous people," and suited "to courtiers and people who use their pen." Earlier in the work, an entire chapter is devoted to each of the eleven colors considered "especially." Pink is the eighth color the author presents:

> Pink is a color very beautiful and gay. It closely approaches red but it is different from it because it calls on white as well. Among flowers, pink closely resembles the carnation and the wallflower. This color . . . signifies health, a short life, nobility, and a person of good temperament. It represents the pleasant, self-confident man. It is also suitable to young women and damsels. In livery, worn with gray, it signifies hope for riches; with purple, good grace toward great men; with tan, happiness and then unhappiness. The color pink is made more by art than by nature.[20]

This last remark is particularly interesting. It leads us to think that pink was seen more often in the workshops of painters and dyers than in the meadows, woods, and gardens. This was a color generally produced by humans rather than nature.

The last sentences in *Blason des couleurs* appear like the questions and answers in a catechism: "What color is the most beautiful?—It is red, because pink is too soon erased. What color is the ugliest? It is tan."[21]

That this "tan" (*tanné*, meaning tanned)—that is, a dark shade of russet—was considered the ugliest of colors is not at all surprising. In the Middle Ages and even the early modern period, russet was a negative color that literary texts and images then associated with liars, hypocrites,

The Pastoral Concert

This famous Venetian painting may have been begun by Giorgione and completed by Titian. Giorgione is supposedly responsible for the wonderful pastoral setting and subtle green tones. Titian is credited with the drawing and painting of the figures, in particular the two naked women whose smooth, slightly orange flesh tones are among the most admired of the sixteenth century. Titian was hardly twenty-three years old when he completed this painting.

Giorgione and Titian, *Le Concert champêtre*, 1510–11. Musée du Louvre, Paris.

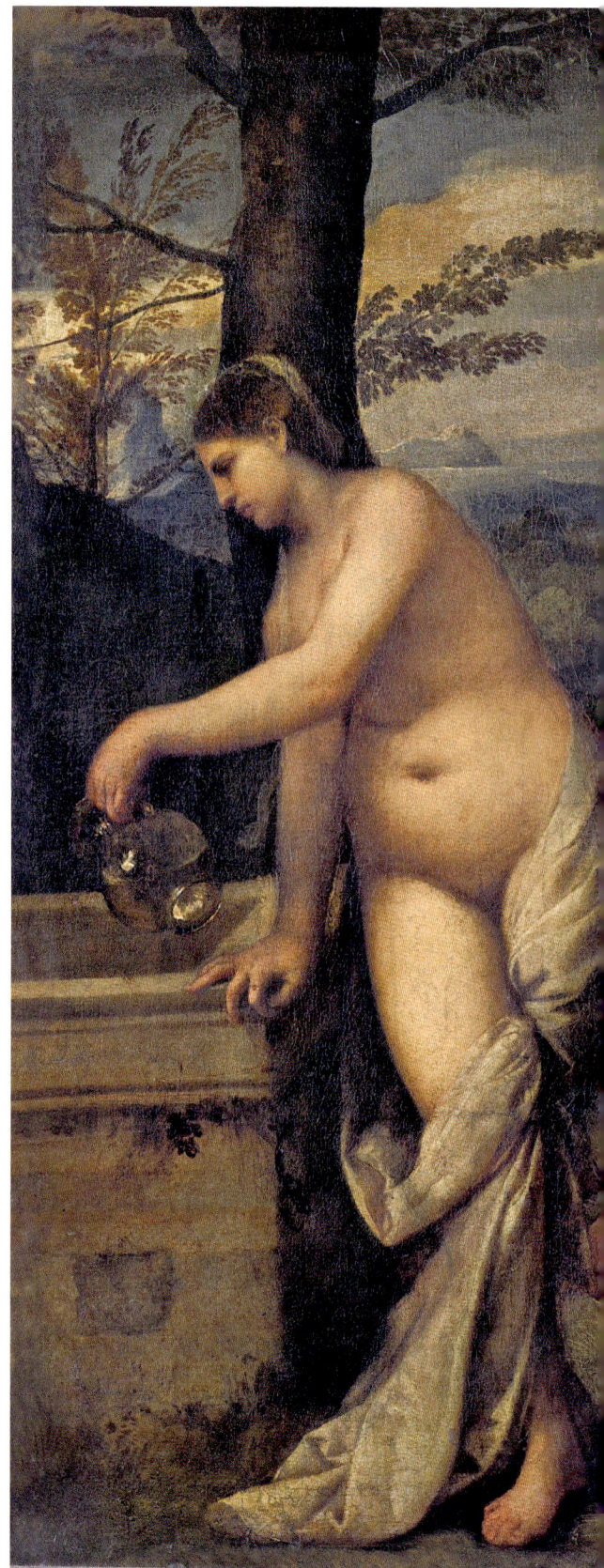

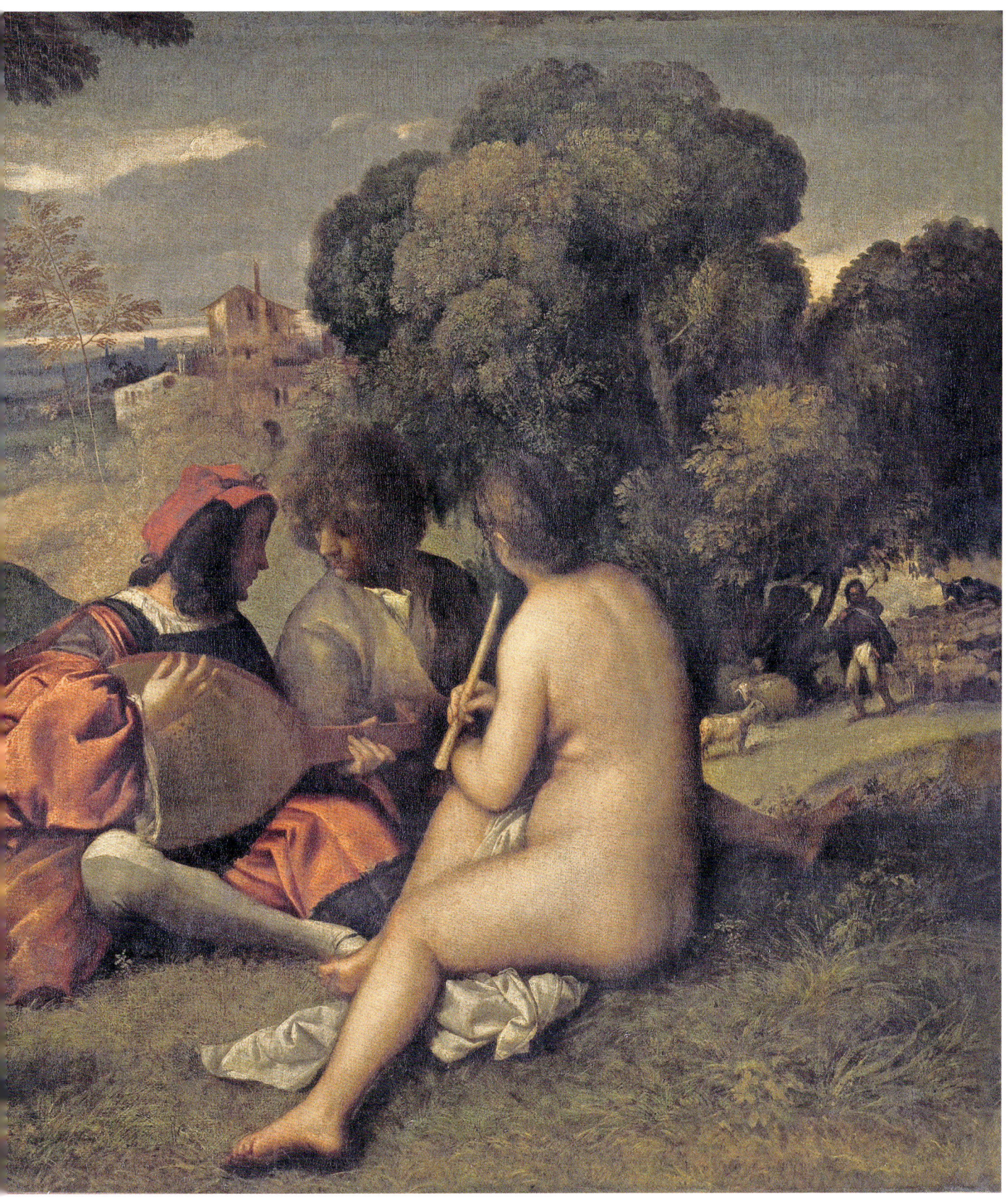

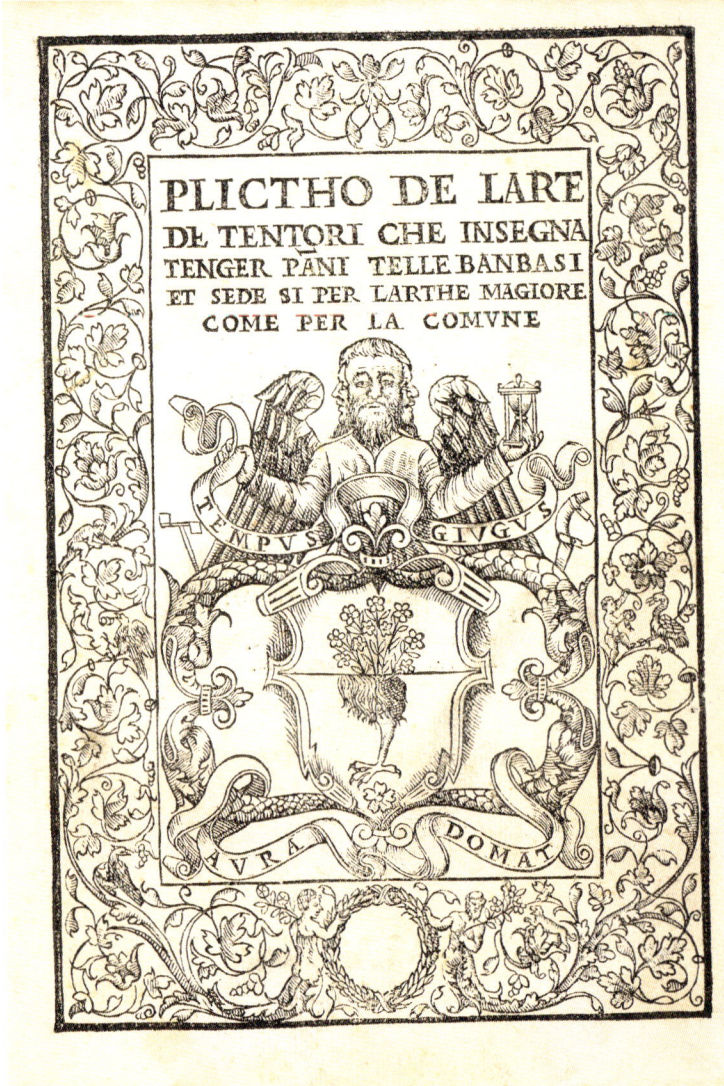

The First Printed Handbook for Dyeing

Starting in the nineteenth century, it was in Venice, the European capital of color, that various expensive colorants arrived from the East to be used by painters and dyers. It was also in Venice that the first technical works intended for those two artisan guilds were printed. The oldest dyeing manual, written by Giovanventura Rosetti and devoted to dyeing wool, was printed there in 1540. Greatly admired in Venice, pink was given two paragraphs in it.

Giovanventura Rosetti, *Plictho de l'arte de tentori che insegna tenger pani telle banbasi et sede si per larthe magiore come per la comune*, F. Rampazetto, printer, 1540, Venice.

prostitutes, deceitful women, and all the traitors who appear in the Bible, chansons de geste, and courtly romances. They all have red hair or red body hair, notably Judas, the disloyal apostle, the traitor par excellence.[22] On the other hand, that pink is presented as the most beautiful color "if it were less evanescent" is new, and a sign that the colors no longer constituted only a code or language, as in heraldry, but also an aesthetic.

In the early modern period, that idea spread among numerous authors. The first half of the sixteenth century witnessed a great output of works devoted to the beauty, harmony, or meaning of colors. Some remained manuscripts, relegated to the silence of libraries, but others were printed as books and even became bestsellers. For examples, let us cite four Venetian publications, reprinted many times, in which our pink is much in evidence: Antonia Telesio, *De coloribus libellus* (1528); Fulvio Pellegrino Morato, *Del significato de colori* (1535); Paolo Pino, *Dialogo di pittura* (1548); and Lodovico Dolce, *Dialogo dei colori* (1565).[23]

It is hardly by chance that these works devoted uniquely to color were published in Venice by authors either native to or working in that city of the doges. Between the fourteenth and eighteenth centuries, Venice was the undisputed capital of color in Europe. It was a commercial city where dyestuffs arrived from the East, sometimes from far away, before being redistributed throughout the West.[24] It was also a city of art, where there were many painters, some of them renowned: the Bellinis, Giorgione, Titian, Tintoretto, and Veronese. In the debates that divided the partisans of drawing from those of color, the Venetians always supported the primacy of color. Moreover, Venice was a great artisanal center where dyeing reigned. No other European city possessed so many workshops, strictly specialized according to fabrics and dyestuffs. The dyeing profession was carefully partitioned, regulated, and controlled.[25] It was in Venice, too, that the first dyeing manual was printed in 1540, the famous *Plictho* by Giovanventura Rosetti, and reissued many times until the end of the eighteenth century.[26] Venice was, in fact, an active city for printing beginning in 1465. A great numbers of books in all areas of literature and learning were published there each year. Books on color numbered among them, whether on dyeing, painting, clothing, aesthetics, or symbolism. A translation of the *Blason des couleurs* was published there in Venetian in 1525, and another in Italian in 1535, and both were reprinted several times before the end of the sixteenth century.[27]

Of the four works cited above, the most instructive one for our purposes is undoubtedly that by Morato (1483–1548), humanist friend of painters.[28] Much of it was certainly borrowed from the recently translated *Blason des couleurs*, but Morato distances himself on various points from the normative discourse on heraldry and social dress codes. Notably, he explains that in matters of pictorial art, "the eye is more important than the mind," and the beauty of the colors takes precedence not only over the perfection of the line but even over the virtues and meanings attributed to those colors as well. For him, the aesthetic trumps the symbolic; surely this marks a rupture with the value systems of the late Middle Ages. Morato recommends to his painter friends many color associations meant solely to give pleasure to the eye and senses, and not to satisfy the mind or morality. According to him, the most beautiful combinations are black with white, blue with orange, gray with fawn (*leonato*), and especially light green with flesh color (*incarnato*) when it is luminous.[29] In his eyes, in a range of light colors, nothing is more beautiful than green with pink.

Also instructive is the small Latin treatise by Telesio (1482–1534), who taught rhetoric and belles lettres in Venice between 1527 and 1529. Telesio was also influenced by the *Blason des couleurs*, but he knew nothing about heraldry and adopts a more philological than symbolic discourse. An admirer of Virgil, Ovid, and Pliny, he

The Most Beautiful Combinations of Colors

In his work *Del significato de colori*, published in Venice in 1535, Fulvio Pellegrino Morato, humanist friend of painters, explains that in matters of color, the eye is more important than the mind and the beauty of colors outweighs the meanings attributed to them. That marks a clear break from medieval value systems. Hence Morato recommends many color combinations meant solely to please the eye and senses: blue with orange, gray with fawn, white with black, and especially light green with pink.

Fulvio Pellegrino Morato, *Del significato de colori e de mazzolli*, 2nd ed., Venice, Giovanni Padovano, 1551, title page.

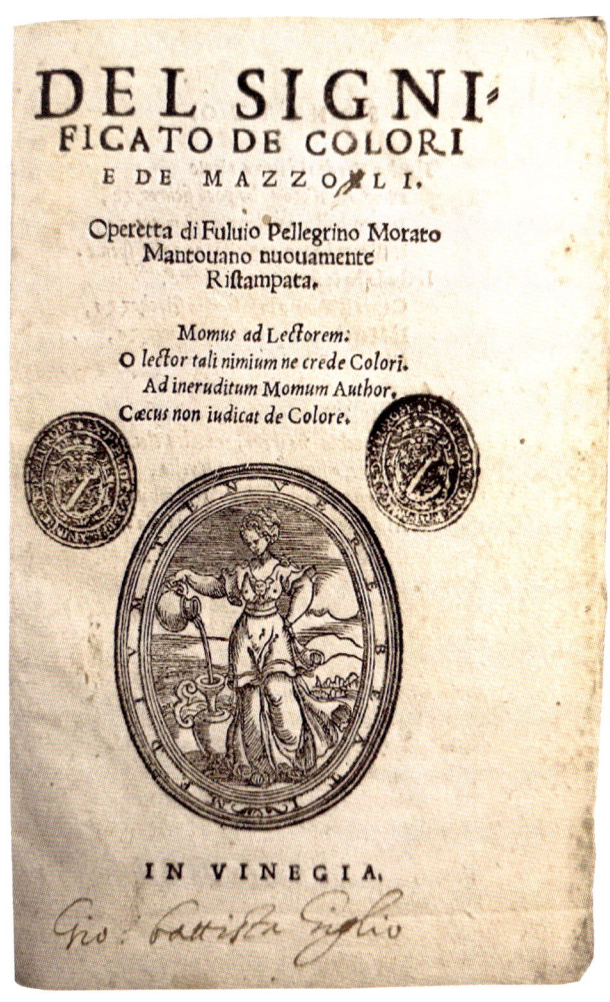

highlights the richness of the Latin vocabulary, analyzing 114 color terms and emphasizing how difficult they are to translate. He also insists that it is impossible, no matter what the language, to name the color of the sky, sea, or eyes (human as well as animal), and, more generally, "everything situated between blue and green." In a final chapter, he proposes various classifications for colors. On the moral plane, he distinguishes the sober colors (*colores austeri*) from the frivolous ones (*colores floridi*), as Pliny had done in his *Natural History*.[30] In the first group, he places white, black, and gray along with "blue and pink when they are soft." On the aesthetic plane, Telesio contrasts the colors that please the eye (*colores suaves*) with those that are disagreeable to look at and seem dirty (*colores sordidi*). Among the first are pink—which he considers "the most beautiful of all the colors"—white, sky blue, and purple (*purpureus*), which—as always the case in Venice—was not purple at all but instead a dark red. Among the second are russet, dull black (*ater*), most browns, and, unexpectedly, dark blue.

The dialogues of Pino (1534–65) and Dolce (1508–68), two wholly Venetian authors, friends of painters, and frequent visitors to Titian's studio, show little interest in morality, none in heraldry, more in symbolism, and much in aesthetics. Pino emphasizes the problems encountered by painters trying to reproduce colors of nature, not only of vegetation but of sky, sea, and fire. He also develops the idea that very costly pigments do not necessarily make beautiful colors. The beauty is in the expertise and genius of the artist, not in the materials.[31] For his part, Dolce, a tirelessly prolific and versatile writer who "wrote in all genres without excelling in any" (Johann Wolfgang von Goethe), lingered over defining what a color is—material, light, sensation, or term—and explaining the notion of harmony. Harmony should depend on contrasts of coloration and saturation rather than shades of the same tone. Nevertheless, to be beautiful, those contrasts should be restrained. He cites as a perfect harmony the juxtaposition of light green, pink, and pale gray. Like both Telesio and Morato, he makes pink the most delicate and appealing of colors, whether it is a matter of flower petals or a young girl's complexion.[32]

At the dawn of the modern period, new sensibilities thus began to develop that no longer made the beauty of colors subject to their ethical, social, or symbolic dimension but only to the pleasure of the eye. These new sensibilities would gradually conquer all of Europe.

The Deposition from the Cross

Famous in his lifetime but a bit disparaged by Giorgio Vasari, Jacopo da Pontormo has not been given the recognition he deserves by posterity. He is one of the great colorists in the entire history of painting. Consider this immense *Deposition* that is found in the funeral chapel of the Capponis (wealthy Tuscan bankers) at the church of Santa Felicita in Florence. The unusual pink of the clothing contrasts with the skin tones of the bodies and faces, but it is in perfect harmony with the subtle greens and magical blues worn by the rest of the group.

Jacopo da Pontormo, *The Deposition from the Cross*, 1526. Church of Santa Felicita, Capponi Chapel, Florence.

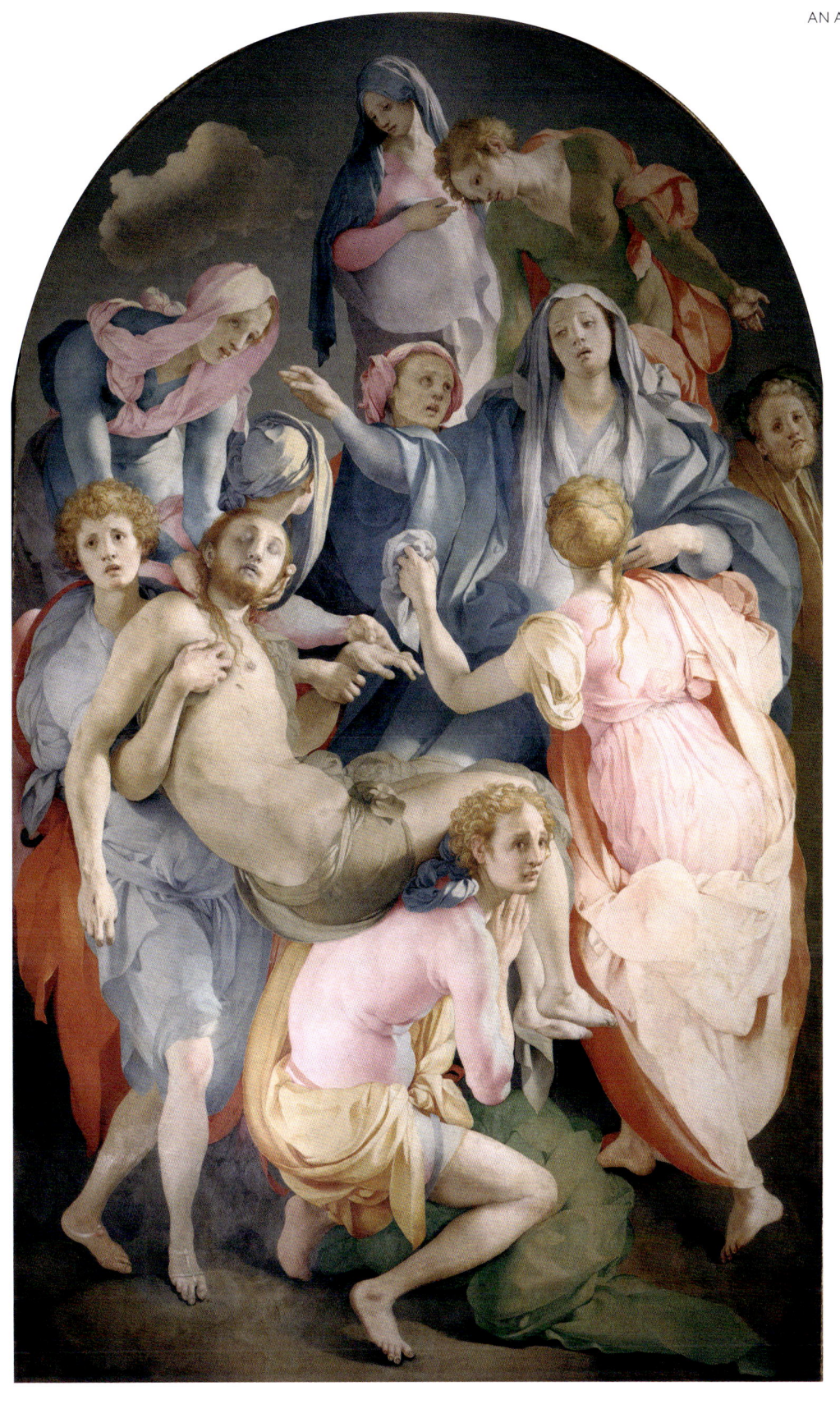

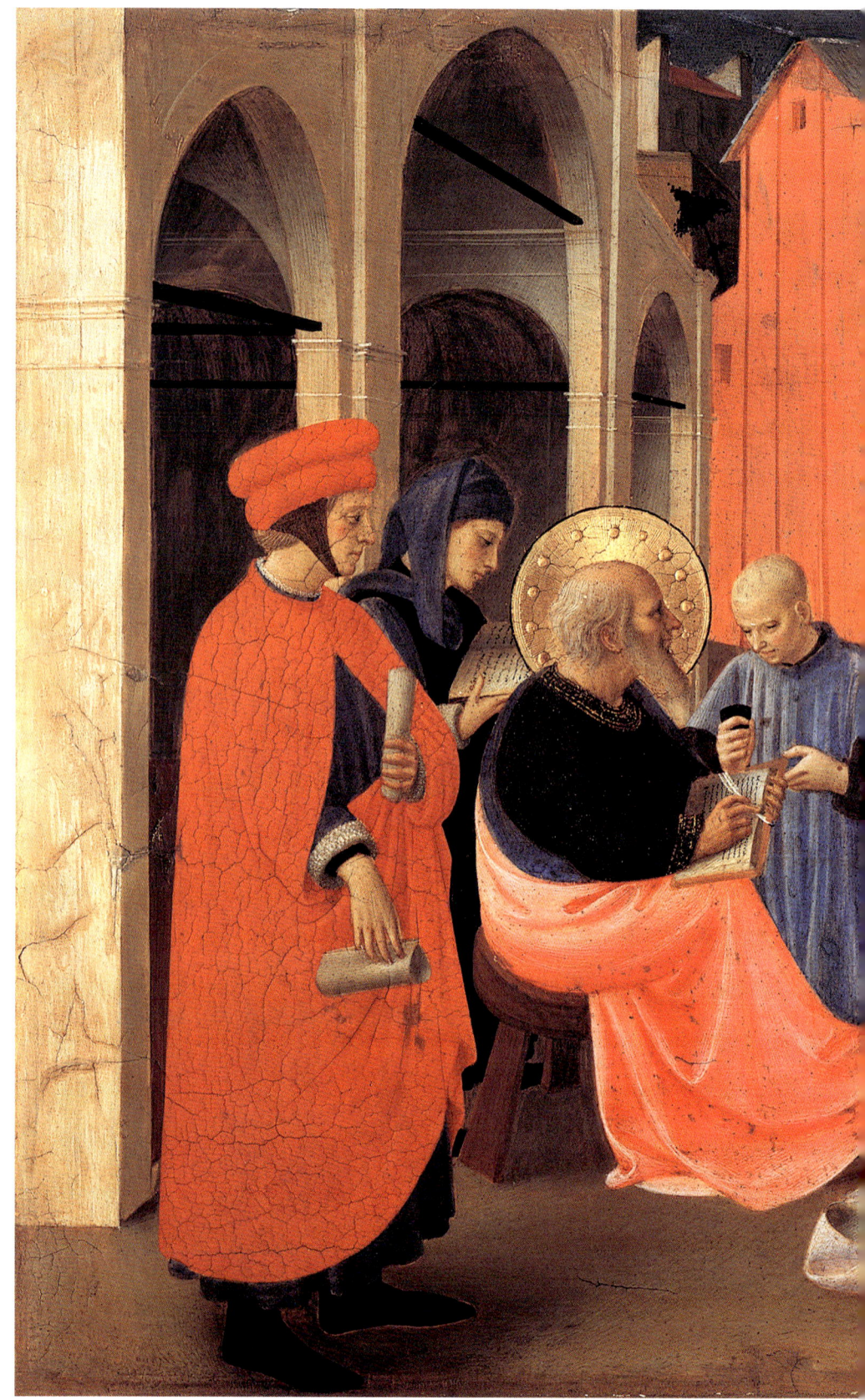

Fra Angelico, *St. Peter
Dictating the Gospel of
St. Mark*, first panel of
the tabernacle of Linaioli
designed by Lorenzo Ghiberti,
ca. 1433. Museo Nazionale
di San Marco, Florence.

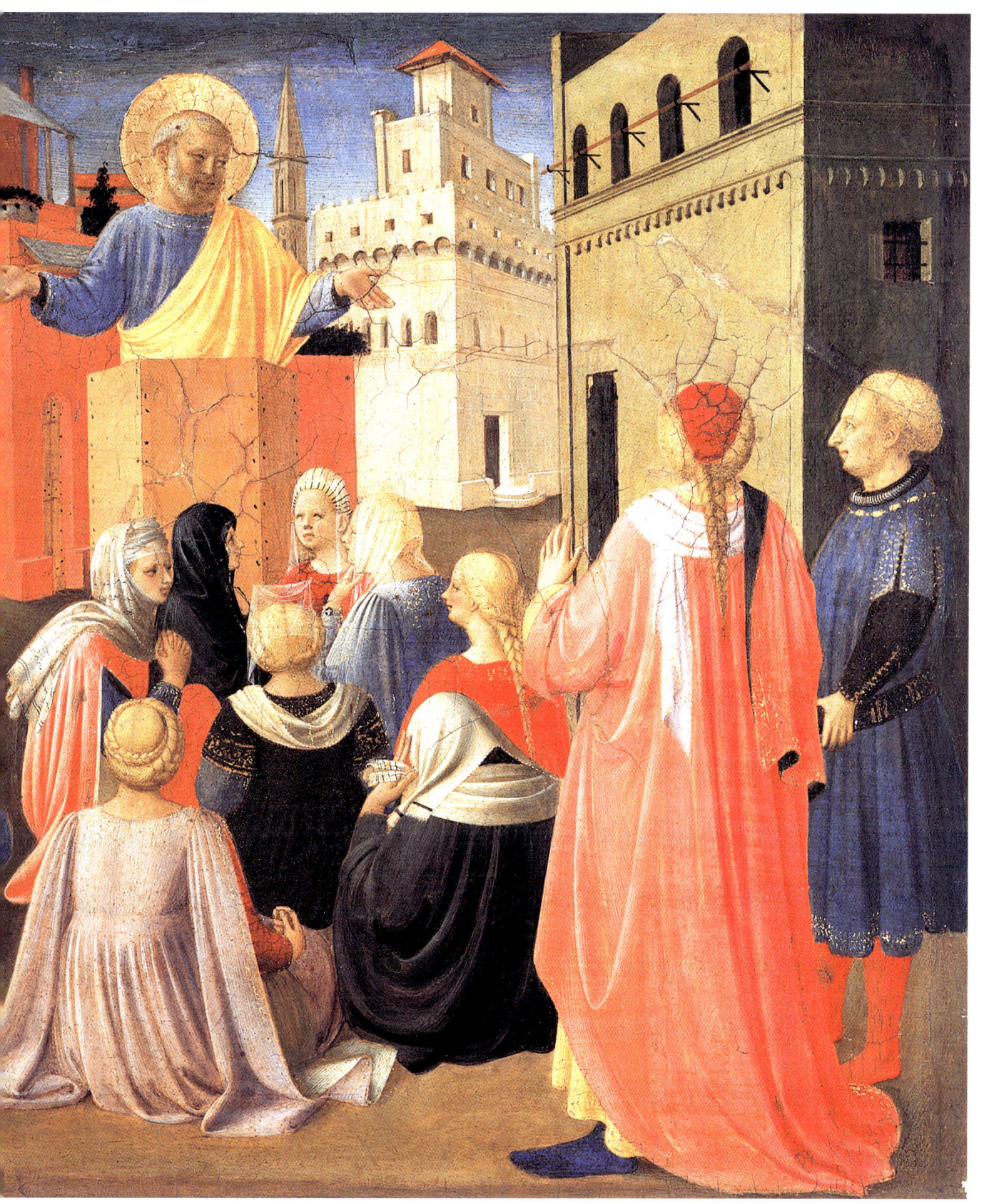

Drawing or Color?

In Renaissance Italy, a question was often asked in the world of artists: Which plays the most important and noble role, drawing or color? The debate was sometimes lively, and involved not only painters but art patrons, collectors, humanists, and philosophers as well. A closer look shows the controversy beginning a few decades earlier. We find the first signs of it in the late fourteenth century in connection with grisaille paintings. Many authors started to argue for the superiority of line over color, like Giovani Conversino (1343–1408), a Paduan humanist and disciple of Petrarch: "Before a painting, a cultivated viewer will appreciate the delicacy of the line, the harmony of proportions, and the general balance of the composition, while the uncultivated viewer will be captivated only by the colors."[33]

In the following century, paintings in grisaille on walls, panels, or parchment gave priority to white, gray, and black over the other colors, attracting some major artists like Pisanello, Paolo Uccello, Andrea Mantegna, and others, who found in this exercise a means of expressing their talent for drawing. Gradually, drawing tended to become an autonomous art form, not simply for making sketches or preparatory works for painting or sculpture. In his famous *De pictura*, completed in 1435, Leon Battista Alberti,

architect and humanist, praised drawing and theorized about a certain number of ideas that would long endure. He explained that painters must be educated, especially in geometry, and the three most important elements in a painting were the drawing, composition, and relationship of light and shadow, the key factor in modeling figures. In his eyes, the artist's most noble task was representing the human body, but he does not discuss colors, not even those of the face, hands, or flesh. Although he speaks endlessly about the body, he ignores the complexion and skin, thus flesh tones and pinks.[34]

These debates were taken up again and expanded in Italy during the second Renaissance, to the point that some artists, more interested than others in theory, began to question specifically the status of color in painting as well as the comparative merits of drawing and color. In Florence, where many painters were also architects and Neoplatonic ideas permeated all forms of artistic creation, drawing was considered to be more exact, precise, and "true." In Venice, where as we have just seen, much was written on colors and pink was frequently considered the most beautiful of them, artists and humanists held the opposite view. The debate had begun. It would last four centuries, impassioning painters, scholars, and art

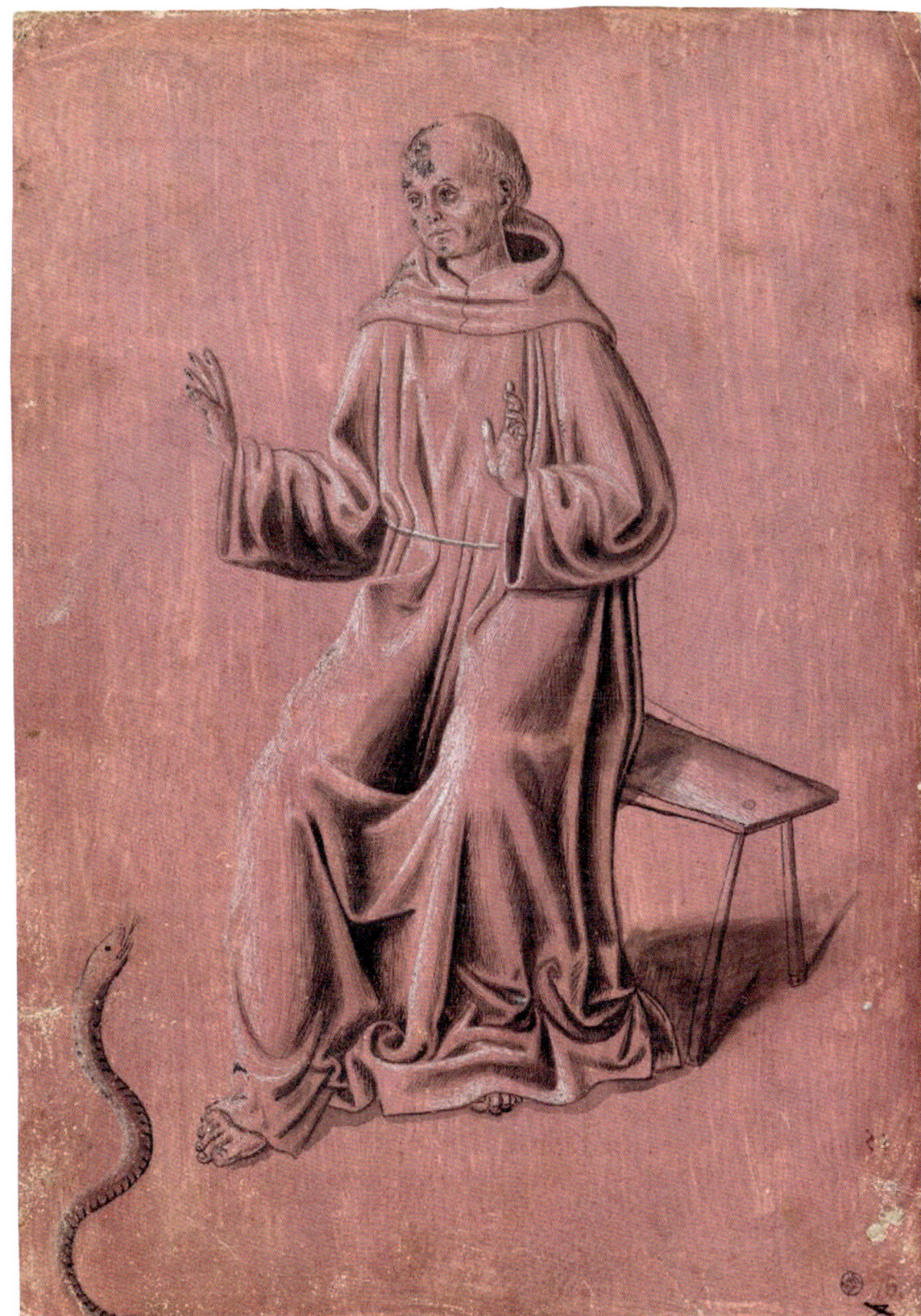

Drawing on Pink Paper

The appearance of printing developed papermaking into a large-scale industry and promoted its use for artistic purposes. Starting in the 1470s and until well into the sixteenth century, drafters and engravers made multiple innovations, and enjoyed using colored paper to soften contrasts or create more subtle tones than the simple opposition of black and white. Rare are the artists, however, who drew their silverpoint sketches on pink paper.

Benozzo Gozzoli, *A Monk Threatened by a Snake*, ca. 1480. Nationalmuseum, Stockholm.

The Union of Drawing and Color

In the painter's work, which is more important, drawing or color? This question was asked constantly from the late fourteenth century until the early twentieth century and gave rise to many debates and controversies. Most of the time, drawing prevailed. Its advocates claimed that it was masculine and appealed to the mind, whereas color, subordinate to it, was feminine, fragile, delicate, and appealed only to the senses.

Guido Reni, *The Union of Drawing and Color* (workshop copy?), ca. 1628–30. Palaces of Versailles and Trianon, Versailles.

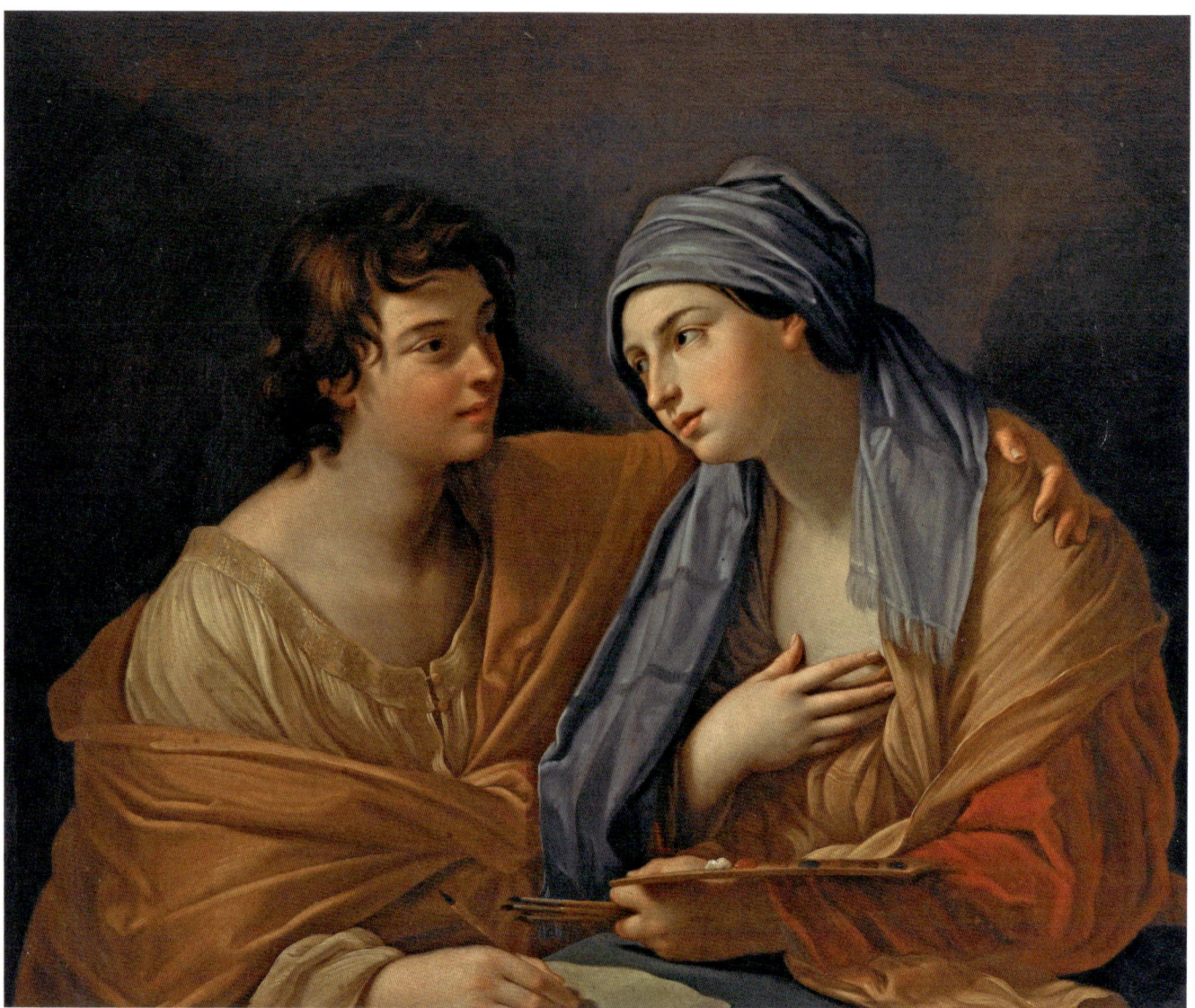

theorists, first in Italy, then in France, and finally throughout Europe.[35]

The opponents of color did not lack arguments. They considered color to be less noble than drawing because unlike the latter, it was not a creation of the mind but instead simply the product of material. Drawing was the extension of an idea; it addressed the intellect and was the "father" of all the arts. As for color, it addressed only the senses; its aim was not to inform but only to captivate. In doing so, it sometimes misled the eye and kept the viewer from clearly discerning contours. Its seductiveness was reprehensible because it was a diversion from the true and therefore the good. In short, it was only makeup, falsity, lying, and treason—old ideas, already presented by Plato, taken up again by the moralists of the Middle Ages and then by the great Protestant reformers. On the other side, the partisans of color emphasized the essential role it played in painting and frescoes, both constructively and iconographically: distinguishing the planes, identifying and hierarchizing the figures, creating the play of combinations or contrasts, and establishing correspondences. But above all, they stressed what drawing alone, deprived of color, failed to convey: not only the emotional, sensual, or musical dimension of the painting, but especially the living nature of the figures, thanks to the flesh tones of faces and bodies. In these areas, the tones tending toward pink played a fundamental role.[36]

In fact, beginning in the sixteenth century, painters paid increasing attention to pink and all of its shades. The humanism of the Renaissance and the anthropocentrism underlying it encouraged the representation of the body, whether realistic or idealized, nude or partially clothed. Thus for many artists, it became a required exercise to paint the complexion of faces, skin of hands and arms, and flesh of torsos, throats, thighs, backs, and buttocks. Gradually it became an accepted idea that a painter could be judged as a colorist by the way all of these flesh tones were conveyed on a mural or panel. Although the thinking on this varied according to the workshop, school, or generation, one idea dominated all others and was constantly put forward for decades, from the first Renaissance until

the middle of the nineteenth century: representing human skin was the hardest task a painter confronted, and the more naked the body, the greater and more difficult the exercise. Nevertheless, even more than the color of bodies, it was usually on the color of faces that most judgments and hierarchies were based.

Reading painting treatises and handbooks, we can see that the materials and processes for producing such colors hardly changed over time. But what differences existed from painter to painter! The principal colors are all cited: white and red first, but also yellow and blue, and sometimes green and even black. What varies are the proportions of each shade, its nuances and combinations, and the way it is applied over another shade. To make the face radiant, the arm or breast creamy, the painter does not mix colors to obtain the suitable shade but rather layers them successively, most often starting with the darkest and ending with the lightest, thereby multiplying the glazes. Glazing is the superimposition of thin, transparent, smooth layers of paint over one or several other layers that have already dried. Layers applied in this way act as optical filters, accentuating the effect of depths while making nuances more delicate and subtle, particularly since the painter can enrich the color obtained by adding highlights or shadows on the last glaze.[37]

Oil painting hugely favored this trend in glazing, impossible with gouache and binders like casein or glue. No doubt improved by Flemish painters in the fifteenth century, glazes were perfected by the Venetians in the early sixteenth century before spreading gradually through most of Europe. They were used especially to convey the swarthy and pinkish tones of facial complexions. Thanks to glazes, faces seemed to be more animated, alive, real, and even, as the humanists claimed, "true."

Handbooks and treatises from the seventeenth and eighteenth centuries offer many recipes for achieving such results, but they all insist as well on the importance of the background and surrounding colors along with those of the hair, clothing, objects, and accessories. Many of them also indulge in making comparisons and establishing winners: Who among the great painters were the best colorists? Who knew best how to enliven the faces and bodies they painted? Two names were unanimous choices: Titian and Peter Paul Rubens. In matters of colors, Titian and the Venetians were considered superior to the Florentines and other Italian painters.[38] As for Rubens, he outmatched all others, whether in Italy, France, Flanders, the Netherlands, or elsewhere, for "painting flesh." In his *Vie de Rubens* (1681), Roger de Piles, painter, engraver, art historian, and critic, claims that Rubens always made male skin darker than female skin, but that an attentive observer can discern in both the use of a great number of different colors, juxtaposed or superimposed in minute touches. Among them, he emphasizes the abundance of bluish touches and, in contrast, fewer pink or orange ones.[39]

The example of Rubens is all the more interesting because in his lifetime, his paintings were better known through engraved reproductions that circulated throughout Europe than through his originals. In the seventeenth century, the reproduction of paintings in black and white played an essential role in public access to art. That was why painters asked the engravers they employed for better representation of their colors on paper through the use of the burin on the copperplate or other techniques such as etching or drypoint engraving. Such demands are repeated constantly in the instructions Rubens gave to his engravers. There were many engravers in Anvers, often very talented ones, and Rubens's correspondence with the most famous of them, Lucas Vorsterman (1595–1675), is instructive in this respect. It informs us especially about their arguments over the rendering of flesh tones in black and white. Rubens proves to be exacting; he wants *vellutato* for the women and *tanné* for the men. Vorsterman, an engraver conscious of his art and sure of his craft, complains, grumbles, and argues; sometimes he quarrels with the painter, and sometimes he complies, corrects, and reworks his colors according to the master's wishes. Sometimes Rubens recognizes the validity of his engraver's remarks and corrects his own colors on the canvas. In the seventeenth century, painting and engraving were closely related, and mutually influenced one another.[40]

Over the course of the centuries, the aim of the great "painters of flesh," whether it was Titian, Rubens, François Boucher, Jean-August-Dominique Ingres, William-Adolphe Bouguereau, or some other artist, was never a realistic representation of the color of bodies and faces. Quite to the contrary, they moved away from realism to better suggest, evoke, enliven, and reveal the flesh. The real and the true were two very different notions. Moreover, to render in painting the exact colors of human skin is an impossible task. All skin is unique, and its color does not depend solely on the quantity or quality of melanin it contains but also on age, sex, latitude, climate, lifestyle, diseases, nutrition, and so on. In addition, that coloration is neither uniform nor static. Its surface varies, and its appearance changes according to the orientation of the light. That is why Titian or Rubens could convey it much more faithfully than any contemporary photograph, even of the highest quality. The skin is a completely singular surface that one can attempt to represent or suggest through painting, but never through photography.

The Rape of the Daughters of Leucippus

Peter Paul Rubens's flesh tones are not those of Titian. They are more naked and sensual, less evanescent, and especially less smooth. They also tend more toward pink than orange. According to a very old practice, already present in ancient painting, the flesh tones of men are distinctly darker and more saturated than the flesh tones of women.

Peter Paul Rubens, *The Rape of the Daughters of Leucippus by Castor and Pollux*, ca. 1617–18. Alte Pinakothek, Munich.

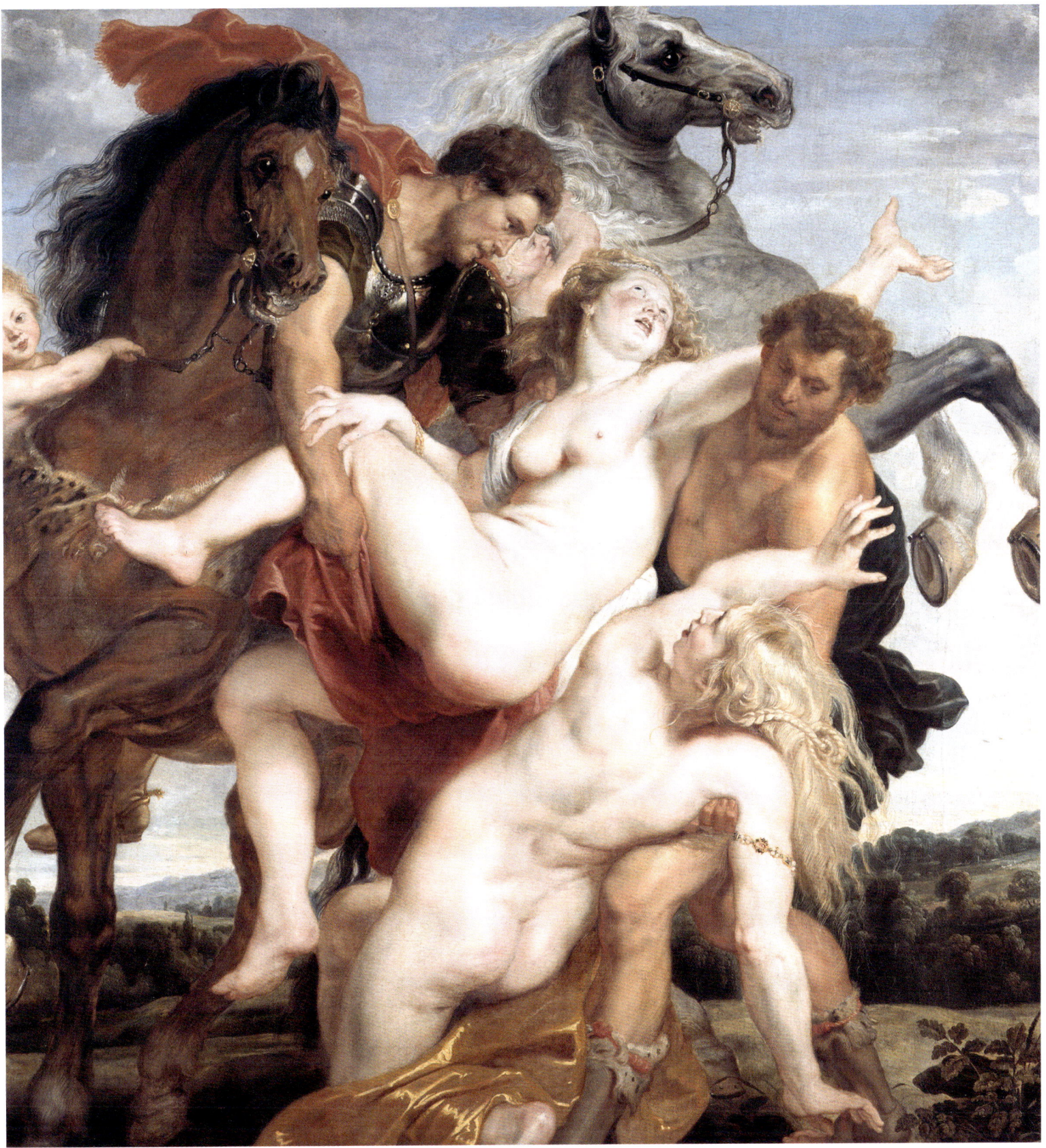

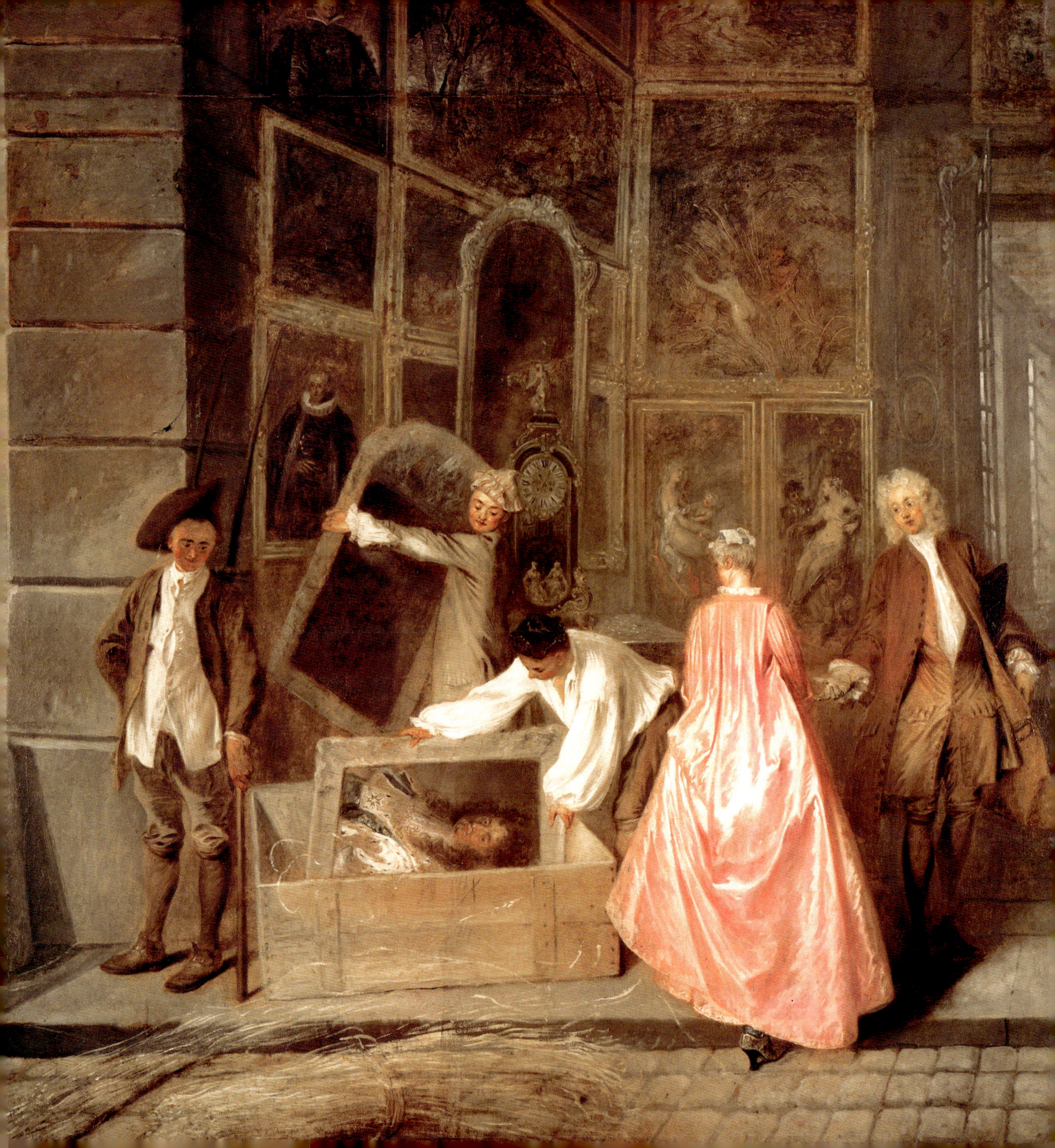

A COLOR IN SEARCH OF A NAME

IN SEARCH

OF A NAME

(16TH TO 18TH CENTURIES)

PAGE 92

L'Enseigne de Gersaint

Despite its fame, this painting by Antoine Watteau, known as *L'Enseigne de Gersaint* (the shop sign of Gersaint), has still not revealed all of its mysteries. Painted in a few days, it first served as advertising for Edme-François Gersaint, art dealer and friend of the painter, whose gallery was on Pont Notre-Dame in Paris. Did Watteau then add to it and finish it himself, or was that the work of some other artist? It is hard to know because the painting quickly passed through the hands of many collectors. In any case, it attests to the fashion for pink in elegant Parisian society at the time of the Regency. This new taste for pink would last until the 1780s.

Antoine Watteau, *L'Enseigne de Gersaint* (detail), 1720. Schloss Charlottenburg, Berlin.

OPPOSITE PAGE

An Exceptional Color Chart

In the last years of the seventeenth century and first years of the eighteenth, color charts started to proliferate on a vast scale, especially those intended for painters. For many decades, the one proposed in 1692 by Dutch artist A. Boogert for watercolors would remain the most expansive ever established, with over five thousand shades! Pink appears there, but remains a discreet color. Only about twenty shades are devoted to it.

A. Boogert, *Traité des couleurs servant à la peinture à l'eau*, 1692. Bibliothèque Méjanes, Aix-en-Provence, ms. 1389 (1228), folio 166.

Let us backtrack a little. The increasing popularity of pinks in textiles and painting beginning in the late fourteenth century raised with renewed urgency an old issue that had never been resolved in an unequivocal way: what to call this color. Ancient Greek and Latin do not possess a single adjective for naming pink, although the Greeks and Romans, like all the peoples of antiquity, had daily opportunities for seeing various shades of pink in nature, whether in flowers, rocks, shells, or simply at dawn or dusk. If we are to believe the poets, it was even a color they seem to have appreciated, without knowing what to call it, much less how to classify it.[1] Where to locate this pink in the ancient *ordo colorum*? Between white and yellow? Between white and red?

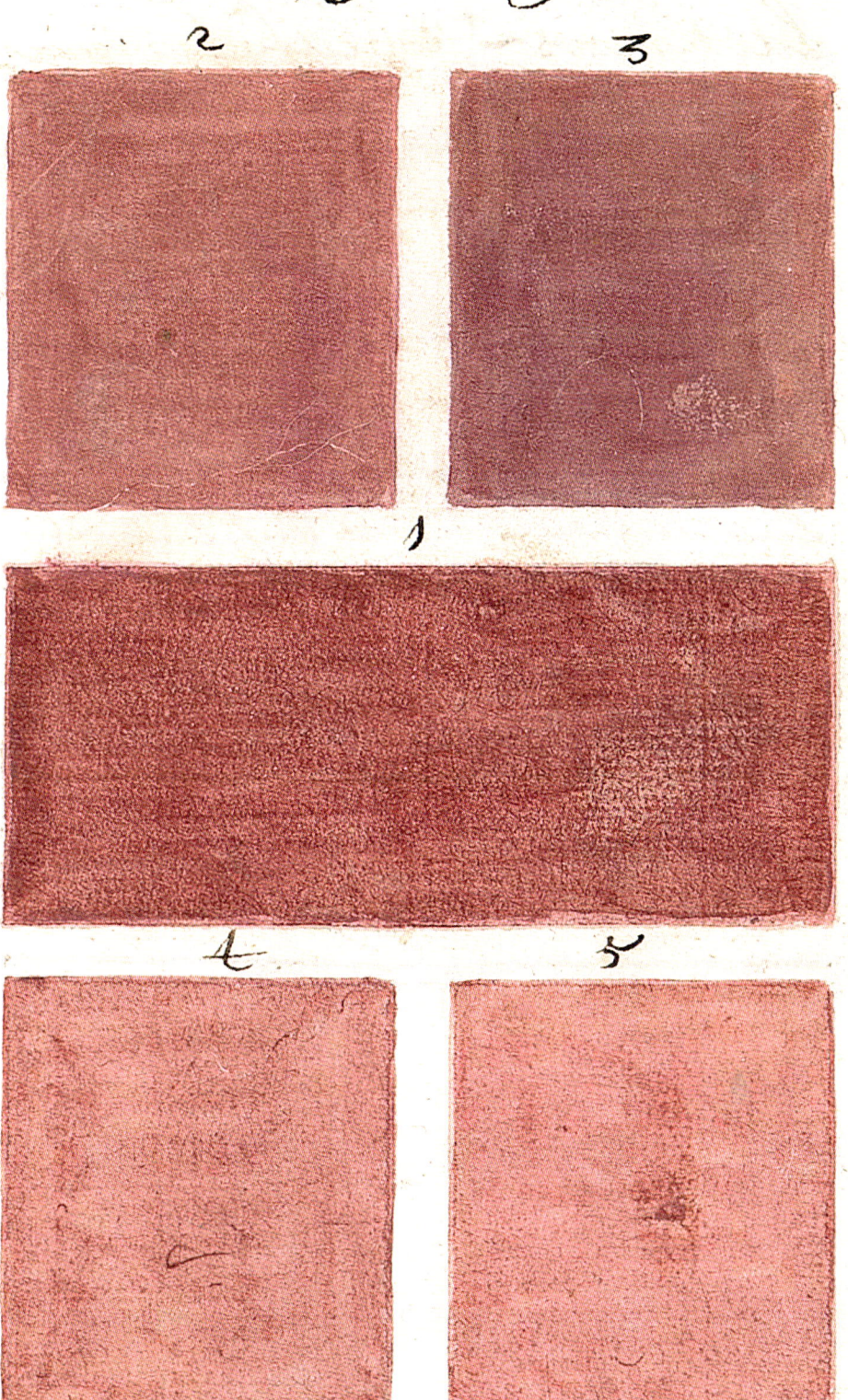

The Hesitations of the Lexicon

Dyeing in Pink

Until the seventeenth century in the textile industry in large cities, the dyeing profession was strictly specialized and regulated. A dyer who worked with red could dye in yellow, orange, or pink, but not in blue, green, or black, and vice versa. To dye in pink, the most common product used was madder to which salts were added along with a powerful mordant. Among the other dyestuffs, brazilwood was much more expensive, and dyes with bases of beetroot juice or various nuts and berries faded quickly.

Brother Conrad Burk of the "Twelve Brothers of Nuremberg" Foundation, dyeing fleece, ca. 1563. Municipal Library, Nuremberg, Amb. 279.2° Folio 50 recto (Landauer I).

An adjective does exist in Greek, *rhodados*, but it is rarely used, and its meaning is not chromatic; it means simply to "be like a rose," or "concerning the rose or rosebush." Moreover, ancient roses were not pink but instead red or white, or more infrequently yellow. Only the wild eglantine was sometimes slightly pinkish white in color. In Latin, the adjective *roseus*, built on the name of the flower (*rosa*), is a false friend that never means "pink," but usually "bright red," "beautiful red," or "vermilion." It was used to describe makeup worn by women and luxury fabrics dyed with kermes.[2] The same is true of its doublet *rosaceus*, which has exactly the same meaning. One particular use of rhodados and roseus describes the dawn—that is, the glow that appears before the sunrise. When Homer attributes "rosy fingers" (*rhododaktulos*) to the dawn in his still-famous poetic phrase, it is not at all a question of the flower or our color pink.[3] Rather it is a symbolic and sensory notation, inspired by the more or less orange reflections that precede the sun when it rises.[4]

Among the Latin poets of the imperial period (Ovid, Martial, and Albius Tibullus), the adjective *roseus* sometimes describes beautiful female skin, pleasing to look at or touch, but its value is more affective than chromatic, and it always expresses an idea of youth and beauty, and sometimes love or sensual delight.[5] Thus whether it was a matter of nature, painting, or dyeing, the pink of ancient times was never called by a color term strictly its own. The Latin adjective that comes closest to it would no doubt be *pallidus* (pale), but that is an imprecise term and hardly chromatic.[6]

The early Middle Ages, which pursued strong, vivid colors, made no new contributions and still could not describe our pink. The shade existed, notably in the world of plants and minerals, but for a long time, it held little interest and never had a name. In medieval Latin, roseus and rosaceus continued to mean "vermilion," and were used especially for cheeks, lips, and makeup. Similarly, in Old and Middle French, the adjective *rose* did exist, but its use was limited. It was used to describe the color of the moon, or a light shade of leather or fabric, sometimes

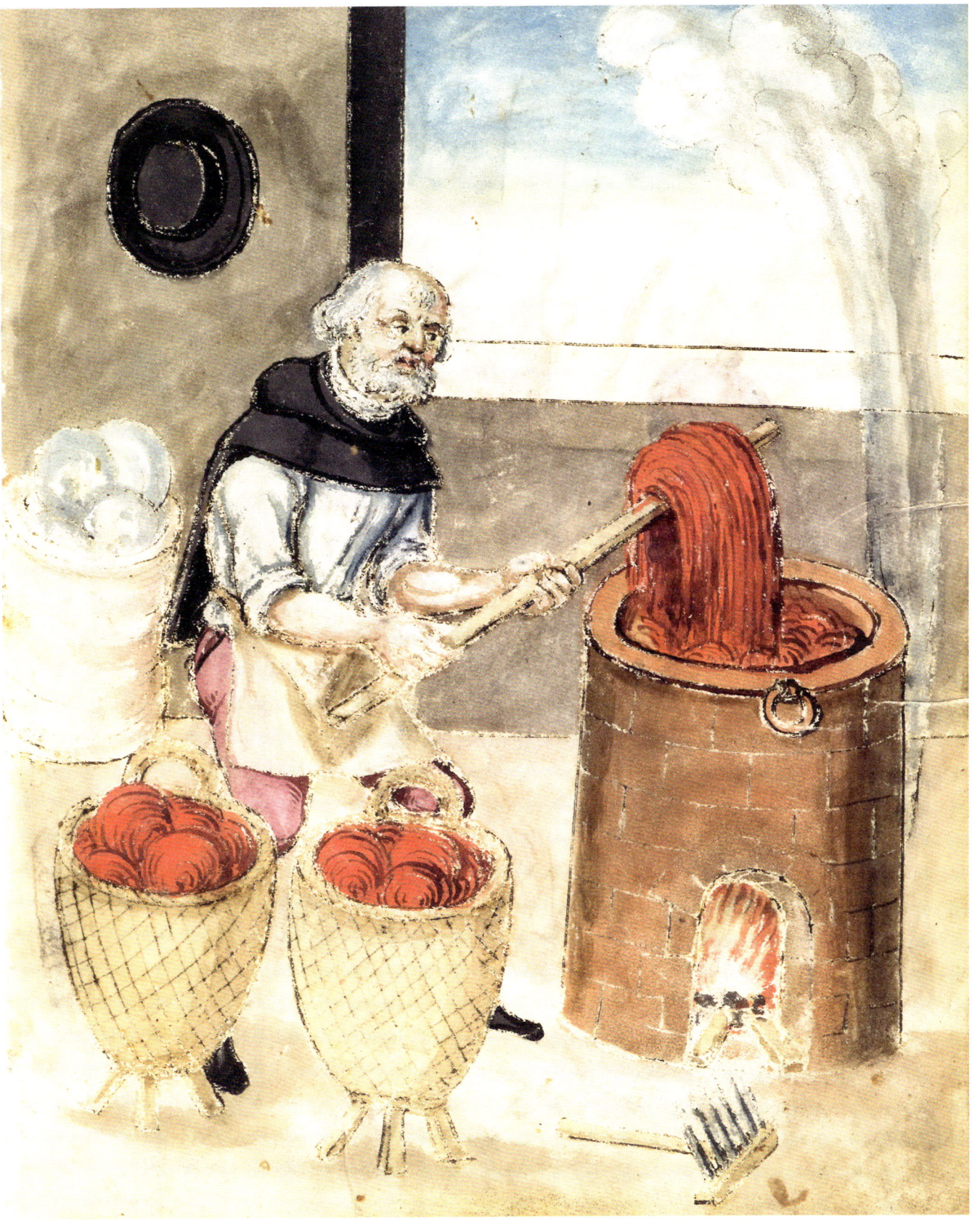

ROSE. fubft. fem. Fleur printaniere qui eft fort odorante. Les *rofes* ordinaires font les *rofes* paſſ s. Les *rofes* de Provins font fort rouges. Il y a des *rofes* blanches , des *rofes* à cent feüilles, des *rofes* de tremiere, d'efglantine, du mufcat de Gueldres. Les *rofes* de Damas qui font blanches furpaffent en vertu toutes les autres. La moins feüilluë des *rofes* produit cinq feüilles, & delà elles vont toûjours en augmentant. On appelle l'*ongle* de la *rofe*, la partie blanche de fa feüille,qui eft la plus proche de fa queuë.On appelle *hymen*, les petites pointes de fa fleur qui enveloppent fon bouton, & qui s'ouvrent, quand elle s'épanoüit ; & le bouton qui refte après que les feüilles font tombées, s'appelle *gratteeu*. Il y a des *rofes* de Hierico, qui étant feches fe confervent pendant un grand nombre d'années , & s'épanoüiffent, quand on trempe leur queuë dans l'eau : les fuperftitieux veulent que ce foit de l'eau benite, & pendant la Meffe de minuit. On tient que la *rofe* de Hierico fert aux femmes en couche, & qu'elles fe délivrent, lorfque la *rofe* s'épanoüit. Matthiole. En Latin *rofa*, en Grec *rhodos*. On dit qu'en la Chine il y a des *rofes* qui changent de couleur deux fois par jour, & qui font tantoft de couleur de pourpre, & tantoft blanches. Saint Bafile dit qu'à la naiffance du monde les *rofes* étoient fans épines, & qu'elles eurent des pointes, à mefure que les hommes mépriferent leur beauté. On appelle eau de *rofe*, celle qui fe fait de *rofes* diftillées. On fait des conferves de *rofes*, des fyrops, des fachets de *rofes*, des teintures de *rofes* avec diverfes preparations de *rofes*.

ROSE , en termes de Blafon, s'appelle *foustenuë* , quand elle eft figurée avec fa queuë. Elle eft quelquefois d'un même, & quelquefois d'un different efmail, mais toûjours épanoüïe , & tantoft avec les pointes de la chaffe d'un efmail different des feüilles.

Noble à la rofe, eft une ancienne monnoye d'Angleterre qui étoit d'or , & marquée d'une *rofe*.

La *Rofe d'or*, eft une rofe que le Pape a couftume de benir à la Meffe du Dimanche de Carefme, où on chante , *Lætare Hierufalem* , qu'il porte après la Meffe en proceffion, & qu'il envoye après à quelque Prince Souverain.

ROSE , fe dit auffi de ce qui eft fait à l'imitation d'une *rofe*, & qui luy reffemble en quelque façon. Les *rofes* des Eglifes font les vitraux de figure ronde , qui font d'ordinaire aux ailes & aux pignons des grandes Eglifes. Des *rofes* de diamants font des joyaux compofez de plufieurs diamants, ou d'autres pierreries difpofées en rond. Une *rofe* de luth, ou d'un autre inftrument , eft une ouverture ronde qui eft au milieu de la table, & d'ordinaire ouvragée, par où fort le fon. Les *rofes* font auffi des ornements d'Architecture, ou de Sculpture, qu'on met dans les frifes, aux corniches, & aux voutes des Eglifes. Et fur tout on appelle *ro è*, celle qui eft au milieu de l'abaque du chapiteau Corinthien. On appelle auffi des nœuds de jartieres, de fouliers, des *rofes*. On appelle encore *rofes*, de petits ouvrages de fil qu'on fait dans les trous d'une toile qu'on veut reparer ; des *rofes*, des colifichets d'écolier.

On appelle auffi fur la *rofe*, le compas de mer , ce qu'on met fous la bouffole , ou fur les cartes hydrographiques , pour marquer les vents, qui eft un cercle divifé en trente deux pointes en forme de *rofe*.

ROSES , fe dit figurément en chofes morales , de ce qui eft doux & agreable. Balzac dit qu'il ne fe veut pas deffendre d'un ennemi qui ne luy jette que des *rofes* à la tefte. On dit qu'on eft couché fur des *rofes*, qu'on ne marche que fur des *rofes*, pour dire,qu'on eft couché mollement, qu'on marche dans un beau chemin. On dit pour bien loüer une femme, qu'elle a un teint de lis & de *rofes* ; que fa bouche eft une *rofe* vermeille, un bouton de *rofe*.

On dit auffi d'une eftude, d'une affaire dont on a effuyé les plus grandes difficultez , Ce n'eft plus que *rofes* ; après les épines on cueille les *rofes*. On dit auffi d'une fille qui a perdu fa fleur de virginité, qu'elle a perdu la plus belle *rofe* de fon chapeau.

the fur of an animal. Its meaning is closer to "pale," "off-white," "beige," or "yellowish" rather than actual "pink."[7] Moreover, it conveyed no positive value.

The first changes took place in the fourteenth century, as we have said, when Italian merchants began importing brazilwood more regularly from Asia—a dyestuff that had long been scorned by European dyers. In about 1340–60, with the use of new mordants, artisans were able to make a more stable dye and obtain new colors from it, never before seen on fabric outside Asia or the Islamic world: pink tones that were truly pink! One problem remained, however: what to call this sophisticated new color, difficult to obtain but now admired throughout the West in all princely circles. Latin and vernacular languages still had nothing to offer in this regard, Arabic little more, and Persian possibly, but who knew Persian in Europe in the fourteenth and fifteenth centuries? In the end, it was a term that existed in Tuscan and Venetian that came to the rescue: *incarnato*. Until that time, this word had only described the facial complexion; henceforth it would be used for all shades of pink, no matter the medium, and would be translated as such into many other European languages. In French, for example, *incarnat*, used as a color term, made its appearance in the years 1400–1410; in Castilian, *encarnado* emerged in the same period; and in English, *carnation* came into use a few decades later. Only German seemed unaware of it.

Thus at the end of the Middle Ages, there was finally a name for this color whose popularity would keep growing, and not only in Italy. On fabric and clothing, it was a

The Flower but Not the Color

Antoine Furetière's French dictionary, published in Amsterdam in 1690–that is, four years before the one by the Académie Française–was interested "not only in words but also in things," like our encyclopedic dictionaries today. If we open it to the entry on *rose*, we find a certain amount of botanical and horticultural information there regarding the flower, but absolutely nothing about the color. It was too early; the flower had not yet given its name to the color. To name the color, it was still necessary to use the word *incarnat*.

Antoine Furetière, *Dictionnaire universel*, vol. 2, Amsterdam, 1690, 496.

sign of high rank, an aristocratic marker, and a youthful attribute. But one other issue remained: where to locate it on the chromatic axis. Aristotle's old classification system, which remained the standard one until Newton's discovery of the spectrum in 1666, went from white to black, passing successively through yellow, red, green, blue, and purple. Where to place this newcomer, pink? If one saw it—as we do today—as a mixture of white and red, its place was already taken, definitively so: between white and red came yellow. On that point all agreed, not only dyers and painters, but all the authors who discussed colors. In about 1500, for example, Jean Robertet, one of the skilled "Grand Rhétoriqueurs" and an elegant versifier, in a lovely poem titled "L'Exposition des couleurs," devotes a quatrain to yellow. He saw it as a mixture of red and white as well as a source of joy:

Yellow
I am composed of red and white,
My coloration resembles the one of worry;
But let him who is happy in love have no worries,
Because he can wear me as seems good to him.[8]

Hence the place between white and red was taken, occupied by yellow. So where to locate this newly fashionable shade that in the sixteenth century became the most beautiful of the colors according to many Venetian authors? For some of them, there was only one solution: to consider this beautiful new *incarnato* as a particularly delicate shade of white mixed with pale yellow and a bit of red—a shade close to what we now call "peach." In 1480, the author of the second part of the *Blason des couleur* uses the expression *fleur de pêcher* (peach blossom) to describe a light, unsaturated *incarnat*.[9]

Thus the pink of the Renaissance seems to be a light, attractive shade, somewhere between white and yellow. In fact, that is its status in various works from the sixteenth century. That does not last long, however. In the following century, pink was again considered a shade of red, sometimes even a bright, saturated shade of that color. That was the opinion of a few language dictionaries and encyclopedias, such as the *Dictionnaire universel* by Antoine Furetière, so useful to the historian, which was published in 1690, two years after the author's death:

> *Incarnat* means the same thing as *incarnadin*: a beautiful red that represents the living and freshly cut flesh. The word comes from the Latin *incarnatum*, which means the color of flesh.[10]

Furetière gives only a single example: a mouth of this color. If we consult the same dictionary for the word *rose*, we find quite a long botanical and horticultural statement on the flower along with a few words on its history and symbolism, but nothing on its color homonym. It was too early. At the end of the seventeenth century, the French term *rose* did not yet have a chromatic meaning. One had to be content, and for many decades to come, with *incarnadin* or *incarnat*, adjectives that have the disadvantage of describing only vivid, saturated tones of the color. To name what we would now consider a pale pink, a "baby" pink, remained a difficult exercise. The expression "rose-colored," which appeared quite early but only became common around 1700–1720, does not describe a pink tone at all but rather a lovely red shade of a more or less sensual flesh color. Moreover, it was used frequently in libertine and erotic literature in the first half of the eighteenth century, in which female flesh was often described or celebrated. So the question remained: what should pale, light, or unsaturated *incarnat* be called?

The solution would come from gardeners who, for many decades already, had been successfully diversifying the floral varieties of roses, offering new shades for garden lovers to enjoy. Among these shades was a light, delicate one that prompted general admiration, and was closer to our present-day pink than the *incarnat* of the Middle Ages or flesh tones of modern painting. It was this subtle, appealing shade that would finally receive the name of the flower itself in French. Before explaining the process and context, let us linger a bit over that flower and its history.

The Queen
of Flowers

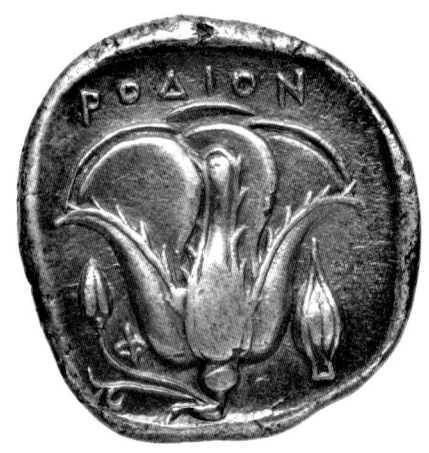

The Rose as Emblem of Rhodes

Many ancient cities chose a flower for an emblem, which they sometimes had engraved on their coins. In Rhodes, it was the rose whose name (*rhodon*) is nearly identical to that of the city (Rhodos). This is a matter of a "speaking" figure, as found abundantly in coats of arms from the Middle Ages. The famous colossus, one of the Seven Wonders of the World, is another emblem of the city; it represents Helios, god of the sun and protector of the island.

Silver tetradrachm struck in Rhodes, reverse, late fourth or early third century BCE. Bibliothèque Nationale de France, Paris, Cabinet des médailles, coll. Chandon de Briailles, no. 539.

For a long time, European roses were not pink; they were white, red, purple, and more rarely yellow. Growing wild for many millions of years, they began to be cultivated around four thousand BCE, first in China, then in Persia, and later throughout the Near East.[11] The Egyptians and Hebrews particularly loved them, though not as much as the Greeks and Romans, who had a passion for roses and associated them with various cults, notably the worship of Aphrodite in Greece and Venus in Rome. For them, the rose was the flower of love and beauty, especially the red rose, which the Greeks cultivated on the island of Samos and which was celebrated throughout the Mediterranean Basin. A Greek author from the third to second centuries, Achilles Tatius, states,

> If Zeus had wished to set a king over the other flowers, the rose would have been the king of flowers. The rose is the embellishment of the earth, the adornment of plants, the eye of the flowers, the flush of the meadow, an astonishing beauty. It exhales desire, procures Aphrodite.[12]

Three centuries later, Ovid reports how Flora, the goddess of flowers, transformed a nymph whom she had loved very much and who had just died into a flower. The goddess asked the other divinities to enrich her creation according to their various powers: Venus granted it eternal beauty; Bacchus bathed it in a subtle nectar to give it the sweetest of scents; and their daughters, the Three Graces, added charm, delicacy, and radiance.[13] In his *Metamorphoses*, Ovid also tells how Venus supposedly wounded herself one day on the thorn of a white rose that had been offered to her and thus had tinted the flower with her blood; henceforth she would only accept red roses as offerings.[14]

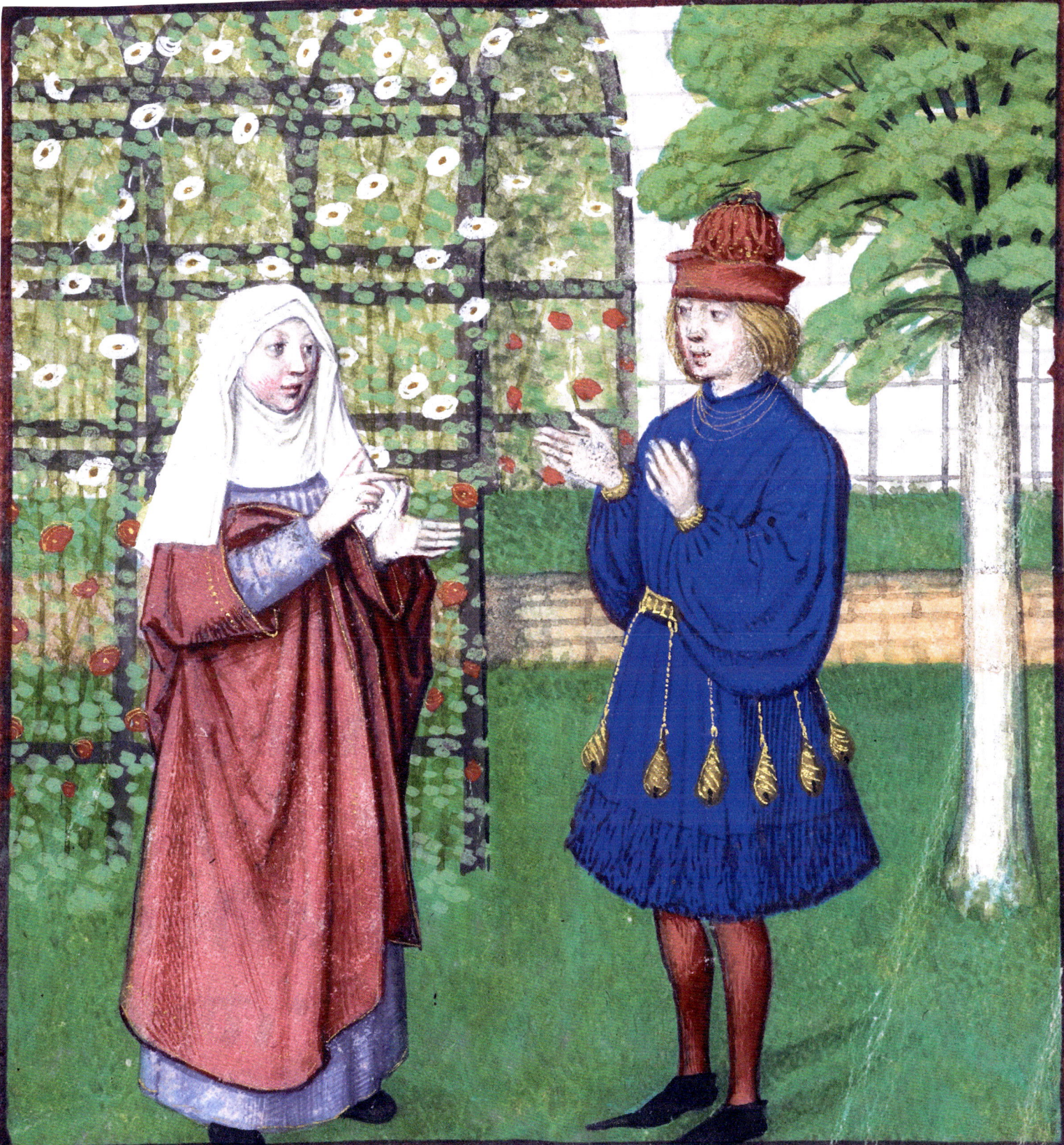

PREVIOUS PAGE

The Trees of Love

In medieval iconography, trees represent a language of love. Before a rosebush, the banter of lovers is chaste; under a linden tree, it becomes flirtatious; under a cherry tree, relations are increasingly daring; and under a pear or fig tree, they turn distinctly more carnal. Indeed, since antiquity, the pear evokes the male genitals, and the fig the female genitals.

Roman de la Rose (Reason and the lover), Bruges, ca. 1490. British Library, London, MS Harley 4425, folio 43 verso.

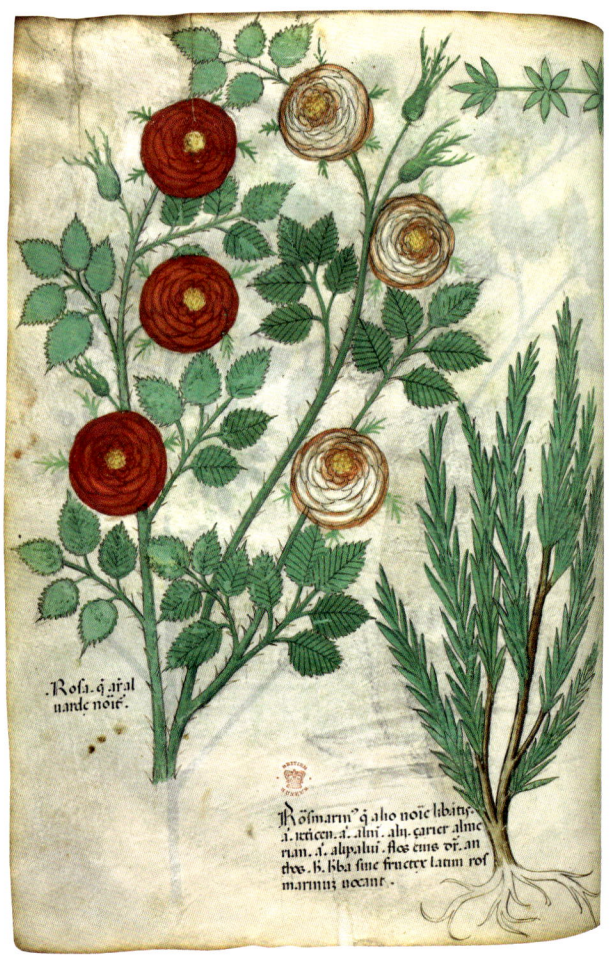

The Romans went through enormous quantities of roses and cultivated rosebushes throughout Italy. In his *Natural History*, Pliny describes twenty different species, classifying them geographically and listing their properties, although, like Theophrastus before him, he hardly mentions the color of the flowers.[15] The Romans also imported both the flowers and petals from great distances and on a grand scale—from Egypt (their principal supplier), Carthage, Libya, Greece, and even Gaul. They extracted an essence from them that they used as perfume, cosmetic, medicine, flavoring, and condiment. But it was especially the petals that sustained large-scale trade and a luxury craft industry. In the wealthiest patricians' homes in Rome and the Vesuvian cities, rose petals were strewn on the ground, used to fill beds and cushions, made into garlands and crowns, and tossed to bless sites, buildings, people, and even certain sacrificial animals. Considerable quantities of roses were offered to the gods and goddesses, especially Venus and Diana, whose statues were always crowned with flowers.

In antiquity, roses had a limited palette: they were white, red, crimson, sometimes yellow, and less frequently some other color.[16] The same was true for much of the Middle Ages, and it was not until the time of the Crusades and acclimatization in the West of new rose varieties from the Near and Middle East that the palette began to be enriched with new shades, notably orange. A widespread but unfounded tradition likes to relate how the count of Champagne, Thibaud IV, returning from the Holy Land in the 1240s, brought back in his helmet a few seeds from the rosebushes of Damascus—the most beautiful in all the Islamic East—and supposedly had them planted in his good town of Provins, where they soon thrived. Because Provins was home to an important trade fair, it was not long before his lovely rosebushes were transplanted in other regions, where, according to the legend, they took root and started a new line.[17]

Whatever its origin, it is indisputable that this rose of Provins was admired throughout the French realm as early as the thirteenth century, mainly because of its beauty and the variety of its shades, from the purest white to the

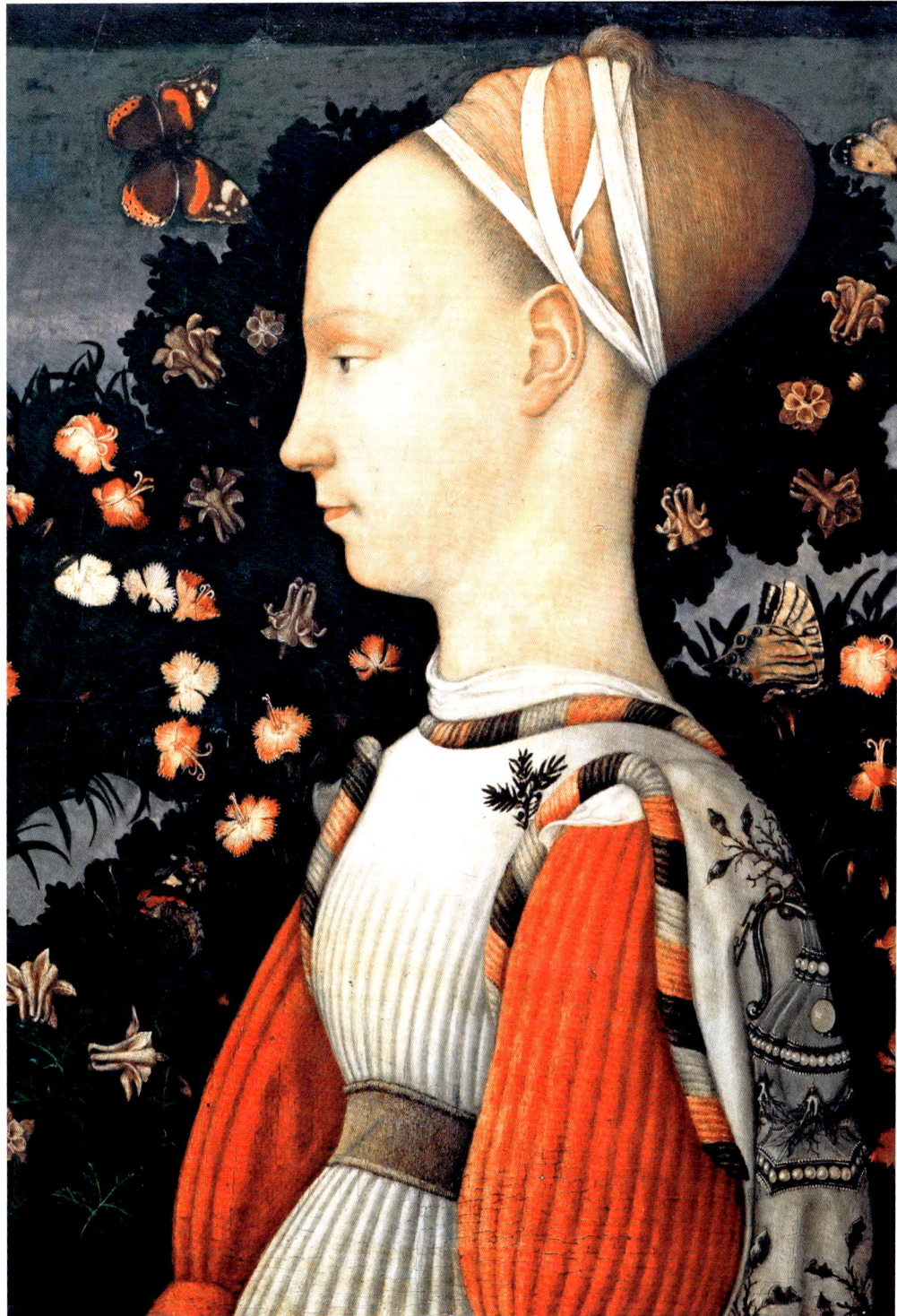

The Colors of the Rose

In the Middle Ages, roses existed that were neither white nor red–yellow ones, for example–but they were rare. In botanical works, when illuminators represented the rose, it was inevitably white or red. And if they made many copies of the work, the same rose was sometimes painted white, and sometimes red.

Anonymous codex, *Tractatus de herbis* (the rose and rosemary), Milan, ca. 1440. British Library, London, MS Sloane 4016, folio 82 verso.

Two Funeral Flowers: Pinks and Columbines

The identity of this princess painted by Pisanello remains a matter of debate. The two-handled vase embroidered on her shoulder suggests that she is a princess of the House of Este, as this object constitutes one of its devices. Similarly, the sprig of juniper visible at the neck of her dress could evoke the Christian name Ginevra, one of the daughters of Niccolò III d'Este. On the other hand, the pinks, columbines, and butterflies present all around the figure are symbols of death. Has this young woman just died?

Pisanello, *Portrait of a Princess of the House of Este*, ca. 1437–40. Musée du Louvre, Paris.

darkest crimson, but also because it has the peculiarity of flowering twice; a second flowering occurs at the end of summer or early autumn, thus earning this flower the nickname of "rose of all seasons" in the late Middle Ages. It was cultivated for its attractiveness, but, as in ancient Rome, for its medicinal value too. In fact, the rose has softening, astringent, healing, tonifying, regenerative, hemostatic, and purgative properties. The Middle Ages knew this and put the rose to use. It was employed in liquid forms as well—wines, syrups, liqueurs, oils, soups, and potions—to soothe sore throats (gargles), care for eyes (eyewashes), ease digestive problems (herbal teas), and beautify the skin (lotions).[18] These practices, all using rosewater as their base, would endure throughout the modern period and still survive today. Medicine, perfumery, and cosmetics have always derived much from this flower, and continue to do so.

But let us stay with the thirteenth century, the time when the rose's symbolism was undoubtedly at its height, signaling beauty, purity, virginity, innocence, fragility, sweetness, goodness, generosity, kindness, piety, love, and passion. This flower had only virtues, and as Pliny had already affirmed, "never does any wrong, never causes any harm."[19] Only yellow roses were sometimes seen in a bad light, symbolizing lying or treachery. In Christian iconography, the red rose is often associated with the blood of Christ and the white rose with the virginity of Mary. Over the decades, the place of the white rose in the Virgin's floriary would expand, to the point of sometimes eclipsing another white flower, the lily, at the end of the Middle Ages; Mary became "the white rose with no thorn."

In literature, the thirteenth century produced *Le Roman de la Rose*, whose considerable success and wide influence extended until the beginning of the modern era. There the rose simultaneously represents the beloved woman, quest of the lover-narrator, and pure poetry, just as another flower would almost six centuries later: Novalis's "blue flower," the emblem of German Romantic poetry. Neither Guillaume de Lorris nor Jean de Meung, the romance's two authors, hesitated over the color of the rosebud, the object of the lover's passion and quest. This rosebud is described as *vermeil*—that is to say, an intense, magnificent red, the most beautiful of all reds—but we learn little more about it, except that it is not pink.[20]

In the time period when the text was composed, between the years 1230 and about 1270–80, rose gardens proliferated in the French realm (Champagne, Picardy, the Loire Valley, and Languedoc), the English realm (Kent, Surrey, and Dorset), and then a large portion of the West. There was great love for this flower, which, thanks to the Crusades and expanding commerce, came in new varieties and an ever wider range of colors. Some roses no longer had five petals, but six, seven, or even more, thanks to the artificial transformation of the stamens. As for the color red, it had now been broken down into numerous, increasingly enchanting shades, with which the lexicon could not keep up, even in Latin. Until the Enlightenment, the Latin lexicon for colors remained much richer than those of vernacular languages, but nevertheless it could not name all the shades of red with precision.

Vermeer's Pink

A magnificent colorist, Johannes Vermeer was particularly delicate and subtle in the application of two shades he rarely used: yellow and pink. Moreover, the two can merge, as in his *View of Delft* with its "little patch of yellow wall" made famous by Marcel Proust (which in fact is a slightly pink roof). Here the silky, saturated pink of the dress, combined with the immaculate white surrounding it, contrasts with all the rest of the painting. In doing so, it highlights the young woman too elegantly dressed for a simple chat over a glass of wine. She seems to be presented not only to the eye of the viewer but also to the ardor of the suitor who holds her hand.

Johannes Vermeer, *The Girl with the Wine Glass*, 1659–60. Herzog Anton Ulrich Museum, Braunschweig (Germany).

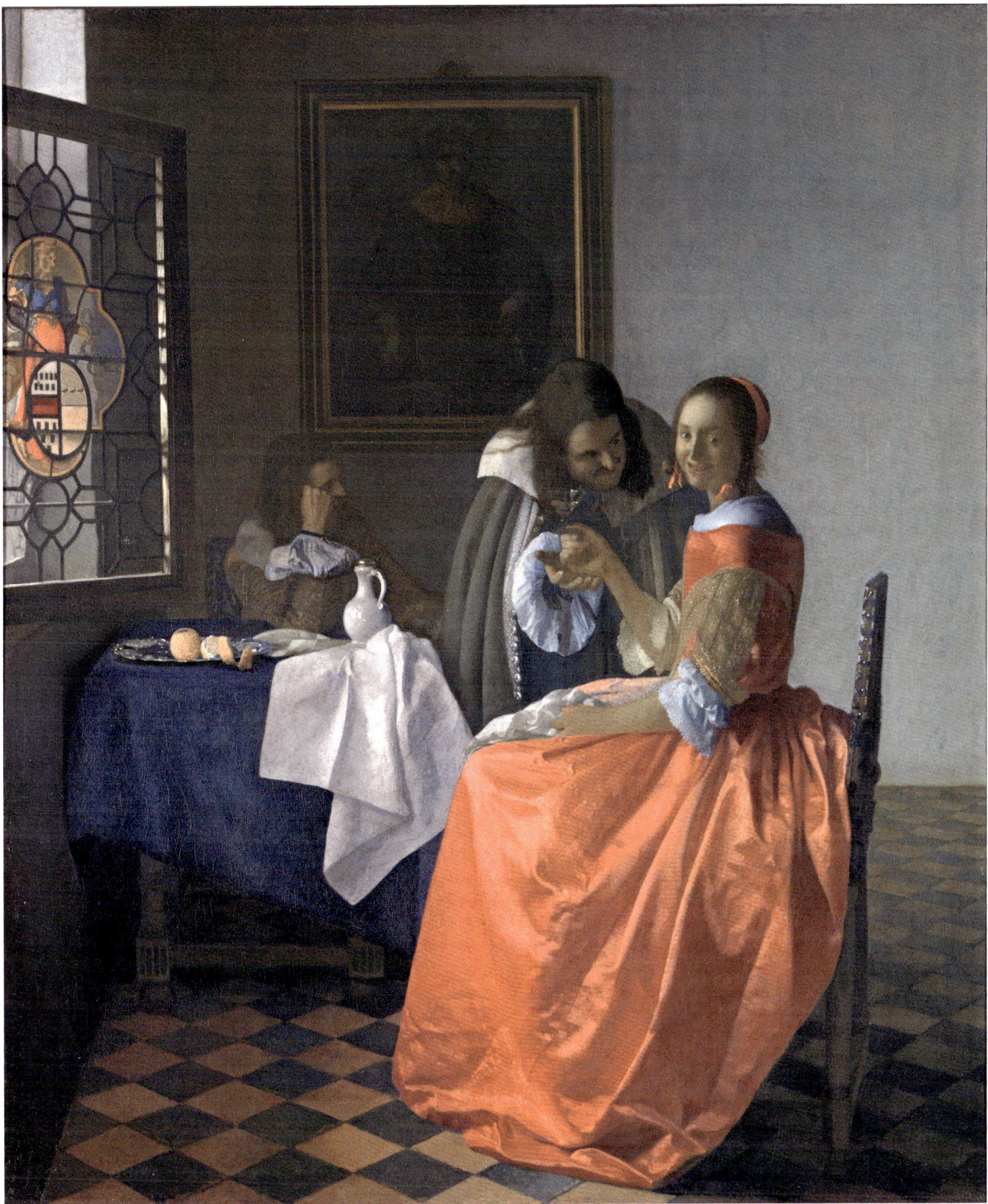

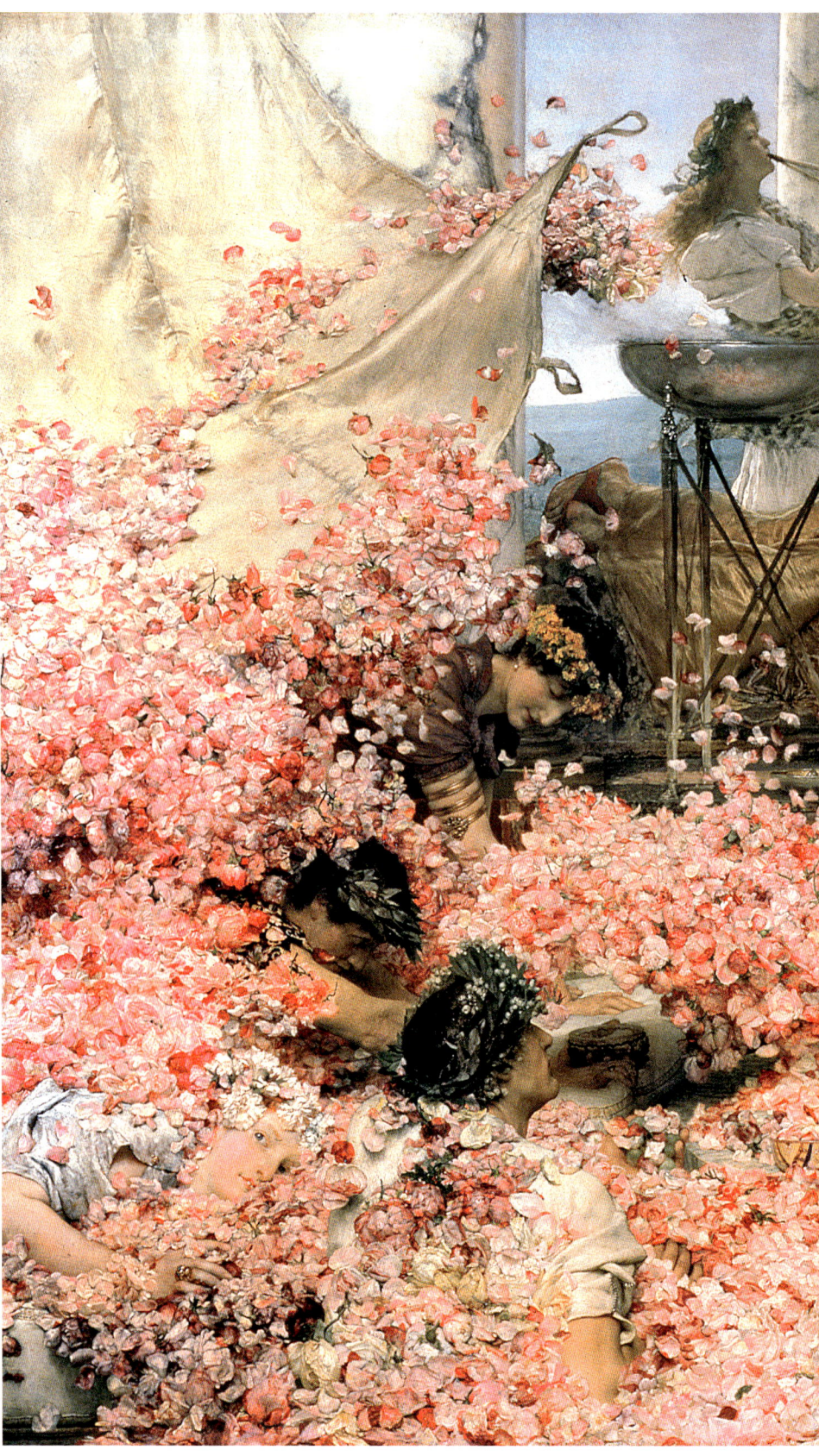

To Die in a Downpour of Roses

The reign of Roman emperor Heliogabalus was brief (218–22) but notorious. The young emperor was degenerate and cruel. Many authors report that during a banquet, as a diversion, he let fall from a false ceiling an enormous quantity of petals, from roses, violets, and other flowers–so many that the guests, unable to move, suffocated beneath them.

Lawrence Alma-Tadema, *The Roses of Heliogabalus*, 1888. Private collection.

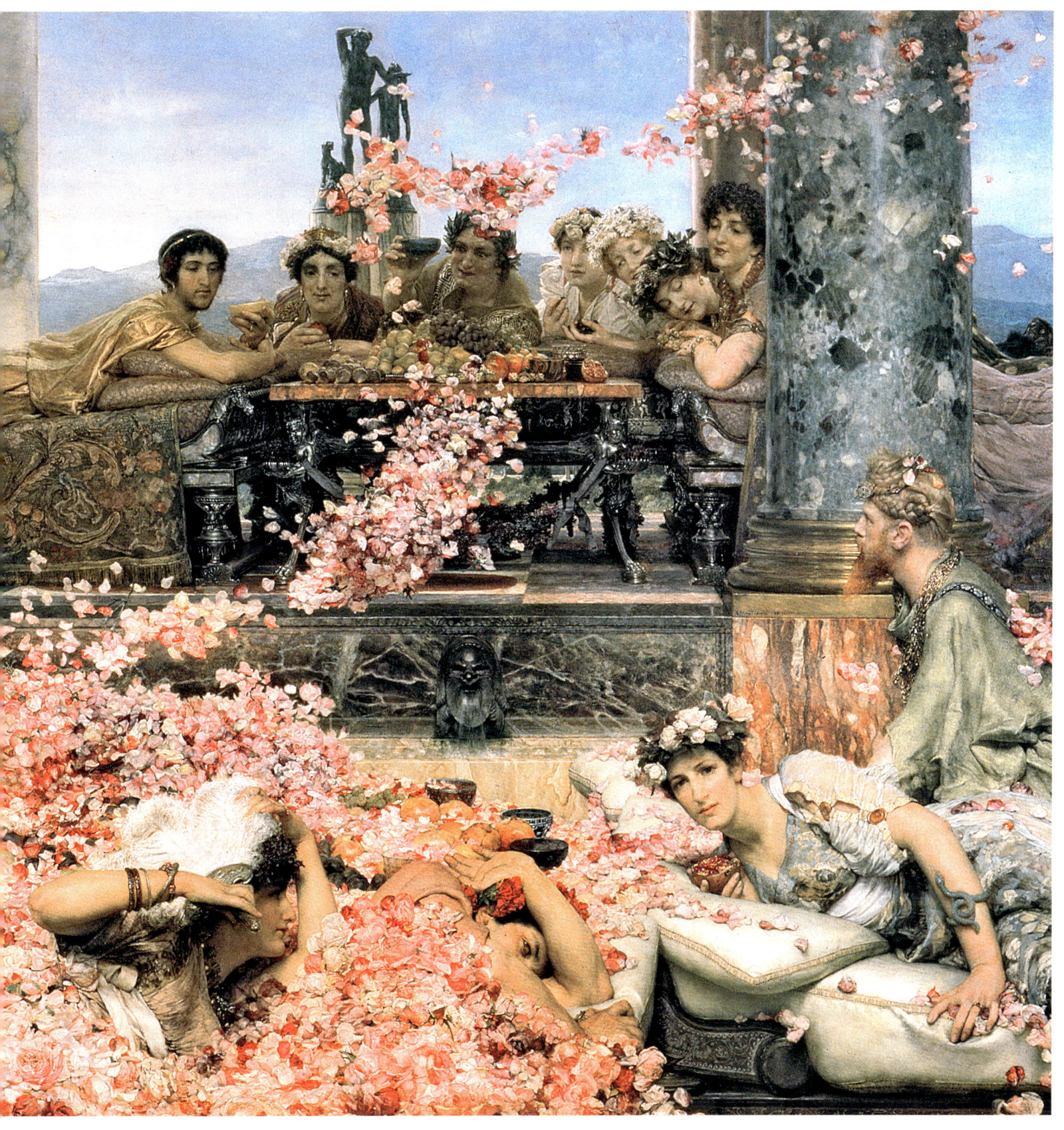

From the Flower to the Color

So it went with the rose up to the modern era, but at the turn of the seventeenth to eighteenth century, the flower entered a new phase of its history. New rosebushes were imported from China and hybridized with those of the West, providing new varieties that were larger, more vigorous, and more resistant to cold, and thus blossomed for a longer time, from June to October. Most important, the shades of their blossoms diversified almost infinitely, especially in the new palette of pink tones, which gradually took the place of reds as the most admired. There would be indirect consequences for the chromatic vocabulary.

In the first decades of the eighteenth century, naming pink remained difficult, as much in French as in other European languages. The adjective *incarnat* remained the usual term, but it could hardly describe pale and light pinks because it was too evocative of flesh. It was closer to red than our contemporary pink. In the domain of fabric and clothing, as in that of furnishings and decoration, it was no longer flesh tones but slightly pink ones, considered soft and delicate, that increasingly pleased the public and became the fashion, thanks to the rococo aesthetic then emerging. Demand prompted dyers to make progress in breaking down these tones into novel new shades, each more refined than the last.

Their task was made easier by the massive and regular importation from the New World of various exotic woods, related to the old brazilwood formerly imported from Asia, but possessing superior dyeing properties. Henceforth woods used for dyeing no longer came from India, Ceylon, or Sumatra, but instead from Brazil and Central America. Despite the long Atlantic crossing, their cost price was lower than that of Indian or Indonesian woods because the workforce employed to exploit tropical forests in the New World was essentially slave labor. The same was true,

The Tastes of Madame de Pompadour

The Marchioness of Pompadour loved pink, that is undeniable, but she was not the one who launched the fashion for pink in the French court. The color had been in vogue there before her arrival in 1745, not only for clothing, but for furnishings. On the other hand, she promoted the trend for combining pale pink with light blue and continued to do so for almost a quarter century. She also relegated to the shadows the dark, saturated pinks of her predecessors and insisted on paler, more delicate tones, close to what is now called *rose dragée*, the color of sugared almonds in France.

Alexandre Roslin, *Madame de Pompadour and Her Brother*, 1754. Gothenburg Museum of Art, Gothenburg (Sweden).

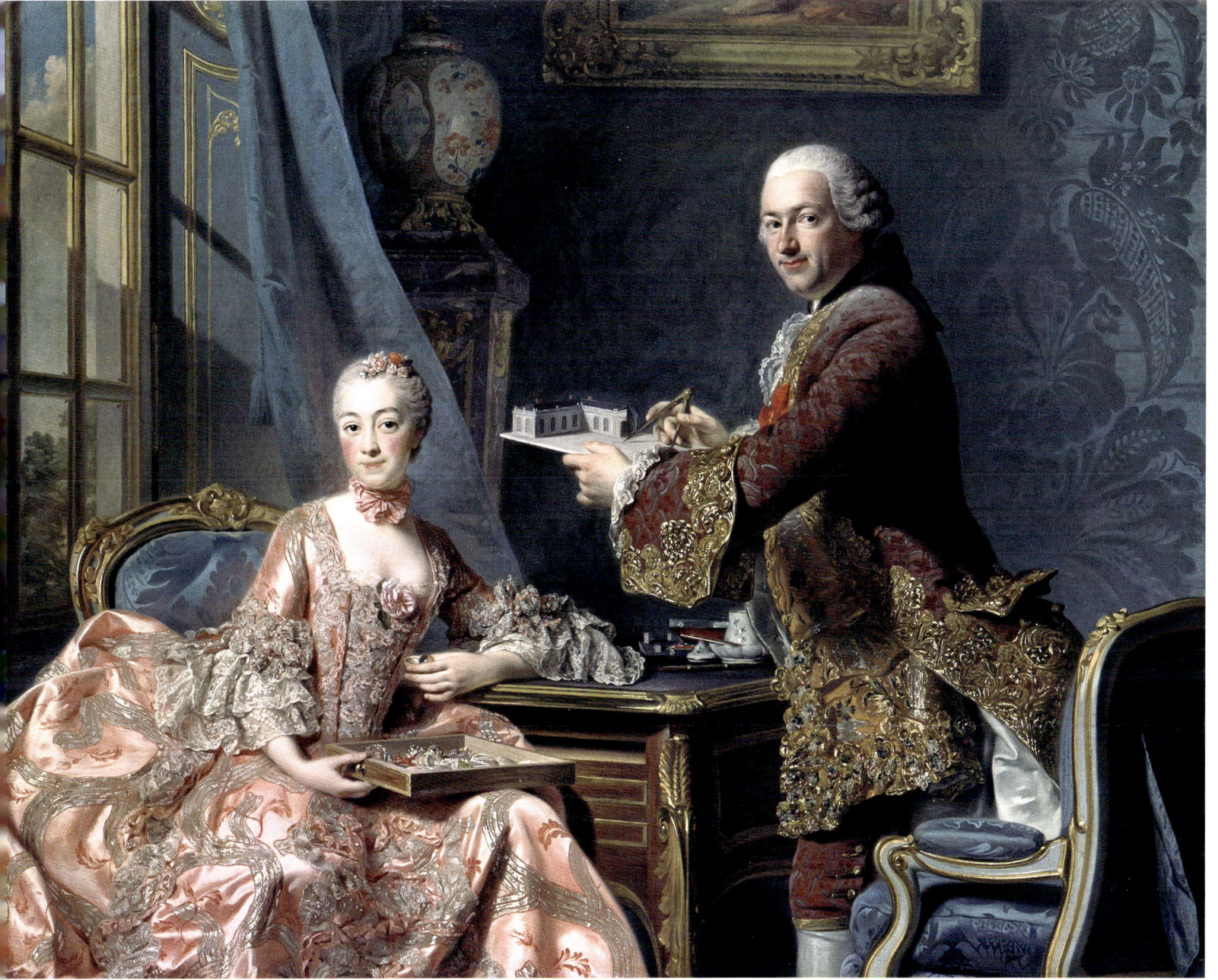

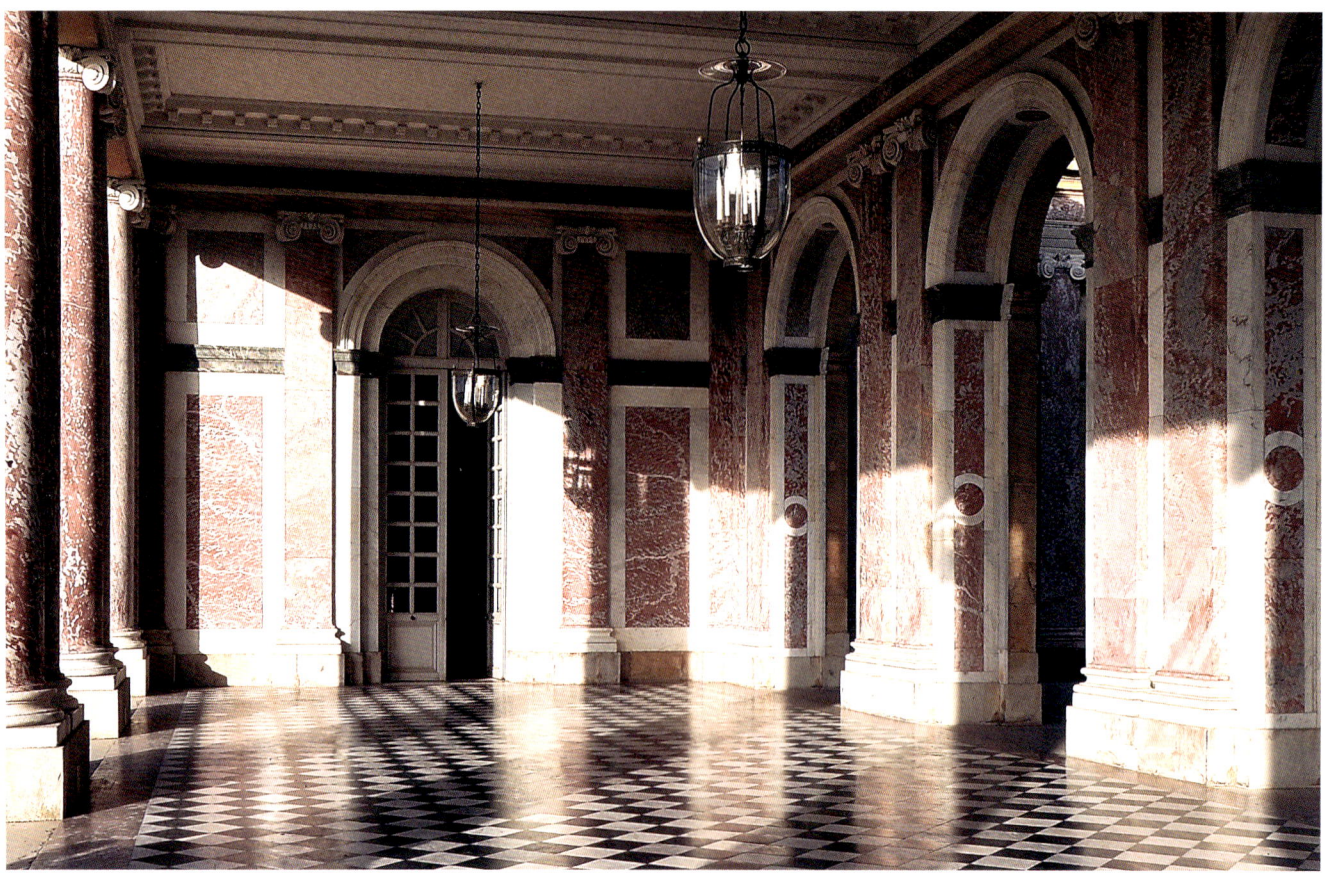

moreover, in the range of blues. American indigo, with dyeing properties superior to those of European woad, cost less because slave labor was used to grow and harvest it. Beginning in the 1730s, indigo as well as brazilwood played a role in the triangular and slave trades, crossing the Atlantic regularly and bringing prosperity to port cities like Liverpool, Bristol, Cadix, Porto, Bordeaux, Nantes, and La Rochelle.

The fashion for pink shades in textiles and clothing reached its height between 1750 and 1780 when the trend became a true social phenomenon, and the most privileged classes sought out pastels, halftones, and ethereal colors as a way of distinguishing themselves from the middle classes, which now had access to bright, strong,

and reliable colors that had once been prohibitively expensive for them. The elites now felt it necessary to avoid being mistaken for their inferiors, resulting in this quest for new, lighter, more subtle, less aggressive, and less saturated shades.

In France, it was the second part of Louis XV's and the first part of Louis XVI's reigns that brought pink to its height, not only in dress, but in the decorative arts and furnishings. Madame de Pompadour launched the fashion for pink in the French court starting in the years 1746 to 1748, and it was immediately imitated in princely circles and foreign courts. Louis XV's mistress particularly loved to combine the new pinks with "celestial" blues (sky blue) or "dove" grays (blue gray). After her death in

OPPOSITE PAGE

The Pink Marble of the Grand Trianon

Marble is everywhere at Versailles, as Louis XIV had a distinct taste for this stone. When he had the Grand Trianon château rebuilt by François Mansart in 1687, he ordered pink marble for the columns and pilasters. This marble was extracted from quarries located at the foot of the Pyrenees in Caunes-Minervois. It was transported by river to Bordeaux and then by sea to Le Havre, before going up the Seine to the building site that was frequently visited and even supervised by the king.

Estate and grounds of Grand Trianon
Peristyle, Versailles.

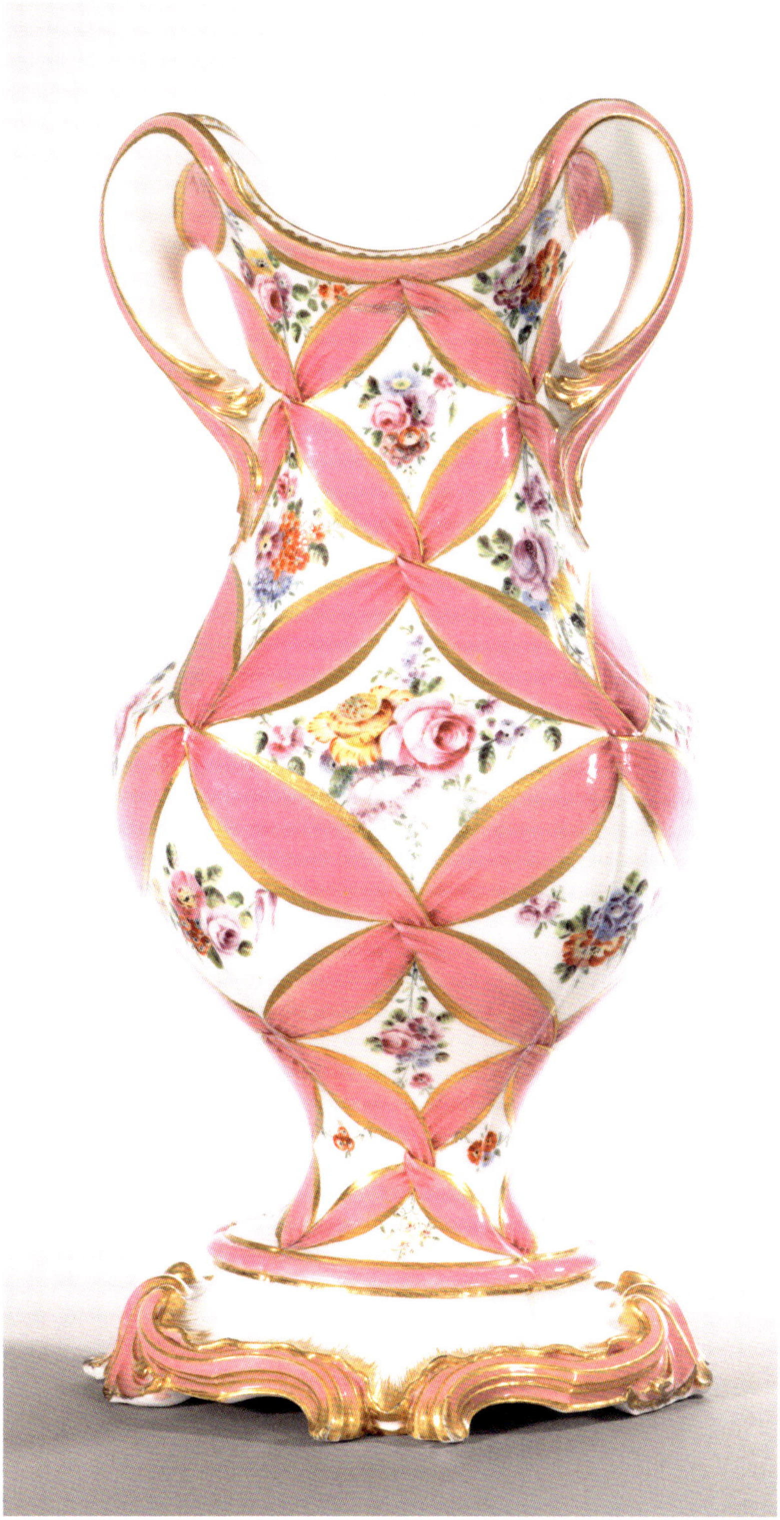

OPPOSITE

Pompadour Pink

It was the painter of porcelain Philippe Xhrouet who seems to have introduced a new shade at Sèvres, the royal porcelain manufacturer, in 1757–58: a soft and delicate lilac pink. It pleased the king so much that he christened it *Pompadour rose* after his mistress, who for many years already had shown a recurrent taste for light, fresh pinks in clothing and furnishings. The success of this new color for porcelain spread rapidly across all of Europe.

Sèvres vase decorated with bows, a gift from Louis XV to the queen. Palaces of Versailles and Trianon collection, Versailles.

1764, Madame du Barry and then the young queen Marie Antoinette would adopt these combinations, often in the form of stripes. For three decades, royal manufacturers (Fontainbleau, Gobelins, Aubusson, and Sèvres) received orders of this kind: to marry blue and pink. At the request of Madame de Pompadour, a certain shade for some porcelains was perfected at Sèvres in 1757–58: a pale, delicate pink with a very slight orange tint, supposed to evoke the complexion of the prettiest women at court.

It was in this same period—about 1740–60—that the French word *rose* finally became a color adjective and quickly replaced the term *incarnat*, whose semantic and chromatic field was less extensive. The new appreciation for pink roses along with the fashion for fabric, clothing, and decor in this shade explains the passage from flower to color. Never cited in dictionaries in the seventeenth century, the adjective *rose* appears in them on various occasions in the following century. One of the first occurrences is found in the work by the Jesuit priest Louis Bertrand Castel, *L'Optique des couleurs*, published in 1740.[21] Later, the great *Encyclopédie* by Denis Diderot and Jean Le Rond d'Alembert, expansive on the colors, uses it in different articles, the first being "Enamel," written by Diderot himself and published in 1755. We find this sentence

A Basket of Flowers

At the beginning of his career, Jan Brueghel the Younger (1601–78), grandson of the great Pieter Brueghel, painted many still lifes with flowers. Pinks and roses are the flowers most frequently represented. But in order to vary the colors, he combined them with a quantity of other flowers, some realistic and others in colors more or less drawn from his imagination. The painters of the late Middle Ages and Renaissance had already done the same, and those of the eighteenth century would continue to do so.

Jan Brueghel the Younger, *Flower Basket and Goblet in Gilded Silver*, still life, 1620. Private collection.

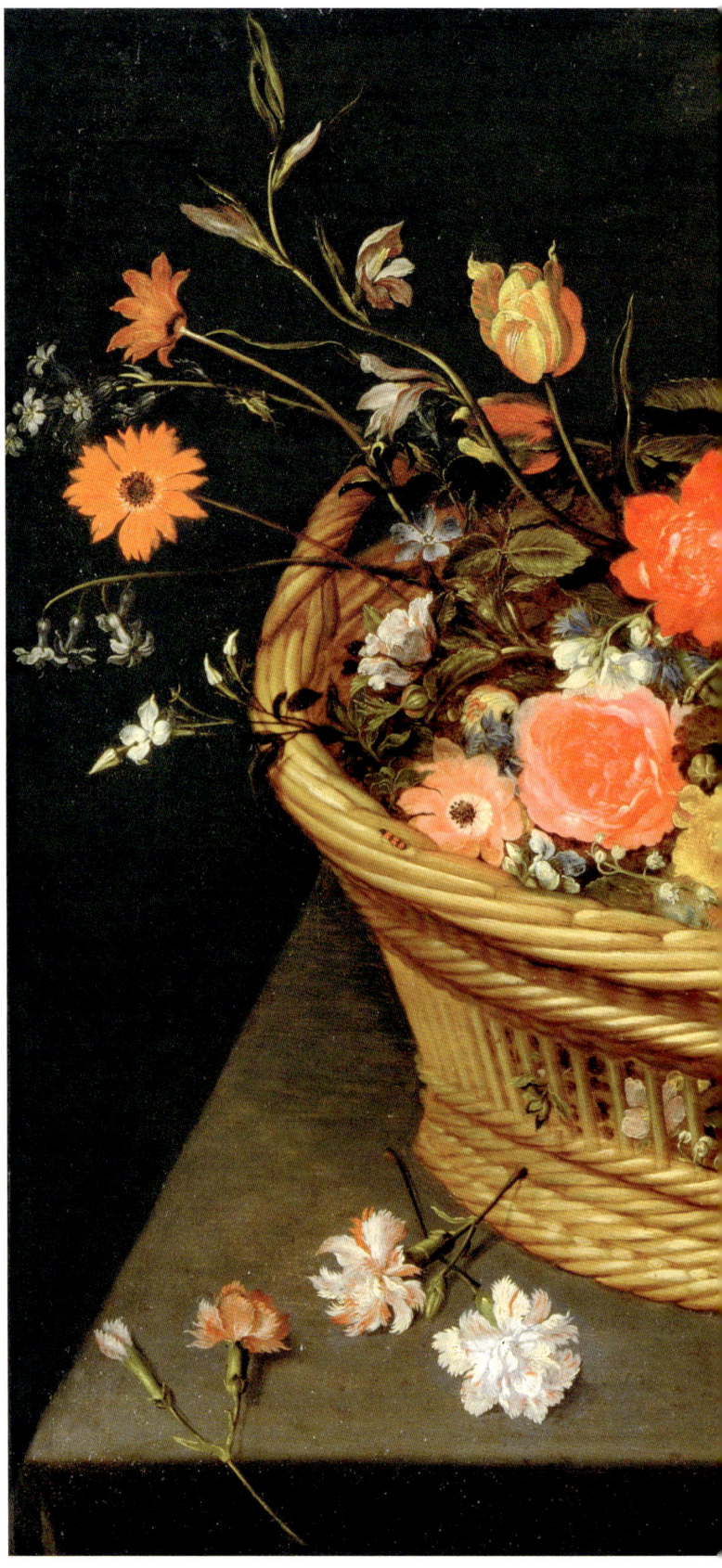

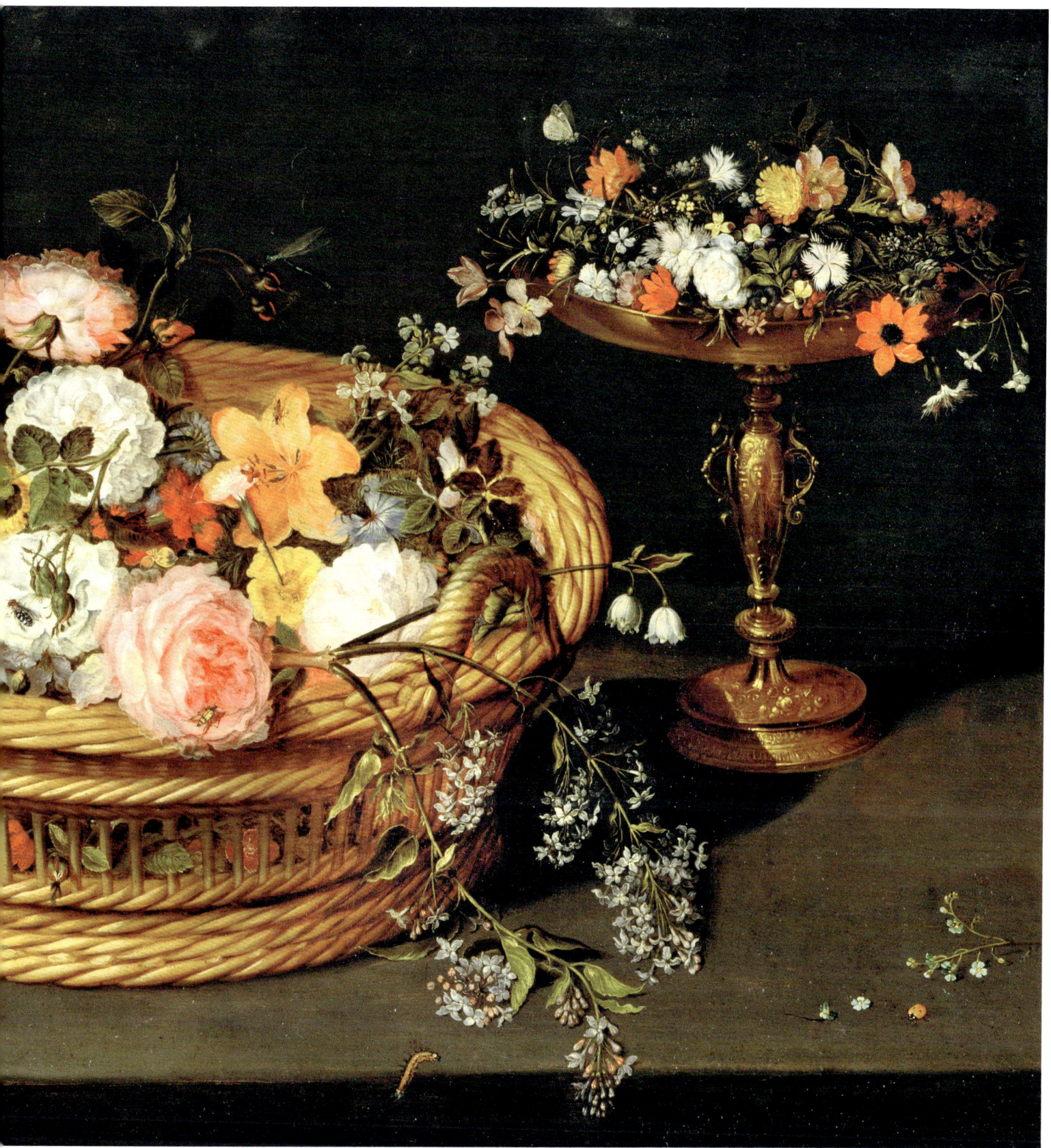

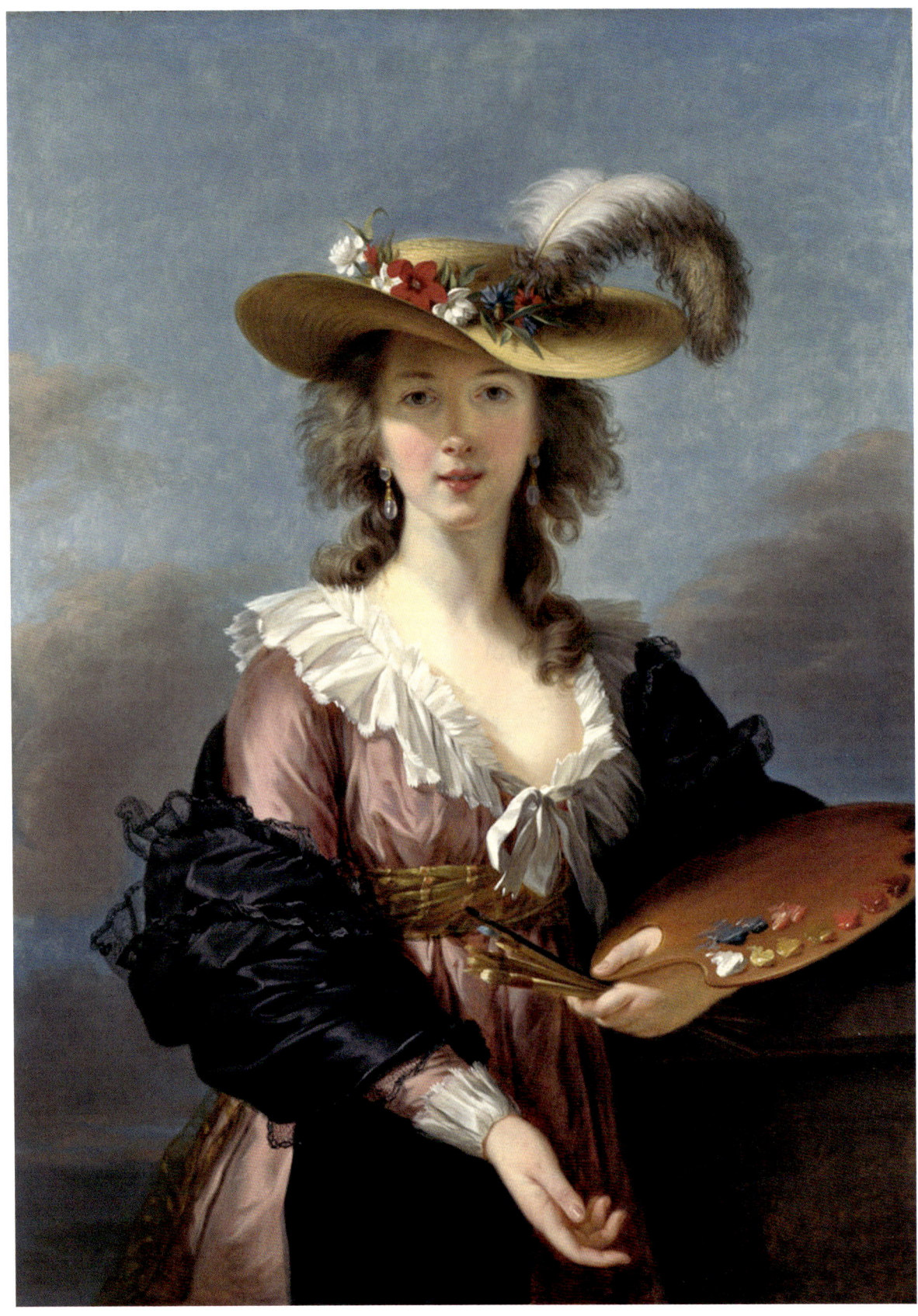

there: "White is the friend of all colors, and mixed with crimson it is the friend of all the colors, and mixed with crimson it gives a pretty pink tint." The adoption of this word as standard usage in the purely chromatic sense occurred quite slowly nevertheless. It was not until the first years of the nineteenth century that the adjective as well as the noun *rose* were definitively established as color terms. The *Dictionnaire de l'Académie française* did not accept them until its sixth edition, published in 1835. That was very late, but it is not the Académie's mission to follow too closely the innovations of the lexicon. Its role is to state good usage and be a sort of conservatory for the French language, not to embrace novelties or passing fads.

In English, the appearance and then circulation of the adjective *pink* follows almost the same chronology. In the language of the sixteenth and seventeenth centuries, this word was always a noun and designated the flower of that name. To describe a shade of pink, *carnation* was used, or less frequently *flesh-colored*, which, like *incarnat* in French, only applied to saturated shades of that color. Naming pale pink was difficult. Many scholars have established a link between *carnation* and *coronation*, arguing that in antiquity it was the custom to crown statues of the goddesses with roses. That is true, but such an etymological connection seems quite tenuous, especially in English. The term *carnation*, like the Italian adjective *incarnato* and all the words derived from it, comes from the Latin *caro* (genitive: *carnis*), the flesh. It is not related to the Latin noun *corona* (from which come *coronation* and *crown*).

In any case, beginning in 1750, the textile fashion for pale pink tones led to the adoption in English of the flower name *pink* as a color adjective, exactly as French had borrowed the term *rose* from the flower in the same period. Let us note in passing that *pink* has no relationship with *ink* or *pig*. As it happens, until the eighteenth century, domestic pigs in Europe were not pink but instead brown, black, gray, beige, or spotted. In the second half of that century, crossbreeding with pigs imported from the Far East gradually led to the animals with the pinkish white coats familiar to us today. For centuries, there was no relationship whatsoever between pigs and the color pink. We will return to this question further on with regard to luxury and pornography.

In Germany, the adjective *rosa*, a loan translation from the French *rose*, took longer to be established. As standard usage, it did not really take hold until the second half of the nineteenth century. Before then, to designate pink, a varied but faltering lexicon was available: *leibfarbe* (color of the body), *fleischfarbe* (color of flesh), *blassrot* (pale red), and *rosenrot* (red like roses). These last two were the adjectives used by Goethe in his epistolary novel *Die Leiden des jungen Werthers* (1774)—a novel we will consider shortly—and his survey on the colors, *Zur Farbenlehre* (1810). This same evolution was even slower in Italian; the modern word *rosa* has never completely eliminated the medieval term *incarnato*.

An Artist More Beautiful Than Her Models

Before the French Revolution, Élisabeth Vigée-Le Brun painted the most beautiful women of the French court and high society in her time. But when she painted herself, she appeared even more beautiful than her models, as if she had cheated and tried to surpass them by embellishing her own image. That was not the case, however. All of her contemporaries agreed on the beauty of this artist, emphasizing that it was equal or superior to the beauty of all the lovely women she painted.

Élisabeth Vigée-Le Brun, *Self-Portrait in a Straw Hat*, ca. 1782. National Gallery, London.

Early Romanticism

eginning in the 1770s, not only in France but in a large part of Europe (Germany, Austria, Poland, and Sweden), pink seemed to invade everything: decor, furniture, clothing, the arts, theater, and literature, at least in elegant, worldly, and cultivated society. Throughout there was an explosion of pink tones as painters, decorators, dyers, tailors, and milliners strove to vary their shades and combinations. In the French language, this capricious invasion contributed to the creation of colorful expressions for naming these novel shades: *pluie de roses* (rain of roses), *cendres de roses* (ashes of roses), and *laurier fané* (faded laurel). It was a difficult task, and sometimes slipped into affectation, preciosity, or even obscurity. Admittedly, pink was not an isolated case here. In fact, this was an era when fashion designers invented names that said nothing in particular about the color, but amused clever minds and delighted beautiful ladies seeking elegance, perfection, and poetry: *poire du matin* (morning pear), *cheveux de la reine* (the queen's hair), *ventre de carmélite* (Carmelite's belly), *dos de puce* (flea's back), and even, for browns, *boue de Paris* (Paris mud) and *caca dauphin* (dauphin's poop).[22] In the range of pinks, we allegedly owe a certain number of locutions to the famous Jean Joseph Beaulard

(ca. 1720–ca. 1781), whose fashion house in Paris rivaled those of Rose Bertin and Mademoiselle Alexandre. Some of them were passed down to posterity: *soupir étouffé*, *secret de Vénus*, *bergère au bain*, *entrailles de petit-maître*, and among the pale pinks, the famous *cuisse de nymphe émue* (stifled sigh, Venus's secret, bathing shepherdess, dandy's entrails, and excited nymph's thigh).[23] A thinly disguised eroticism underlies this lexical palette, which lacks any actual color information and seems to have inherited the affectations of the seventeenth century.

Quickly, however, the salacious connotations of pink that accompanied the rococo aesthetic and a few racy midcentury stories (for example, *Bijoux indiscrets* by

Pink Silk and Its Highlights

Throughout Europe in the mid-eighteenth century, pink was worn by both men and women of fashionable society and the aristocracy. Pink was most elegant on silk because dyers by then were able to produce luminous, shimmering tones, difficult to obtain on cotton, much less wool. Painters enjoyed reproducing all the shades and highlights of those silks that seemed to them to play with light in entirely new ways.

Alexandre Roslin, *Baroness of Neubourg-Cromière*, 1756. Nationalmuseum, Stockholm.

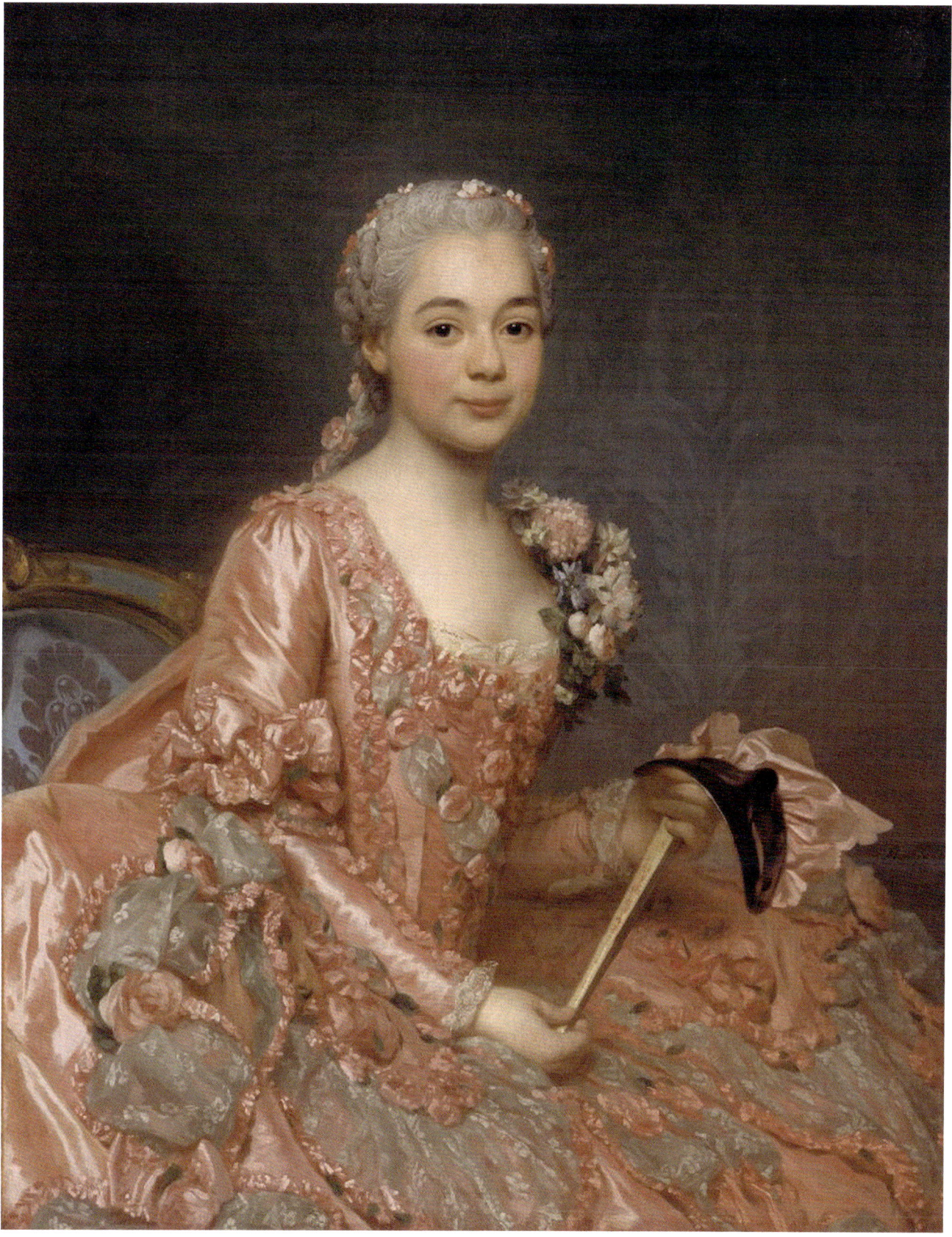

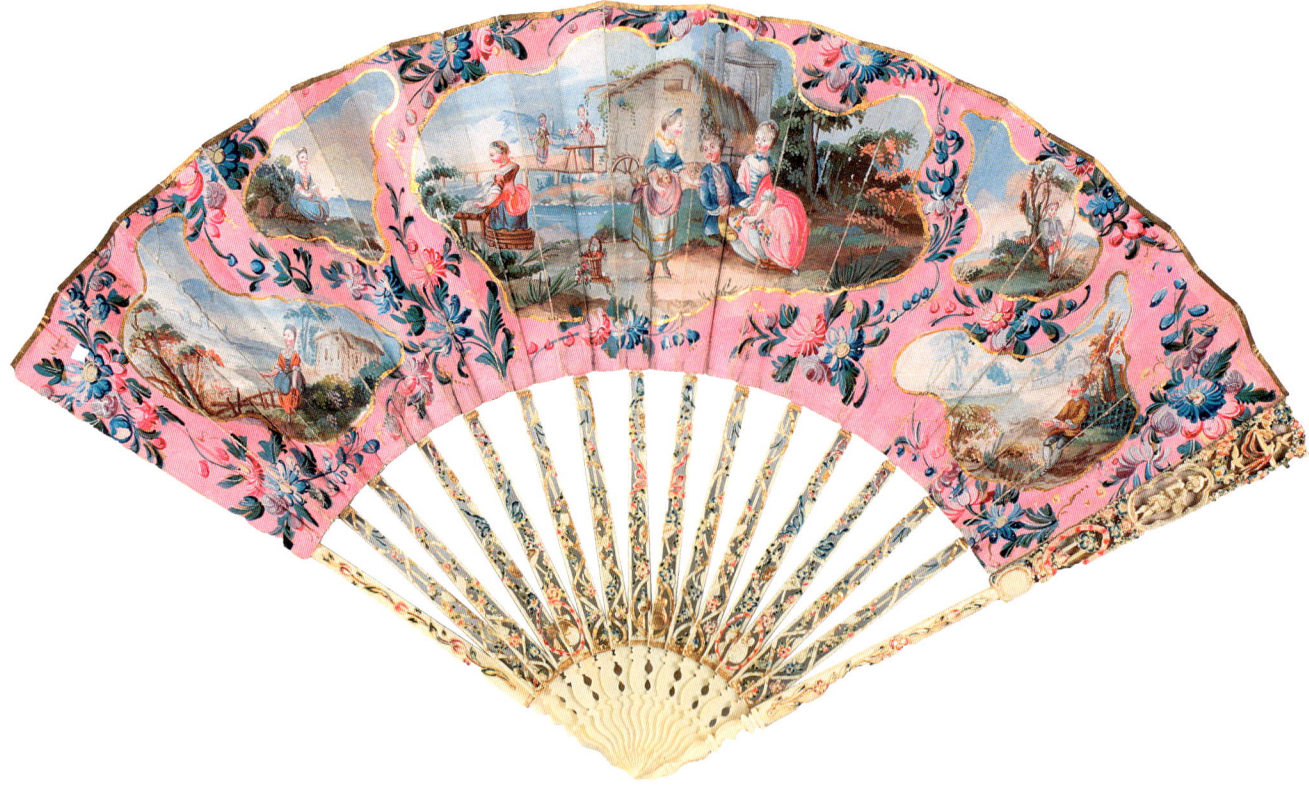

A Fashionable Fan

In the second half of the eighteenth century, the fan was no longer an object of great luxury reserved for the aristocracy. Its use had become much more widespread. Romantic and pastoral scenes were then replacing mythological subjects and reproductions of famous paintings. When fans were made of ivory and meticulously hand-painted, however, they remained costly.

Fan in ivory and paper, ca. 1770–80. Palais Galliera, Musée de la Mode de la Ville de Paris.

Diderot) gave way to a different tonality. Romanticism was dawning, and the pink of flesh was about to be replaced by the pink of the heart. Every artistic and literary movement has its palette, and there is no denying that the first Romantics paid special attention to light blue and pink. Painting provides evidence of this, as does literature, perhaps earlier in Germany than in France. Consider, for example, the epistolary novel by Goethe, *The Sorrows of Young Werther*, published in Leipzig in 1774. It launched the fashion throughout Europe, lasting for many decades, of blue morning coats for young men and white dresses with pink ribbons for young women. The novel was so successful that in Germany and Europe at large, all romantic youths wanted to dress like Werther and Charlotte, Goethe's two heroes. The "Wertheromania" that followed the book's publication extended this fashion to the plastic, graphic, and decorative arts, theater and the opera, and even social behavior. Not only did reading the work unleash a wave of suicides, but sometimes the suicides were on Christmas Day, in blue morning coats and yellow breeches, like Werther.[24]

Let us pause to consider Charlotte's dress, still popular in the 1830s, with some modifications, of course. Goethe describes it quickly the first time Werther sees the girl, as preparations are being made for a country ball. Since the death of her mother, Charlotte, the daughter of a modest bailiff in the region of Wetzlar, takes care of her brothers and sisters, and this quasi-maternal sight moves the hero, who immediately falls in love:

I crossed the courtyard to a well-built house and, climbing the flight of steps in front, opened the door and beheld the most charming scene I had ever set eyes on. In the hallway, six children aged between eleven and two were milling about a girl with a wonderful figure and of medium height, wearing a simple white dress with pink ribbons at the sleeves and breast. She was holding a loaf of rye bread and cutting a piece for each of the little ones about her, according to their age and appetite.[25]

The King's Chamber

The Petit Trianon château, built in the park at Versailles, is one of the first examples of French neoclassical architecture. Designed by Ange-Jacques Gabriel, it was commissioned by Louis XV in 1762. Madame de Pompadour rarely had time to stay there, but Madame du Barry often did between 1769 and 1774. Subsequently, it was Marie Antoinette who resided there regularly. Entirely upholstered in pink, the room called "the king's chamber" was redecorated many times, but always in that same color range. Louis XV slept there a few times; Louis XVI never.

The king's chamber, 1764–68. Petit Trianon, Versailles.

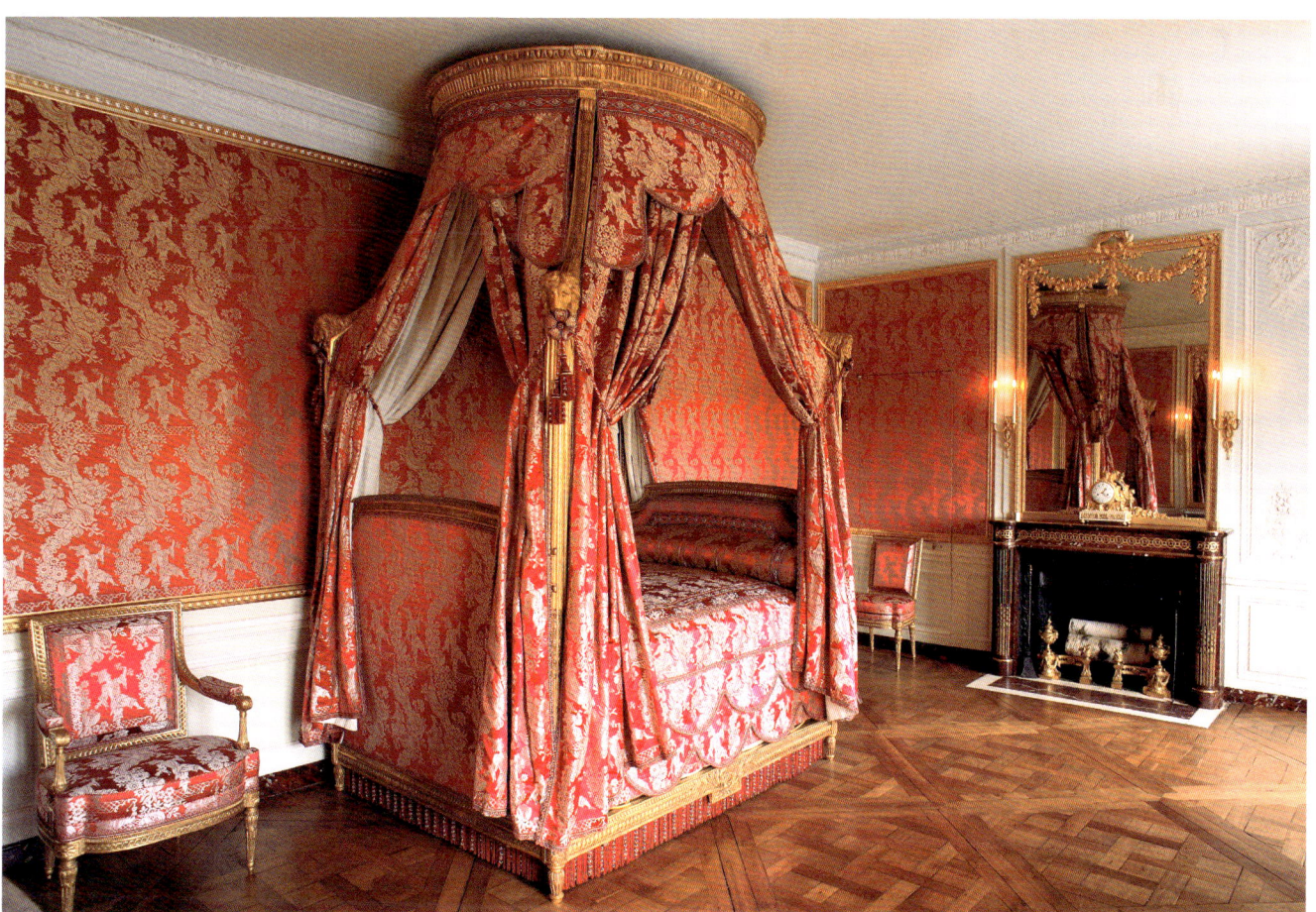

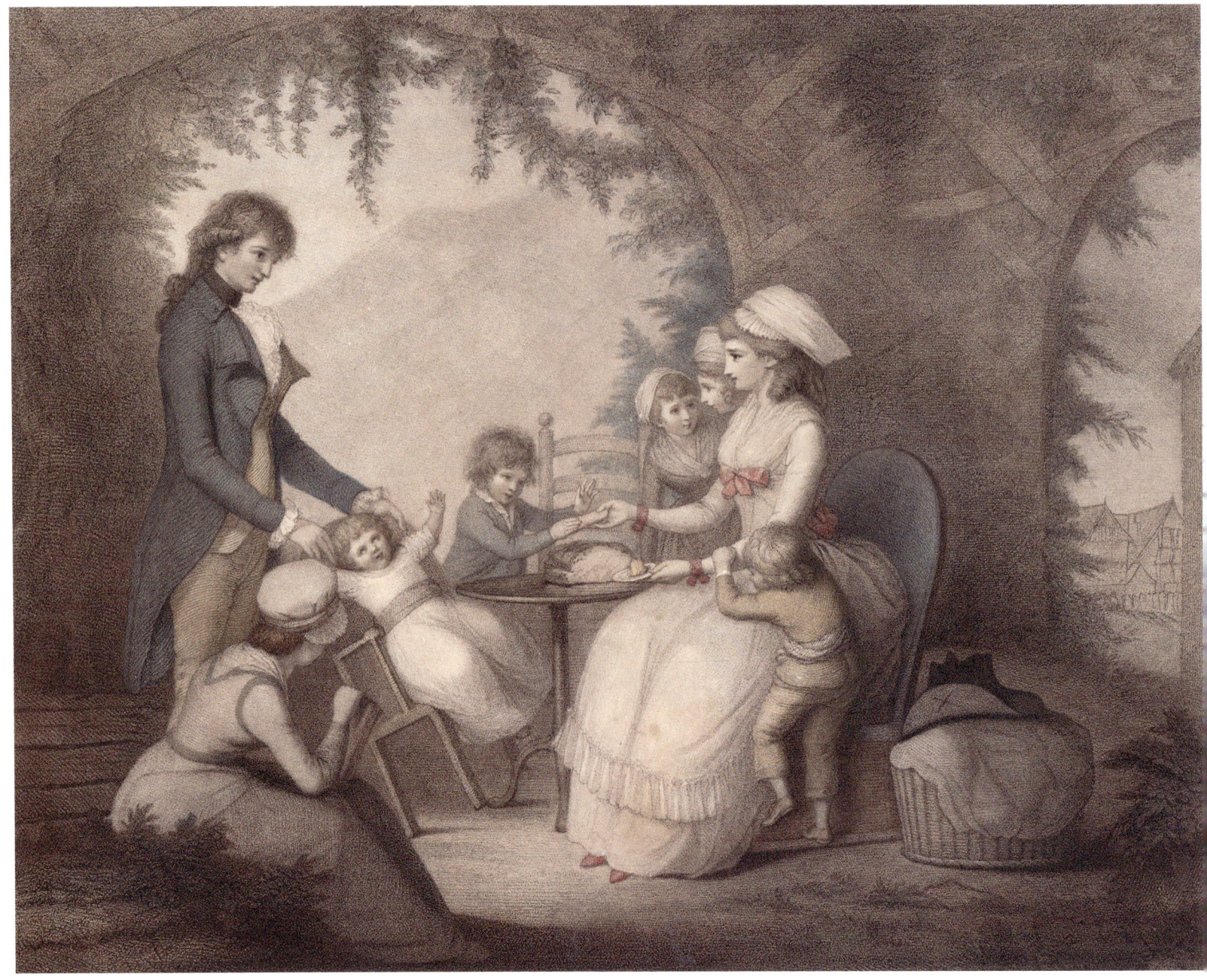

The Famous Pink Ribbons

Johann Wolfgang Goethe's epistolary novel *The Sorrows of Young Werther* (*Die Leiden des jungen Werthers*), published in 1774, was the greatest bestseller of the eighteenth century. Throughout Romantic Europe, it launched two clothing fashions that would last for many generations: the blue morning coat with yellow breeches worn by young men, and the white dress modestly trimmed with pink ribbons for young women.

Henry William Bunbury, *The First Interview of Werther and Charlotte*, 1782. Metropolitan Museum of Art, New York.

Goethe provides no more details, but that brief description ensured the dress's immortality, and not just in literature. The presence of the dark bread contrasts with the light colors of the dress, and gives the white and pink an almost virginal dimension because it is very much a matter of pink bows, not red ones. Goethe uses the compound adjective *blassrot*.[26] In this period, *blassrot* really did mean pink, even a pale pink, and not "light red," as it was translated by many commentators who wanted to see a sensual or sexual allusion in this color, supposedly more alluring than simple pink. There is a great risk here of overinterpretation: it is not a matter of stockings or garters, or even a sash, but rather a simple white dress with bows that Charlotte is wearing, and moreover, before having ever met Werther. It is, in fact, a very modest dress, and the color of these ribbons is not at all enticing but instead charming and discreet. As for Werther, he is a romantic hero, and like all romantic heroes, he is completely in love with being in love. What he seeks is not carnal possession of his beloved but rather desire. He desires only desire.

Those pink ribbons return in many episodes and prompt a kind of fetishism in Werther. Charlotte is imprudent enough to give in to Werther's repeated requests for one of them; she offers it to him on his birthday. "The most beautiful gift I have ever received," he writes to his friend Wilhelm. Werther cherishes that ribbon beyond all measure. Later, when he realizes his love is without hope because Charlotte is engaged to another and does not want to break her promise, he decides to commit suicide and, symbolically, do it on Christmas Day. He leaves instructions for being buried in his blue morning coat and yellow breeches, with his most precious possession, this pink ribbon, in one pocket:

> I wish to be buried in these clothes, Lotte; you touched them and they are sacred; I have made the request of your father also. My soul will keep watch over my coffin. I do not want anyone going through my pockets. This pink ribbon you wore at your breast the first time I saw you amongst your children—oh, give them a thousand kisses and tell them the fate of your wretched friend. . . . This ribbon is to be buried with me. You gave it to me on my birthday. I could not get enough of it all!—Ah, I little thought my path was leading me this way![27]

Werther is the first romantic hero of European literature and perhaps the most emblematic of a kind of sensibility that would endure for many decades. But in a few texts predating Goethe's masterpiece, we already find the recourse to colors for highlighting the feelings of characters in love or despair. That is the case in Jean-Jacques Rousseau's *Julie ou la Nouvelle Héloïse* (1761), an epistolary novel that was also a great success.[28] Of course the author proved characteristically hostile to colors and even painting. Color notations are rare and generally involve the complexions of young women—especially Julie, who has "a rosy freshness"—and the makeup that some of them use to excess. When Julie sends her portrait to Saint-Preux, her tutor, who loves her as she loves him, he responds with a severe critique of the painting that expresses everything Rousseau thinks about the artifices of color and how pink, because of its paleness, is truer than excessive, artificial red:

> Vainly has the painter supposed he could render your eyes and features exactly; he has not rendered that sweet sentiment that gives them life, and without which, charming as they are, they would be nothing. It is in my heart, dear Julie, that your face's fard is to be found and such a one cannot be imitated. This is due, I admit, to the insufficiency of art; but the artist is at least to blame for not being exact in all that lay within his power. . . . He has

neglected the purple branches created in that location by two or three small veins under the skin, rather like those of the irises we were observing one day in the garden at Clarens. The color in the cheeks is too close to the eyes, and does not blend delightfully into rose lower in the face as in the model. One would take it for an artificial rouge plastered like the carmine of the women in this country.[29]

Following Rousseau and Goethe, numerous authors in the Romantic period found occasions to express such flights of the heart through color, especially in English literature and German poetry. From the poetic and symbolic perspective, pink gained its autonomy with respect to red and sometimes even became its opposite. When it appeared in the Romantic universe, it was associated with female beauty and gentleness as well as delicate feelings, youth, charm, and gaiety, but also with the fragility of happiness and fleeting nature of love. Similar examples can be found in the French novel, such as in *Paul et Virginie* by Bernardin de Saint-Pierre (1788) or *Oberman* by Étienne Pivert de Senancour (1804).

The Romantic infatuation with pink lasted two or three generations, after which it ran out of steam, diminished, and became a caricature of itself. Later Romantics, like Stendhal, preferred red and black to pink and blue. Pink, which had been the sign of candor or innocence, gradually became bland, sentimental, and maudlin. The feminine ideals that pink represented became adolescent girls' dreams, and in the second half of the nineteenth century, the Romantic novels that young men and women swooned over three generations earlier had transformed into "rosewater" literature.

That pejorative expression *à l'eau de rose* appeared in France about 1880. In the same era, one spoke of "sugar novels" in English. Today these expressions have become cruder and crueler: in English, sugar novels are now "saccharine novels," underlining the artificial nature of such work, whereas in French, rosewater literature is sometimes called *cucul la praline*, a colorful term meaning "sappy," and evoking the special relationship that bare flesh and sweets both have with the color pink. In Great Britain, the

high priestess of this type of romance novel was Barbara Cartland (1901–2000). She wrote over seven hundred such novels, and the color pink plays a much emphasized role in them. In the second half of her life, she herself flaunted her immoderate taste for pink, especially "candy pink," in her eccentric outfits and excessive makeup.[30]

But let us step back in time a bit. Born of a pink full of charm and optimism, the expression *voir la vie en rose* (to see life in pink), which exists in many variations, appeared in 1830. Thus it came well before the song "La vie en rose," made famous throughout the world by Édith Piaf beginning in 1945.[31] It may be that the German expression *Alles sehen durch rosenrote Brillen* (to see everything through rose-colored glasses) dates back even further by a few years. Thus in the early nineteenth century, pink already seemed to lead toward heaven on earth. A century and a half later, that would become an artificial heaven: alcohol and hallucinogens would push the color to even greater extremes, as the colorful expression "seeing pink elephants" attests. In French, those pink elephants are flying: *voir voler des éléphants roses*, but the expression's origin remains unknown, or at least a matter of debate.[32]

Julie and Saint-Preux

Published in 1761, thirteen years before *The Sorrows of Young Werther*, Jean-Jacques Rousseau's novel *Julie or the New Heloise* (*Julie ou la Nouvelle Héloïse*) was also a great success. Until the 1830s, it inspired numerous paintings, engravings, and drawings that, one after the other, offered representations of all the greatest scenes in the novel, particularly the one in which Julie shows her portrait to Saint-Preux, who sharply criticizes the colors in it.

Pierre Alexandre Wille, *Les Étrennes de Julie*, 1783. Wimpole Hall, Cambridge (England).

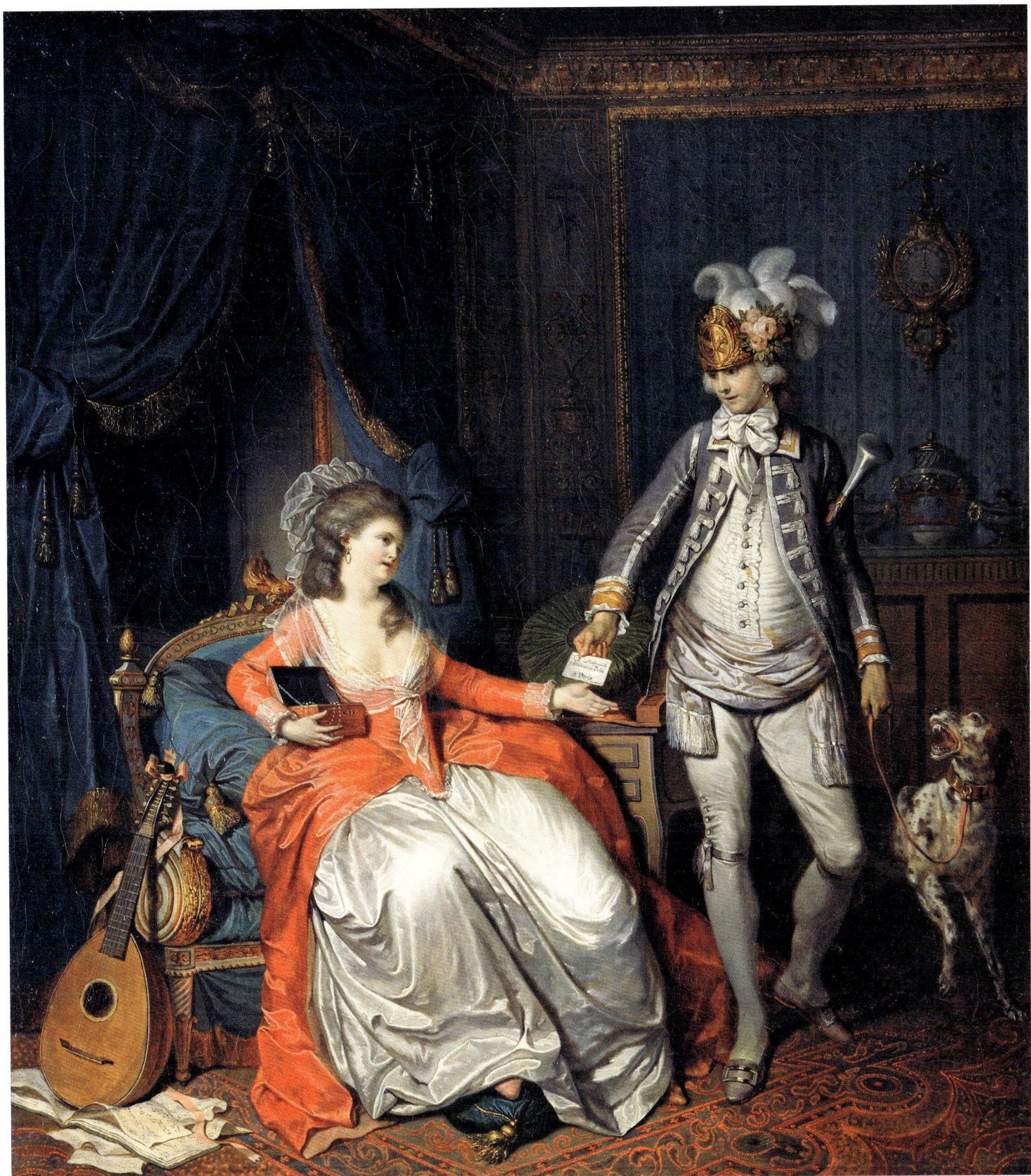

AN AMBIGUOUS COLOR

(18TH TO 21ST CENTURIES)

PAGE 124

The Music of Pink

Each painting by Mark Rothko considered by itself imposes a certain silence. Juxtaposed with other paintings, on the other hand, it participates in the composition of a kind of symphonic work, based entirely on colors. Red, pink, purple, and orange combine to form the main harmonies.

Mark Rothko, *Red and Pink on Pink*, ca. 1953.
Museum of Fine Arts, Houston.

OPPOSITE PAGE

Lyrics Abstraction in Pink, Beige, and Blue

Quite well-known in the United States, Richard Diebenkorn (1922–93) is much less recognized in Europe. A great colorist, he moved from representation to abstract expressionism and finally to geometric abstraction. His prolific series titled *Ocean Park* was so successful that in the years 1970–80, he sold some of his paintings even before he had painted them.

Richard Diebenkorn, *Ocean Park no. 135*, 1954. North Carolina Museum of Art, Raleigh.

Pink romanticism is essentially a feminine romanticism, and thus seems to have played a decisive role in the origins of the feminization of that color, long gender neutral. It may also be that the phenomenon was reversed, though, and that the gradual feminization of pink in society made it into a romantic color. Technical mutations, like artistic and literary innovations, are always born of their time and directly linked to social transformations. Whatever the case, in the eighteenth century, in aristocratic and princely circles, women were far from the only ones to wear pink; men wore it as well.

In France, for example, the inventories and documents we possess on the wardrobes of Louis XV and the young Louis XVI show that this color was very much present in their attire. Moreover, we have numerous portraits of young French, English, German, and Austrian aristocrats who dressed in pink, sometimes into their mature years. Only old people avoided it.

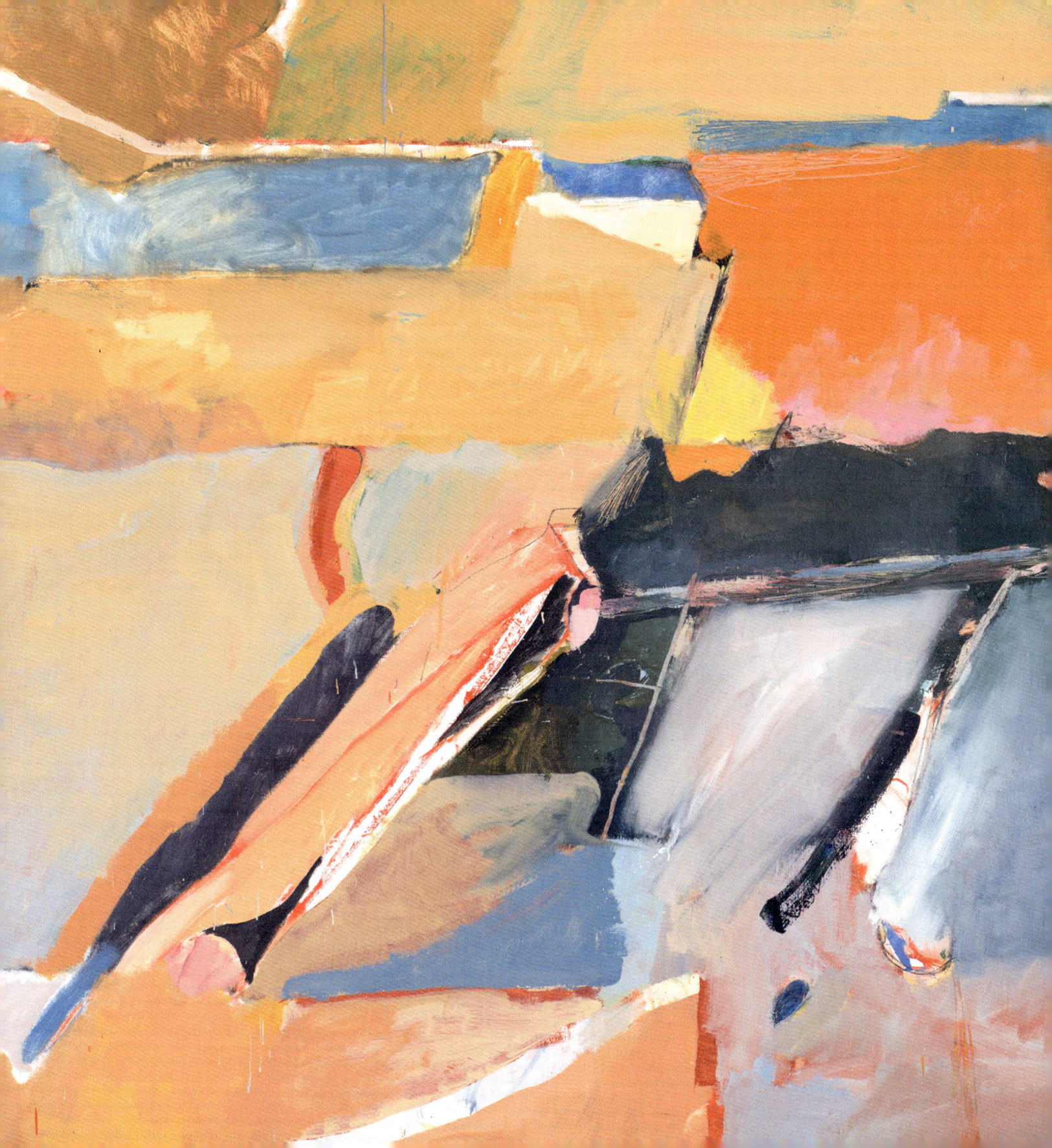

From Masculine to Feminine

The Pink Prince

Charles Joseph de Ligne (1735–1814), marshal of the army of the Holy Roman Empire, was nicknamed "the pink prince" because of the color of his livery, unusual for princely emblems, even if this saturated pink was closer to red than to white. A military man and diplomat as well as author, scholar, memorialist, friend of the arts, and great ladies' man, he charmed his contemporaries for more than half a century with his elegance, wit, and lively conversation.

After Josef Kreutzinger, *Charles Joseph de Ligne*, 1807.

He was a prince whom all of Europe nicknamed "the pink prince" (*der rosarote Prinz*): Charles Joseph de Ligne (1735–1814), marshal of the army of the Holy Roman Empire, diplomat, thinker, writer, scholar, and a great ladies' man. His courtly manner, wit, elegance, and gaiety charmed all the European courts. His nickname came from the traditional livery of his house along with his personal taste for pink, notably in clothing and furnishings, but also from his optimism and good humor. Hence we have proof that in the late seventeenth century, the color pink, symbolically, already evoked joie de vivre, pleasure, and lightheartedness, a pink that was not pale and delicate, but strong and saturated, closer to a light, vivid red.[1]

The example of the prince of Ligne remains the exception, however, and comes somewhat late. During the French Revolution, masculine pink was clearly less common, and in the first years of the nineteenth century, pink became almost exclusively feminine. Around 1820, in the midst of Romantic ferment, men no longer wore pink except for shock value. Nevertheless, this was not a matter of the color signaling masculine homosexuality. Here again, it would be anachronistic to see a sign of homosexuality or effeminate behavior in the wearing of

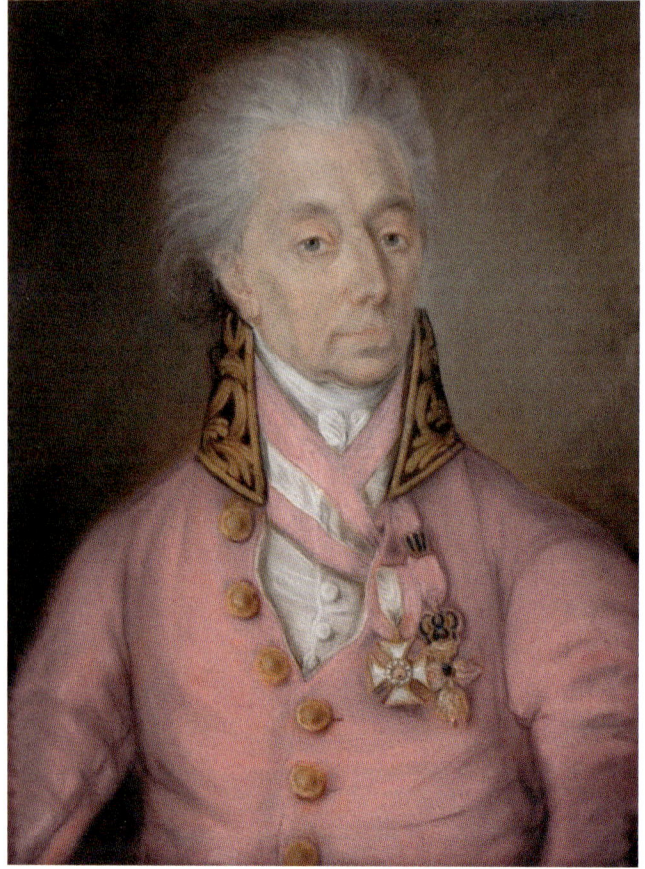

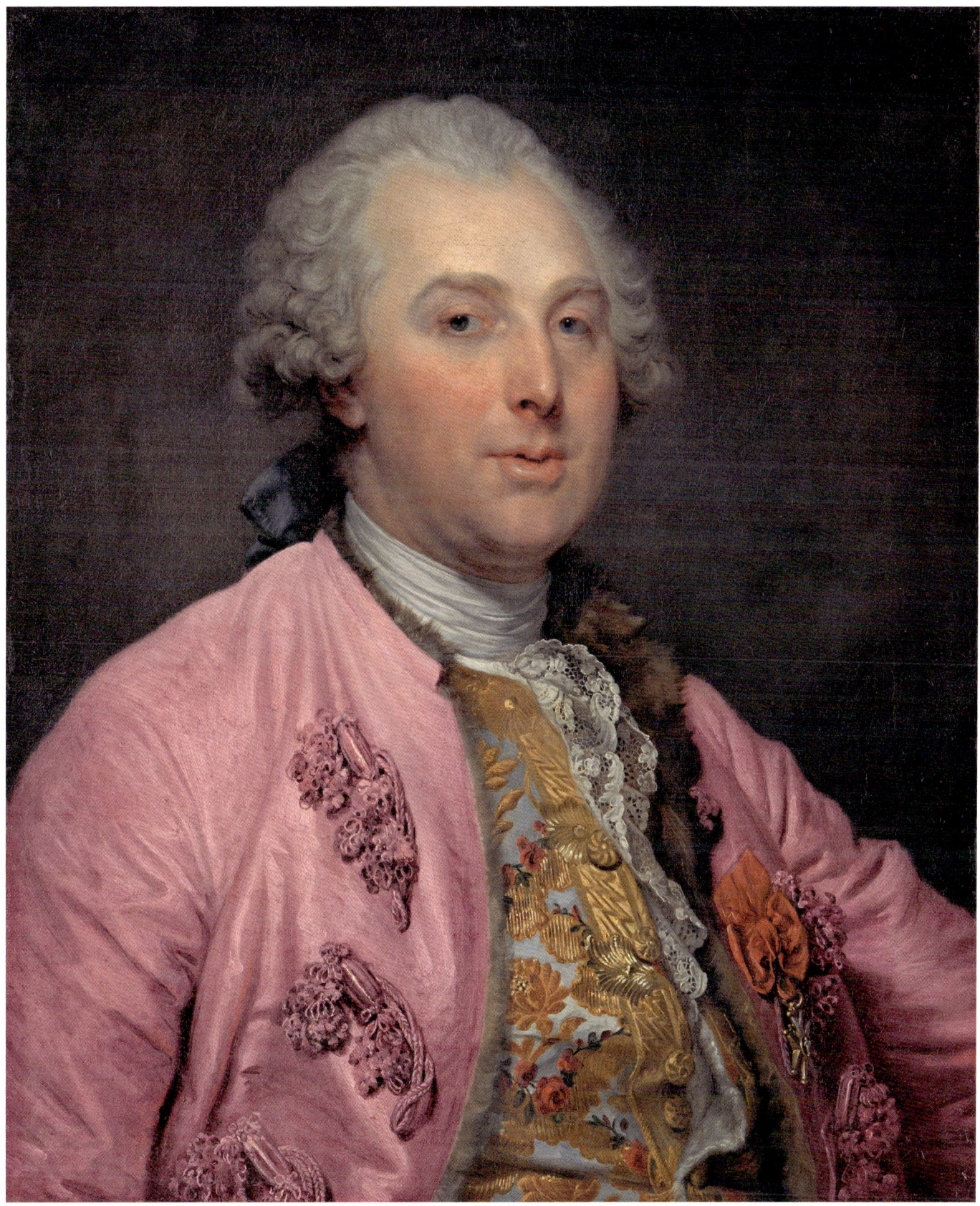

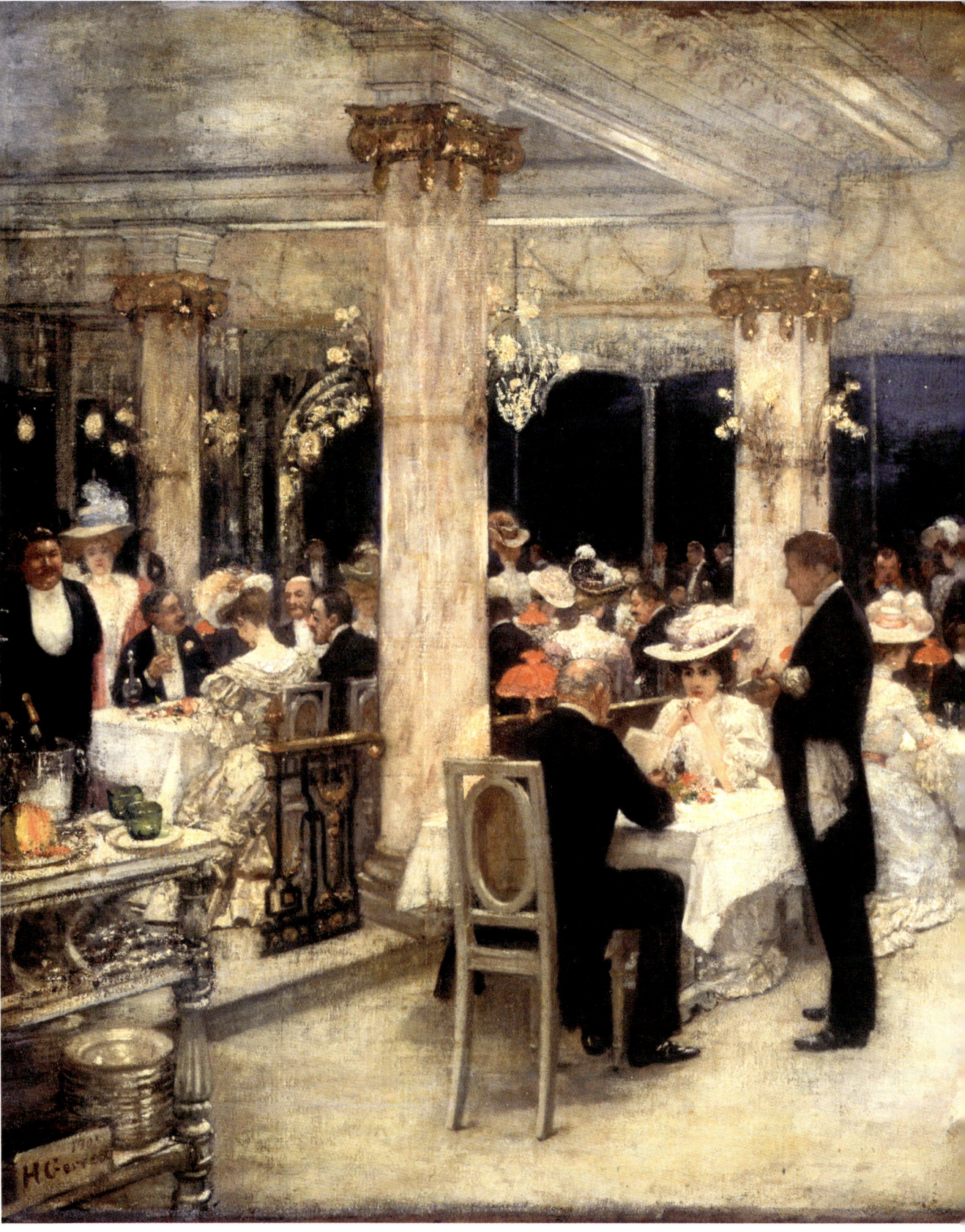

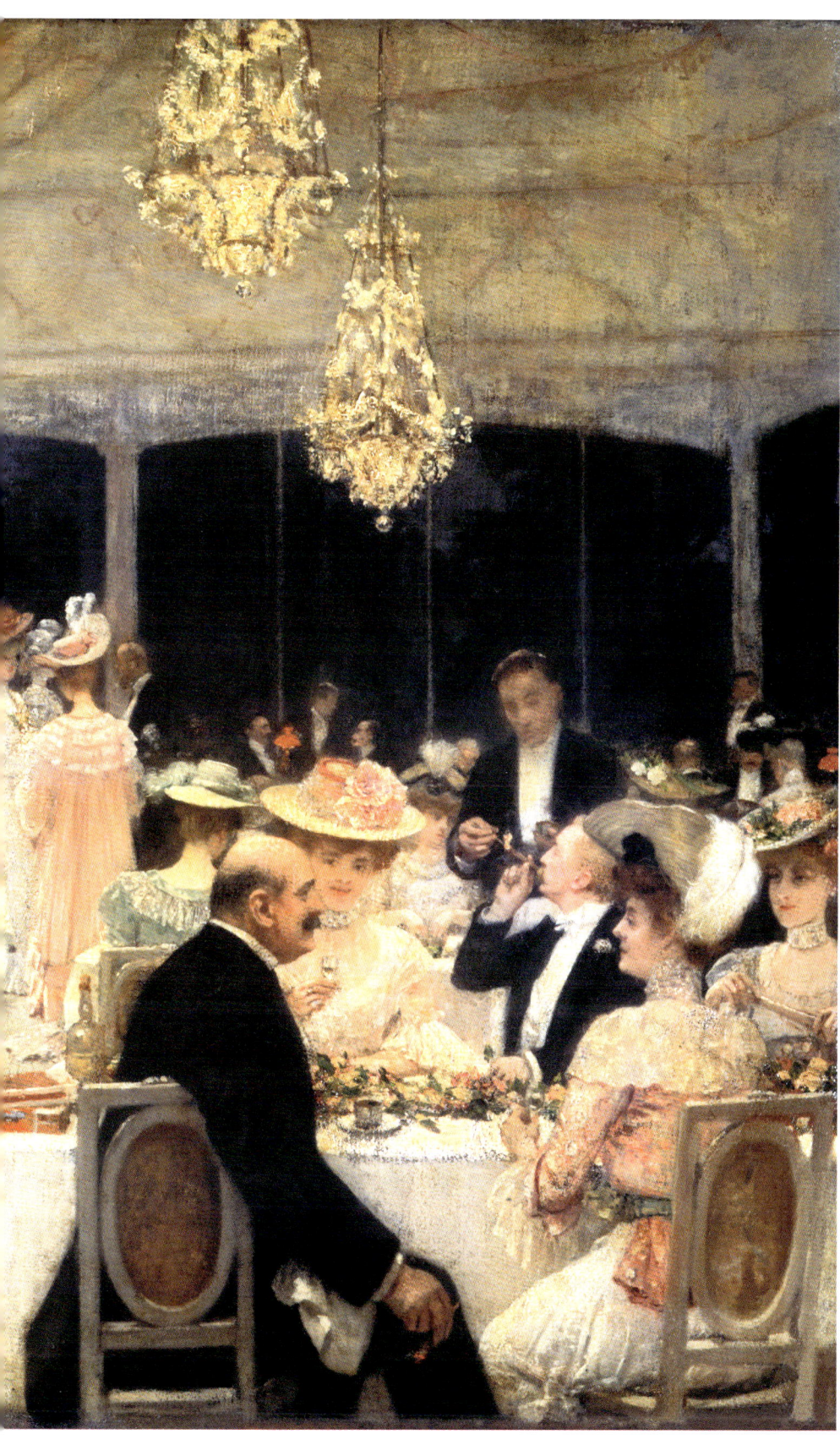

Henri Gervex, *Armenonville,
le soir Grand-Prix*, 1905.
Musée Carnavalet, Paris.

Pink for Men

It would be a mistake to see the pink of the ancien régime as a feminine color. In the eighteenth century, there were many men of the aristocracy who wore pink, especially in the years 1760–70, after which russet, or *feuille morte* (dead leaf), tones took over.

Jean-Baptiste Greuze, *Charles Claude de Flahaut, Comte d'Angiviller*, 1763. Metropolitan Museum of Art, New York.

Melancholy in Pink

The café scene in Édouard Manet's *La Prune* was not painted in situ but rather in a setting reconstructed at his studio, probably representing the Café de la Nouvelle Athènes where Manet and his friends (Auguste Renoir and Edgar Degas) were in the habit of meeting. The young woman is the actress Ellen Andrée, who posed regularly for them. They loved her silhouette, face, and especially, wrote Manet, "her generous patience."

Édouard Manet, *La Prune*, 1877 or 1878. National Gallery of Art, Washington, DC.

pink by men in the second half of the eighteenth century or first years of the nineteenth century.[2] Furthermore, it would be absurd. The prince of Ligne himself, who happily wore this color for many decades, had sixteen children by his wife and multiple affairs with women throughout Europe. All women found him charming. In 1808, when he was seventy-three years old and hosted Germaine de Staël at his home in Vienna, she wrote to her dear friend Juliette Récamier, "This man, the nicest man on earth, treats me like a daughter. Like his daughter . . . , alas!"[3]

In addition, with the end of the ancien régime along with the disappearance or transformation of life at court, men's use of makeup and powder declined. It was still the custom in France at the end of Louis XV's reign, yet less so during the following reign. Elsewhere in Europe, notably in Protestant countries, men rarely wore powder and makeup. Gradually makeup once again became the business of women. In the same period, the dramatic reds women used excessively in the mid-eighteenth century became more discreet, giving way to more delicate tones on cheeks and lips, in keeping with the new codes of society. Pinks—all pinks—held a place of honor and would continue to do so for a long time. Of course, red did not disappear from makeup practices, but it was limited to the lips alone, at least among those who were then called "honest women."

Beginning in the years 1860 to 1880 and until World War II, only those women who made a profession of debauchery and a few who wanted to make a scene continued

to paint their faces red. Many great painters, fascinated by those living at the margins of the social order, left us some famous images of them. These include Édouard Manet, Henri de Toulouse-Lautrec, Kees van Dongen, Amedeo Modigliani, Otto Dix, and others. Women of polite society were more discreet, but did not give up using red for the lips. In fact, after World War I, its use became more democratic, and lipstick became an object of true mass consumption. Now sold in tubes with a turning mechanism, it was available in a great many shades. These were given names having less and less to do with the color, whether it was red or pink. In the past, words like *cherry*, *strawberry*, or *poppy*, perhaps accompanied by a simple adjective (*light*, *dark*, *matte*, or *glossy*), sufficed. Now red shades were designated by phrases meant to be poetic or catchy, without the least attempt to name the precise color, but rather to surprise, intrigue, or conjure dreams: *Morning Peony*, *Andrinople Beauty*, *Midsummer Night*, and *Opera Festival*. Brands competed in their inventiveness, captivating women not only with the vast array of shades and the quality of their new products but also with the originality of their names. At the same time, many makeup testers were made available to serve as guides or for advertising. They constituted veritable little lexicons of red and pink; no other color, in any other domain, offered anything like this.

But let us go back once more to the moment when the fashion for romantic pink was in decline, and then displaced and transgressed. Following that, in the second half

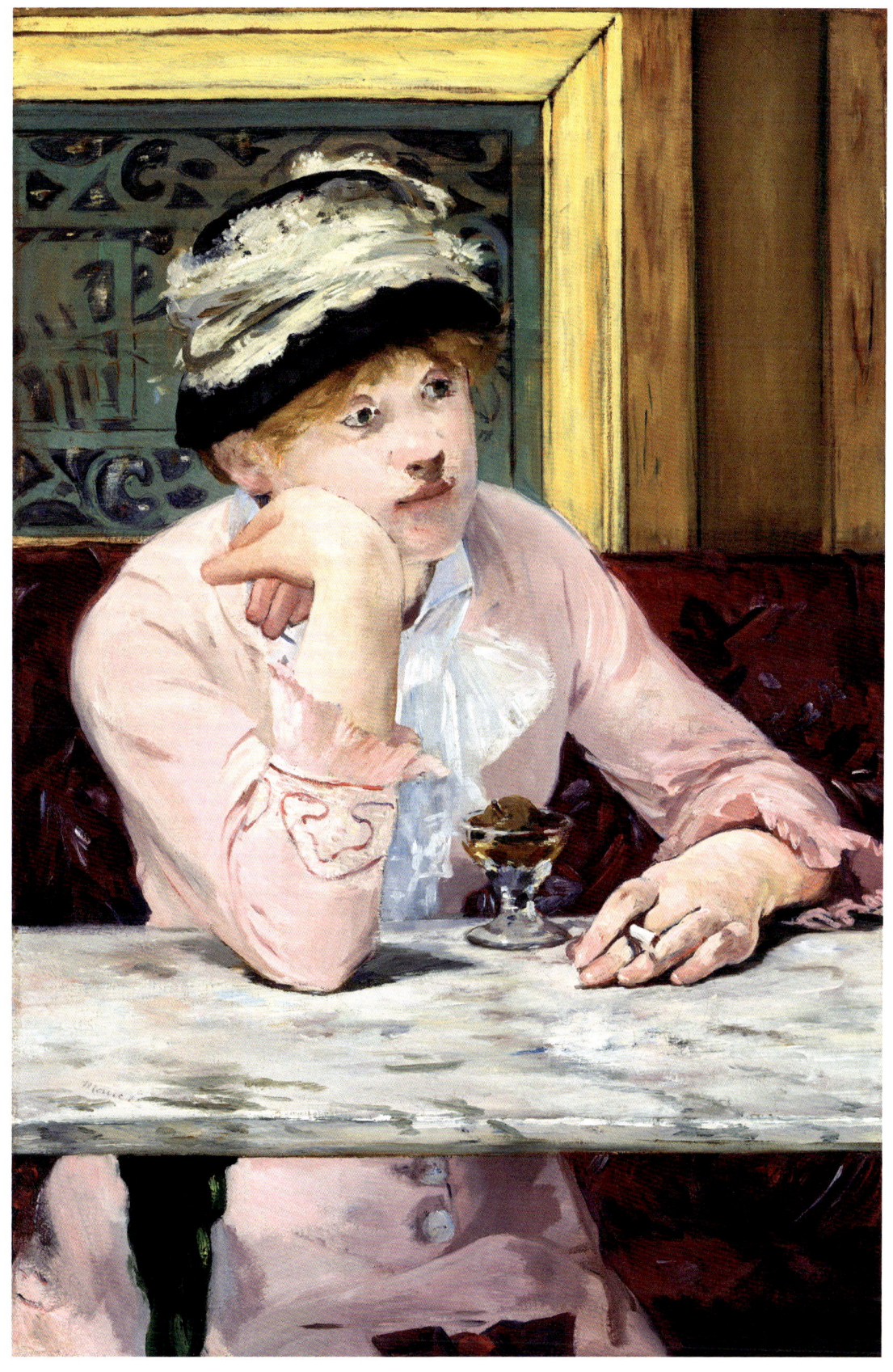

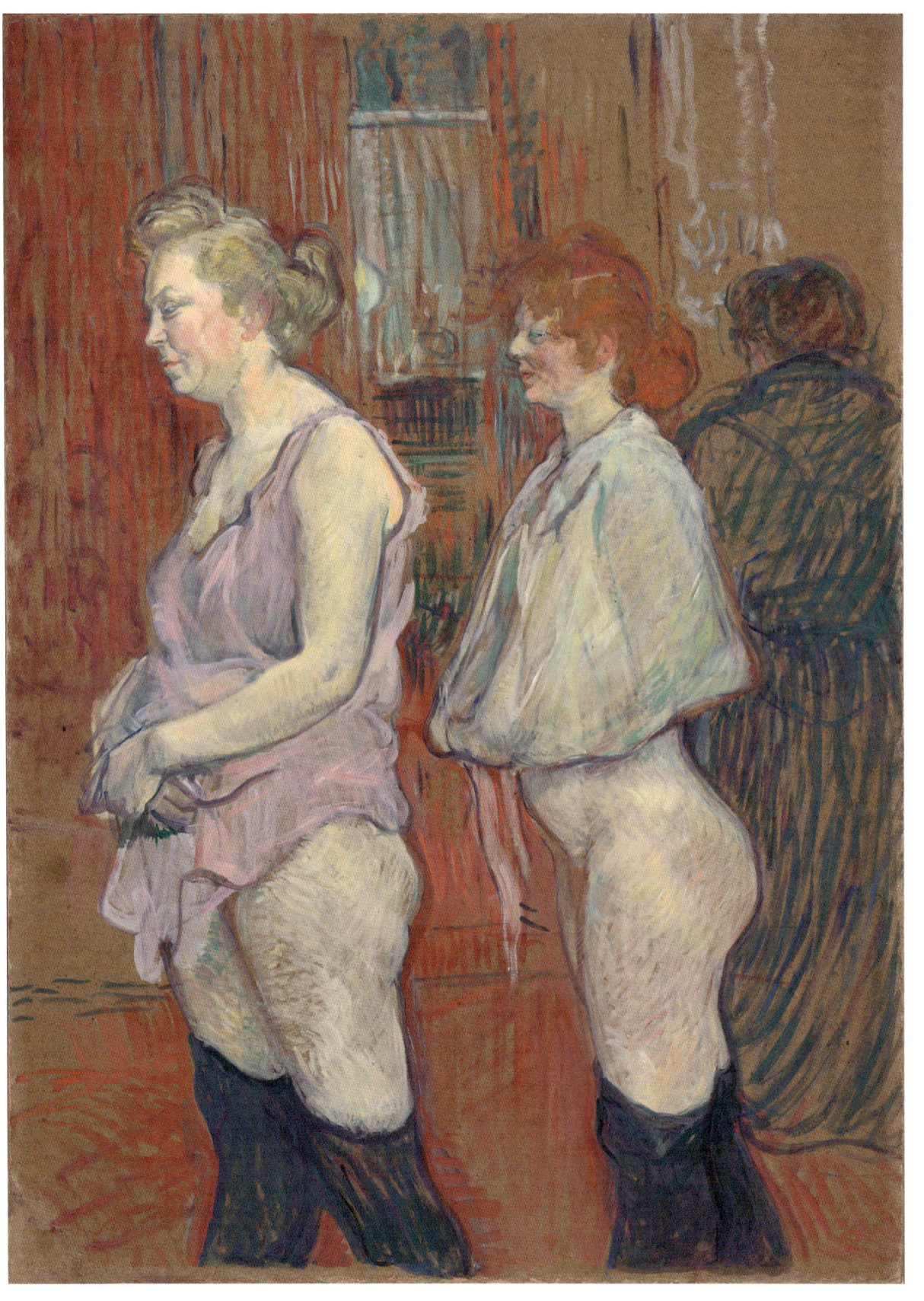

OPPOSITE

The Colors of Prostitution

Like other painters of his era, Henri de Toulouse-Lautrec frequented brothels. He painted many pictures showing the cozy "sitting rooms" of those places as well as their residents. The range of colors he used is always the same: abundant red, pink, purple, black, sometimes orange, and a bit of white, but rarely blue or green. The women have red hair and ample pink flesh. Debauchery delights in warm colors.

Henri de Toulouse-Lautrec, *Rue des Moulins*, 1894. National Gallery of Art, Washington, DC.

OPPOSITE PAGE

Pink among the Fauvists

In the years 1905–10, young artists (André Derain, Henri Matisse, Albert Marquet, Kees van Dongen, and Maurice de Vlaminck) exalted pure color and sought to free it from all the constraints that drawing had imposed on it since the Renaissance. They all seem to have been stricken with a true "colorist fever" and applied tones arbitrarily: any element in a painting could be any color. The execution was rapid, the touch violent, the forms simplified, and the contrasts stark and resonant. The nickname "fauvists" was given to them on the occasion of the Salon d'Automne in 1905.

André Derain, *Woman in a Chemise*, 1906. Statens Museum for Kunst, Copenhagen.

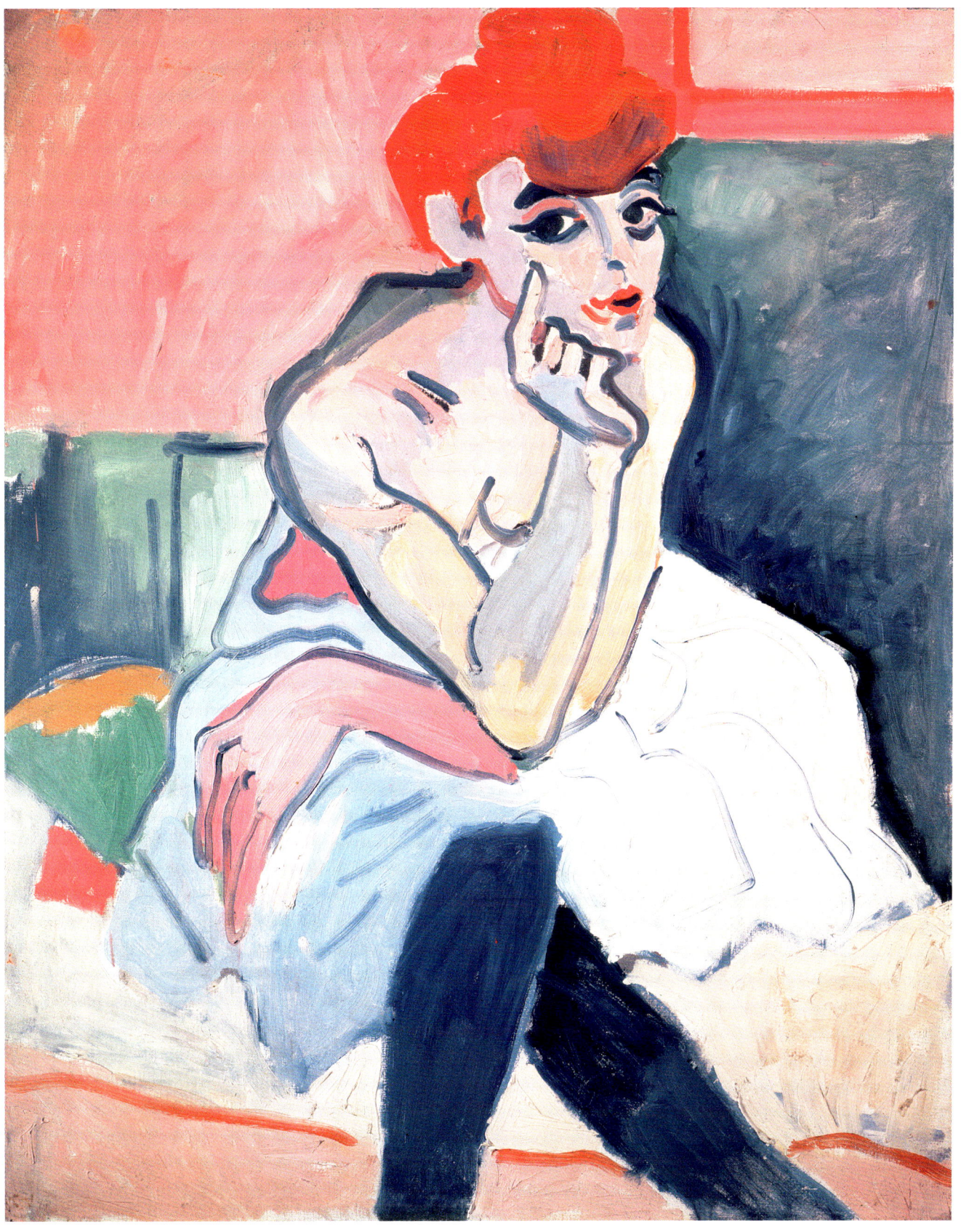

BELOW

Makeup and Cosmetics

As early as the years 1760–80, the makeup and cosmetic industry had launched advertisements vaunting various products meant to protect or beautify the skin of both sexes. In the nineteenth century, that advertising began to target a female clientele exclusively. It grew exponentially in the following century and provides the color historian with a multitude of makeup displays that offer an almost infinite variety of reds, pinks, pale or whitish oranges, cream tones, flesh tones, and salmon tones, with iridescent, opalescent, or nacreous options.

Advertising card for makeup products by the Helena Rubinstein company, ca. 1925.

OPPOSITE PAGE

Pastel Colors

For centuries, all fabrics that touched the body had to be undyed or white, for reasons both hygienic and moral. Then, starting in the late nineteenth century, those fabrics slowly shifted from white to colors. They did so in two ways: by means of either stripes (white plus one other color) or pastel shades. The latter, ubiquitous in women's lingerie, were pale and drab–"colors" that did not dare say their name.

Lingerie and nightclothes, "White" catalog from the Grands Magasins du Printemps, Paris, January 1935.

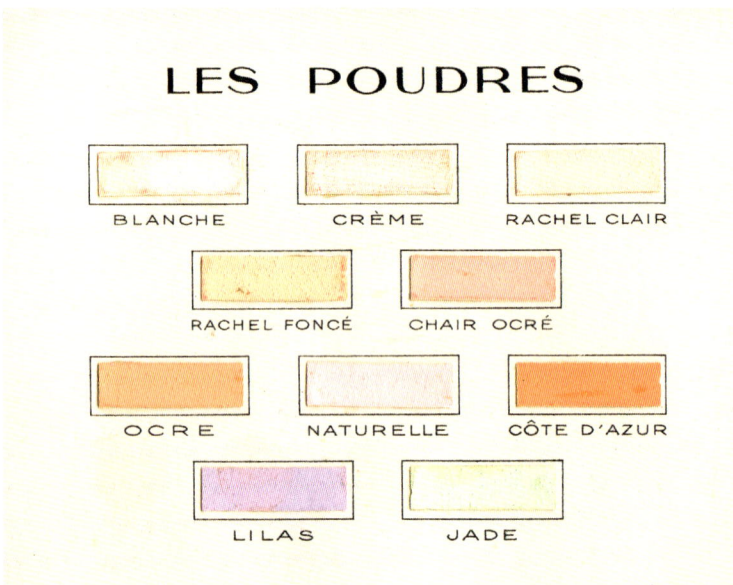

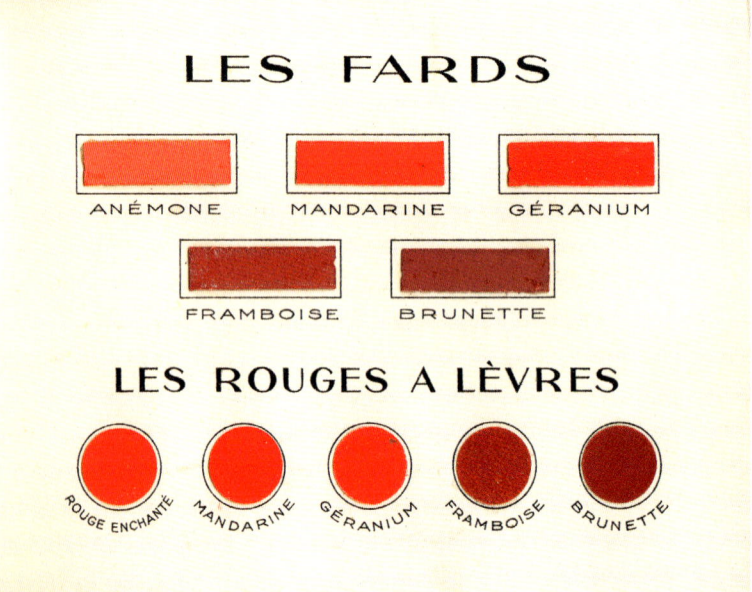

of the nineteenth century, came a certain discrediting of the color in clothing as in furnishings and the decorative arts. Pink became sentimental, petit bourgeois, and old-fashioned, if not insipid. Elegant ladies in high society henceforth relegated it to women of the middle classes, or even to shopgirls and lowly seamstresses. As for men, they mistakenly believed this color to still be in fashion when it had long been passé, or they complacently saw the future as rosy when dark days lay ahead. About 1900, many authors turned to irony in the face of so much naïvete or foolishness:

The bourgeois man must have pink, that is his color. His daughters dress in pink and so does his wife, until she is over sixty. He himself is rosy and joyful as a young pig when business is good. He insists on seeing everything

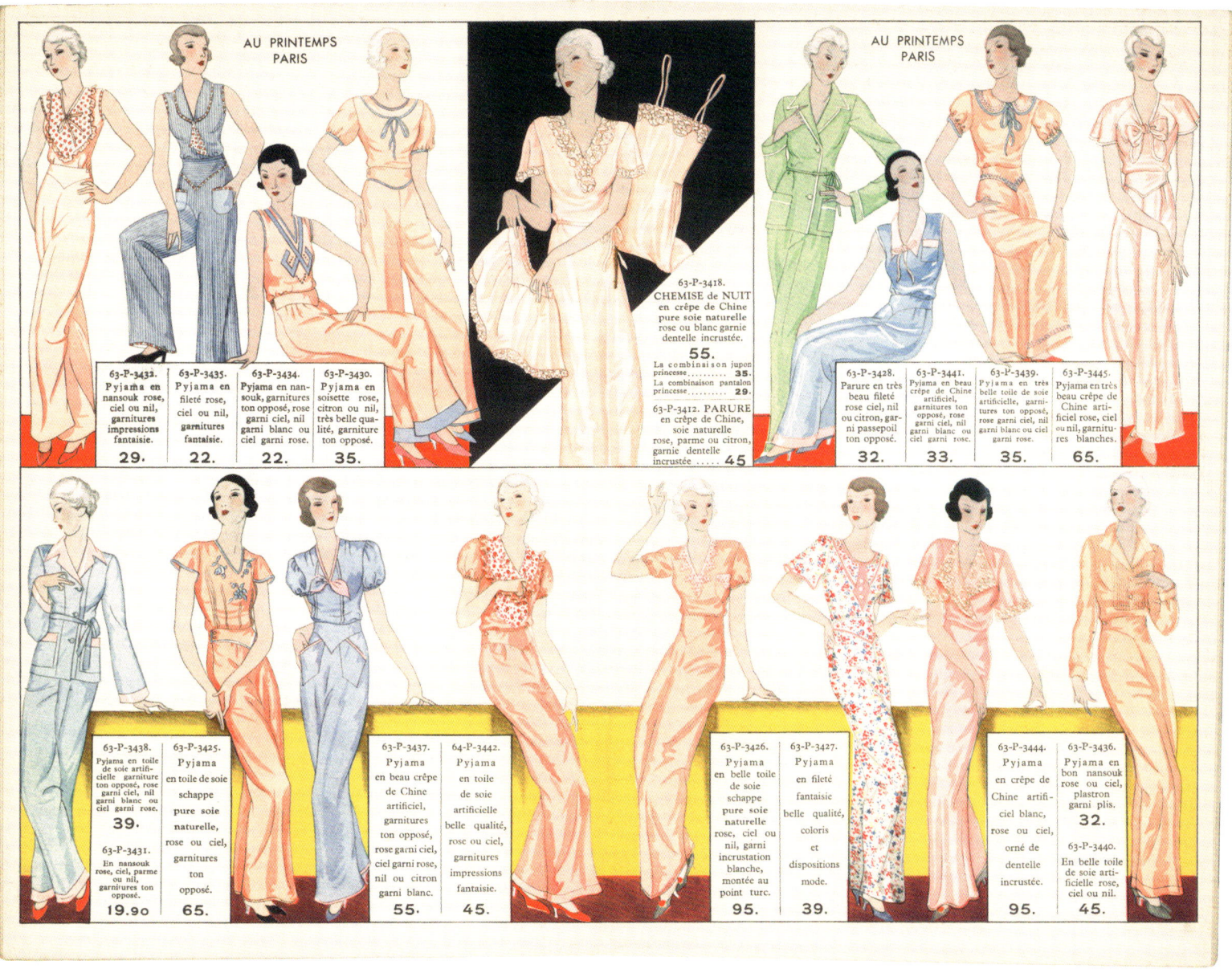

63-P-3432.
Pyjama en
nansouk rose,
ciel ou nil,
garnitures
impressions
fantaisie.
29.

63-P-3435.
Pyjama en
fileté rose,
ciel ou nil,
garnitures
fantaisie.
22.

63-P-3434.
Pyjama en nan-
souk, garnitures
ton opposé, rose
garni ciel, nil
ou ciel garni rose.
22.

63-P-3430.
Pyjama en
soisette rose,
citron ou nil,
très belle qua-
lité, garniture
ton opposé.
35.

63-P-3418.
CHEMISE de NUIT
en crêpe de Chine
pure soie naturelle
rose ou blanc garnie
dentelle incrustée.
55.
La combinaison jupon
princesse . . . . **35.**
La combinaison pantalon
princesse . . . . **29.**

63-P-3412. PARURE
en crêpe de Chine,
soie naturelle
rose, parme ou citron,
garnie dentelle
incrustée **45**

63-P-3428.
Parure en très
beau fileté
rose ciel, nil
ou citron, gar-
ni passepoil
ton opposé.
32.

63-P-3441.
Pyjama en beau
crêpe de Chine
artificiel,
garnitures ton
opposé, rose
garni ciel, nil
ou ciel garni rose.
33.

63-P-3439.
Pyjama en très
belle toile de soie
artificielle, garni-
tures ton opposé,
rose garni ciel, nil
ou ciel garni rose.
35.

63-P-3445.
Pyjama en très
beau crêpe de
Chine arti-
ficiel rose, ciel
ou nil, garnitu-
res blanches.
65.

63-P-3438.
Pyjama en toile
de soie artifi-
cielle garniture
ton opposé, rose
garni ciel, nil
garni blanc ou
ciel garni rose.
39.

63-P-3431.
En nansouk
rose, ciel, parme
ou nil,
garnitures ton
opposé.
19.90

63-P-3425.
Pyjama
en toile de soie
schappe
pure soie
naturelle,
rose ou ciel,
garnitures
ton
opposé.
65.

63-P-3437.
Pyjama
en beau crêpe
de Chine
artificiel,
garnitures
ton opposé,
rose ou ciel,
ciel garni rose,
nil ou citron
garni blanc.
55.

64-P-3442.
Pyjama
en toile
de soie
artificielle
belle qualité,
rose ou ciel,
garnitures
impressions
fantaisie.
45.

63-P-3426.
Pyjama
en belle toile
de soie
schappe
pure soie
naturelle,
rose, ciel ou
nil, garni
incrustation
blanche,
montée au
point turc.
95.

63-P-3427.
Pyjama
en fileté
fantaisie
belle qualité,
coloris
et
dispositions
mode.
39.

63-P-3444.
Pyjama
en crêpe de
Chine artifi-
ciel blanc,
rose ou ciel,
orné de
dentelle
incrustée.
95.

63-P-3436.
Pyjama en
bon nansouk
rose ou ciel,
plastron
garni plis.
32.

63-P-3440.
En belle toile
de soie arti-
ficielle rose,
ciel ou nil.
45.

through rose-colored glasses and wants everything to be in the pink. . . . Following so many poets, he alone still dares to speak of "the rosy fingers of dawn."[4]

This discrediting of pink explains why, at the turn of the century, it starts to be hidden, passing from women's outer garments to their undergarments. The first half of the twentieth century was indeed the time of pink under-clothes, and not an enticing or exciting pink but instead a discreet, dull, slightly beige pink meant to more or less evoke the color of Caucasian skin tones. Corsets, pantalets, stockings, garters, and then, later, underpants, slips, and bras increasingly adopted this distinctly unseductive but serviceable shade, abandoning white to young women of the upper class and red and black to professional women prostitutes. Later, in the 1960s and 1970s, this beige pink gave way to pastel shades of different colors (sky blue, pale yellow, and sea green), before white made its big return, followed by that of more vivid colors. Today, according to statistics, it is black that prevails. Not only is there absolutely nothing erotic or provocative about it, but for synthetic fabrics, it is the color that stands up longest to repeated machine washings.

The Palette of Pinks

Félix Vallotton was a marvelous colorist. Beginning with a limited palette, he offers the viewer a particularly rich and appealing range of pinks here. He also shows how the shades of that color easily blend with other colors and are enriched by proximity with them. For a painter, a pink used alone holds little interest, but in combination with browns, grays, blues, greens, and even reds, it can be magnificent. That is the case in this painting, which has such powerful appeal that it was stolen in 1978.

Félix Vallotton, *Woman Combing Her Hair*, 1900. Musée d'Orsay, Paris.

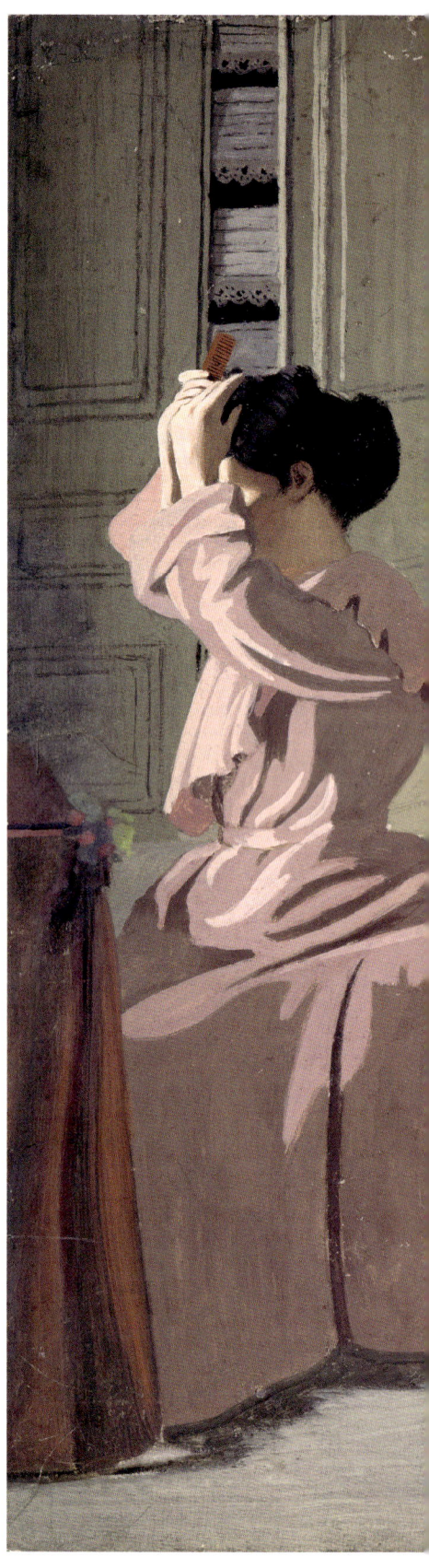

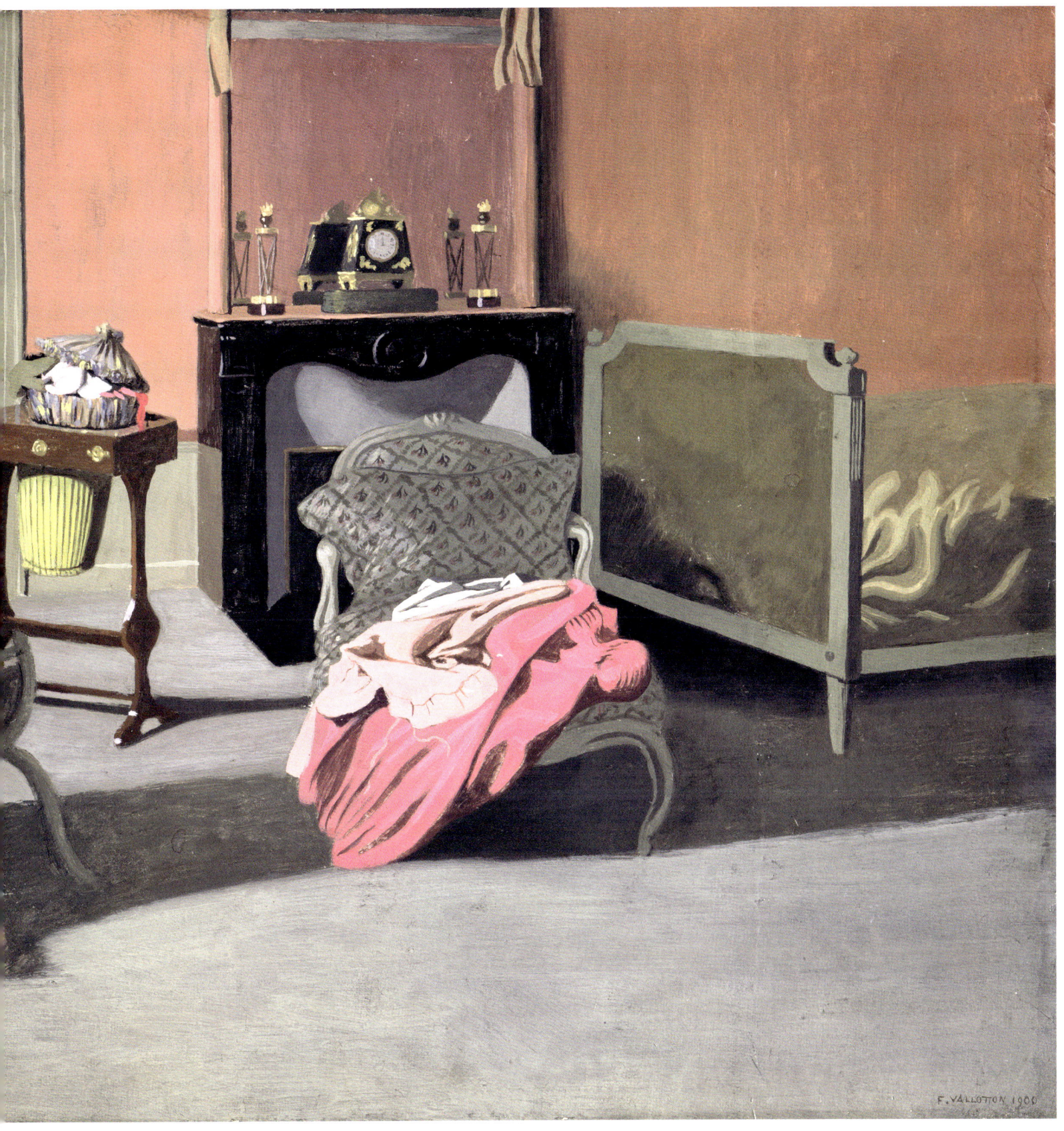

F. VALLOTTON 1900

From Ladies to Little Girls

In that same time period, that is, the mid-nineteenth to the mid-twentieth century, pink clothing passed from young women to girls to little girls, who were assigned to pink well before little boys were assigned to sky blue. As early as the eighteenth century, nursery rhymes and songs told how boys were born in the cabbage patch and girls among the roses. Here as well, passing to the color from the flower was easy, but from the vegetable, more difficult. Throughout the nineteenth century, documentation abounds attesting to the custom of dressing little girls in pink, but not until the end of the century do we find evidence of the fashion for dressing infants and young children in pink and sky blue. It seems to have appeared in Victorian England before spreading across the European continent. Contrary to what has sometimes been written, the patronage of the Virgin Mary had absolutely nothing to do with this custom. In fact, it was a practice that first involved Protestant countries before expanding slowly throughout all Western societies. Moreover, for a long time, it was not neatly divided by gender; little girls and boys alike could be dressed in either pink or blue. And male children seem to have been dressed more frequently in pink than in blue, if we are to believe the paintings of fashionable society prior to World War I.[5]

Originally this custom was limited to the court, aristocracy, and upper middle class. In other social classes, infants and young children were always dressed in white, as they had been for centuries. It was not until the 1930s and the appearance of durable color fabrics resistant to repeated laundering in boiling water that the use of pink and sky blue became widespread, first in the United States, and later in Europe. Subsequently, the increasing availability of washing machines and synthetic fabrics promoted this phenomenon. That was when a stricter gender division was established: pink for girls, and blue for boys. Pink was no longer considered the young boy's version of the old masculine red of warriors and hunters. Henceforth this color was feminine, entirely feminine, whereas in the eighteenth century it had frequently been masculine.

In the contemporary period, even more than the clothing of infants and young children, it is undoubtedly the famous Barbie doll, plus all of her accompanying toys and accessories, that we must identify with the feminization of pink. For over half a century, she has played a decisive role in it. Barbie (a diminutive of Barbara) made her appearance in 1959, launched by the US company Mattel, which specializes in toys and games. She was an imitation of Bild Lilli, a German doll and the first doll mannequin,

Birth in a Rose

An ancient tradition holds that boys are
born in the cabbage patch and girls
in the roses. It is attested in the Middle
Ages (but not in ancient Greece as one
often reads). The cabbage was then a
common symbol of fertility; the rose a
feminine flower. It is hard to say much
more about it. Around the end of the
nineteenth century, that tradition, having
lost favor, experienced a revival thanks
to postcards and birth announcements.
That phase lasted until the 1940s.

"A Rose," postcard, 1900.

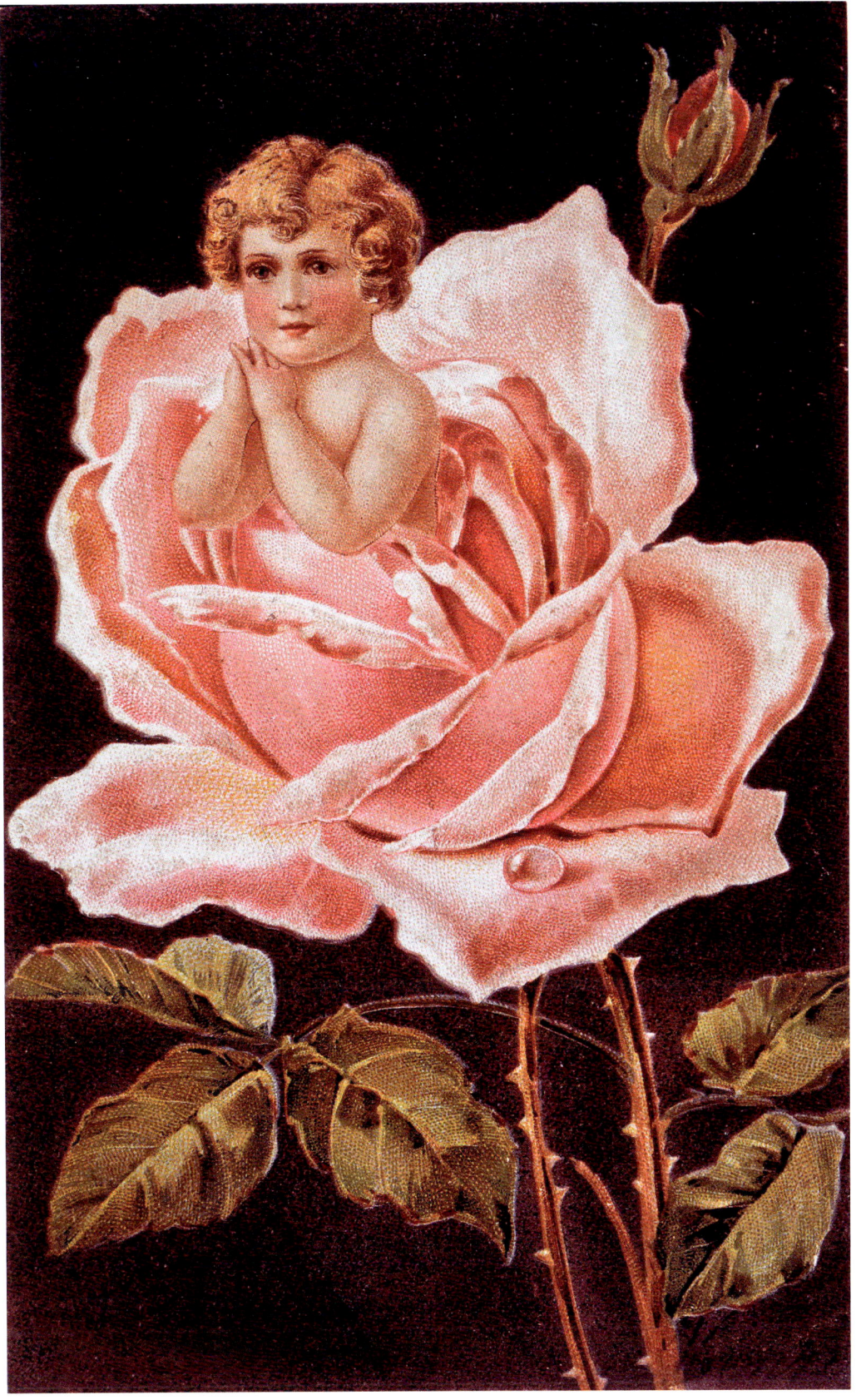

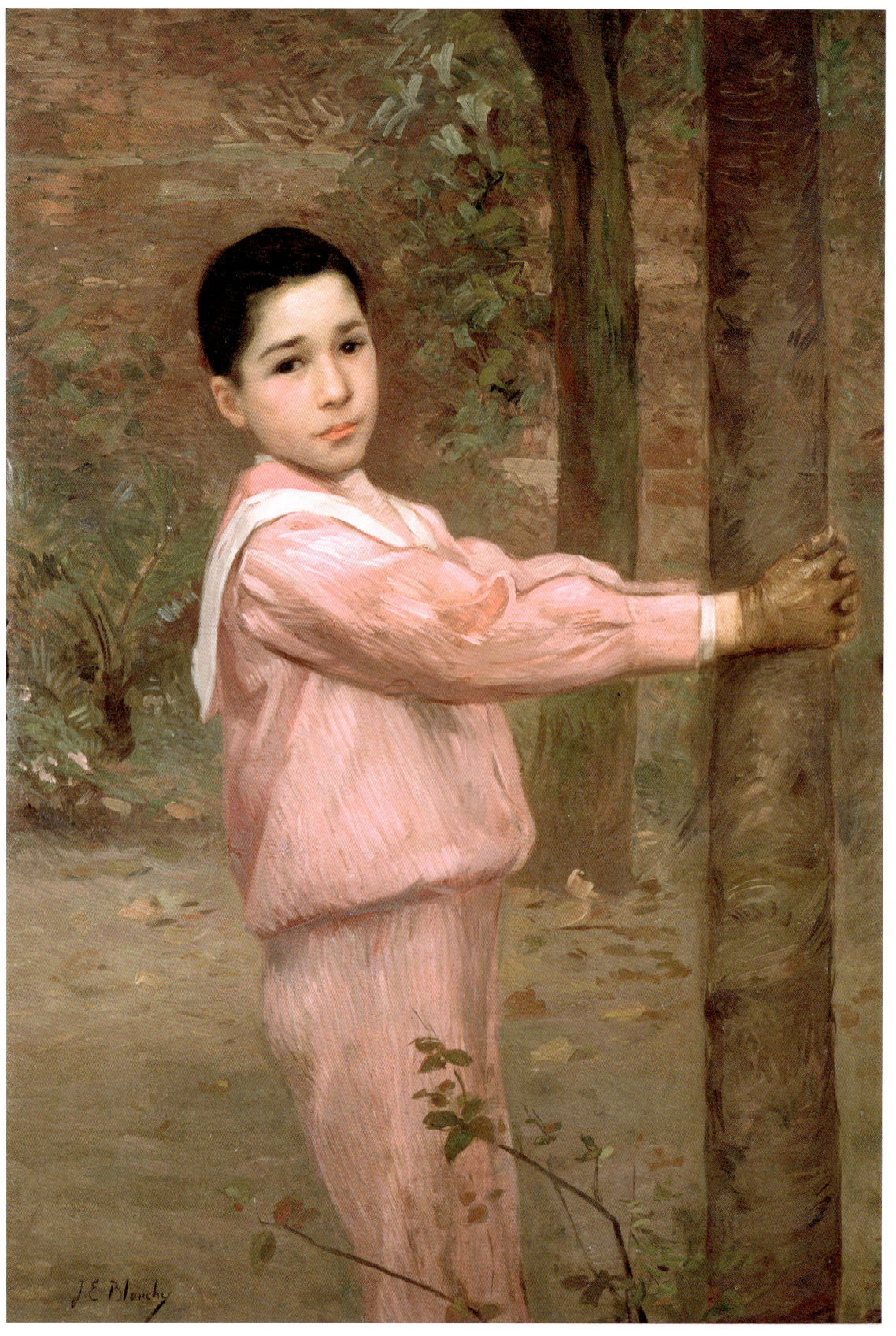

J.E.Blanche

"Gendered" Colors:
A Late and Limited Code

Dressing little girls in pink and little boys in blue was a rare practice before the appearance of colorfast fabrics and the washing machine. It involved primarily the privileged classes and only "Sunday best" clothing. Moreover, the color code long remained uncertain; illustrated documents from the late nineteenth or early twentieth century that show small boys dressed entirely in pink are not uncommon.

Jacques-Émile Blanche, *Portrait of a Boy in a Pink Sailor Suit*, undated. Private collection.

created in 1955. At the beginning, the ties between Barbie and pink were subtle. Of course her skin was flesh color, but her wardrobe presented a relatively varied palette. It was especially in the 1970s that pink became dominant, and in the 1990s, it took on an insistent and even aggressive aspect. What were the reasons for this? Were they social? Ideological? Commercial? Sexual? It is hard to find an answer. For the historian, the most remarkable thing is how the intensified presence of "Barbie pink" occurs at the moment when in the United States as in Europe, various feminist movements started to protest against everything that too strongly distinguished girls from boys, notably colors. Since then the phenomenon has only expanded, to the point that today in the Western world, it has become politically incorrect to attribute pink to girls and blue to boys. For a long time, Barbie has represented the polar opposite of this position and has prompted hostility from feminist movements, principally in Germany, Great Britain, and Scandinavia, advocating in all domains the end of chromatic distinctions between men and women.

So is "Barbie pink" a "shocking pink"—that is, a deliberate provocation with regard to such movements, and as such, a defense of a certain moral conservatism? A way of proclaiming loud and strong that a girl is a girl? We must continually keep in mind that this is a US toy—that is, a toy originating in a country where morals and counterviews from all sides play a different social role than in Europe. But perhaps more mundanely, it is a matter of a new marketing strategy, aimed less at conquering Europe than another continent where pink is admired and thought to bring good luck: Asia. In fact, this famous doll now enjoys considerable success there. Unless, even more hypocritically, the real goal of this increasingly immodest pink is to eroticize Barbie, not only by accentuating her femininity, but by making it vaguely provocative? Because Barbie is not a little girl but rather a young woman with an adult body, her hips are exaggerated, and her bust is pronounced. Though a mannequin doll, she is presented as a young wonder woman, able to do all sorts of jobs and activities, as some of her clothes and accessories underscore: nurse, flight attendant, teacher, veterinarian, jockey, horsewoman, race car driver, and so on.[6] Her car is pink, as are her suits, jewelry, and makeup. That said, can Barbie really evoke anything erotic? She is much too artificial to do that and hardly arouses desire, with her fixed smile and inexpressive big blue eyes.

Nevertheless, the essential thing here is the influence exerted by Barbie and other toys made for little girls—a considerable influence, running counter to a general defeminizing of the color palette and contributing to the feminization of pink. One only has to scan the toy shelves of a large store or supermarket to see this; everything meant to interest little girls is pink and packaged in pink boxes. The phenomenon is not new; it is at least twenty years old and stems in part from "Barbie pink," which has contaminated or eradicated other colors. Pink shades are all affected, and have increasingly taken on less and less childlike tones: salmon, fuchsia, violet, and magenta. For many years, the pinks on toys for little girls—or marketed as such—have tended to become harsher, purpler, and more saturated, thereby losing all suggestion of childhood. These pinks are aimed at older girls, already aware of their sexuality. For a certain clientele, they transform the dolls dressed in them into seductive princesses, and if the pink tends too close to purple, into fairies, sorceresses, or even witches. A whole ensemble of accessories in the same color range accompany them, from deep purple slippers to mauve magic wands spangled with gold or silver stars. The poor quality of the plastic materials from which these toys are made only accentuates the vulgarity of their fuchsia or purplish tones. The former "glamorous side" that some dolls occasionally possessed in the 1960s and 1970s seems largely to have disappeared today.[7]

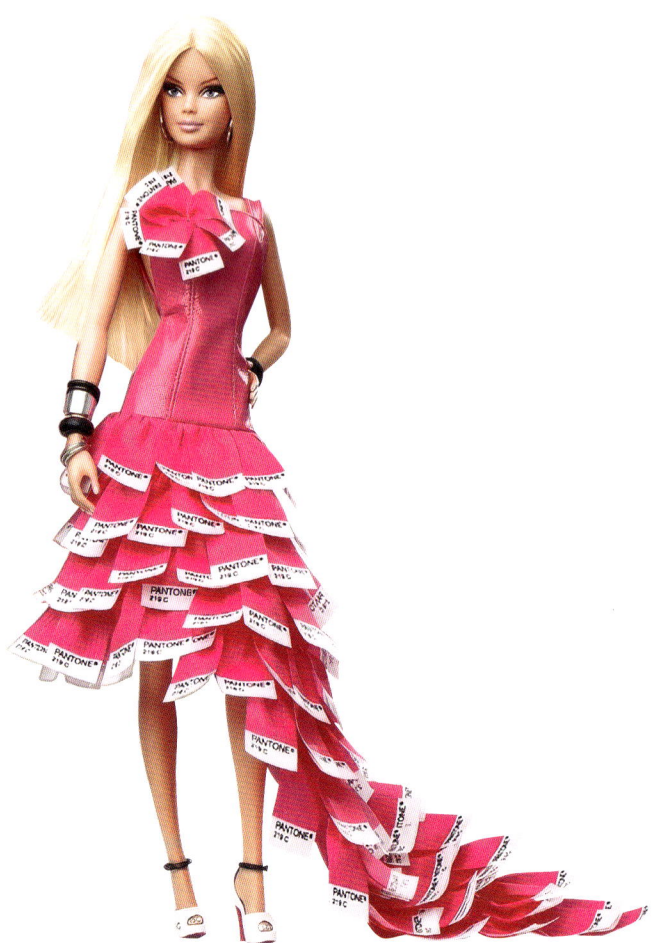

Pink Barbie

Born in 1959, the Barbie doll has long had a special relationship with the color pink. After a brief period when she was dressed only in black and white, pink became her favorite color for clothing, accessories, and even for her signature, serving as the logo for her brand. That pink, originally relatively pale and modest, became more saturated and flashy over the years, finally taking on a mauve tone far removed from the world of childhood. Through the evolution of her color alone, the doll ceased being a toy to become a symbol.

Collector Barbie doll "Pink in Pantone," 2011. Mattell W3376.

Scene from the film *Barbie* by Greta Gerwig with Margot Robbie and Ryan Gosling, 2023.

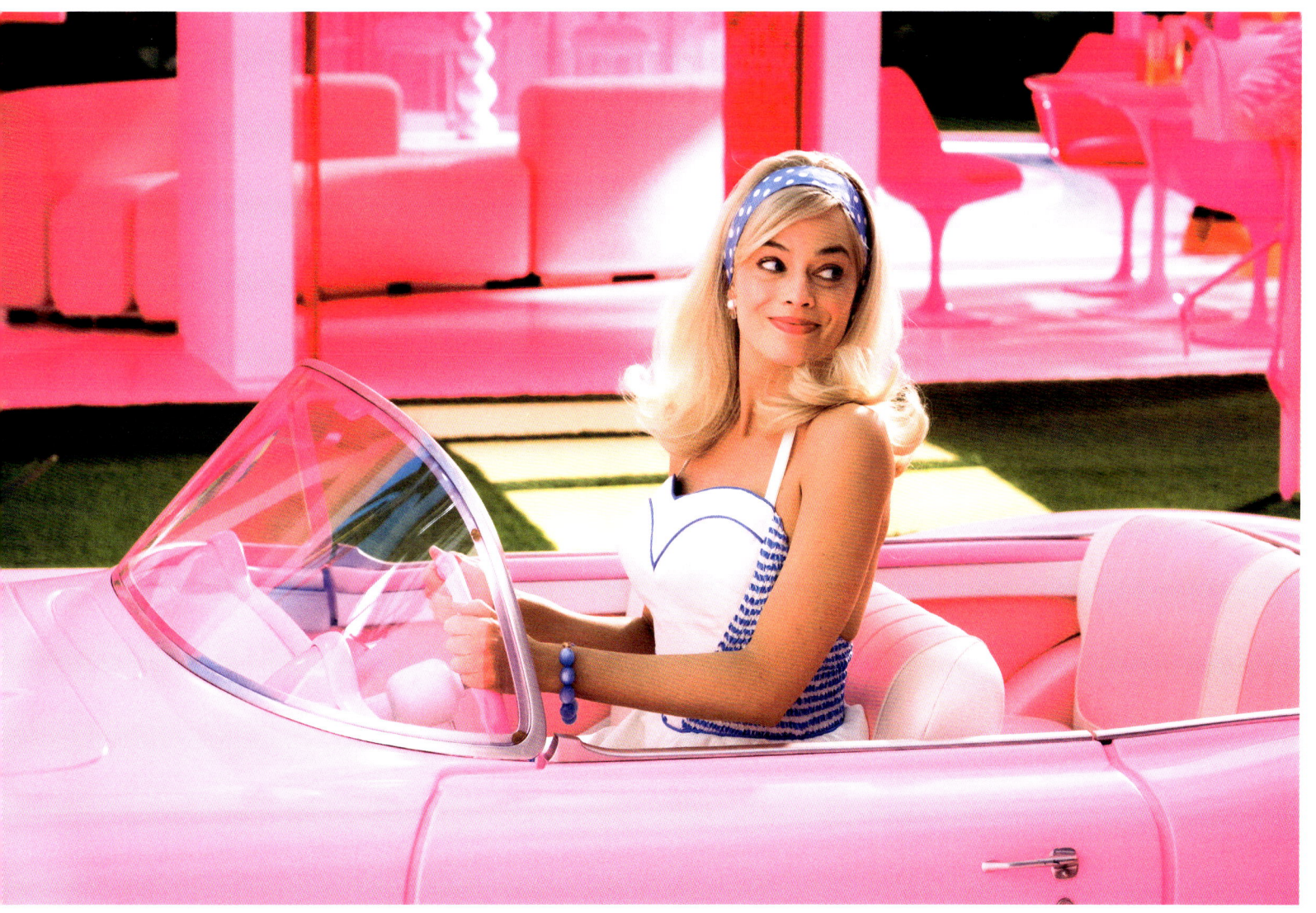

Bad Taste, Debauchery, and Pornography

In our time, on the symbolic level, pink, like all the other colors, is ambivalent. There is a good and bad pink, like there is a good and bad red, or a good and bad black. For most of the other colors, their positive and negative aspects seem to counterbalance each other, but with regard to pink, at least in Europe, its negative aspects seem to prevail. All opinion polls conducted over more than a century demonstrate this: pink is unpopular. When a wide and significant sample of individuals was asked about favorite colors, pink was never cited. On the other hand, when it was a question of detested colors, pink shared first place with purple and brown.[8]

For the historian, the most remarkable thing about these opinion polls—always considered circumspectly, of course—is that the results on favorite colors do not change from one decade to the next. For as long as they have existed—that is, since the 1880s—blue always comes in first, followed by green and red; pink, purple, and brown always tie for last place. Not only are these results consistent over time, but they hardly vary throughout European countries, from Ireland to Poland and from Greece to Norway. Nothing seems to affect favorite or least favorite colors, not climate, history, religions, or cultural traditions, much less political regimes or levels of economic development. Everywhere, blue wins, hands down, while pink is rejected. And even more surprisingly, the most and least popular colors are the same for men and women, various socioprofessional categories, and pretty much the same for each age group. Only young children poll somewhat differently, sometimes preferring red to blue, with little girls having a certain predilection for pink. Purple is often rejected by children of both sexes, on the other hand; for some, it is even a color that "brings bad luck."[9]

Those are the results in Europe and the West. Elsewhere it is a different story. In Japan, for example, white, black, and red come in first, but pink, very much appreciated there, comes in fourth, before blue. The same is true in China, where pink has been highly regarded by women

The Colors of Pigs

Domestic pigs have not always been pink. Until the eighteenth century in Europe, their coats were dark, most often black, gray, or brown, and sometimes beige or spotted. These pigs were crossbred with ones from Asia, and, beginning in the years 1760–80, gave birth to piglets with lighter coats. Today the pig has become the archetypal pink animal, even though the true color of its fur tends more toward off-white than pink. This color accounts for the link between dirty jokes (*cochonneries*), eroticism, and pornography.

Félicien Rops, *Pornokratès*, 1878. Musée provincial Félicien Rops, Namur (Belgium).

and girls for some twenty years.[10] Elsewhere in Asia and Africa the parameters that define color can be so different from those in modern-day Europe that it is difficult to conduct comparable studies. In sub-Saharan Africa, for example, for a given color, it is often more important to know if it is dry or moist, smooth or rough, matte or glossy, than to determine whether it belongs to the range of reds, blues, greens, or yellows. Color is not something in and of itself, an abstraction, separable from its medium or materiality. That is why "Western-type" surveys on favorite or detested colors have little significance there; they are too ethnocentric in their conceptions, methods, and aims.[11]

Thus let us stay with Europe. Why is pink so little appreciated today? The reasons are varied, most certainly, but one idea is frequently associated with them, at least if we look once again to opinion polls: bad taste or even vulgarity.[12] Rarely present in nature and daily life, pink, especially when it is chosen for clothing, stands out from its surroundings and thereby attracts attention. Now whatever one says, or whether one likes it or not, to draw attention to oneself is still considered vain, indecent, immoral, or ridiculous today, at least for the common run of mortals. Why show off? Why want to be different from others? Such behaviors violate the social order. Even if market strategies try to claim otherwise, even if the media, fashion designers, and advertisers promote changes, innovations, and updates in color shades and ranges, a significant part of the population—if not the majority—want their everyday life to be "like everyone else's" and "like usual." To claim otherwise is to deny the obvious.

Another reason for rejecting pink may be linked to our earlier discussion on the Barbie doll: too much rose soils the rose, as in the case of that (alleged) toy, formerly beloved, now considered banal. Until recently in Europe in the beauty and fashion industries, it was widely held that young blond women should not wear pink; it was considered to be in bad taste. Whereas Barbie is blond and dresses in pink!

All of this is a matter of undeniable subjectivity and no doubt offends those readers who sincerely love pink. May they forgive me; I am only citing the results of opinion polls, which does not mean I share those opinions, especially since there are more concrete reasons behind the unpopularity of pink. The first is a particularly painful historical reason: Nazi concentration camps used pink to distinguish male homosexuals by making them wear a large pink triangle (*rosa Winkel*).[13] The memory of that infamous mark—its shape and color—has not disappeared. Some homosexual communities have even subverted the code recently by embracing the pink triangle as an identity symbol to ensure that the memory of those persecuted and deported in the 1930s and 1940s will not vanish forever.[14]

The second reason, widely attested, though more indirect and harder to pinpoint, is the link between the color pink and debauchery, pornography, and even pedophilia. No doubt it is this connection that has done the most harm to that color in the contemporary era. In Europe, pink evokes the skin and flesh, and also, by extension, nudity, especially female nudity, physical love, and sexual intercourse. In French, the anagrammatic wordplay between *rose* and *eros* goes back quite far, but for a long time, it only involved the flower. At the end of the eighteenth century, it began to include the color as well. Such wordplay may be tame and poetic, not calling up attraction or desire, but it can be more risqué or even sensual, if not downright salacious. Starting in the years 1860 to 1880, it became highly sexual and even pornographic. Hence *littérature rose* was not a matter of books for little girls; much to the contrary, it presented them in abominable situations, combining pornography and pedophilia. The second half of the twentieth century would revive that tradition, becoming the era of the *ballet rose*, *messagerie rose*, and *minitel rose*, all sordid expressions as well as practices that brought no honor to the color—just the opposite.[15]

Regarding the link between pink and lechery or sexuality, it is likely that the pig played a role in it as well, a belated but decisive role. In the modern period, that poor animal, already burdened with many vices thanks to the Bible and medieval Christian authors (filthiness, voraciousness, stupidity, and impiety), found itself charged with a new depravity: lust. Other animals had preceded it in this role, however: the goat, ass, monkey, and especially dog. For centuries, from antiquity to the dawn of modernity, in matters of lust and sex, it was the dog, not the pig, that was deemed the dirtiest creature, considered particularly unclean by Mediterranean societies and absolutely vile throughout the West in terms of its sexual behavior. The female dog especially was considered singularly lustful, even more so than the sow. Like the she-wolf, she long embodied prostitution or depravation.[16]

It was not until the end of the Middle Ages or even the beginning of the modern era that the swine became the "dirty pig," taking on the vices of lechery and lust in addition to its other alleged vices, while the dog rapidly redeemed itself in European societies and definitively became "man's best friend," as is still the case today. But for the dog's redemption to be complete and entire, it had to clear its reputation as a sexually dirty and repugnant animal—a stigma it had borne since antiquity. Thus between the fifteenth and seventeenth centuries, a symbolic transfer gradually took place involving the dog and pig. Although there is absolutely nothing especially dirty or remarkable about the actual sexual behavior of the pig, it nevertheless became the shameless, lustful animal par excellence.[17] Little by little, any man making salacious remarks, indulging in obscene practices, or harassing women began to be called a "pig." In France, such men (cochons) also started to make cochonneries, which became the word for dirty jokes, although it did not take

on that sexual meaning until the eighteenth century (before then it simply designated the task of raising piglets). Over the course of the following century, it gained a companion term, the somewhat precious doublet, cochoncetés. Between 1780 and 1840, when European pigs gradually ceased to be black, brown, and spotted, becoming more or less pink following crossbreeding with Asian pigs, that color, like the animal, also began to be associated with the vice of lust and everything related to debauchery.

That is still true in part today, and if there is something sexual about pink, the pig is partly responsible—very much in spite of itself, most certainly. The mating practices of this animal are not particularly dirty. From the human perspective, those of the dog seem much more repugnant. Hence the French expression vieux cochon (dirty old man) seems unfounded, at least to the historian. Likewise, the contemporary feminist slogan of the French Me Too movement, balance ton porc (denounce your pig), seems a poor choice; it would be better

Triangle of Infamy

In the Nazi concentration camps, various categories of deportees and condemned prisoners were forced to wear marks of infamy on their clothing. Male homosexuals, considered undesirable, antisocial, or dangerous, were marked with a pink triangle. Since the years 1980–90, through an inversion of values, this triangle has become a symbol of commemoration and a community emblem.

Poster depicting the classification of insignias worn by detainees in deportation and concentration camps, Germany, 1933–45.

BELOW

The Demimondaines

During the Second Empire and belle epoque, there were many pretty young women who, without being actual prostitutes, lived more or less by their charms. They were called *les cocottes*. When they were seen in elegant, wealthy social circles, they became the women of the demimonde, *les demimondaines*. Pink was their favorite color for clothing, if not in reality, at least in the iconography and imagination.

Liane de Pougy, colored photographic print, ca. 1900.

to say *balance ton chien* (denounce your dog). That would be more accurate based on the actual behavior of those two animals, and would dissociate the color pink from the idea of debauchery and pornography with which it is too often linked.[18]

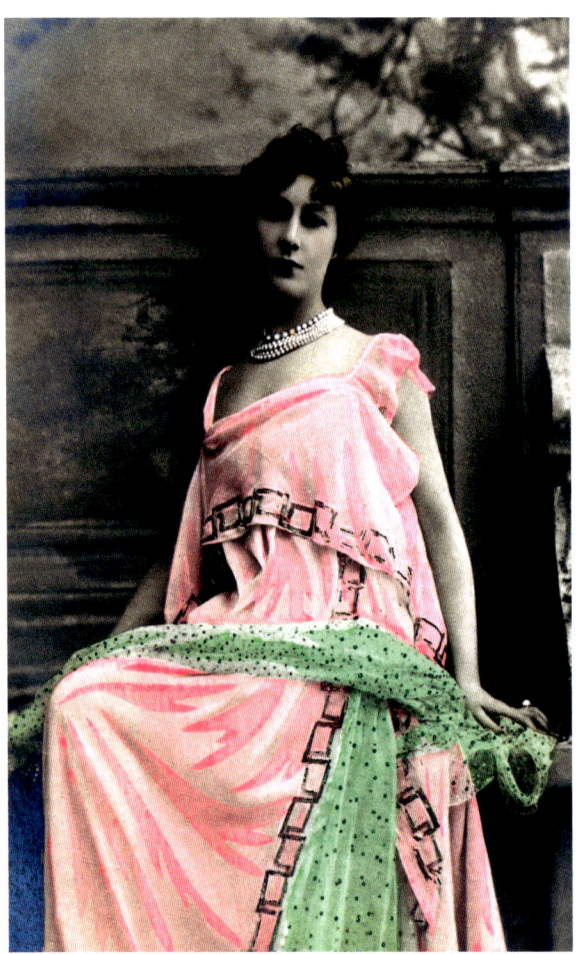

OPPOSITE PAGE

Picasso's Pink Period

Pablo Picasso was not a great colorist; he acknowledged this himself. Nevertheless, early on, critics designated his production in the years 1901–4 and 1904–7 as, respectively, the "blue period" and "pink period" based on the dominant color in his paintings. To the pink period belongs the famous *Les Demoiselles d'Avignon*. That city plays no part in the origin of the painting, which first bore the name of a brothel located on a street in Barcelona, the Carrer de Avinyó. Who renamed the work and gave it its definitive title? An art dealer? A critic? Writer and poet André Salmon, a friend of the painter?

Pablo Picasso, *Les Demoiselles d'Avignon*, 1907. Museum of Modern Art, New York.

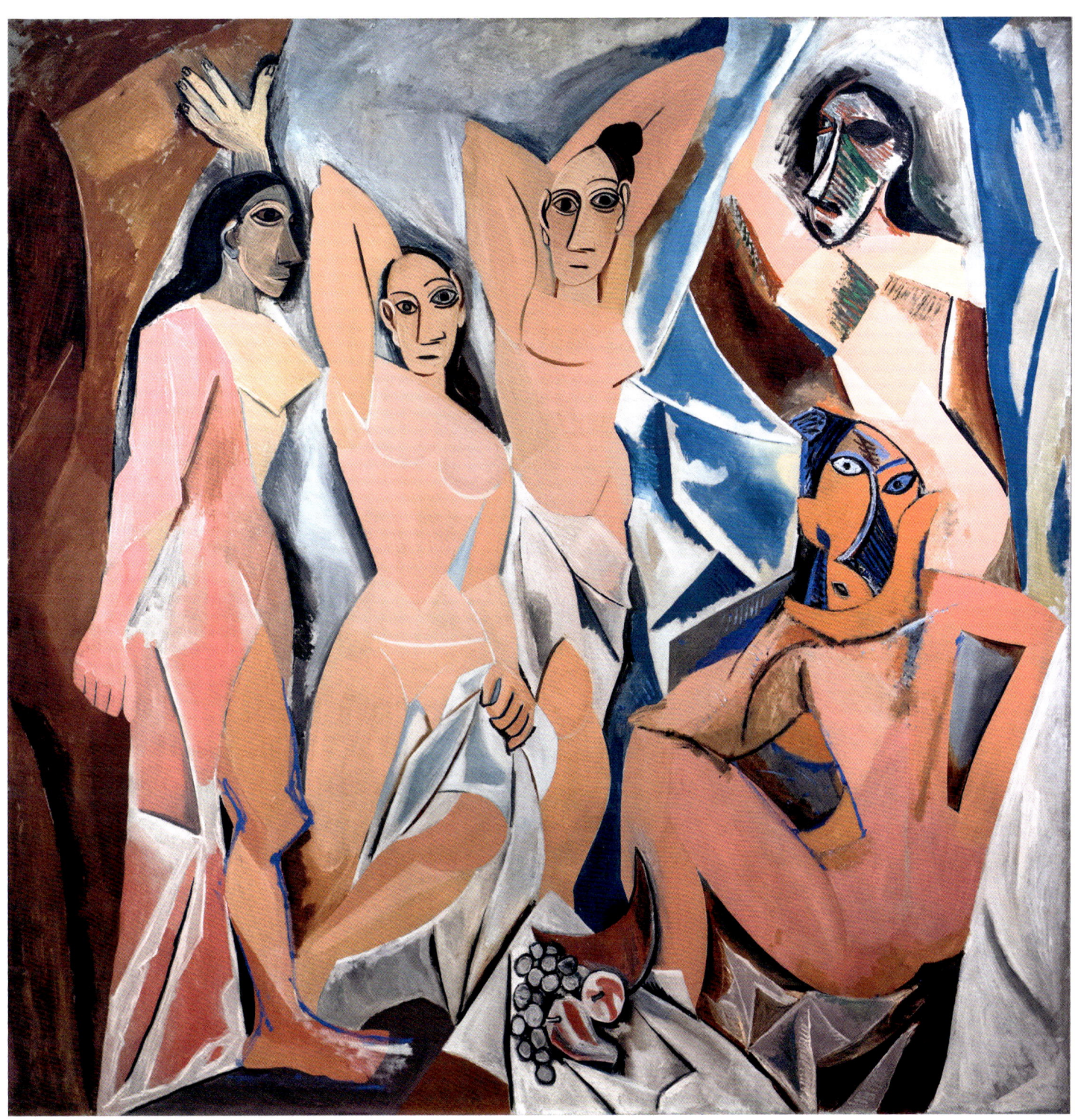

Gentleness, Pleasure, and Modernity

With all of contemporary pink's ambivalence, it would only be fair now to highlight its positive dimensions. There are not too many of them. The first ones again involve the relationship we have already noted between pink and the body, skin, and nudity. But contrary to what was just discussed, not everything about that relationship is sexual; beauty, gentleness, hygiene, and cleanliness play a part in it too, and no less of a part than eroticism or lust.

The issues of makeup, cosmetics, and lingerie have been covered. We must add here the one of hygiene, beginning with soap. Soap hardly changed in composition between the thirteenth century, when vegetable oils replaced the traditional animal fats, and the Romantic period, when considerable advances were made in the chemistry of soda and ammonias, and when the forms, fragrances, and colors of "soap cakes" started to diversify, not only for the wealthiest clientele, but for what we now call the middle classes. Beginning in the 1830s, soaps intended for personal hygiene ceased being uniformly white, ecru, or grayish, and took on pastel shades. Pink was the dominant shade, especially for bar soap meant for women. Not all soaps released a rose fragrance, but they were all expensive products as soap was still heavily taxed. Thus pink gradually became a color linked to hygiene and cleanliness because what was true for soap extended to various accessories for women's bathrooms, notably towels and washcloths, sometimes brushes, washbowls, bidets, and all categories of receptacles for personal use.

Today, soaps and soap bars are no longer luxury objects, and pink or pastels are often considered less elegant colors for them than white. That is how the pendulum swings in the history of colors: what was expensive and chic in one period ceases to be so, and fashion trends reverse or revert to the past. With regard to pink and cleanliness,

A Color to Shock

In the fashion world and advertising, it is necessary to stand out to attract public attention; color is a good means for doing so. Not long after opening her fashion house in Place Vendôme, Paris, in the mid-1930s, Elsa Schiaparelli adopted a particularly intense and saturated fuchsia pink as her emblematic color and gave it the name Shocking Pink. Shortly after that, she marketed a perfume with the same name, sold in bottles in the shape of a female bust–shocking in color and form. That was the intended goal.

Advertising poster for Elsa Schiaparelli's Shocking perfume, 1940.

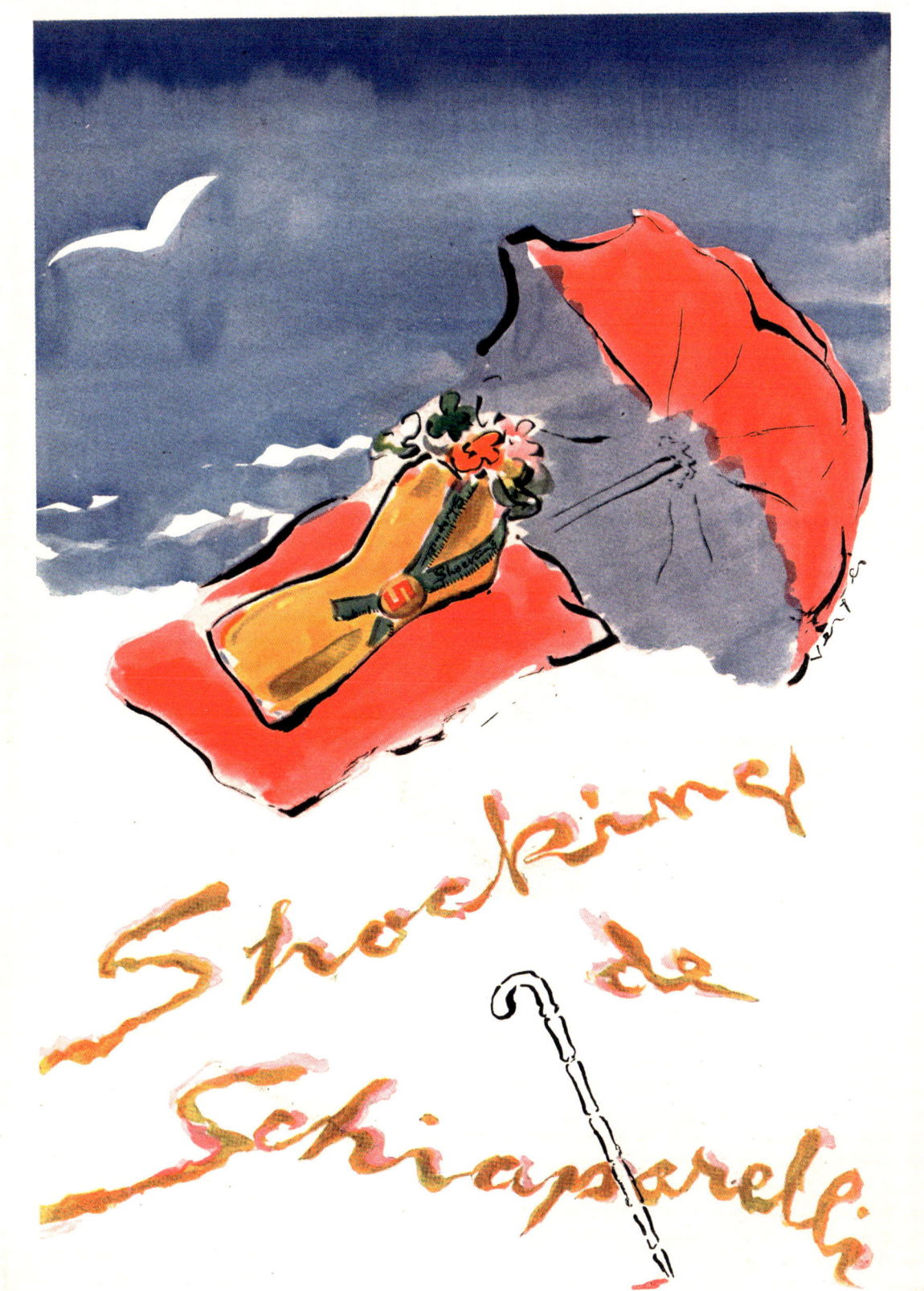

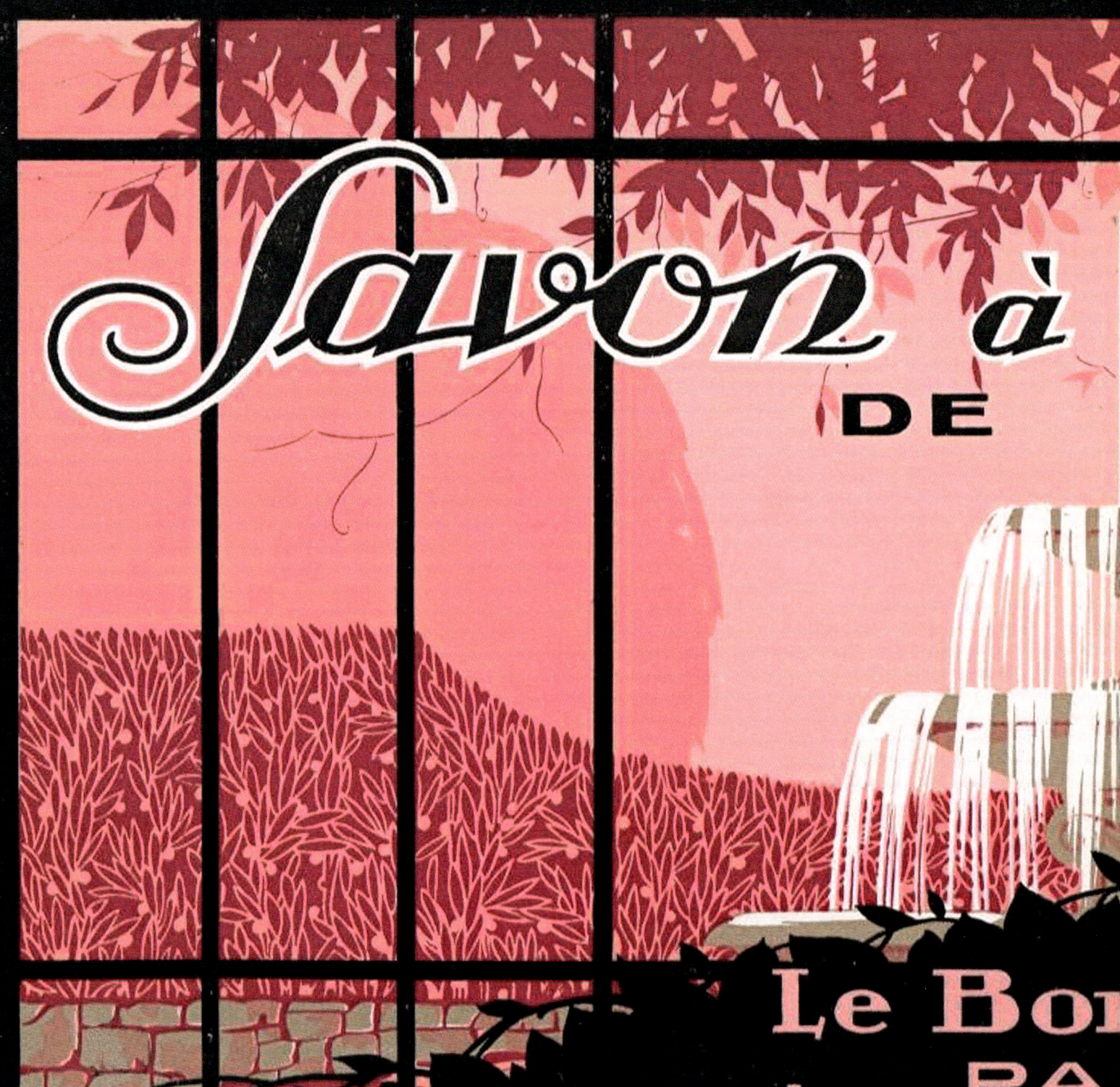

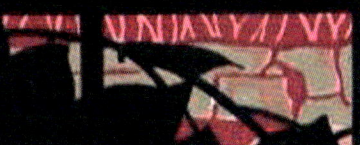

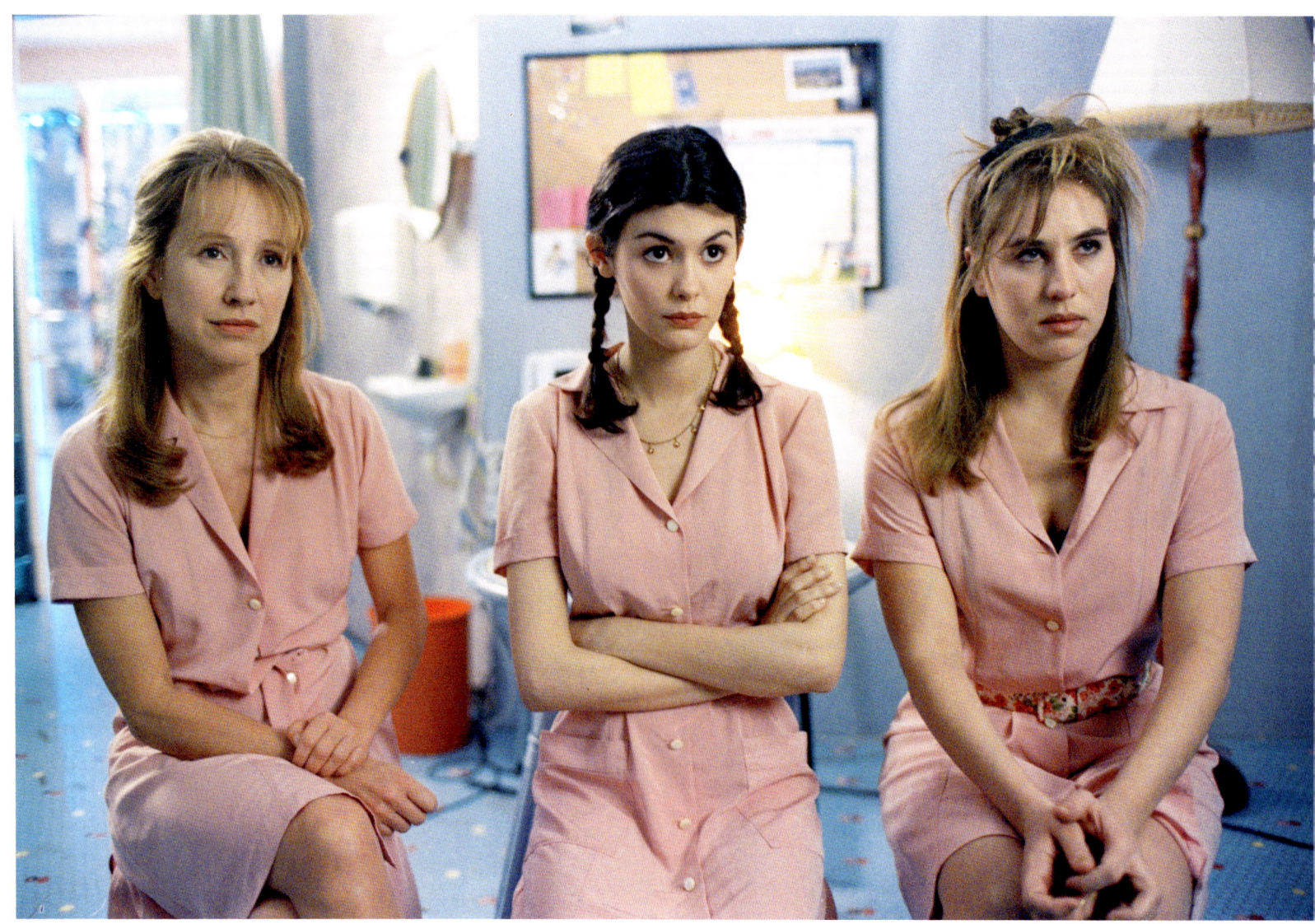

PREVIOUS PAGE SPREAD

Hygienic Pink

A long time ago, soaps did not come in different colors. Toward the end of the eighteenth century a few pastel shades made their appearance, but it was only in about 1830–50 that pink soaps, meant especially for women, began to be distributed on a large scale. Subsequently, pink became a color associated with hygiene and cleanliness, and started to compete with white in this domain. Gradually bathroom fixtures, toiletries, towels, and even toilet paper adopted this color.

Advertisement for a brand of soap made in Nice, ca. 1925. Bibliothèque Forney, Paris.

toilet paper provides another good example here. When toilet paper started to replace newspaper, it was thick, rough, and an indefinable shade of beige, brown, or gray. Then thinner, softer paper appeared, no longer in rolls but in pastel-colored sheets, usually pink. In the 1950s and even 1960s, pink toilet paper was considered more elegant than ordinary toilet paper, which still tended more or less toward a dirty beige. It cost more too. Then, in its turn, it became commonplace and had to compete with other shades, such as sky blue, light green, pale yellow, or mauve, which also became commonplace, if not vulgar, after which came a return to white. Today, what is chic for this mundane product is no longer a matter of color—white is still the thing—but instead its thickness, softness, strength, and environmental friendliness. Everywhere, white has once again become more hygienic than pink; it seems to clean better, whether it is a matter of soaps, sinks, toilets, tubs, towels, washcloths, or toilet paper. That was not the case fifty years ago; in the 1970s—the

OPPOSITE PAGE

Working in a Pink Smock

Men have never worn pink smocks, but women have done so frequently, starting in the 1920s and until the 1950s. For little girls, that began early, in elementary school (while boys wore gray or blue smocks), and then continued in many professions connected to bodily hygiene, medicine, beauty care, cooking, and diet.

Image from Tonie Marshall's film *Venus Beauty Institute* (1999), which takes place partly in a beauty salon.

"vulgar years," as they are sometimes called—pink held a place of honor in many bathrooms.

That was true as well in many other places, notably those connected to beauty care for women: hair and nail salons, perfume shops, facial and body care centers, and so on. Female practitioners and clients both wore pink smocks there, as protection for their clothing and to identify them, as some of them must have worn as schoolgirls, less stylish of course, but already meant to distinguish them from the boys wearing blue or gray. Here again, the link between pink, the body, and cleanliness is clear. We also find this "clean" pink on different items used directly on the skin for hygiene, protection, or health, such as wound dressings like band-aids, adhesive strips, and compresses. Nonetheless, in these areas as in many others today, the trend has often reverted back to white from pink.

This hygienic or medical pink is not exclusive to the skin; strangely, it applies to the inside of the mouth as well. As proof, consider the color of certain toothpastes and gum creams, or that of the base for dentures, made of a hard pink plastic material that imitates the color of the palate and gums. This prosthetic pink is more disturbing than appealing, however; it is almost unfit to be seen. Cleaning dentures must be done with the greatest discretion; taking them out or displaying them in public is absolutely taboo. Therefore advertising must resort to subterfuge when promoting denture cleaners through words or images.

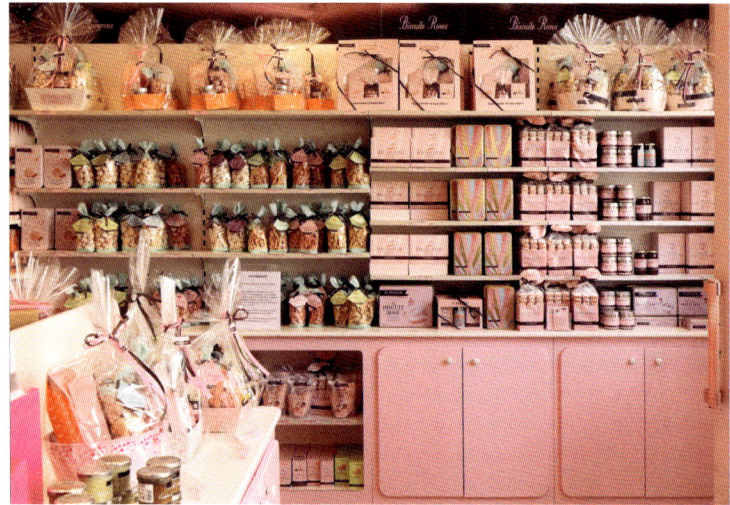

A good example of this is an advertisement for a denture cleaner that appeared on French television a few years ago. It showed a tall, clear glass full of water into which an anonymous hand dropped two white effervescent tablets; pretty bubbles then formed in the glass. That same hand then introduced into the precious liquid the dentures to be cleaned. Actually, not the dentures themselves, a horrifying prosthetic pink color, but the letters of the word *appareil* (dentures), all in uppercase, blue, and joined together as if they were a set of teeth. Everything about this sequence is instructive, beginning with the fact that a set of dentures is an object that cannot appear on-screen; it is too personal, degrading, and repugnant. Anything can be shown on television, including the worst atrocities, but not dentures. They must be replaced by their name, and not by the name usually used: *dentier*—a term just as taboo as the object it designates—but by their most proper name, the one used in oral medicine offices and specialized publications: *appareil*, a term generally followed by the adjective

that specifies its use: *dentaire*. But here, that adjective is omitted, probably because it evokes the horrible word *dentier*. That is a lot of taboos to work around. Thus the ingenious strategies of the advertisers do not stop there. To top the whole thing off and get away with this ad concealing a great number of taboos, they choose blue, a quiet, consensual color, and not just any blue but rather a lovely sky blue exuding calm, silence, and serenity. Pink would have called up the actual color of the dentures and their prosthetic function. That type of pink must not be seen.[19]

It is just the opposite, though, with treats and candies of this color, which are also put in the mouth. There are quite a number of them, delicate, sweet, and always a source of pleasure. Some have a long history as well, like sugared almonds and marshmallows. These were both medicines before becoming treats (in the sixteenth century), white before becoming pink (in the eighteenth century), and offered on the occasion of a ceremony (first marriage and then baptism) before being consumed as

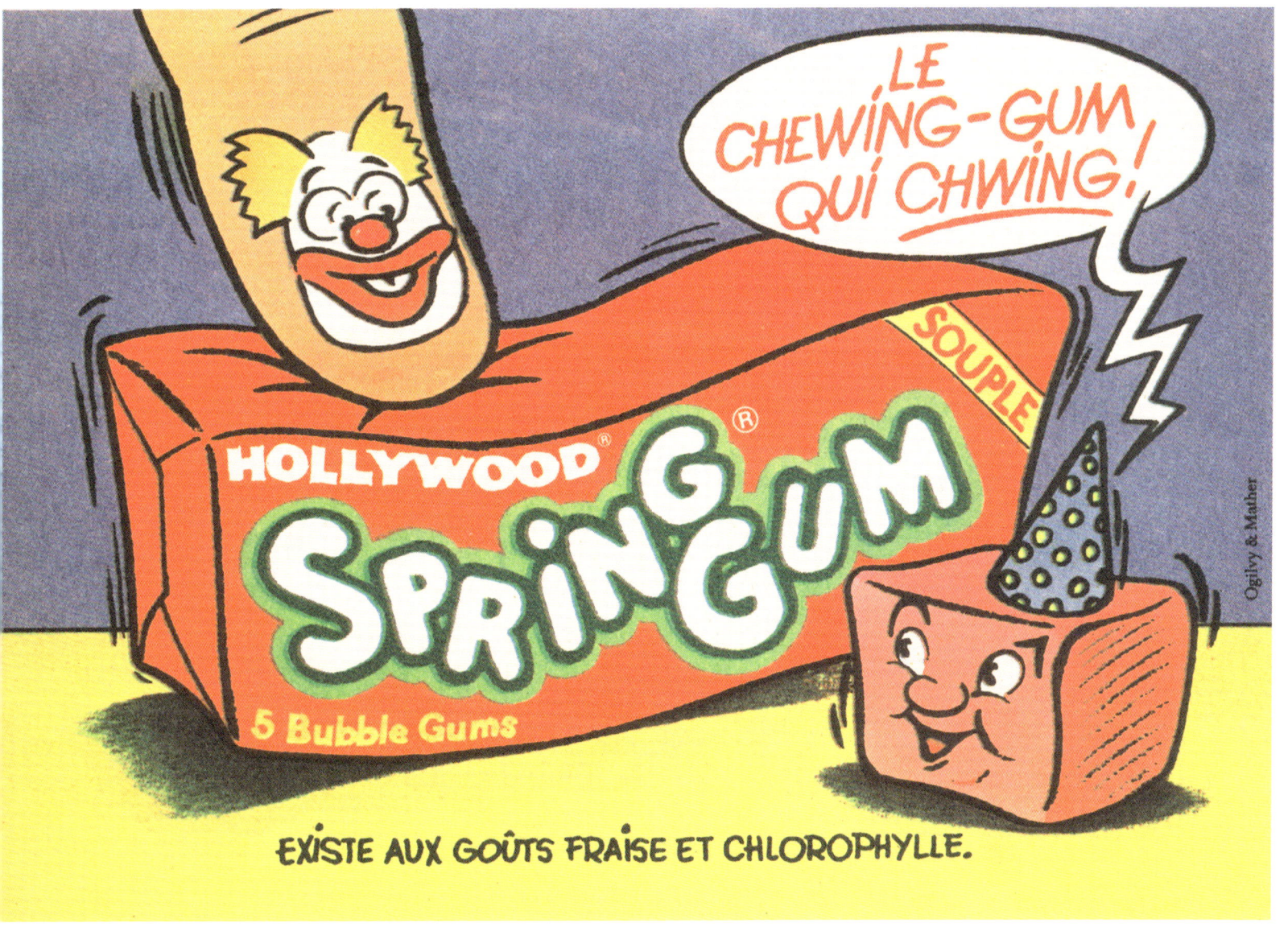

BELOW

Driving and Showing Off in Pink

A firmly established tradition holds that people drive faster in red cars and have more accidents. But what about pink cars? Such a color is more likely to attract attention than to enhance speed. Pink gets noticed because it is unusual. If most cars were pink, it would undoubtedly take a gray car to stand out and catch our eye.

Pink Cadillac that belonged to Elvis Presley, 1957.

OPPOSITE PAGE

A Pink Suit with a Sad Memory

Beginning in 1961, fashion icon and faithful Chanel client Jackie Kennedy loved to wear a pink suit with a navy blue collar, complete with a hat of the same shade, especially during official trips in cold weather. She was wearing it in Dallas, Texas, on November 22, 1963, when her husband was assassinated. The suit, spattered with the blood of the president of the United States, became a mythical object and even a relic.

President John F. Kennedy and his wife, Jackie, arriving at the Dallas airport, 1963.

simple sweets. Chewing gum, which appeared in the United States in 1871, is certainly a more recent development, but takes a similar course. For a long time it remained pink and slightly sweet before taking on whitish or greenish shades related to its mint flavor.

To the list of pink sweets and candies must be added pastries of all kinds that are decorated in pink to be enticing, please the eye, promise a sweet, sugary taste, make the mouth water, and prompt a choice; in a dish of multicolored candies, the pink ones have a good chance of being chosen first, especially among children. This is not the pink of happiness, but it closely resembles it. Pleasure and happiness frequently merge today, and pink has become their color.

In an entirely different domain, there is a contemporary pink that can also be considered positively, at least for a portion of the population that likes what seems modern, new, and original: this is the pink of haute couture. Originally, it was a matter of a rather transgressive color, meant to attract attention, break with habits or conventions, innovate, shock, and especially prompt comments. In the 1930s, fashion designer Elsa Schiaparelli, a friend of the surrealist painters, launched a line of clothing in an intense, saturated fuchsia pink as well as perfume packaged in the same color, its bottle in the provocative form of a nude female bust. It was all called Shocking Pink and unleashed a scandal.[20] It was not so much because the female bust was nude but rather because of the way pink

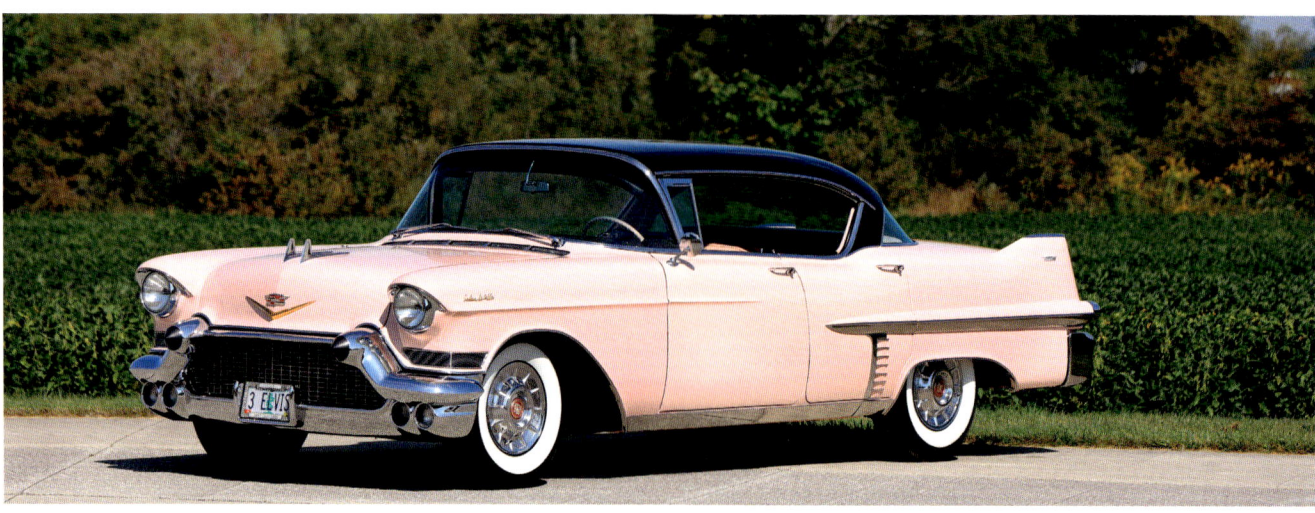

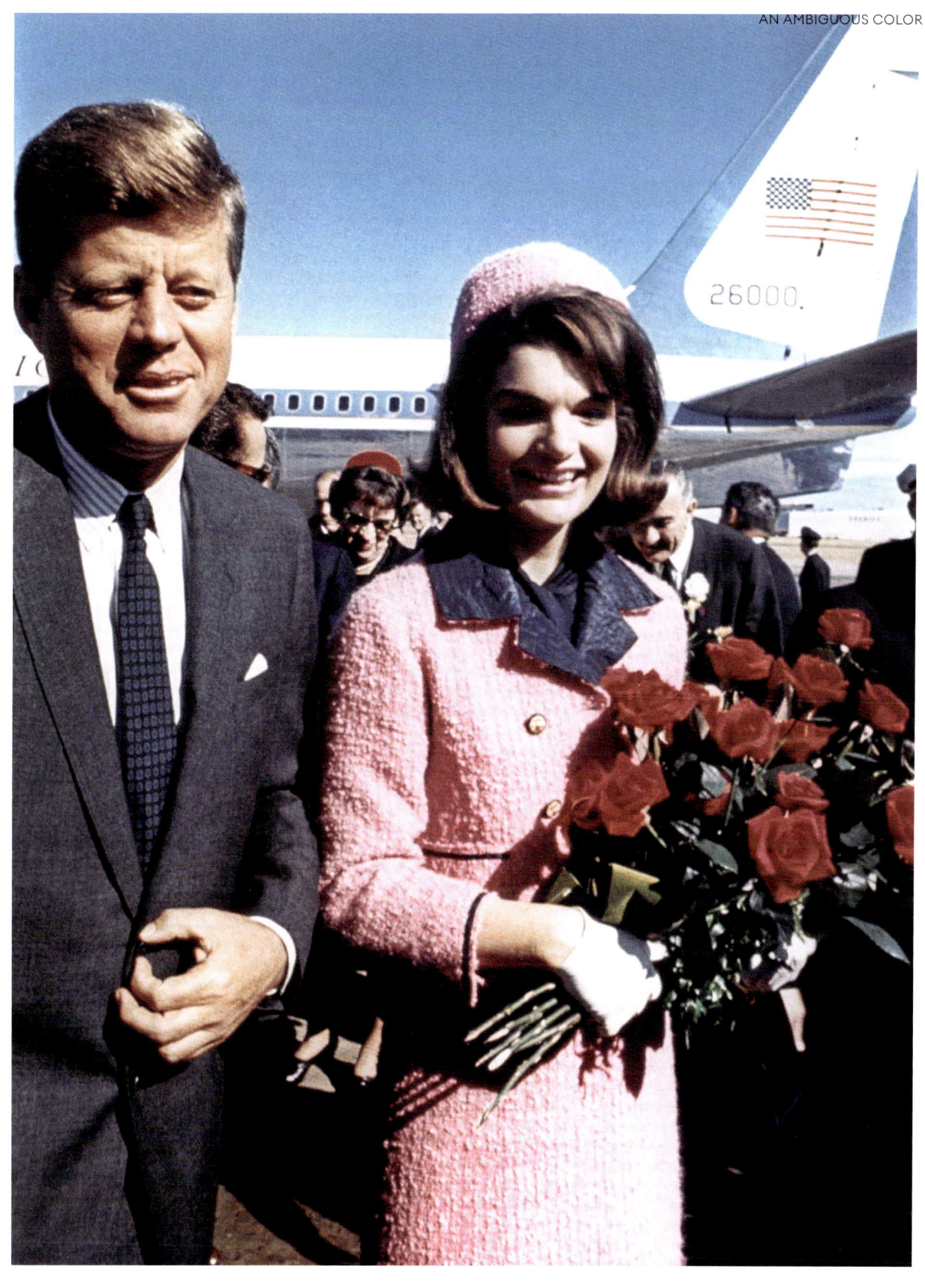

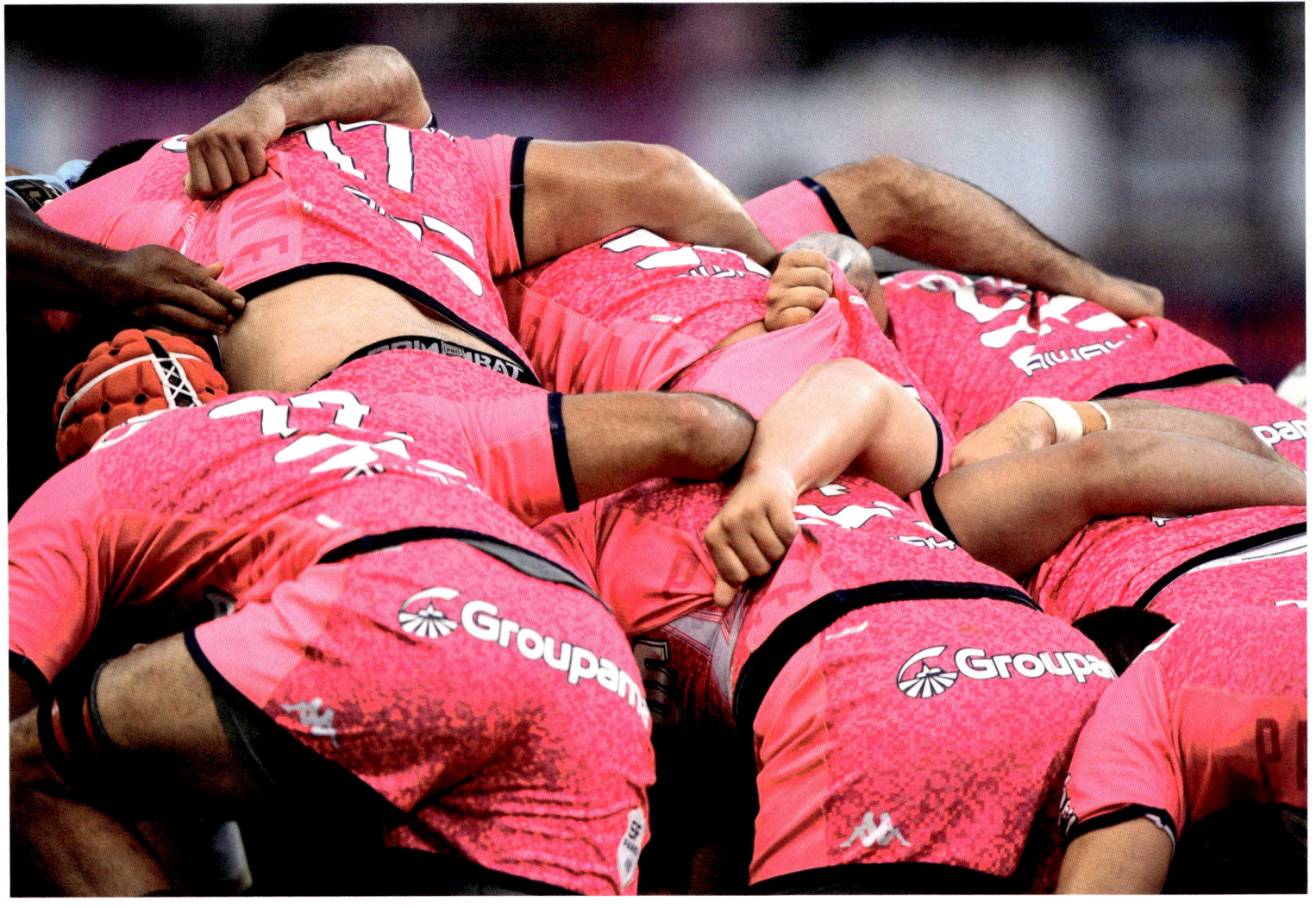

was being used. This was no longer a sweet, charming, delicate pink; this was a pink deliberately meant to be aggressive, flashy, and loud.

After World War II, that pink did not disappear from haute couture (or what claimed to be so), but its power and originality diminished, and it even became somewhat kitsch. This was the era when Marilyn Monroe, blonder than ever, had photographs taken in pink dresses or bathing suits, and the era when film or media stars drove pink Rolls-Royces or Cadillacs. On soccer and then rugby fields, referees gradually stopped wearing their traditional black jerseys to adopt yellow or pink ones, making them more visible on television, but costing them a share of their authority. A bit later, on those same playing fields, the teams themselves displayed a flashy pink sometimes combined with white, blue, green, or black stripes, transforming the players into wandering minstrels. With pink, everything becomes spectacle. The final blow was struck by pop art, which made this extreme pink into a kind of agenda to brighten up life. Pop art also used it perversely, delighting in presenting pink dragons and sharks, pink hammers and pipes, and even—transgression of transgressions!—pink hearts and flowers! [21]

Thus the playful side of the contemporary "pinkathon" continues. It is undeniable, and unlike most of the childishness and eccentricities of a kind of falsely artistic high fashion, its success spans decades. Its emblem is a fictional creature who, as soon as it appeared, won nothing but sympathy: the Pink Panther. Actually, this feline more closely resembles a puma or jaguar, or even a large cat, rather than a true panther. But above all it is a cartoon character: rangy silhouette, thin limbs, hands with four fingers, and eyes located at the top of the head. As for its body, it is entirely pink, its belly, muzzle, and the inside

Pink on the Rugby Field

The array of colors worn on the sports field has never stopped diversifying over the course of the decades. But it was color television that, starting in the years 1970–80, dealt the decisive blow. Referees gave up their black uniforms to dress in orange, yellow, or green, and pink made its appearance on jerseys and shorts, even among rugby players–a transformation that was inconceivable fifteen years earlier.

The Stade Français team entering a scrum against Perpignan, October 8, 2022.

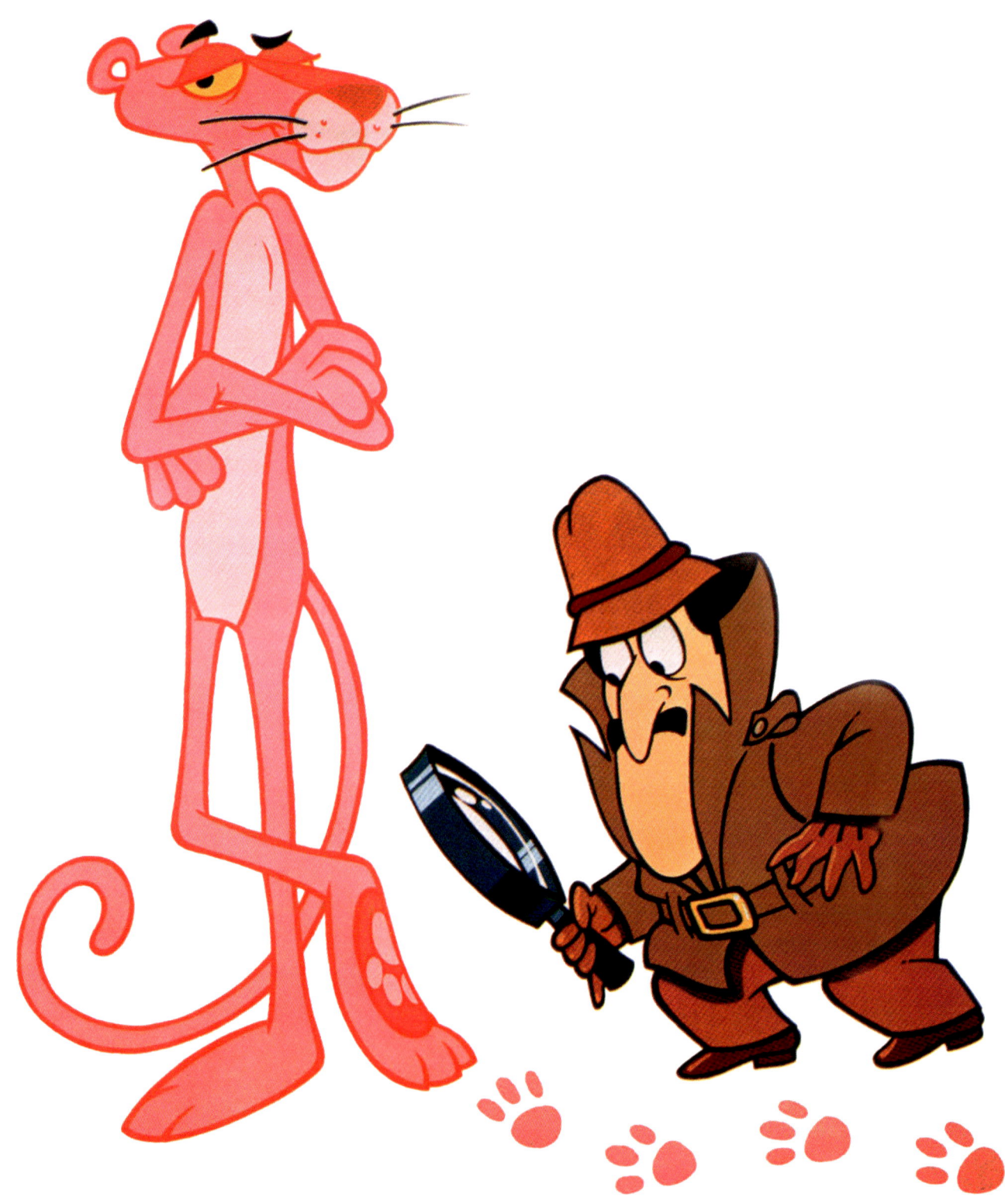

of its ears a slightly lighter pink than the other parts. This animal appeared for the first time in 1963 in the credits at the end of a comedy detective film by Blake Edwards, *The Pink Panther*, the name of a famous stolen jewel sought by the hilarious inspector Jacques Clouseau. An immediate success, the animal became the star of many short films, and then television series, cartoons, video games, and spin-off products of all kinds.[22] In films, each of its appearances is accompanied by the same theme music of a couple notes, which itself has become emblematic of a certain playful absurdity appropriate to our modern societies. Its composer, Henry Mancini, is famous for the music he wrote for films.

This endearing panther, calm, phlegmatic, and mute, whose gestures and movements are more a matter of mime than action, has done more for the glory of pink than all the merchandising for little girls or eccentricities of pop art. Let us leave to it the task of closing out this history of a color all of its own, both prim and rowdy, romantic and eccentric, adored by some of our contemporaries, rejected by others.

A Famous Panther

A slender feline with long limbs, a flat head, yellow eyes, and a pale belly, the Pink Panther is a cartoon character that appeared for the first time on-screen in 1963. Its success was immediate, all the more so because each of its appearances was accompanied by a few notes, always the same, serving as its sonorous attribute. For over half a century, this silent, surreal panther has contributed more to the popularity of pink than any other figure, image, creation, or fiction.

Image drawn from the trailer of the film by Blake Edwards, *The Pink Panther*, 1963.

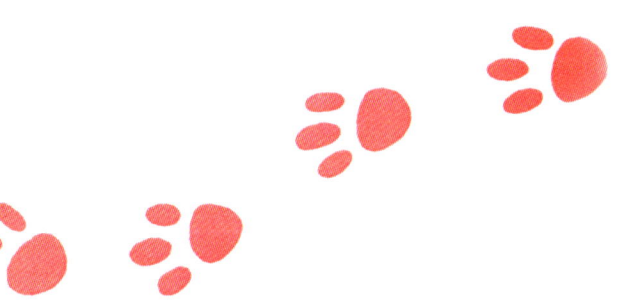

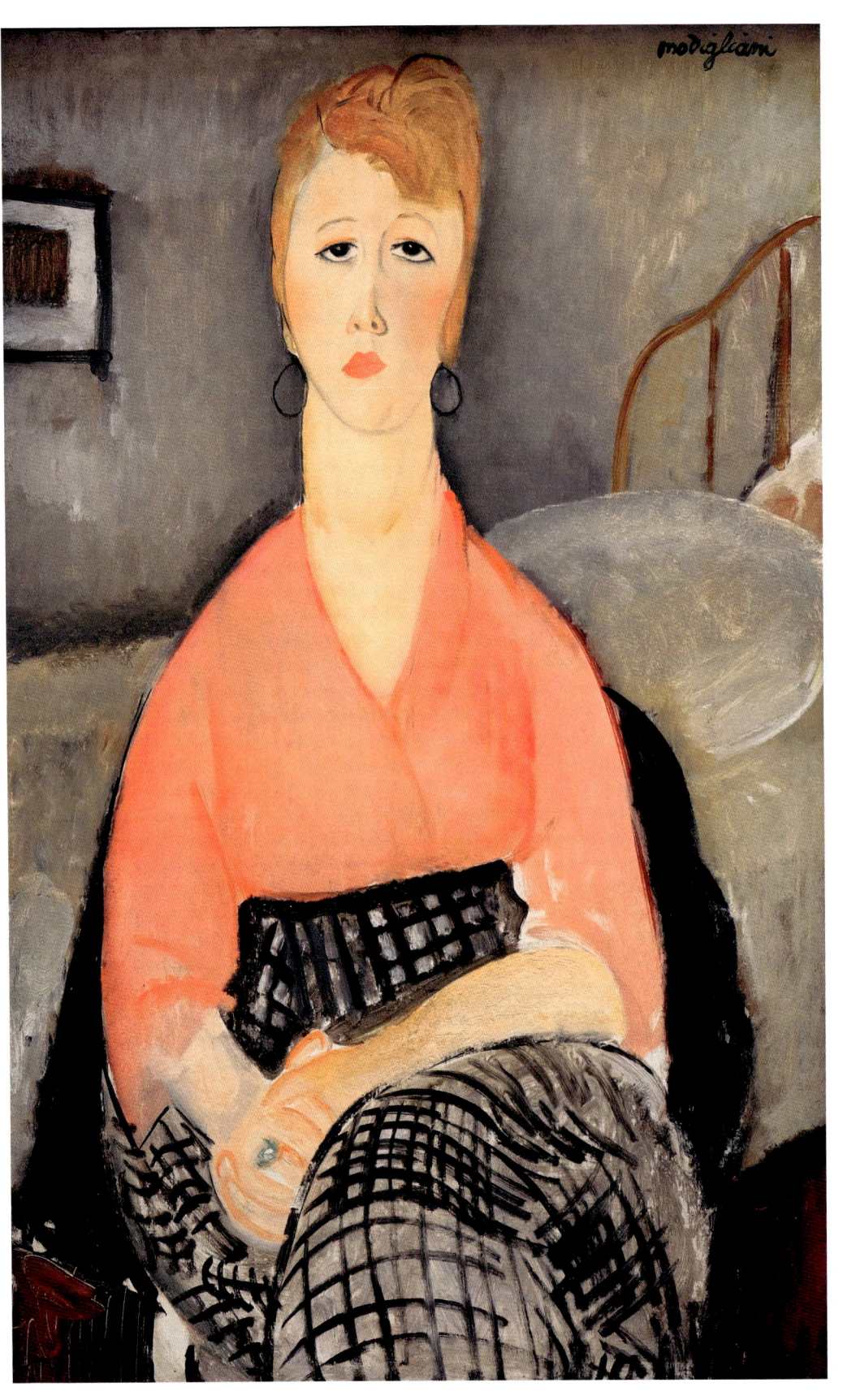

From Orange to Pink

Amedeo Modigliani was a great painter of oranges and red tones, but he also excelled in the range of pinks, less common on his palette and sometimes merging with the other two. This woman in a pink blouse is a superb example. It is one of the last portraits he painted, a few months before his death. He was not yet thirty-six years old.

Amedeo Modigliani, *Pink Blouse*, 1919. Musée Angladon–Collection Jacques Doucet, Avignon.

Conclusion

Historians are neither physicists nor neurologists. For them, what "makes" colors is not the light, nor is it the eye-brain mechanism in conjunction with the perceptive phenomena it processes. It is society, with its definitions, classifications, laws, and practices, often different from those of science. Thus the history of colors is essentially a social history, and the number of colors is not limited to seven, as in the solar spectrum—where they form a continuum, moreover—but instead includes four more, at least in contemporary Western culture.

For the social sciences, there are in fact eleven colors, six principal ones—white, red, black, green, yellow, and blue—and five often described as "half colors"—pink, orange, purple, gray, and brown. After that, there are no more, only shades and shades of shades that number in the thousands, and have no history or symbolism of their own. Furthermore, those shades vary constantly according to light, material, medium, technique, the eye of the viewer, and the hour of the day. They are not colors—that is to say, abstract categories that exist without needing to be materialized; they are only ranges or variations of the eleven basic colors. To speak on the radio of red, green, or blue without any visuals presents no problem for listeners.

On the other hand, to speak of Bismarck red, government green, or the blue of the South Seas without an image or color sample is more problematic.

The first six volumes of the present collection were each devoted to one of the principal colors. The seventh, entirely dedicated to pink, has just introduced the series for the colors of the second group. I am using that vague wording intentionally to avoid any inappropriate connotations. "Secondary colors" would be a bit depreciatory, and "complementary colors" would put too much emphasis on scientific theories that are reductive and now outdated (notably the ones that exclude green from the "primary" colors, or deny black and white the status of colors in their own right). The expression half colors is more fitting if we consider that pink, purple, orange, gray, and brown are frequently obtained through mixing colors, yet that fact must not let us deem them any less valuable. They really are true colors, as the history of pink has just fully demonstrated.

That history has also allowed me to highlight the distinctive characteristics belonging to this second group—characteristics that constitute almost as many difficulties, and ones that this historian did not encounter in studying the six principal colors. It is worthwhile to mention them here, not only by way of concluding this long inquiry into pink, but by way of introducing the volumes that will follow, because we will encounter them again with regard to orange, gray, purple, and brown.

As in the case of pink, the history of these four half colors is neither continuous nor homogeneous but instead presents many chronological "parentheses" and thematic "voids," essentially due to gaps in the documentation. No such gaps existed for red, green, yellow, or blue, much less for white and black. With regard to the colors in the second group, on the other hand, there are periods about which the historian, lacking evidence—whether archaeological, textual, lexical, or pictorial—has nothing to say, except to repeat that the lack of documentation can in itself have documentary value. That does not lead very far and hardly provides opportunity for expansion. In the European history of pink, as we have just seen, the gaps involve time periods prior to the fourth century BCE, when the first pigments in this color appeared in Macedonian paintings. They also involve a later period, the several centuries that separate paleo-Christian art from Ottonian illumination dating from about the year 1000. In that long slice of time, pink is practically absent from images and artworks, just as it is absent from the lexicon and texts. Finally they involve, although to a lesser degree, most of the seventeenth century, as much for the study of daily life as for that of artistic creation. How to trace the history of pink between the end of mannerism and appearance of the rococo style? Documentation is lacking, especially if we compare it to the following period. Now what is true for pink will be true similarly for orange, gray, and purple for those same periods, and even for other, longer, or more numerous ones. Here again, the historian must confront the silence of the sources, not a difficulty encountered for the six principal colors, continually and abundantly documented from the time of ancient Greece to the twenty-first century.

These gaps and silences probably explain why the few available works devoted to the history of pink are limited to the contemporary period and focus, as it were, on only one issue: the relationship between color and gender. This is certainly an interesting question, particularly within the context of a problem linked to the most recent current events, but it is a question that clearly represents only a small part of the history of pink in European societies. Why limit that history to modern, gender-related uses of the color? There is much more to say about the history of pink, as this book hopes to have demonstrated. With regard to orange, we must not fall into the same trap, repeating the standard lines on redheads, the red fox, or vitamin C. As for the symbolism of purple, it will extend far beyond liturgical practices, bishops' robes (which were green for a long time before becoming purple), and feminist emblems. Reducing the history of a color to the most recent periods is a common mistake that, understandable as it is, must be avoided. When, for the lack of sufficient documents, a subject cannot be treated by tracing it through the centuries, there is great temptation to artificially exaggerate the importance of a particular point or moment to the detriment of the general ideas and ordinary course of history. The anecdotal, circumstantial, exceptional, and sometimes provocative then supplant true historical synthesis.

Another consequence of uneven documentation and discontinuity in source material is the more limited choice of iconography for the half colors as compared to the principal ones. In this area as well there are gaps and absences that did not exist for white, black, red, green, yellow, or blue. Locating a few color documents from the Roman Republic or feudal period that display a bit of pink has not been an easy task.

Nevertheless, that is not the essential difficulty, which clearly lies in the uncertain nature of the chromatic fields of the five half colors. Over the course of its history, pink, as I have noted, maintained relatively fluid boundaries with red, orange, yellow, and white. Likewise, purple shares ill-defined borders even today with blue on one side and red on the other, as it did in earlier times with black, gray, or brown. Now, corresponding to these somewhat unstable chromatic fields are semantic and symbolic fields that fluctuate just as much, sometimes wavering between many poles, all far removed from one another. Incarnadine and baby pink—to take two examples that have just been discussed—belong to the same chromatic field, but not to the same social or symbolic fields. It is no simple task to determine what connects them historically. Similarly, to demonstrate the relationship between candy pink, lascivious pink, and socialist pink requires several detours even while emphasizing the richness of the meanings linked to this color. Such obstacles existed for the six principal colors, but their definitions and boundaries were better established and did not have to be revisited.

Things will go differently for the half colors. Their history is certainly just as instructive and exciting, but it is trickier to trace. Pink has been a particularly telling example in this regard.

NEXT PAGE SPREAD

The Deceptive Plenitude of Rose Skies

When Nicolas de Staël discovered the light of Provence and then Sicily, his palette underwent a transformation. Formerly a great painter of grays, he opted for warmer, more vivid colors. Pink played a role here. At the same time, his paintings became less tactile, less thick, and smoother. Thick, layered impasto with "visible seams" gave way to large, flat, uniform surfaces with hardly any relief, as if a certain serenity now accompanied the painter. Nothing could have been further from the truth.

Nicolas de Staël, *Agrigente*, 1954. Private collection.

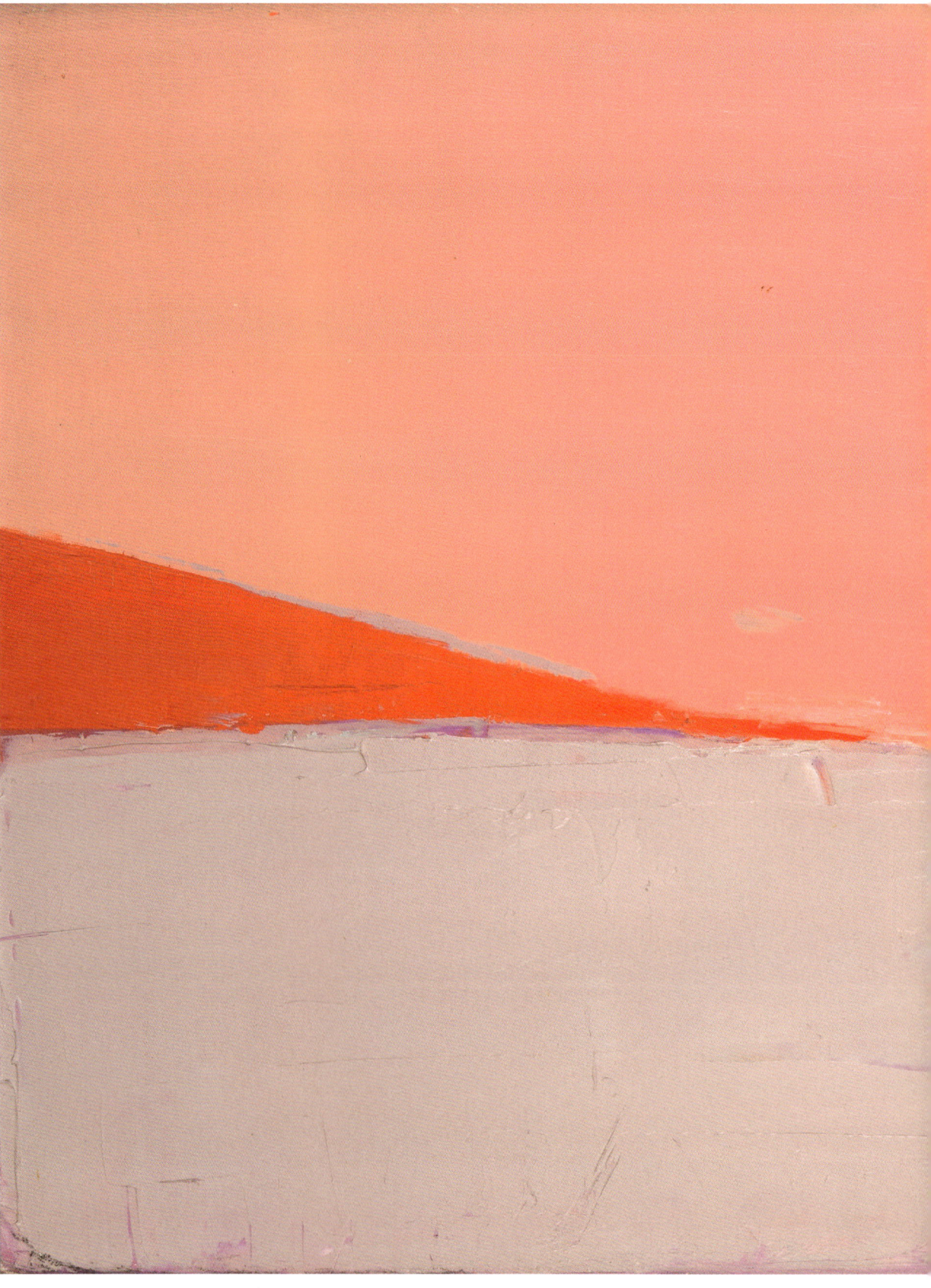

Notes

A DISCREET COLOR

1. Egyptian painting, on the other hand, reveals earlier pink tones, as do Chinese and Indian painting. But they are far removed from Europe. Further on we will consider the Fayum mummy portraits of Roman Egypt in which the faces present flesh tones that can be included in the range of pinks.

2. On this painted funerary decor, which has greatly enriched and renewed our knowledge of ancient Greek painting, see for the question of pigments and colors H. Brécoulaki, *La Peinture funéraire de Macédoine: Emplois et fonctions de la couleur, V[e]–IIe s. avant J.-C.*, 2 vols. (Paris, 2006).

3. S. Descamps-Lequime, ed., *Peinture et couleur dans le monde grec antique* (Paris, 2007).

4. C. Blanc, *Grammaire des arts du dessin: Architecture, sculpture, peinture . . .* (Paris, 1867).

5. A lacquer is a pigment of both plant and mineral origin. To obtain it, pieces of cloth dyed with a good colorant had to be reprocessed by extracting the remaining dyestuff from them and then chemically precipitating it onto a mineral base (kaolin or aluminum salts). Finely grinding all of this resulted in a good-quality pigment, solid and stable in the light. Yet it was difficult to use over a large surface. In the Middle Ages, lacquers involved primarily red tones (madder, kermes, or brazilwood lacquers), blue tones (indigo lacquer), and yellow tones (weld lacquer).

6. For example, they used a lighter skin tone for men of higher social status, a darker one for slaves, and a swarthy tone for East Asians.

7. J. Riederer, "Egyptian Blue," in *Artists' Pigments*, ed. E. W. Fitzhugh (Oxford, 1997), 3:23–45; F. Delamare, *Bleus en poudres: De l'art à l'industrie* (Paris, 2008).

8. Rubrica is a red makeup with a base of ocher or clay rich in iron oxide.

9. Fucus is a red makeup with an orcein base.

10. Ovid, *The Art of Love*, bk. 3, 210. Trans. J. Michie (New York, 2002).

11. It is time to put an end to the idea that during the Middle Ages, the poorest classes wore shabby, undyed, soiled, torn clothing, close to rags. That is not true.

All clothes were dyed, but with the most modest clothing, dyes took badly and soon faded.

12. Our Lady of Chartres Cathedral, north window devoted to the story of Noah, bay 47, completed ca. 1210–15.

13. See the recipes proposed by the monk Theophilus and compiled around 1120 in his *De diversis artibus*, ed. J. G. Hawthorne and C. S. Smith (Oxford, 1989), bk. 1, chap. 1.

14. F. Cabrol, *Dictionnaire d'archéologie chrétienne et de liturgie* (Paris, 1914), vol. 3, cols. 3003–4; S. P. Paci, *Storia delle vesti liturgiche* (Milan, 2008), 145–46; J. P. Brooke-Little, *Boutell's Heraldry* (London, 1978), 34–35; A. M. Hildebrandt, *Wappenfibel* (Neustadt an der Aisch, 1981), 17th ed., 26–28.

15. On the ancient and medieval rainbow, see C. B. Boyer, *The Rainbow: From Myth to Mathematics* (New York, 1959); B. S. Eastwood, "Robert Grosseteste's Theory of the Rainbow: A Chapter in the History of Non-Experimental Science," *Archives internationales d'histoire des science* 19 (1966): 313–32; D. C. Lindberg, "Roger Bacon's Theory of the Rainbow: Progress or Regress?," *Isis* 17 (1968): 235–48; M.-T. Lorcin, "L'arc-en-ciel au XIIIe siècle," *Senefiance* 24 (1988): 229–51; M. Blay, *Les Figures de l'arc-en-ciel* (Paris, 1995); B. Maitte, *Histoire de l'arc-en-ciel* (Paris, 2005).

16. Among scientists, philosophers, and theologians who were interested in the rainbow in the thirteenth century, let us mention Robert Grosseteste, John Pecham, Roger Bacon, Thierry de Freiberg, and Witelo.

17. There are a few elements worth noting in older works. See F. Bock, *Geschichte der liturgischen Gewänder im Mittelalter*, 3 vols. (Berlin, 1859–69); J. W. Legg, *Notes on the History of the Liturgical Colours* (London, 1882) (addresses especially the modern period); J. Braun, *Die liturgische Gewandung in Occident und Orient* (Frieburg im Briesgau, 1907); G. Haupt, *Die Farbensymbolik in der sakralen Kunst des abendländischen Mittelalters* (Leipzig, 1844) (often cited, always disappointing). For the paleo-Christian period, some information can be found in *Dictionnaire d'archéologie chrétienne et de liturgie*, vol. 3 (1914), cols. 2999–3001. On pontifical uses, see B. Schimmelpfennig, *Die*

Zeremonienbücher der römischen Kurie im Mittelalter (Tübingen, 1973), 286–88, 350–51; M. Diekmans, *Le Cérémonial papal* (Brussels, 1977), 1:223–26. Allow me to cite as well a short passage on liturgical colors in my study, "L'Église et la couleur des origines à la Réforme," *Bibliothèque de l'École des chartres* 147 (1989): 203–30; I discuss a few elements from it here.

18. See, for example, the short Irish treatise in Gaelic (eleventh century?) edited by J. Moran, *Essays on the Origin, Doctrines, and Discipline of the Early Irish Church* (Dublin, 1864), 171–72, and the subject of a study by D. Barbet-Massin, "Le traité irlandais sur les couleurs liturgiques du *Leabhar Breac*," in *Corona monastica: Moines bretons de Landévennec: Histoire et mémoire celtique. Mélanges offerts au père Marc Simon*, ed. L. Lemoine and B. Merdrignac (Rennes, 2004), 101–10.

19. Lacking a newer edition, which would be extremely welcome, we may still consult the one printed by J.-B. Migne in his *Patrologia latina*, vol. 217, cols. 774–916 (colors = cols. 779–802).

20. Migne, *Patrologia latina*, vol. 217, col. 813.

21. The text of Durand's chapter on the liturgical colors (*De coloribus libellus*, bk. 3, chap. 18) can be read in the beautiful scholarly edition of the *Rationale* by A. Davril and T. M. Thibodeau (Turnhout, 1995), 223–29 (*Corpus christianorum, continuatio medievalis*, vol. 140). More verbose than Cardinal Lothar on purple (229), Durand does not use a noun to designate it—it was undoubtedly too early for this somewhat imprecise shade—but rather the phrase *color violaceus*.

22. A. Ott, *Étude sur les couleurs en vieux français* (Paris, 1899), 94–95; J. André, *Étude sur les termes de couleur dans la langue latine* (Paris, 1949), 195–99; A. M. Kristol, *Color: Les langues romanes devant le phénomène de la couleur* (Berne, 1978), 155–58, 223–43; W. Jervis Jones, *German Colour Terms: A Study in Their Historical Evolution from Earliest Times to the Present* (Amsterdam, 2013), 372–405.

23. Nonetheless, we do not know the colors of many coats of arms. On wax seals, for example, a principal source for studying medieval coats of arms, nothing indicates the colors, not even the workshop practice of using a code of

hachures or guilloche patterns to express one color or another. Such codes did not appear until the early seventeenth century, and then only on engraved images, not on seals. Therefore we encounter this difficulty in various parts of Europe, for various individuals, families, or communities that bore monochromatic or *plain* shields—that is, void of figures, parts, or partitions.

24. D. L. Galbreath and L. Jéquier, *Manuel du Blason* (Lausanne, 1977), 91–100; M. Pastoureau, *Traité d'heraldique*, 2nd ed. (Paris, 1995), 100–121; C. Boudreau, *L'Heritage symbolique des hérauts d'armes* (Paris, 2006), 1:494–503; M. Pastoureau, *L'Art héraldique au Moyen Âge* (Paris, 2009), 77–92.

25. These terms belonging to French (and Anglo-Norman) did not all appear at the same time: *or*, *argent*, *azur*, and *gueules* existed from the beginning, meaning the mid-twelfth century; *sable* is more recent; and *sinople* began being used as a synonym for green only in the second half of the fourteenth century.

26. K. Nyrop, "*Gueules*, histoire d'un mot," *Romania* 48, no. 592 (1922): 559–70.

27. Nyrop, "*Gueules*, histoire d'un mot," 560. See also A. Chéruel, *Dictionnaire historiques des institutions, moeurs et coutumes de la France* (Paris, 1874), 1:513.

28. In the eighteenth century, the coat of arms for Manosque in Provence included this color: *écartelé d'azur et de gueules à quatre mains de carnation* (in quarters of blue and red with four hands of pink).

AN ADMIRED COLOR

1. Archivo di Stato, Florence, Guidice degli appelli di nulitta, ms. 117. The volume includes 308 pages and measures 30 × 24 cm. The title *Prammatica* (meaning "regulatory practices") seems to have been given to it in the sixteenth century.

2. For a first approach, see L. Gérard-Marchant, "Compter et nommer l'étoffe à Florence au Trecento (1343)," *Médiévales* 29 (1995): 87–104. The manuscript, copied on paper, was badly damaged when the Arno flooded in 1966 and remains

difficult to read. Despite skillful restoration, about 10 percent of the text was permanently lost.

3. L. Eisenbart, *Kleiderordnungen der deutschen Städte* (Göttingen, 1962); A. Hunt, *A History of Sumptuary Laws* (New York, 1996); M. A. Ceppari Ridolfi and P. Turrini, *Il mulino delle vanità* (Sienna, 1996); M. G. Muzzarelli, *Guardaroba medievale: Vesti e società dal XIII al XVI secolo* (Bologna, 1999).

4. See above notes 2 and 3.

5. L. Gérard-Marchant, C. Klapisch-Zuber, et al., *Draghi rossi e querce azzurre: Elenchi descrittivi di abiti di lusso, Firenze, 1343–1345* (Florence, 2013) (SISMEL, *Memoria scripturarum* 6, *testi latini* 4). Thanks to Laurence Gérard-Merchant and the Italian Archives for the courage to publish this entire document on paper.

6. Beginning in the mid-twelfth century, dyeing with madder became a true industry. Madder was grown intensively in certain regions heavily engaged in textile production (Brabant, Flanders, Zealand, Normandy, Lombardy), to be exported throughout Europe. Many medieval authors describe madder cultivation in detail: the soil had to be cool, calcareous, well irrigated; seeds were planted in March; after eighteen months the plant was tall enough to provide leaves and stems that served as fodder (which dyed a light red the milk of cows and sheep), but it was three years before the roots could be dug; and the roots were then dried, peeled, and ground through a mill. The powder thus obtained was used for dyeing. Growing madder was relatively easy but required rigorous protection against rats; the plant bore blackish berries that those animals loved to eat. On cloth, madder produced beautiful red tones, but they were dull and lackluster. That was why kermes was preferred for luxury cloths and silks, despite madder's lower cost and great stability as a dye. See M. Pastoureau, *Rouge: Histoire d'une couleur* (Paris, 2016), 36–39, 96–100. See also the English edition: M. Pastoureau, *Red: The History of a Color*, trans. J. Gladding (Princeton, 2017), 37–39, 90–93.

7. The insects of the Mediterranean are different from those of eastern Europe (Poland, Russia, and Ukraine). For those areas, it is better to call them "cochineal."

8. Orcein, the dyestuff, was a relatively expensive product because of the difficulty of obtaining and complexity of transforming orcinol. But it produces beautiful light tones tending toward pink or purple, and requires a weak mordant.

9. To mordant consists of adding to the dye bath a *mordant*, an astringent substance that rids wool of its impurities and helps to make the dyestuff deeply penetrate the fibers of thread, yarn, or cloth. Without a mordant, dyeing is impossible or will not take. The main mordants used for medieval dyeing were alum (for luxury dyeing), tartar (a salt deposit that wine leaves on the bottom and sides of casks), lime, vinegar, urine, and the ash of certain wood (walnut or chestnut). Certain mordants work better for certain dyes or textiles. According to proportions, combinations (alum and tartar, for example), and practices, any particular tone or shade can be obtained within the range of a given color. With madder, for instance, the palette can be extensive, from orange to purple, and include all the pinks, crimsons, dark reds, and scarlets. If the mordant is successful, all of these tones are extremely solid.

10. As mentioned earlier, to transform a colorant into a pigment, a certain amount of concentrated dyestuff had to be collected on fabric and chemically precipitated onto a mineral base (usually aluminum salts). With grinding, dilution, and various additives, a lacquer was obtained.

11. On recipe collections, see M. P. Merrifield, *Original Treatises Dating from the XIIth to the XVIIIth Centuries on the Art of Painting*, 2 vols. (London, 1849); G. Loumyer, *Les Traditions techniques de la peinture médiévale* (Brussels, 1920); D. V. Thompson, *The Materials of Medieval Painting* (London, 1936); H. Roosen-Runge, *Farbgebung und Technik frühmittelalterlicher Buchmalerei*, 2 vols. (Munich, 1967); E. E. Ploss, *Ein Buch von alten Farben: Technologie der Textilfarben im Mittelalter*, 6th ed. (Munich, 1989); D. Bomford et al., *Art in the Making: Italian Painting before 1400* (London, 1989); R. Halleux, "Pigments et colorants dans la *Mappae Clavicula*," in *Pigments et colorants de l'Antiquité et du Moyen Âge, Colloque international du CNRS*, ed. B. Guineau (Paris, 1990), 173–80; F. Brunello, *De arte illuminandi e altri trattati sulla tecnica della miniature medievales*, 2nd ed. (Vicenza, 1992); M. Clarke, *The Art of All Colours: Medieval Recipe Books for Painters and Illuminators* (Chicago, 2001); B. Guineau, *Glossaire des matériaux de la couleur et des termes techniques employés dans les recettes de couleurs anciennes* (Turnhout, 2005); M. Clarke, *The Medieval Painter's Materials and Techniques: The Montpellier Liber Diversarum Artium* (Chicago, 2011).

12. Archivio di Stato, Lucca, Archivio Arnolfini, XXIII, Contratti 1389–98, C. 8 (translation by the author).

13. The oldest manuscript, now housed at the Laurentian Library in Florence, is dated 1437. There is no autograph, as was long believed, and the book was not written in prison, as a persistent legend holds.

14. C. Cennini, *Il libro dell'arte*, ed. F. Brunello and L. Magagnato (Vicenza, 1971; 2nd ed. 1982; 3rd ed. 1997); C. Cennini, *Le Livre de l'art*, trans. C. Deroche (Paris, 1991). Strangely, the work ends with a few remarks on engraving coins and seals along with the casting of medals.

15. Cennini, *Il libro dell'arte*, chap. 39. Translation and adaptation by the author, following the edition by F. Brunello, *Il libro dell'arte*, (Vicenza, 1971; 2nd ed. 1982; 3rd ed. 1997).

16. Verdaccio is a light grayish green, unsaturated, often serving as an undercoat, and generally made from a mixture of light yellow ocher, green earth, and a bit of charcoal black, all diluted.

17. Cennini, *Il libro dell'arte*, chap. 147.

18. G. Saffroy, *Bibliographe généalogique, héraldique et nobiliaire de la France*, vol. 1 (Paris, 1968), no. 1999–2020.

19. Saffroy, *Bibliographe généalogique*, no. 2012–13. A new edition of the *Blason des couleurs* would be welcome. We are forced to resort to the old edition by H. Cocheris, published in Paris by A. Aubrey in 1860. This mediocre edition was based on printed copies and not on manuscripts, whereas there are many variants between them.

20. H. Cocheris, *Le Blason des couleurs en armes, livrées et devises* (Paris, 1860), 125–26.

21. Cocheris, *Le Blason des couleurs*, 89.

22. R. Mellinkoff, "Judas's Red Hair and the Jews," *Journal of Jewish Art* 9 (1982): 31–46; M. Pastoureau, "L'homme roux: Iconographie médiévale de Judas," in *Une histoire symbolique du Moyen Âge* (Paris, 2004), 197–212.

23. Printed in Venice by Bernardino Vitalis in 1528, *De coloribus libellus* was reprinted the following year, and then two more times before the author's death in 1534. Lazare Baïf, ambassador to Venice, brought a copy of the work to France and introduced it to his circles. Robert Estienne printed it in France in 1549. A modern edition of it was recently offered by M. Indergand and C. Viglino (Paris: Presses de l'École Estienne, 2010). For the modern edition of *Del significato de colori*, see P. Barocchi, *Scritti d'arte del Cinquecento* (Milan, 1971), 2:217–76. For the modern edition of P. Pino, *Dialogo di pittura* (Venice, 1548), see E. Camesasca, *Dialogo di pittura* (Milan, 1954). I used the second edition of L. Dolce, with a longer title and more extensive remarks: *Dialogo nel quale si ragiona della qualità, diversità e proprietà dei colori* (Venice, 1565).

24. The Venice-Nuremberg, Venice-Milan-Lyon, and Venice-Cologne-Brussels axes were essential with regard to the distribution of pigments, dyestuffs, and the expertise accompanying them. See M. B. Hall, ed., *Color and Technique in Renaissance Painting: Italy and the North* (New York, 1987).

25. F. Brunello, *L'arte della tintura nella storia dell'umanita* (Vicenza, 1968); F. Brunello, *Arti e mestiera a Venezia nel medioevo e Rinascimento* (Vicenza, 1981); M. Pastoureau, "Les teinturiers médiévaux: Histoire social d'un métier réprouvé," in *Une histoire symbolique du Moyen Âge occidental* (Paris, 2004), 173–96.

26. Edition and study by S. M. Evans and H. C. Borghetty, *The "Plictho" of Gioventura Rosetti* (Cambridge, MA, 1969). For the collections of dyeing recipes and manuals compiled in Venice that survive as manuscripts, see G. Rebora, *Un manuale di tintoria del Quattrocento* (Milan, 1970).

27. Saffroy, *Bibliographe généalogique*, no. 2012–13.

28. See J. Gage, *Couleur et culture: Usages et significations de la couleur de l'Antiquité à l'abstraction* (Paris, 2008), 119–20. Original English edition: J. Gage, *Colour and Culture: Practice and Meaning from Antiquity to Abstraction* (London, 1993).

29. Gage, *Couleur et culture*, 120.

30. Pliny, *Historia naturalis*, bk. 35, chap. 12; bk. 36, chap. 45.

31. Pino, *Dialogo di pittura*, 47–54, 62–73.

32. On Dolce's aesthetic ideas regarding painting, see M. Roskill, *Dolce's Aretino and Venitian Art Theory of the Cinquecento* (London, 1968).

33. G. Conversino, *De fortuna aulica*, ed. L. and D. Cortese (Padua, 1978), 15, cited in M. Krieger, *Grisaille als Metapher: Zum Enstehen der Peinture in Camaieu im frühen 14. Jahrhundert* (Vienna, 1995), 27.

34. L. B. Alberti, *La Peinture*, ed. and trans. T. Golsenne, B. Prévost, and Y. Hersant (Paris, 2004), 73.

35. There was an initial pause in the debate, however, in Italy toward the middle of the sixteenth century. Many authors, like Giorgio Vasari, emphasized that the union of *disegno* and *colorito* was necessary for painting to really be painting. A bit later, around 1620, the great artist of Bologna Guido Reni made a painting celebrating this almost conjugal union, *The Union of Drawing and Color*, now housed in Paris at the Louvre.

36. On these opposing arguments and the positions underlying them, see the great book by Jacqueline Lichtenstein, *La Couleur éloquente: Rhétorique et peinture à l'âge classique* (Paris, 1989).

37. A glaze is a thin layer of transparent oil paint applied over a thicker layer of paint. The superimposition of the two (or even more) layers allows colorful effects to be obtained—impossible with gouache or similar materials.

38. M. Brusatin, *Histoire des couleurs*, 2nd ed. (Paris, 2009), 79–102.

39. R. de Piles, *Abrégé de la vie des peintres, avec des réflexions sur leurs ouvrages* (Paris, 1699), 393–412.

40. M. Pastoureau, "La couleur en noir et blanc (XVᵉ–XVIIIᵉ siècle)," in *Le Livre et l'historien: Études offertes en l'honneur du Professeur Henri-Jean Martin* (Geneva, 1997), 197–213.

A COLOR IN SEARCH OF A NAME

1. J. André, *Études sur les termes de couleur dans la langue latine* (Paris, 1949), 106–7.

2. André, *Études sur les termes de couleur*, 111–12, 116–17.

3. See the relevant remarks in Adeline Grand-Clément, *La Fabriques des couleurs: Histoire du paysage sensible des Grecs anciens (VIIIᵉ s.–début du Vᵉ s. avant J.-C.)* (Paris, 2011), 103–5.

4. "When the child of morning, rosy-fingered Dawn, appeared." In many books of the *Odyssey*, Homer uses this line as an expression to begin the storytelling again or introduce new developments.

5. H. Blümmer, *Die rote Farbe im Lateinischen* (Leipzig, 1889), 402–3.

6. Other adjectives might also be suitable for naming pink: *pallescens*, *rubellus*, and *subrubeus*, but these terms are rare. See André, *Études sur les termes de couleur*, 139–47 passim.

7. A. Ott, *Étude sur les couleurs en vieux français* (Paris, 1899); B. Schäfer, *Die Semantik der Farbedjektive im Altfranzösischen* (Tübingen, 1987).

8. J. Robertet, *Oeuvres*, ed. M. Zsuppàn (Geneva, 1970), epistle 16, 139.

9. H. Cocheris, *Le Blason des couleurs en armes, livrées et devises* (Paris, 1860), 99: "There is another beautiful color that is commonly called peach blossom, it is like pale, slightly brownish pink." In seventeenth- and eighteenth-century French, the word *jaune* (yellow) itself can sometimes be translated into modern French as *rose* (pink) and not as yellow.

10. A. Furetière, *Dictionnaire universel* (Amsterdam, 1690), 1:158 (at the end of the entry for *chair* [flesh]).

11. The hypothesis that makes the cultivated rose the descendant of the wild eglantine tends to have been abandoned today by paleobotanists.

12. A. Tatius, *Leucippe and Clitophon*, trans. T. Whitmarsh (Oxford, 2009), 20.

13. Ovid, *Fasti* 5, lines 193–228. On the Roman rose, see the texts collected by J.-C. Belfiore, *Dictionnaire des croyances et symboles de l'Antiquité* (Paris, 2010), 856–58.

14. Ovid, *Metamorphoses* 10, verses 299–323. A less poetic legend explains that her son Cupid was responsible for the red of the roses offered to Venus. As a clumsy child, he had once spilled a glass of wine on a white rose offered to the goddess; the flower turned a crimson shade, and from that day on, Venus would only accept red roses as offerings.

15. Pliny the Elder, *Historia naturalis*, bk. 16, chap. 71; bk. 21, chap. 10 passim.

16. C. Joret, *La Rose dans l'Antiquité et au Moyen Âge: Histoire, légendes et symbolisme* (Paris, 1892), 123–26.

17. C. Taittinger, *Thibaud le Chansonnier, comte de Champagne* (Paris, 1987), 308.

18. M. Touw, "Roses in the Middle Ages," *Economic Botany* 36, no. 1 (1982): 71–83.

19. Pliny the Elder, *Historia naturalis*, bk. 21, chaps. 10, 16.

20. There is a vast bibliography on *Le Roman de la Rose*. For an initial approach, see D. Poirion, *Le Roman de la Rose* (Paris, 1974); J.-C. Payen, *La Rose et l'utopie* (Paris, 1976); A. Strubel, *Le Roman de la rose* (Paris, 1984).

21. L. B. Castel, *L'Optique des couleurs, fondée sur les simples observations et tournée surtout à la pratique de la peinture, de la teinture et des autres arts coloristes* (Paris, 1740), 35.

22. The color term *puce* also means "flea" in French. Fashionable in 1775–80 for clothing and textiles, it originally designated a shade of reddish brown that was slightly gray. It was broken down further, extravagantly, into various shades naming various parts of the flea: *dos de puce* (flea's back, a brown beige color), *ventre de puce* (flea's belly, a brownish pink color), and so on.

23. See all the examples cited in E. de Goncourt and J. de Goncourt, *La Femme au XVIIIᵉ siècle* (Paris, 1862).

24. On this style of dress "à la Werther," see A. Gaillard, "Le rose de Lumières (identités visuelle, sociale et sexuée du rose)," *Lumières* 36, no. 2 (December 2020): 31–64.

25. J. W. von Goethe, *The Sorrows of Young Werther*, trans. M. Hulse (London, 1989), 37. In German: J. W. von Goethe, *Die Leiden des jungen Werther* (Berlin, 2014), 35.

26. With regard to Charlotte's dress, in the original 1774 edition, Goethe writes only that she wore "ein simples weisses Klied mit blassroten Schleifen an Arm und Brust" (a simple white dress with pink bows on the arms and breast). The passage was modified slightly in the 1787 edition, but the color terms remained unchanged.

27. Goethe, *The Sorrows of Young Werther*, 133.

28. On its success, see C. Labrosse, *Lire au XVIIIᵉ siècle: La Nouvelle Héloïse et ses lecteurs* (Lyon, 1985).

29. J.-J. Rousseau, *Julie, or, The New Heloise*, trans. P. Stewart (Hanover, NH, 1997), 174.

30. H. Cloud, *Barbara Cartland: Crusader in Pink* (London, 1979); G. Robyns, *Barbara Cartland: An Authorised Biography* (London, 1987).

31. The initial title of the song, said to have been written and composed in part by Piaf herself, was "Les choses en rose" (things in pink).

32. A. Mollard-Desfour, *Le Dictionnaire des mots et expressions de couleur: Le rose* (Paris, 2002), 58, 85, 91.

AN AMBIGUOUS COLOR

1. On the prince of Ligne, see M. Oulié, *Le Prince de Ligne: Un grand seigneur cosmopolite au XVIIIᵉ siècle* (Paris, 1926); P. Mansel, *Le Charmeur de l'Europe: Charles-Joseph de Ligne (1735–1814)* (Paris, 1992); P. Grenaud, *Le Charmant prince de Ligne, prince de l'Europe* (Paris, 1999).

2. On this subject, I do not share Aurélia Gaillard's views, which it seems to me rely on a few isolated literary examples. But I may be wrong. See A. Gaillard, "Le rose des Lumières (identités visuelle, sociale et sexuée du rose)," *Lumières* 36, no. 2 (December 2020): 31–64.

3. Cited in J. Chastenet, *Commémoration du 150ᵉ anniversaire de la mort du Prince de Ligne* (Paris, 1964), 3.

4. L. Bloy, *Exégèse des lieux communs* (Paris, 1902), 162.

5. Let us cite for examples: George Romney, Franz Xaver Winterhalter, Jacques Joseph Tissot, Mary Cassatt, and Henry Caro-Delvaille.

6. I had finished writing this book when Barbie, the 2023 film by Greta Gerwig, was released. It has been a huge success throughout the world. I am not competent to judge its cinematic qualities, but I did note with pleasure that it constituted a veritable hymn to the color pink. I observed, on the other hand, that green was totally absent from it, which

must be the only case of this in the whole history of color films.

7. For all the preceding information, allow me to cite M. Pastoureau, "Rose Barbie," in *Barbie*, ed. A. Monier (Paris, 2016), 92–98.

8. E. Heller, *Psychologie de la couleur: Effets et symboliques* (Paris, 2009), 4–9, 177–88.

9. A few years ago, I was invited to give a talk on colors at an elementary school in the Marais district in Paris. It was a class of students between eight and ten years old. For my visit, the teacher had wanted to divide the class into five teams: the blues, reds, yellows, greens, and purples. She asked the children, girls and boys, to choose a team and try to keep the teams fairly equal in number. The exercise proved to be impossible; none of the students wanted to join the purple team. Not one out of twenty-seven or twenty-eight students! Of course we wanted to find out why. Many of the students said that purple "was not a color for children." What they meant was that it was a color for "old people." One of them even added that a friend of her grandmother had purple hair. A larger number said that

purple was not a "true color," meaning that for them, purple was not on the same level as blue, red, yellow, and green. Thus to belong to the purple team was perceived as demeaning. One student stood out in this class generally hostile to purple. He did not want to join the purple team either, of course, especially not by himself, but he refused to say why. Although the teacher and I were willing to let him keep his secret, his classmates immediately decided to force it out of him. Their mockery, gibes, and promises finally worked, and the shy boy declared quietly, "Purple brings bad luck." Far from laughing or objecting, most of the other children nodded in agreement: yes, purple brings bad luck.

10. P. W. Fregonese, *L'Invention du rose: Couleur Japon, histoire monde* (Paris, 2023).

11. On field surveys done in Africa and Asia on colors, and on the absurdity of using the ranges of shades conceived in the West, see the proceedings of the stimulating conference directed by Serge Tornay, *Voir et nommer les couleurs* (Nanterre, 1973).

12. Heller, *Psychologie de la couleur*, 184–85.

13. H. Heger, *Die Männer mit dem rosa Winkel: Der Bericht eines Homosexuellen über seine KZ-Haft von 1939–1945* (1972; repr., Hamburg, 2014); J. Le Bitoux, *Les Oublies de la mémoire: La persécution des homosexuels en Europe au temps du nazisme* (Paris, 2002); R. Schlagdenhauffen, *Triangle rose: La persécution nazie des homosexuels et sa mémoire* (Paris, 2011).

14. See F. Martel, *Le Rose et le Noir: Les homosexuels en France depuis 1968*, 3rd ed. (Paris, 2008).

15. B. Duteurte, *Ballets roses* (Paris, 2009).

16. In classical and medieval Latin, the word *lupa* designates both the she-wolf and prostitute. In Middle French, the term *chienne* was used for a lustful, depraved woman as early as the fifteenth century and still possessed that meaning in the twentieth century.

17. M. Pastoureau, *Le Cochon: Histoire d'un cousin mal aimé*, 2nd ed. (Paris, 2009), 64–75.

18. M. Pastoureau, "Sale et lubrique comme un porc," in *Histoires des préjugés*, ed. X. Mauduit and J. Guérout (Paris, 2023), 317–24.

19. M. Pastoureau, *Une couleur ne vient jamais seule: Journal chromatique*

2012–2016 (Paris, 2017), "August 2012" chap.

20. F. Baudot, *Elsa Schiaparelli* (Paris, 1998); D. E. Blum, *Shocking* (New Haven, CT, 2003); E. Schiaparelli, *Shocking Life* (London, 2007) (the original English and US editions date from 1954, and the original French edition, also from 1954, is titled *Shocking, souvenirs d'Elsa Schiaparelli*); Y. Kerlau, *Les Secrets de la mode* (Paris, 2013); Y. Kerlau, *Le Dynasties du luxe* (Paris, 2016); M.-S. Carron de la Carrière, ed., *Les Mondes surréalistes d'Elsa Schiaparelli* (Paris, 2022).

21. On pink and the flashy or glamorous colors of pop art, see B. Nemitz, *Pink: The Exposed Color in Contemporary Art and Culture* (Ostfildern-Stuttgart, 2006); V. Steele, *Pink: The History of a Punk, Pretty, Powerful Color* (New York, 2018), 1177–203.

22. M. A. Collins, *The Pink Panther* (London, 2005); J. Beck, *Pink Panther: The Ultimate Guide to the Coolest Cat in Town* (London, 2006).

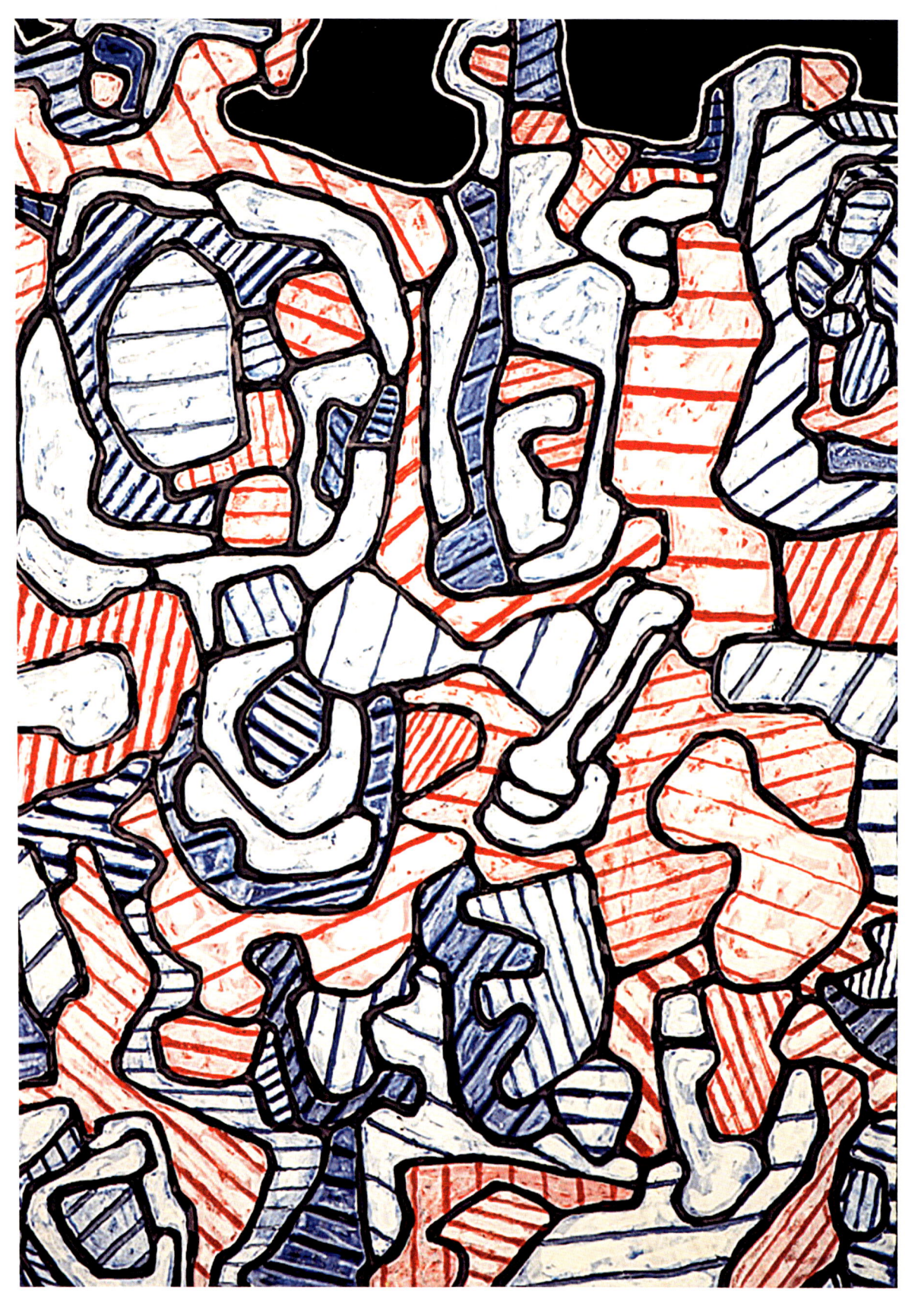

Making Pink without Pink

Juxtaposing red lines and white lines more or less closely was enough for Jean Dubuffet to produce the impression of pink. The mixing takes place in the eye of the viewer. In 1839, Michele Eugène Chevreul was the first to theorize about this optical phenomenon, already familiar to painters in ancient Rome.

Jean Dubuffet, *Dispositif aux vaisselles* (*Dishwasher*), 1965. National Galleries of Scotland, Edinburgh.

Bibliography

GENERAL WORKS

Berlin, Brent, and Paul Kay. *Basic Color Terms: Their Universality and Evolution*. Berkeley, CA, 1969.

Birren, Faber. *Color: A Survey in Words and Pictures*. New York, 1961.

Brusatin, Manlio. *Storia dei colori*. 2nd ed. Turin, 1983. Translated as *Histoire des couleurs*. Paris, 1986.

Conklin, Harold C. "Color Categorization." *American Anthropologist* 75, no. 4 (1973): 931–42.

Eco, Renate, ed. "Colore: Divietti, decreti, discute." Special issue, *Rassegna* (Milan) 23 (September 1985).

Gage, John. *Colour and Culture: Practice and Meaning from Antiquity to Abstraction*. London, 1993.

Heller, Eva. *Wie Farben wirken: Farbpsychologie, Farbsymbolik, Kreative Farbgestaltung*. 2nd ed. Hamburg, 2004.

Indergand, Michel, and Philippe Fagot. *Bibliographie de la couleur*. 2 vols. Paris, 1984–88.

Meyerson, Ignace, ed. *Problèmes de la couleur*. Paris, 1957.

Pastoureau, Michel. *Blanc: Histoire d'une couleur*. Paris, 2022.

———. *Bleu: Histoire d'une couleur*. Paris, 2000.

———. *Dictionnaire des couleurs de notre temps: Symbolique et société*. 4th ed. Paris, 2007.

———. *Jaune: Histoire d'une couleur*. Paris, 2020.

———. *Noir: Histoire d'une couleur*. Paris, 2007.

———. *Rouge: Histoire d'une couleur*. Paris, 2016.

———. *Vert: Histoire d'une couleur*. Paris, 2013.

Portmann, Adolf, and Rudolf Ritsema, eds. *The Realms of Colour: Die Welt der Farben*. Leiden, 1974.

Pouchelle, Marie-Christine, ed. "Paradoxes de la couleur." Special issue, *Ethnologie française* (Paris) 20, no. 4 (October–December 1990).

Rzepinska, Maria. *Historia coloru u dziejach malatstwa europejskiego*. 3rd ed. Warsaw, 1989.

Tornay, Serge, ed. *Voir et nommer les couleurs*. Nanterre, 1978.

Valeur, Bernard. *La Couleur dans tous ses états*. Paris, 2011.

Vogt, Hans Heinrich. *Farben und ihre Geschichte*. Stuttgart, 1973.

Zahan, Dominique. "L'homme et la couleur." In *Histoire des mœurs*, edited by Jean Poirier, 115–80. Vol. 1 of *Les Coordonnées de l'homme et la culture matérielle*. Paris, 1990.

Zuppiroli, Libero, ed. *Traité des couleurs*. Lausanne, 2001.

ANTIQUITY AND THE MIDDLE AGES

Beta, Simone, and Maria Michela Sassi, eds. *I colori nel mondo antiquo: Esperienze linguistiche e quadri simbolici*. Siena, 2003.

Bradley, Mark. *Colour and Meaning in Ancient Rome*. Cambridge, UK, 2009.

Brinkmann, Vinzenz, and Raimund Wünsche, eds. *Bunte Götter: Die Farbigkeit antiker Skulptur*. Munich, 2003.

Brüggen, Elke. *Kleidung und Mode in der höfischen Epik*. Heidelberg, 1989.

Carastro, Marcello, ed. *L'Antiquité en couleurs: Catégories, pratiques, représentations*. Grenoble, 2008.

Cechetti, Bartolomeo. *La vita dei Veneziani nel 1300: Le veste*. Venice, 1886.

Centre Universitaire d'Études et de Recherches Médiévales d'Aix-en-Provence. *Les Couleurs au Moyen Âge*. Vol. 24 of *Senefiance*. Aix-en-Provence, France, 1988.

Ceppari Ridolfi, Maria A., and Patrizia Turrini. *Il mulino delle vanità: Lusso e cerimonie nella Siena medievale*. Siena, 1996.

Descamps-Lequime, Sophie, ed. *Peinture et couleur dans le monde grec antique*. Paris, 2007.

Dumézil, Georges. "*Albati, russati, virides*." In *Rituels indoeuropéens à Rome*, 45–61. Paris, 1954.

Frodl-Kraft, Eva. "Die Farbsprache der gotischen Malerei: Ein Entwurf." *Wiener Jahrbuch für Kunstgeschichte* 30–31 (1977–78): 89–178.

Grand-Clément, Adeline. *La Fabrique des couleurs: Histoire du paysage sensible des Grecs anciens*. Paris, 2011.

Haupt, Gottfried. *Die Farbensymbolik in der sakralen Kunst des abendländischen Mittelalters*. Leipzig-Dresden, 1941.

Istituto Storico Lucchese. *Il colore nel Medioevo: Arte, simbolo, tecnica: Atti delle Giornate di studi*. 2 vols. Lucca, 1996–98.

Luzzatto, Lia, and Renata Pompas. *Il significato dei colori nelle civiltà antiche*. Milan, 1988.

Pastoureau, Michel. *Les Couleurs au Moyen Âge. Dictionnaire encyclopédique*. Paris, 2022.

———. "L'Église et la couleur des origines à la Réforme." *Bibliothèque de l'École des chartes* 147 (1989): 203–30.

———. "Voir les couleurs au XIIIe siècle." In *View and Vision in the Middle Ages*, 2:147–65. Vol. 6 of *Micrologus: Nature, Science and Medieval Societies*. Florence, 1998.

Rouveret, Agnès. *Histoire et imaginaire de la peinture ancienne*. Paris, 1989.

Rouveret, Agnès, Sandrine Dubel, and Valérie Naas, eds. *Couleurs et matières dans l'Antiquité: Textes, techniques et pratiques*. Paris, 2006.

Sicile, héraut d'armes du XVe siècle. *Le Blason des couleurs en armes, livrées et devises*. Edited by H. Cocheris. Paris, 1860.

Tiverios, Michales A., and Despoina Tsiafakis, eds. *The Role of Color in Ancient Greek Art and Architecture (700–31 B.C.)*. Thessaloniki, 2002.

Villard, Laurence, ed. *Couleur et vision dans l'Antiquité classique*. Rouen, 2002.

MODERN AND CONTEMPORARY TIMES

Batchelor, David. *La Peur de la couleur*. Paris, 2001.

Birren, Faber. *Selling Color to People*. New York, 1956.

Brino, Giovanni, and Franco Rosso. *Colore e città: Il piano del colore di Torino, 1800–1850*. Milan, 1980.

Laufer, Otto. *Farbensymbolik im deutschen Volsbrauch*. Hamburg, 1948.

Lenclos, Jean-Philippe, and Dominique Lenclos. *Les Couleurs de la France: Maisons et paysage*. Paris, 1982.

———. *Les Couleurs de l'Europe: Géographie de la couleur*. Paris, 1995.

Noël, Benoît. *L'Histoire du cinéma couleur*. Croissy-sur-Seine, 1995.

Pastoureau, Michel. "La couleur en noir et blanc (XVe–XVIIIe siècle)." In *Le Livre et l'Historien: Études offertes en l'honneur du Professeur Henri-Jean Martin*, 197–213. Geneva, 1997.

———. "La Réforme et la couleur." *Bulletin de la Société de l'histoire du Protestantisme français* 138 (July–September 1992): 323–42.

———. *Les Couleurs de nos souvenirs*. Paris, 2010.

Varichon, Anne. *Nuanciers. Éloge du subtil*. Paris, 2023.

PROBLEMS OF PHILOLOGY AND TERMINOLOGY

André, Jacques. *Étude sur les termes de couleurs dans la langue latine*. Paris, 1949.

Brault, Gerard J. *Early Blazon: Heraldic Terminology in the Twelfth and Thirteenth Centuries, with Special Reference to Arthurian Literature*. Oxford, 1972.

Crosland, Maurice P. *Historical Studies in the Language of Chemistry*. London, 1962.

Giacolone Ramat, Anna. "Colori germanici nel mondo romanzo." *Atti e memorie dell'Academia toscana di scienze e lettere La Colombaria* (Florence) 32 (1967): 105–211.

Gloth, Walther. *Das Spiel von den sieben Farben*. Königsberg, 1902.

Grossmann, Maria. *Colori e lessico: Studi sulla struttura semantica degli aggetivi di colore in catalano, castigliano, italiano, romano, latino ed ungherese*. Tübingen, 1988.

Irwin, Eleanor. *Colour Terms in Greek Poetry*. Toronto, 1974.

Jacobson-Widding, Anita. *Red-White-Black, as a Mode of Thought*. Stockholm, 1979.

Jacquesson, François. "Les mots de la couleur en hébreu ancien." In *Histoire et géographie de la couleur*, edited by P. Dollfus, F. Jacquesson, and M. Pastoureau, 67–130. Vol. 13 of *Cahiers du Léopard d'or*. Paris, 2013.

Jones, William Jervis. *German Colour Terms: A Study in Their Historical Evolution from Earliest Times to the Present*. Amsterdam, 2013.

Kristol, Andres M. *Color: Les Langues romanes devant le phénomène de la couleur*. Berne, 1978.

Maxwell-Stuart, P. G. *Studies in Greek Colour Terminology*. Vol. 2 of *XAPOIIOE*. Leiden, 1998.

Meunier, Annie. "Quelques remarques sur les adjectifs de couleur." *Annales de l'Université de Toulouse* 11, no. 5 (1975): 37–62.

Mollard-Desfour, Annie. *Le Dictionnaire des mots et expressions de couleur*. 6 vols. Paris, 2000–2012.

Ott, André. *Études sur les couleurs en vieux français*. Paris, 1899.

Schäfer, Barbara. *Die Semantik der Farbadjektive im Altfranzösischen*. Tübingen, 1987.

Sève, Robert, Michel Indergand, and Philippe Lanthony. *Dictionnaire des termes de la couleur*. Paris, 2007.

Wackernagel, Wilhelm. "Die Farben- und Blumensprache des Mittelalter." In *Abhandlungen zur deutschen Altertumskunde und Kunstgeschichte*, 143–240. Leipzig, 1872.

Wierzbicka, Anna. "The Meaning of Color Terms: Semantics, Culture, and Cognition." *Cognitive Linguistics* 1, no. 1 (1990): 99–150.

THE HISTORY OF DYES AND DYERS

Brunello, Franco. *Arti e mestieri a Venezia nel medioevo e nel Rinascimento*. Vicenza, 1980.

——. *L'arte della tintura nella storia dell'umanita*. Vicenza, 1968.

Cardon, Dominique. *Le Monde des teintures naturelles*. Paris, 1994.

——. *Mémoires de teinture: Voyage dans le temps chez un maître des couleurs*. Paris, 2013.

Cardon, Dominique, and Gaëtan Du Châtenet. *Guide des teintures naturelles*. Neuchâtel, 1990.

Chevreul, Michel-Eugène. *Leçons de chimie appliquées à la teinture*. Paris, 1829.

Evans, M., and Hector C. Borghetty. *The "Plictho" of Giovanventura Rosetti*. London and Cambridge, MA, 1969.

Gerschel, Lucien. "Couleurs et teintures chez divers peuples indo-européens." *Annales ESC* 21 (1966): 608–63.

Hellot, Jean. *L'Art de la teinture des laines et des étoffes de laine en grand et petit teint*. Paris, 1750.

Jaoul, Martine, ed. *Des teintes et des couleurs*. Paris, 1988.

Lauterbach, Fritz. *Geschichte der in Deutschland bei der Färberei angewandten Farbstoffe, mit besonderer Berücksichtigung des mittelalterlichen Waidblaues*. Leipzig, 1905.

Legget, William F. *Ancient and Medieval Dyes*. New York, 1944.

Lespinasse, René de. *Histoire générale de Paris: Les métiers et corporations de la ville de Paris*. Vol. 3 of *Tissus, étoffes. . . .* Paris, 1897.

Pastoureau, Michel. *Jésus chez le teinturier: Couleurs et teintures dans l'Occident médiéval*. Paris, 1998.

Ploss, Emil Ernst. *Ein Buch von alten Farben: Technologie der Textilfarben im Mittelalter*. 6th ed. Munich, 1989.

Rebora, Giovanni. *Un manuale di tintoria del Quattrocento*. Milan, 1970.

Varichon, Anne. *Couleurs: Pigments et teintures dans les mains des peuples*. 2nd ed. Paris, 2005.

THE HISTORY OF PIGMENTS

Ball, Philip. *Histoire vivante des couleurs: 5000 ans de peinture racontée par les pigments*. Paris, 2005.

Bomford, David, et al. *Art in the Making: Impressionism*. London, 1990.

———. *Art in the Making: Italian Painting before 1400*. London, 1989.

Brunello, Franco. *"De arte illuminandi" e altri trattati sulla tecnica della miniatura medievale*. 2nd ed. Vicenza, 1992.

Feller, Robert L., and Ashok Roy. *Artists' Pigments: A Handbook of Their History and Characteristics*. 2 vols. Washington, DC, 1985–86.

Guineau, Bernard, ed. *Pigments et colorants de l'Antiquité et du Moyen Âge*. Paris, 1990.

Harley, Rosamond D. *Artists' Pigments (c. 1600–1835)*. 2nd ed. London, 1982.

Hills, Paul. *The Venetian Colour*. New Haven, CT, 1999.

Kittel, Hans, ed. *Pigmente*. Stuttgart, 1960.

Kühn, Hermann, et al. *Reclams Handbuch der künstlerischen Techniken*. Vol. 1 of *Farbmittel, Buchmalerei, Tafel- und Leinwandmalerei*. Stuttgart, 1960.

Laurie, Arthur P. *The Pigments and Mediums of Old Masters*. London, 1914.

Loumyer, Guy. *Les Traditions techniques de la peinture médiévale*. Brussels, 1920.

Merrifield, Mary P. *Original Treatises dating from the XIIth to the XVIIIth Centuries on the Art of Painting*. 2 vols. London, 1849.

Montagna, Giovanni. *I pigmenti: Prontuario per l'arte e il restauro*. Florence, 1993.

Roosen-Runge, Heinz. *Farbgebung und Technik frühmittelalterlicher Buchmalerei*. 2 vols. Munich, 1967.

Smith, Cyril S., and John G. Hawthorne. "*Mappae clavicula*: A Little Key to the World of Medieval Techniques." In *Transactions of the American Philosophical Society* 64, no. 4. Philadelphia, 1974.

Technè: La science au service de l'art et des civilisations. Vol. 4 of *La couleur et ses pigments*. 1996.

Thompson, Daniel V. *The Material of Medieval Painting*. London, 1936.

THE HISTORY OF CLOTHING

Baldwin, Frances E. *Sumptuary Legislation and Personal Relation in England*. Baltimore, MD, 1926.

Baur, Veronika. *Kleiderordnungen in Bayern von 14. bis 19. Jahrhundert*. Munich, 1975.

Boehn, Max von. *Die Mode: Menschen und Moden vom Untergang der alten Welt bis zum Beginn des zwanzigsten Jahrhunderts*. 8 vols. Munich, 1907–25.

Boucher, François. *Histoire du costume en Occident de l'Antiquité à nos jours*. Paris, 1965.

Bridbury, Anthony R. *Medieval English Clothmaking: An Economic Survey*. London, 1982.

Eisenbart, Liselotte C. *Kleiderordnungen der deutschen Städte zwischen 1350–1700*. Göttingen, 1962.

Harte, N. B., and Kenneth G. Ponting, eds. *Cloth and Clothing in Medieval Europe: Essays in Memory of E. M. Carus-Wilson*. London, 1982.

Harvey, John. *Men in Black*. London, 1995. Translated as *Des hommes en noir: Du costume masculin à travers les âges*. Abbeville, 1998.

Hunt, Alan. *Governance of the Consuming Passions: A History of Sumptuary Laws*. London, 1996.

Lurie, Alison. *The Language of Clothes*. London, 1982.

Madou, Mireille. *Le Costume civil: Typologie des sources du Moyen Âge occidental*, vol. 47. Turnhout, 1986.

Mayo, Janet. *A History of Ecclesiastical Dress*. London, 1984.

Nixdorff, Heide, and Heidi Müller, eds. *Weisse Vesten, roten Roben: Von den Farbordnungen des Mittelalters zum individuellen Farbgeschmak*. Berlin, 1983.

Page, Agnès. *Vêtir le prince: Tissus et couleurs à la cour de Savoie (1427–1447)*. Lausanne, 1993.

Pellegrin, Nicole. *Les Vêtements de la liberté: Abécédaires des pratiques vestimentaires françaises de 1780 à 1800*. Paris, 1989.

Piponnier, Françoise. *Costume et vie sociale: La cour d'Anjou, XIVe–XVe siècles*. Paris, 1970.

Piponnier, Françoise, and Perrine Mane. *Se vêtir au Moyen Âge*. Paris, 1995.

Quicherat, Jules. *Histoire du costume en France depuis les temps les plus reculés jusqu'à la fin du XVIIIe siècle*. Paris, 1875.

Roche, Daniel. *La Culture des apparences: Une histoire du vêtement (XVIIe–XVIIIe siècles)*. Paris, 1989.

Roche-Bernard, Geneviève, and Alain Ferdière. *Costumes et textiles en Gaule romaine*. Paris, 1993.

Vincent, John M. *Costume and Conduct in the Laws of Basel, Bern, and Zurich*. Baltimore, MD, 1935.

THE PHILOSOPHY AND HISTORY OF SCIENCE

Albert, Jean-Pierre, et al., eds. *Coloris Corpus*. Paris, 2008.

Blay, Michel. *La Conceptualisation newtonienne des phénomènes de la couleur*. Paris, 1983.

———. *Les Figures de l'arc-en-ciel*. Paris, 1995.

Boyer, Carl B. *The Rainbow from Myth to Mathematics*. New York, 1959.

Goethe, Johann Wolfgang von. *Materialen zur Geschichte der Farbenlehre*. 2 vols. Munich, 1971.

———. *Zur Farbenlehre*. 2 vols. Tübingen, 1810.

Halbertsma, Klaas Tjalling Agnus. *A History of the Theory of Colour*. Amsterdam, 1949.

Hardin, Clyde L. *Color for Philosophers: Unweaving the Rainbow*. Cambridge, MA, 1988.

Lindberg, David C. *Theories of Vision from Al-Kindi to Kepler*. Chicago, 1976.

Magnus, Hugo. *Histoire de l'évolution du sens des couleurs*. Paris, 1878.

Newton, Isaac. *Opticks or a Treatise of the Reflexions, Refractions, Inflexions, and Colours of Light*. London, 1704.

Pastore, Nicholas. *Selective History of Theories of Visual Perception, 1650–1950*. Oxford, 1971.

Romano, Claude. *De la couleur*. Paris, 2020.

Sepper, Dennis L. *Goethe contra Newton: Polemics and the Project of a New Science of Color*. Cambridge, UK, 1988.

Sherman, Paul D. *Colour Vision in the Nineteenth Century: The Young-Helmholtz-Maxwell Theory*. Cambridge, UK, 1981.

Westphal, John. *Colour: A Philosophical Introduction*. 2nd ed. London, 1991.

Wittgenstein, Ludwig. *Bemerkungen über die Farben*. Frankfurt am Main, 1979.

THE HISTORY AND THEORIES OF ART

Aumont, Jacques. *Introduction à la couleur: Des discours aux images*. Paris, 1994.

Ballas, Guila. *La Couleur dans la peinture moderne: Théorie et pratique*. Paris, 1997.

Barasch, Moshe. *Light and Color in the Italian Renaissance Theory of Art*. New York, 1978.

Dittmann, Lorenz. *Farbgestaltung und Farbtheorie in der abendländischen Malerei*. Stuttgart, 1987.

Fischer, Hervé. *Les Couleurs de l'Occident, de la Préhistoire au XXIe siècle*. Paris, 2019.

Gavel, Jonas. *Colour: A Study of Its Position in the Art Theory of the Quattro- and Cinquecento*. Stockholm, 1979.

Hall, Marcia B. *Color and Meaning: Practice and Theory in Renaissance Painting*. Cambridge, MA, 1992.

Imdahl, Max. *Farbe: Kunsttheoretische Reflexionen in Frankreich*. Munich, 1987.

Kandinsky, Vassily. *Über das Geistige in der Kunst*. Munich, 1912.

Le Rider, Jacques. *Les Couleurs et les mots*. Paris, 1997.

Lichtenstein, Jacqueline. *La Couleur éloquent: Rhétorique et peinture à l'âge classique*. Paris, 1989.

Roque, Georges. *Art et science de la couleur: Chevreul et les peintres de Delacroix à l'abstraction*. Nîmes, 1997.

Shapiro, Alan E. "Artists' Colors and Newton's Colors." *Isis* 85 (1994): 600–630.

Teyssèdre, Bernard. *Roger de Piles et les débats sur le coloris au siècle de Louis XIV*. Paris, 1957.

ABOUT THE COLOR PINK

Beauvalet-Boutouyrie, Scarlett, and Emmanuelle Berthiaud. *Le Rose et le Bleu: La fabrique du féminin et du masculin, cinq siècles d'histoire*. Paris, 2015.

Bideaux, Kévin. *Rose: Une couleur aux prises avec le genre*. Amsterdam, 2023.

Boutet, Claude. *Traité de la peinture en mignature*. The Hague, 1708.

Chansigaud, Valérie. *Une histoire des fleurs: Entre nature et culture*. Paris, 2014.

Fregonese, Pierre William. *L'Invention du rose*. Paris, 2023.

Gaillard, Aurélia. "Le rose des Lumières (identités visuelle, sociale et sexuée du rose)." *Lumières* 36, no. 2 (December 2020): 31–64.

Gaillard, Aurélia, and Catherine Lanoë, eds. "La couleur des Lumières." *Dix-huitième siècle* 51 (2019).

Hyde, Melissa. "Beautés rivales: les portraits de Mme Du Barry et de la reine Marie-Antoinette." In *Cultures de cour, cultures du corps, XIVe–XVIIIe siècle*, edited by Catherine Lanoë and Mathieu Da Vinha, 185–205. Paris, 2011.

Joret, Charles. *La Rose dans l'Antiquité et au Moyen Âge: Histoire, légendes et symbolisme*. Paris, 1892.

Kaufmann, Caroline. "Zur Semantik der Farbadjektive rosa, pink und rot." PhD diss. Munich, 2006.

Kovács, Katalin. "La couleur et le sentiment de la chair dans les premiers 'Salons' de Diderot." *Diderot Studies* 30 (2007): 125–41.

Lanoë, Catherine. *La Poudre et le fard: Une histoire des cosmétiques de la Renaissance aux Lumières*. Seyssel, 2008.

———. "Une dynastie de parfumeurs du roi: Les Gallois/Huet et la fabrique des apparences de la cour à la ville, 1689–1789." *Artefact* 12 (2020): 317–48.

Mollard-Desfour, Annie. *Le Dictionnaire des mots et expressions de couleur du XXe siècle: Le Rose*. Paris, 2002.

Nemitz, Barbara. *Pink: The Exposed Color in Contemporary Art and Culture*. Ostfildern-Stuttgart, 2006.

Pastoureau, Michel. "Sur les marges du rouge: Le rose." In *Rouge: Histoire d'une couleur*, 144–51. Paris, 2016.

Ripoll, Élodie. *Penser la couleur en littérature: Explorations romanesques des Lumières au réalisme*. Paris, 2018.

Steele, Valerie. *Pink: The History of a Punk, Pretty, Powerful Color*. New York, 2018.

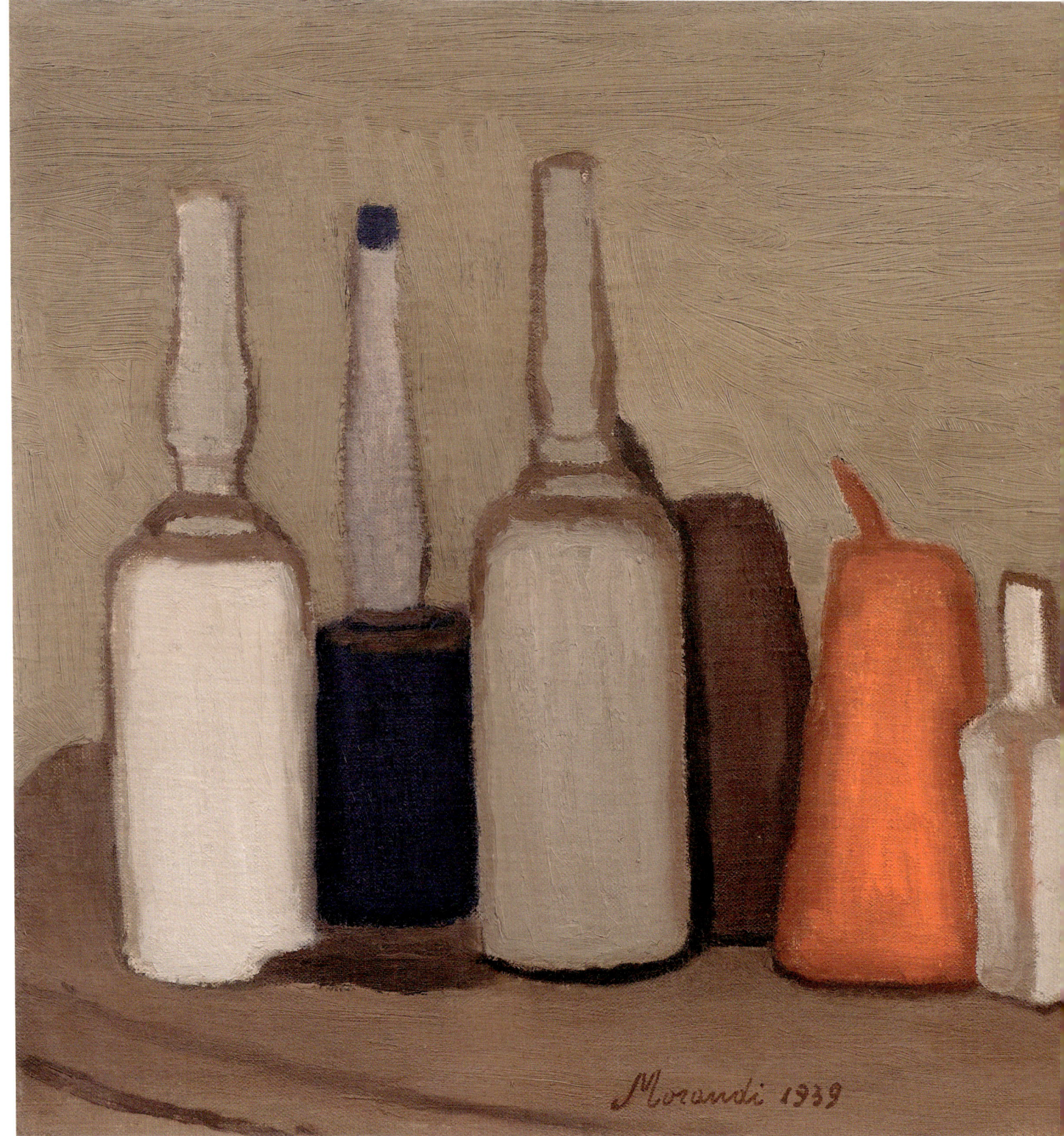

Morandi 1939

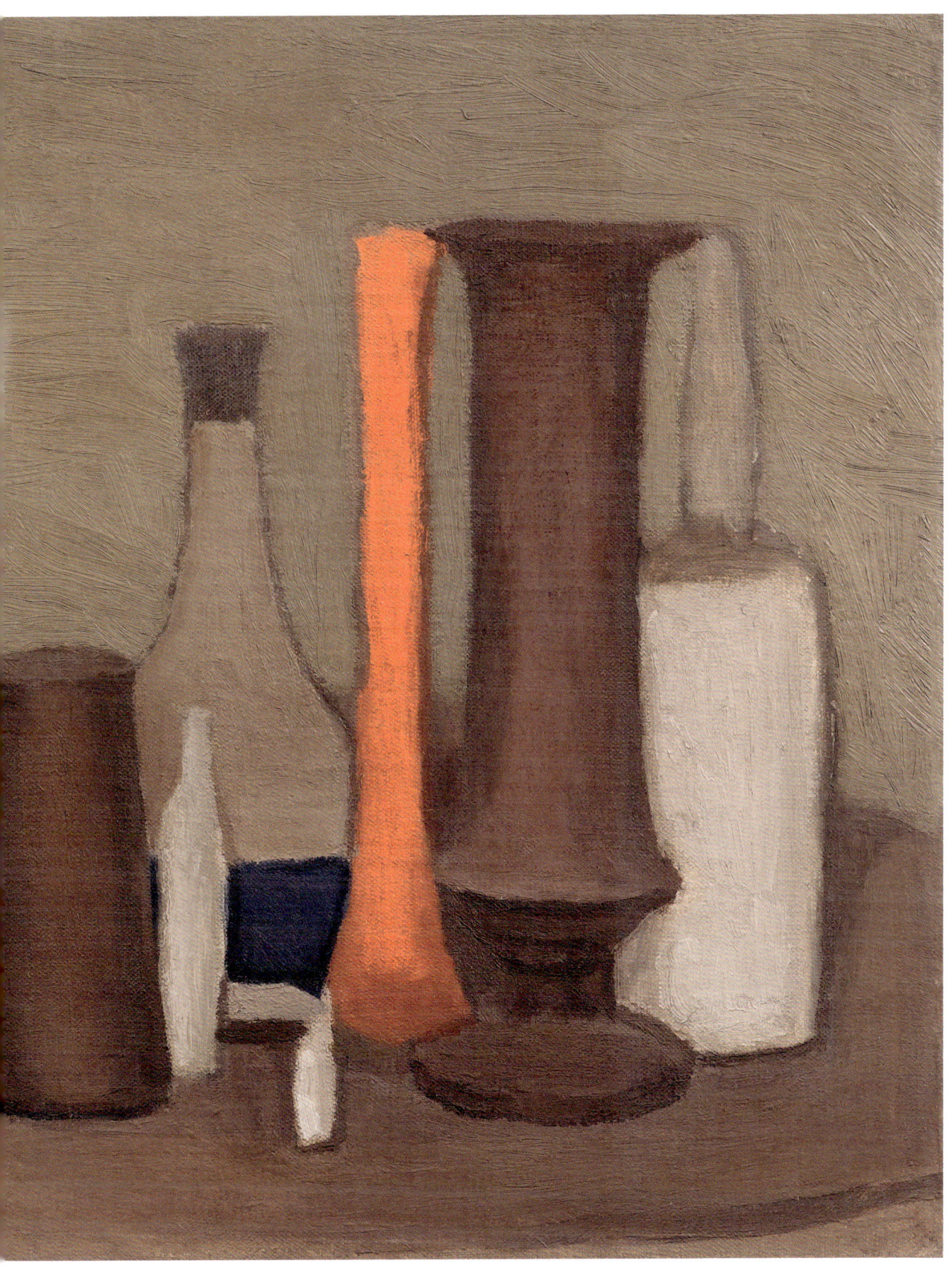

Giorgio Morandi,
Still Life, 1939.
Private collection.

Endpapers: Bauhaus motif wallpaper, 1929. Kassel (Allemagne), Deutches Tapetenmuseum.

Credits

Acknowledgments

Before taking the form of a book, this history of the color pink in European societies constituted—as did those of the other colors—the subject of my research and teaching for more than half a century. It goes without saying, of course, that I did not study the colors one by one, one after the other, which would be absurd. A color never occurs alone; it takes on meaning insofar as it is combined or contrasted with one or many other colors. That is why to speak of pink is necessarily to speak of red, white, yellow, blue, and even green, violet, and black. I study these colors together, as they are presented in documentation and as they have been the subject of my seminars at the École Pratique des Hautes Études, the École des Hautes Études en Sciences Sociales, and the École des Chartes. If I give each of my works a main theme centered on one color in particular, it is for both didactic and editorial reasons.

I thank all my students and auditors for the fruitful exchanges we had over many long years. I would also like to thank all those close to me—friends, relatives, colleagues, students—whose advice, comments, and suggestions I have benefited from, especially Thalia Brero, Denis Bruna, Brigitte Buettner, Pierre Bureau, Perrine Canavaggio, Yvonne Cazal, Marie Clauteaux, Claude Coupry, François Jacquesson, Christine Lapostolle, Christian de Mérindol, Claudia Rabel, Anne Ritz-Guilbert, and Olga Vassilieva-Codognet.

Thanks as well to Éditions du Seuil, especially to the Beaux Livres team: Nathalie Beaux and Caroline Fuchs for publishing the work; Marie-Anne Méhay and Karine Benzaquin for the iconography; Elisabetta Trevisan for the foreign editions; François-Xavier Delarue for the book design; Carine Ruault for the production; Renaud Bezombes and Silvain Chupin for proofreading. Everyone has worked to make the present volume a very beautiful one. Thanks finally to my faithful and efficient publishing assistants Marie-Claire Chalvet and Laetitia Correia who, as with its predecessors, will make this work known to a wide readership.